PandoraHearts ❹

JUN MOCHIZUKI

Translation: Tomo Kimura • Lettering: Alexis Eckerman

PandoraHearts Vol. 4 © 2008 Jun Mochizuki / SQUARE ENIX CO., LTD. All rights reserved. First published in Japan in 2008 by SQUARE ENIX CO., LTD. English translation rights arranged with SQUARE ENIX CO., LTD. and Hachette Book Group through Tuttle-Mori Agency, Inc.

Translation © 2011 by SQUARE ENIX CO., LTD.

Yen Press
Hachette Book Group
1290 Avenue of the Americas, New York, NY 10104

www.HachetteBookGroup.com
www.YenPress.com

Yen Press is an imprint of Hachette Book Group, Inc. The Yen Press name and logo are trademarks of Hachette Book Group, Inc.

First Yen Press Edition: January 2011

ISBN: 978-0-316-07611-1

10 9 8

BVG

Printed in the United States of America

D0061806

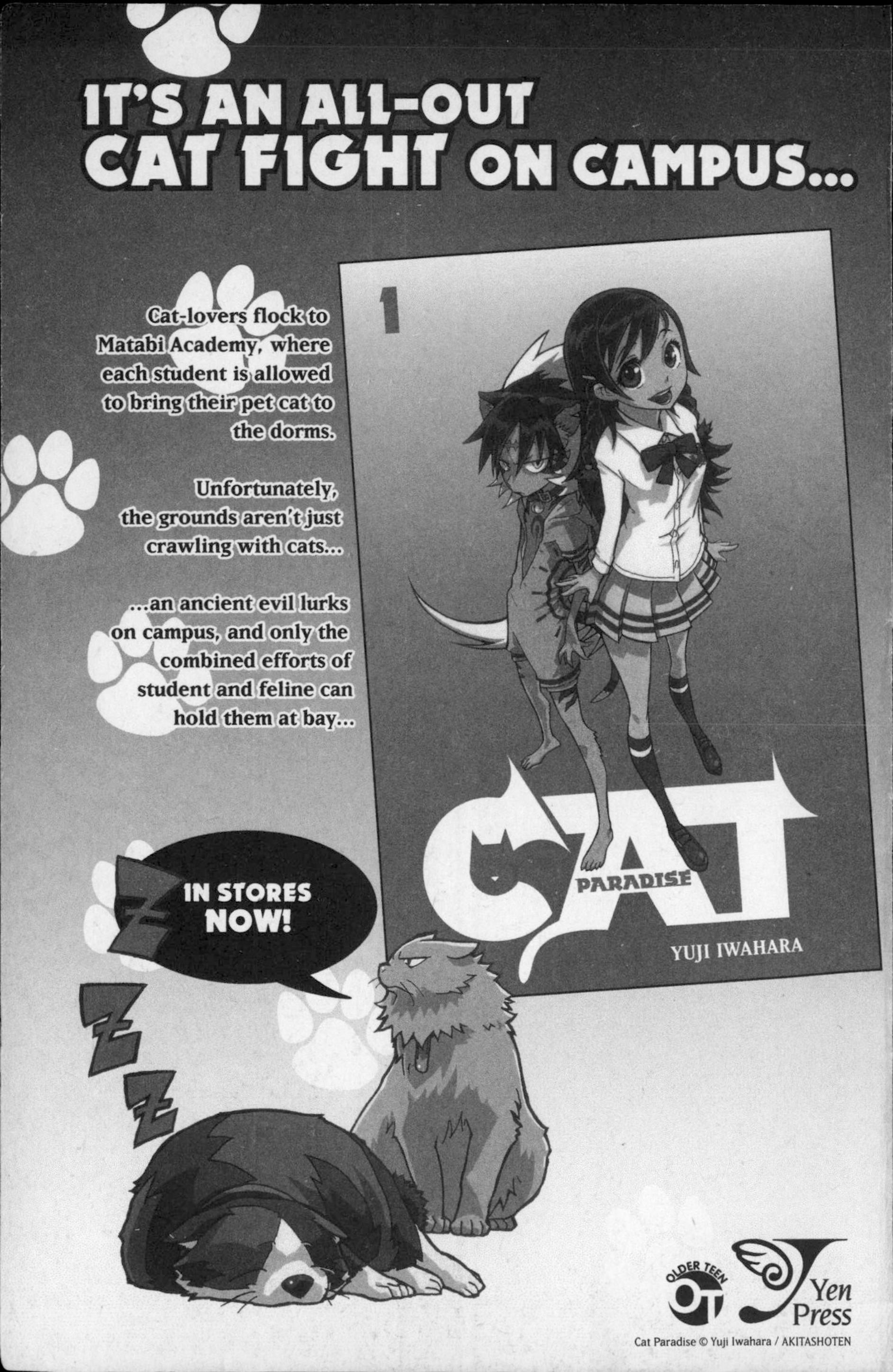
IT'S AN ALL-OUT CAT FIGHT ON CAMPUS...
Cat-lovers flock to Matabi Academy, where each student is allowed to bring their pet cat to the dorms.
Unfortunately, the grounds aren't just crawling with cats...
...an ancient evil lurks on campus, and only the combined efforts of student and feline can hold them at bay...
1
CAT PARADISE
YUJI IWAHARA
IN STORES NOW!
OLDER TEEN OT
Yen Press
Cat Paradise © Yuji Iwahara / AKITASHOTEN

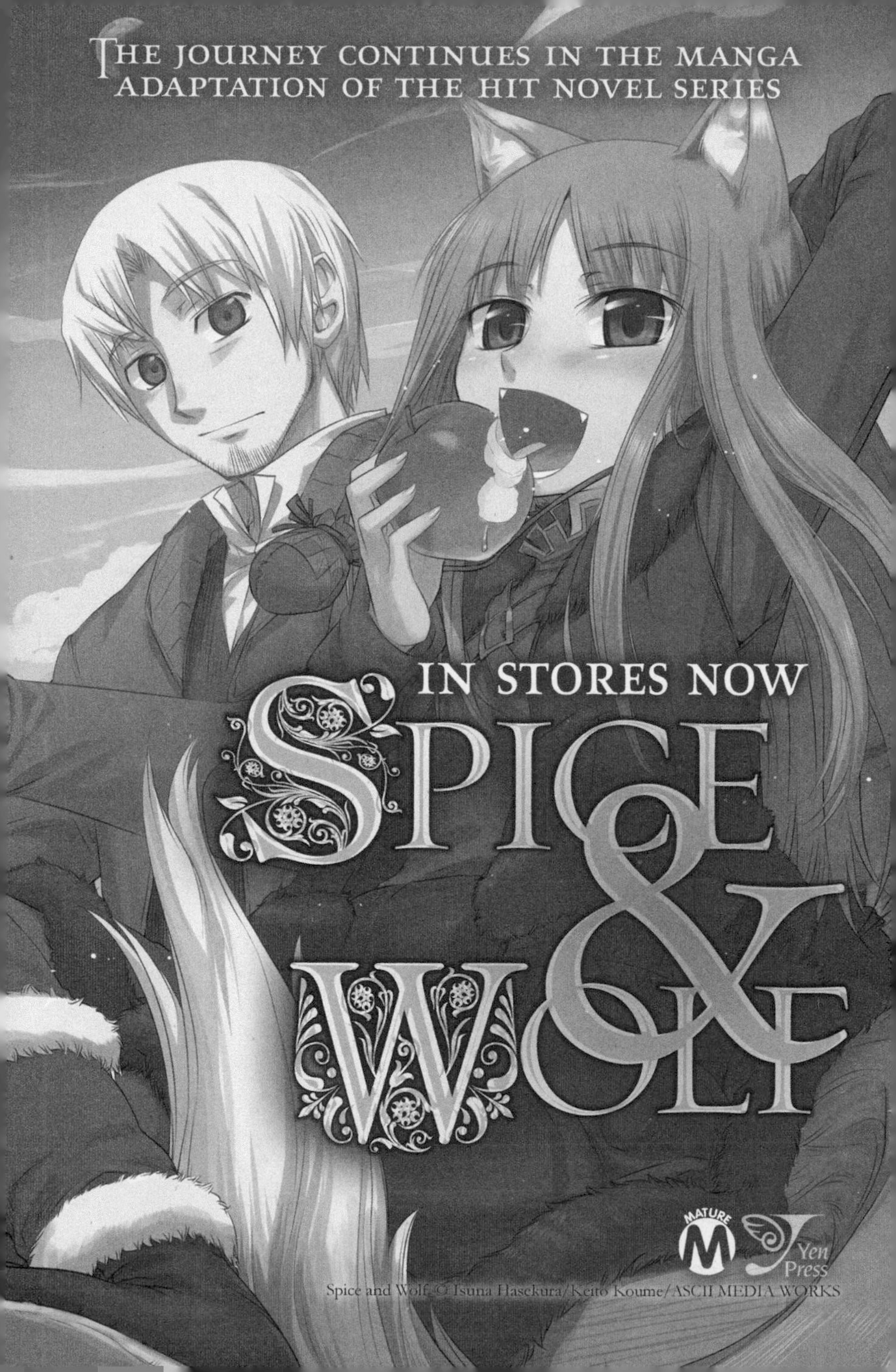
THE JOURNEY CONTINUES IN THE MANGA
ADAPTATION OF THE HIT NOVEL SERIES
IN STORES NOW
SPICE & WOLF
MATURE M
Yen Press
Spice and Wolf © Isuna Hasekura/Keito Koume/ASCII MEDIA WORKS

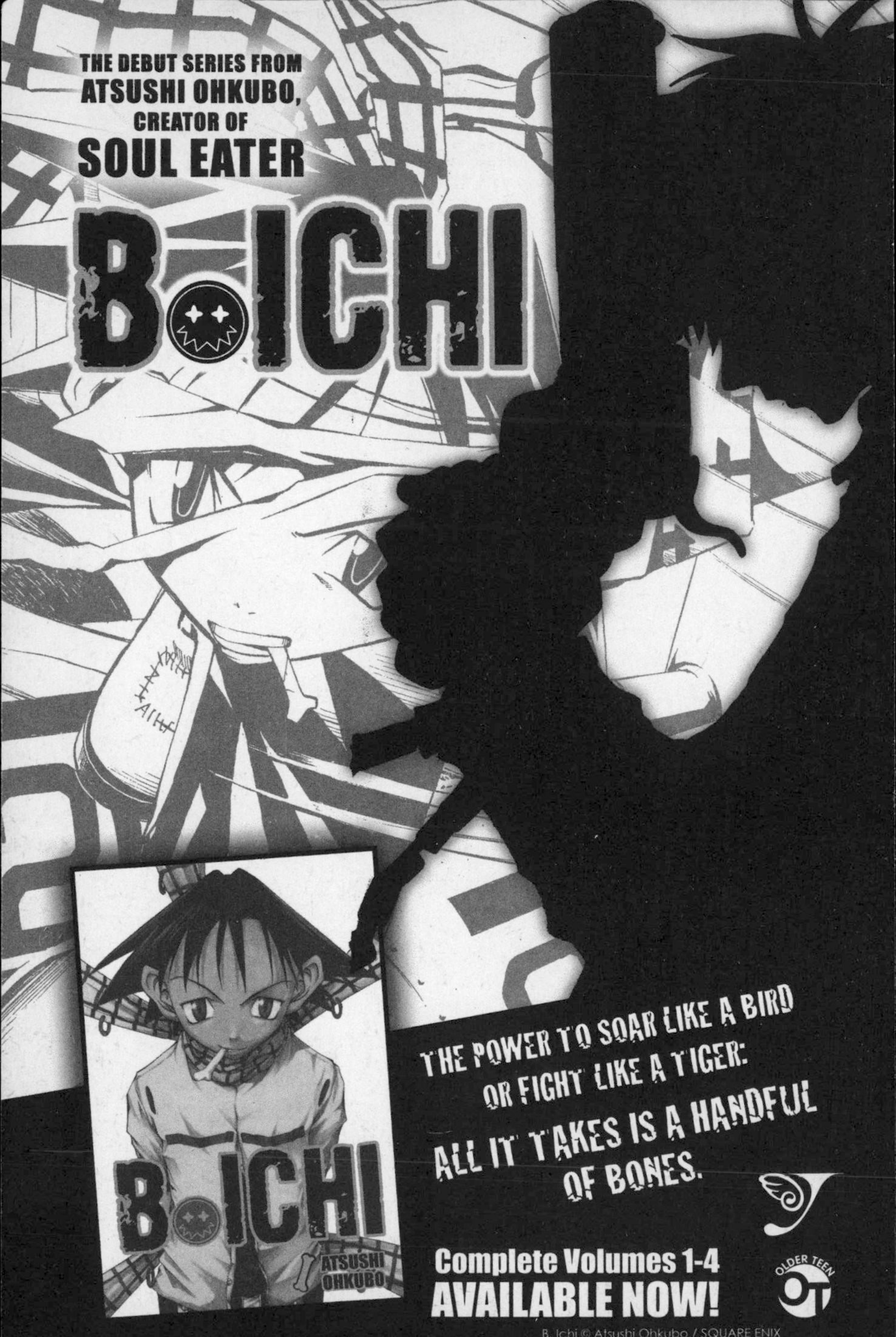
THE DEBUT SERIES FROM
ATSUSHI OHKUBO,
CREATOR OF
SOUL EATER
B. ICHI
B. ICHI
ATSUSHI OHKUBO
THE POWER TO SOAR LIKE A BIRD
OR FIGHT LIKE A TIGER:
ALL IT TAKES IS A HANDFUL
OF BONES.
Complete Volumes 1-4
AVAILABLE NOW!
OLDER TEEN
OT
B. Ichi © Atsushi Ohkubo / SQUARE ENIX

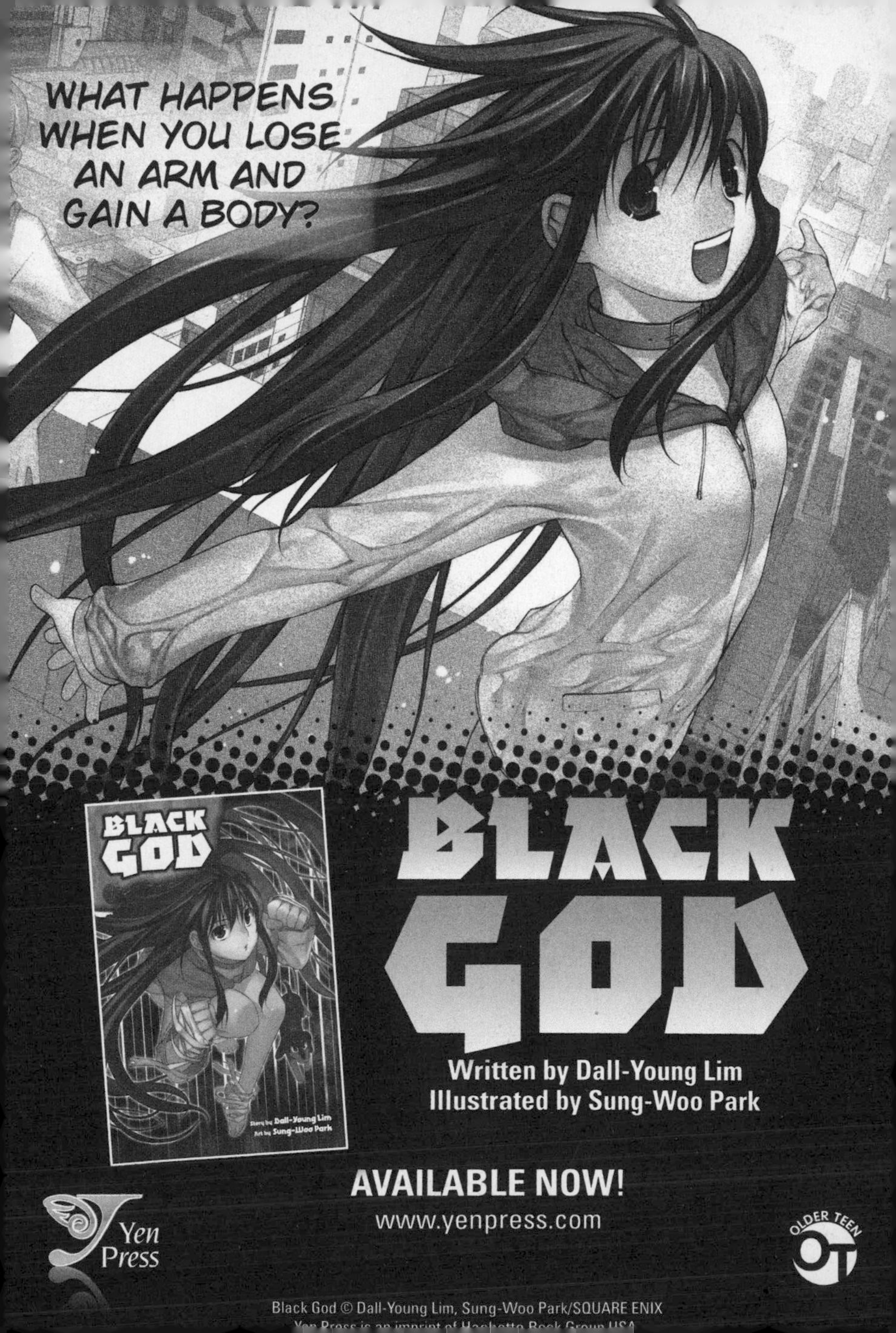
WHAT HAPPENS WHEN YOU LOSE AN ARM AND GAIN A BODY?
BLACK GOD
Story by Dall-Young Lim
Art by Sung-Woo Park
BLACK GOD
Written by Dall-Young Lim
Illustrated by Sung-Woo Park
AVAILABLE NOW!
www.yenpress.com
Yen Press
OLDER TEEN
OT
Black God © Dall-Young Lim, Sung-Woo Park/SQUARE ENIX

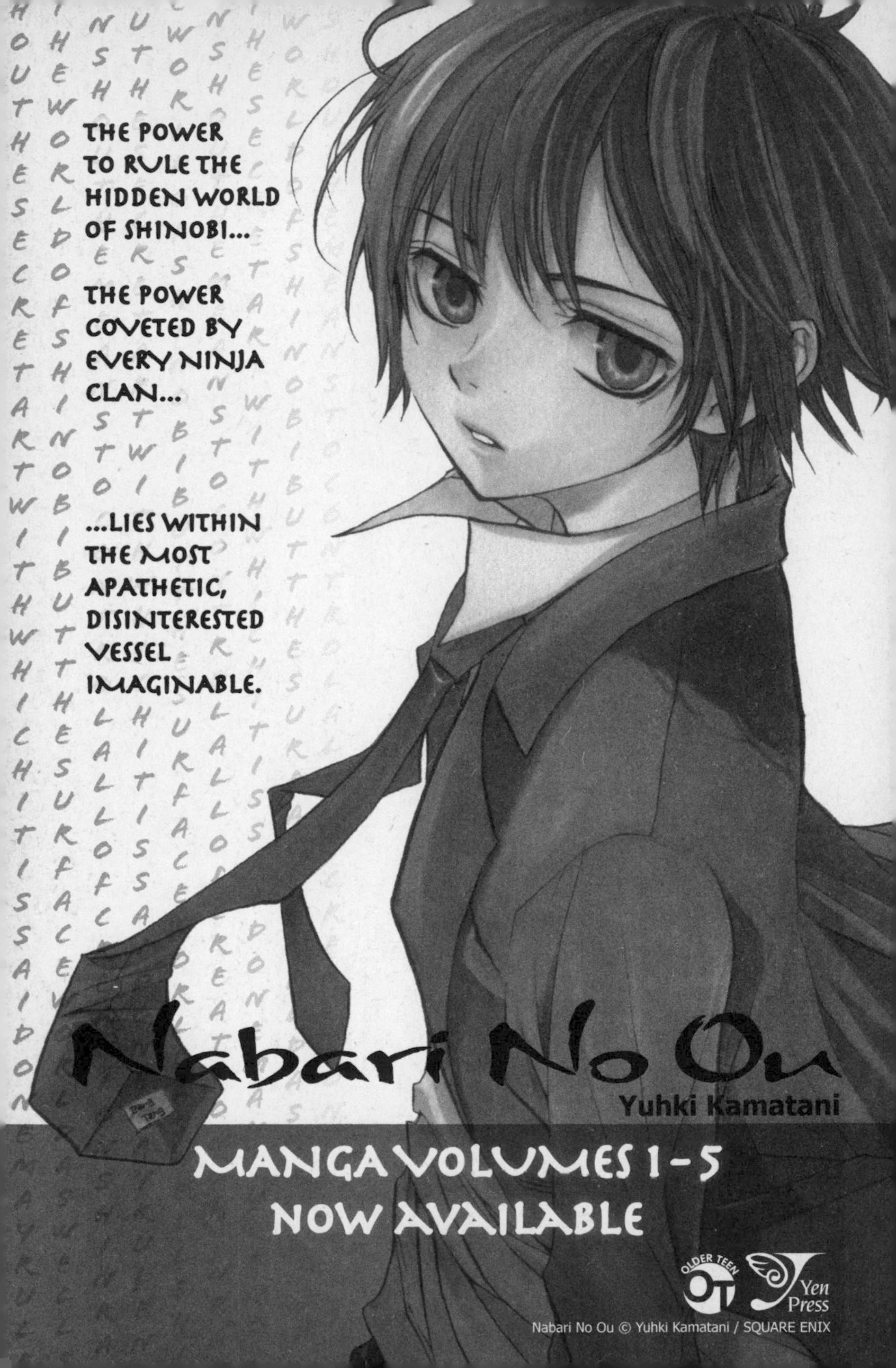
THE POWER TO RULE THE HIDDEN WORLD OF SHINOBI...
THE POWER COVETED BY EVERY NINJA CLAN...
...LIES WITHIN THE MOST APATHETIC, DISINTERESTED VESSEL IMAGINABLE.
Nabari No Ou
Yuhki Kamatani
MANGA VOLUMES 1-5 NOW AVAILABLE
OLDER TEEN OT
Yen Press
Nabari No Ou © Yuhki Kamatani / SQUARE ENIX

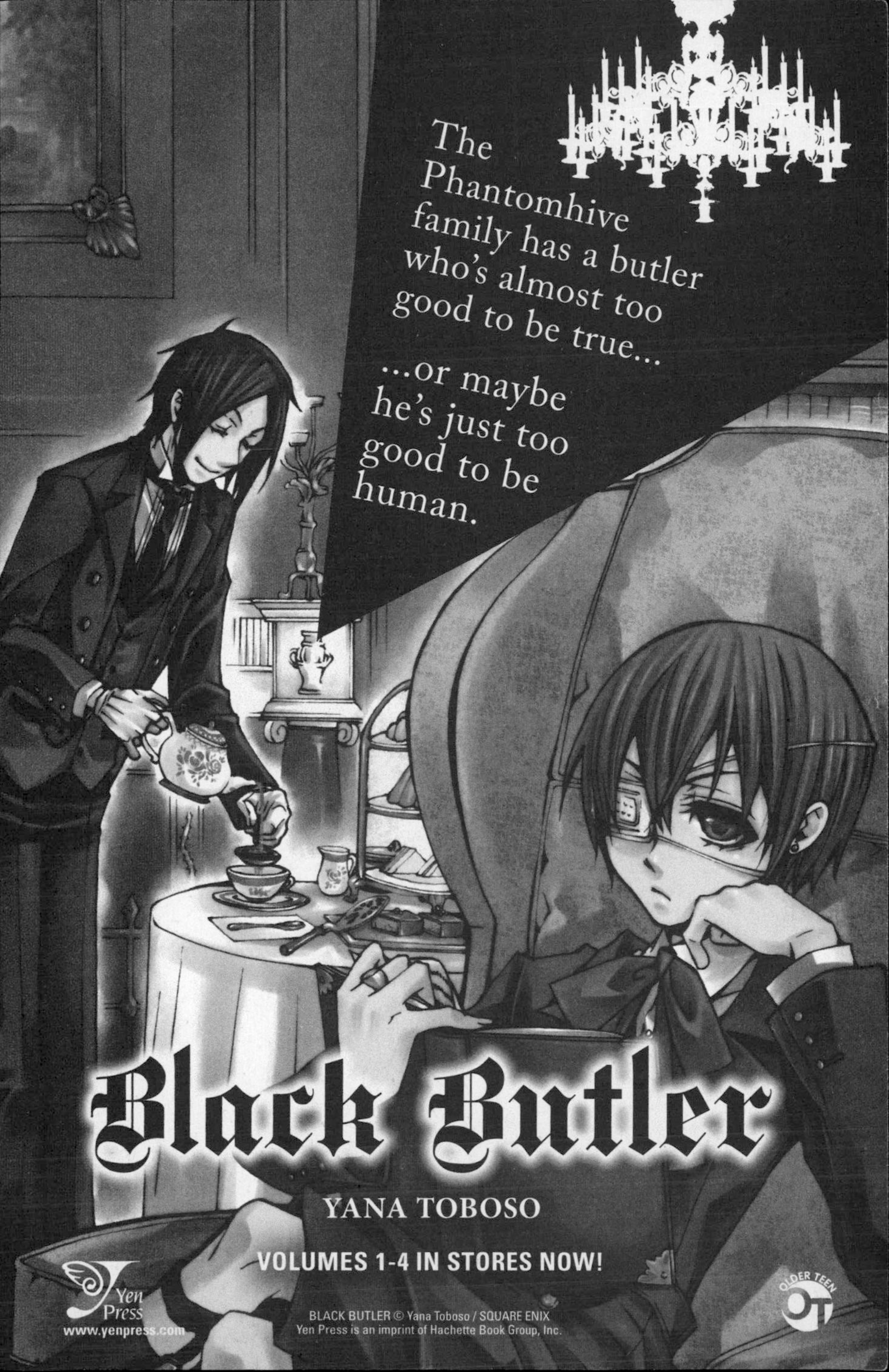
The Phantomhive family has a butler who's almost too good to be true...
...or maybe he's just too good to be human.
Black Butler
YANA TOBOSO
VOLUMES 1-4 IN STORES NOW!
Yen Press
www.yenpress.com
OLDER TEEN
OT
BLACK BUTLER © Yana Toboso / SQUARE ENIX
Yen Press is an imprint of Hachette Book Group, Inc.

PandoraHearts

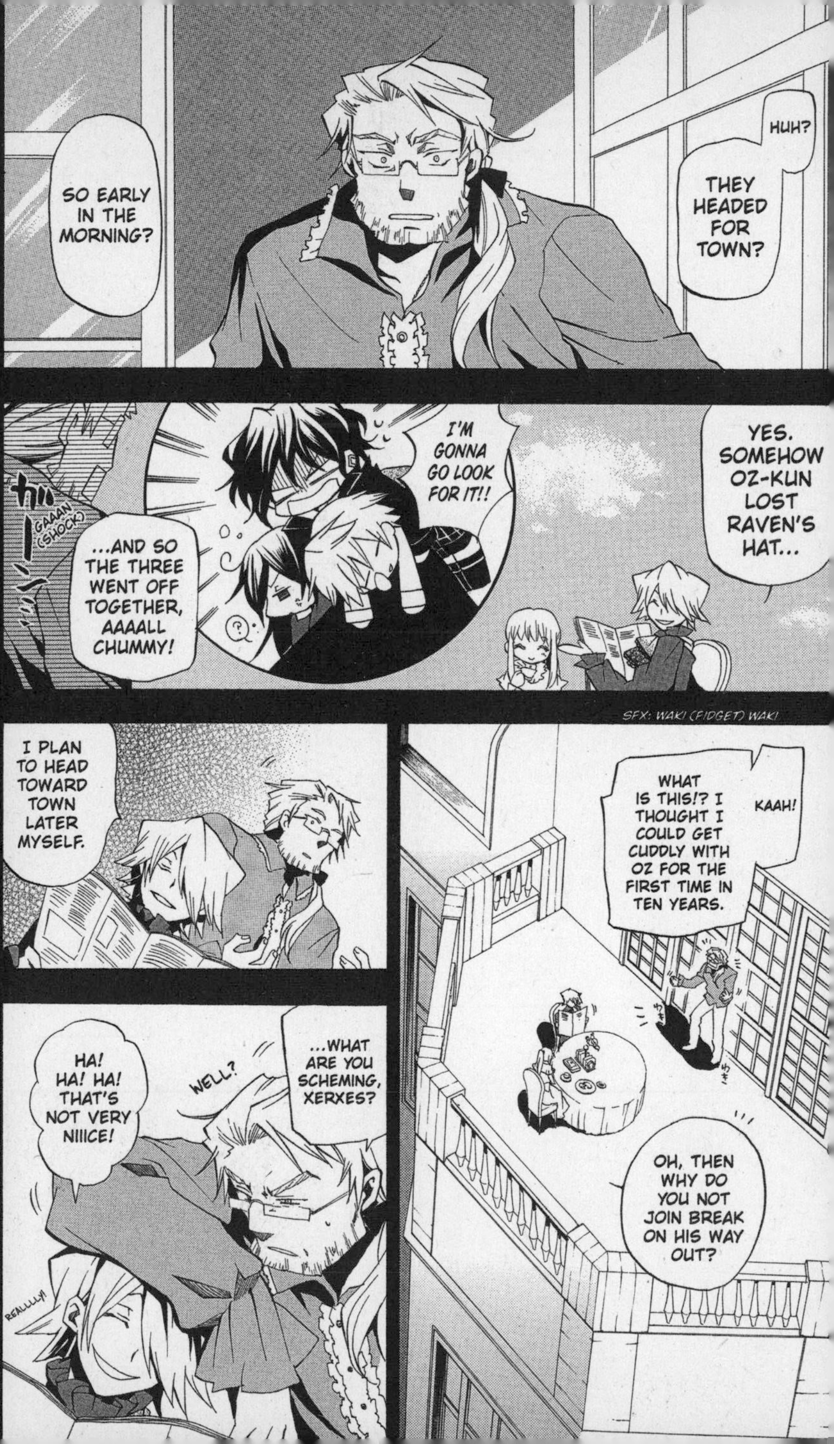
HUH?
THEY HEADED FOR TOWN?
SO EARLY IN THE MORNING?
YES. SOMEHOW OZ-KUN LOST RAVEN'S HAT...
I'M GONNA GO LOOK FOR IT!!
...AND SO THE THREE WENT OFF TOGETHER, AAAALL CHUMMY!
GAAAN (SHOCK)
SFX: WAKI (FIDGET) WAKI
WHAT IS THIS!? I THOUGHT I COULD GET CUDDLY WITH OZ FOR THE FIRST TIME IN TEN YEARS.
KAAH!
OH, THEN WHY DO YOU NOT JOIN BREAK ON HIS WAY OUT?
I PLAN TO HEAD TOWARD TOWN LATER MYSELF.
...WHAT ARE YOU SCHEMING, XERXES?
WELL?
HA! HA! HA! THAT'S NOT VERY NIIICE!
REALLLLY!

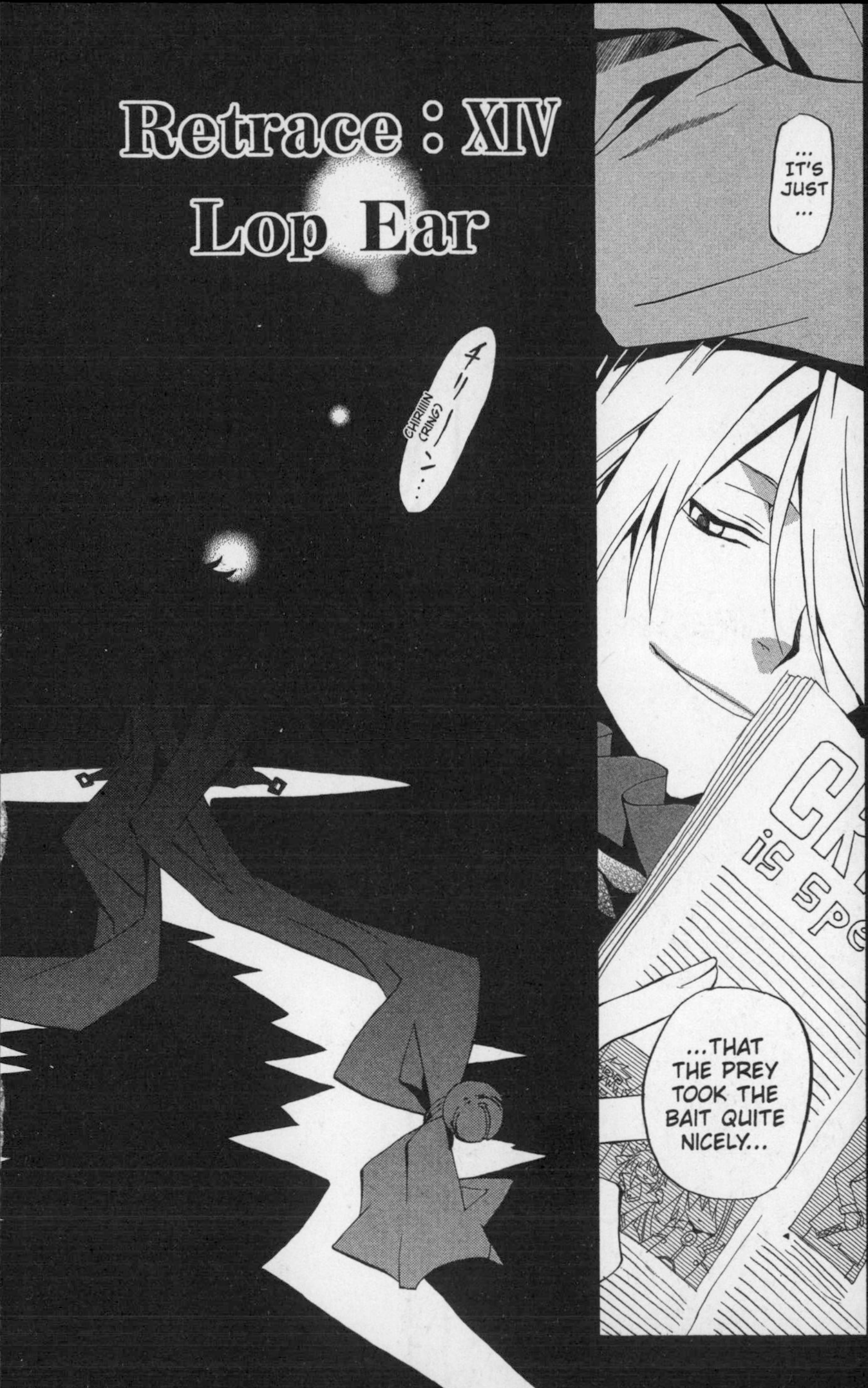

...IT'S JUST...
...THAT THE PREY TOOK THE BAIT QUITE NICELY...
Retrace : XIV
Lop Ear
CHIRIIIN (RING)

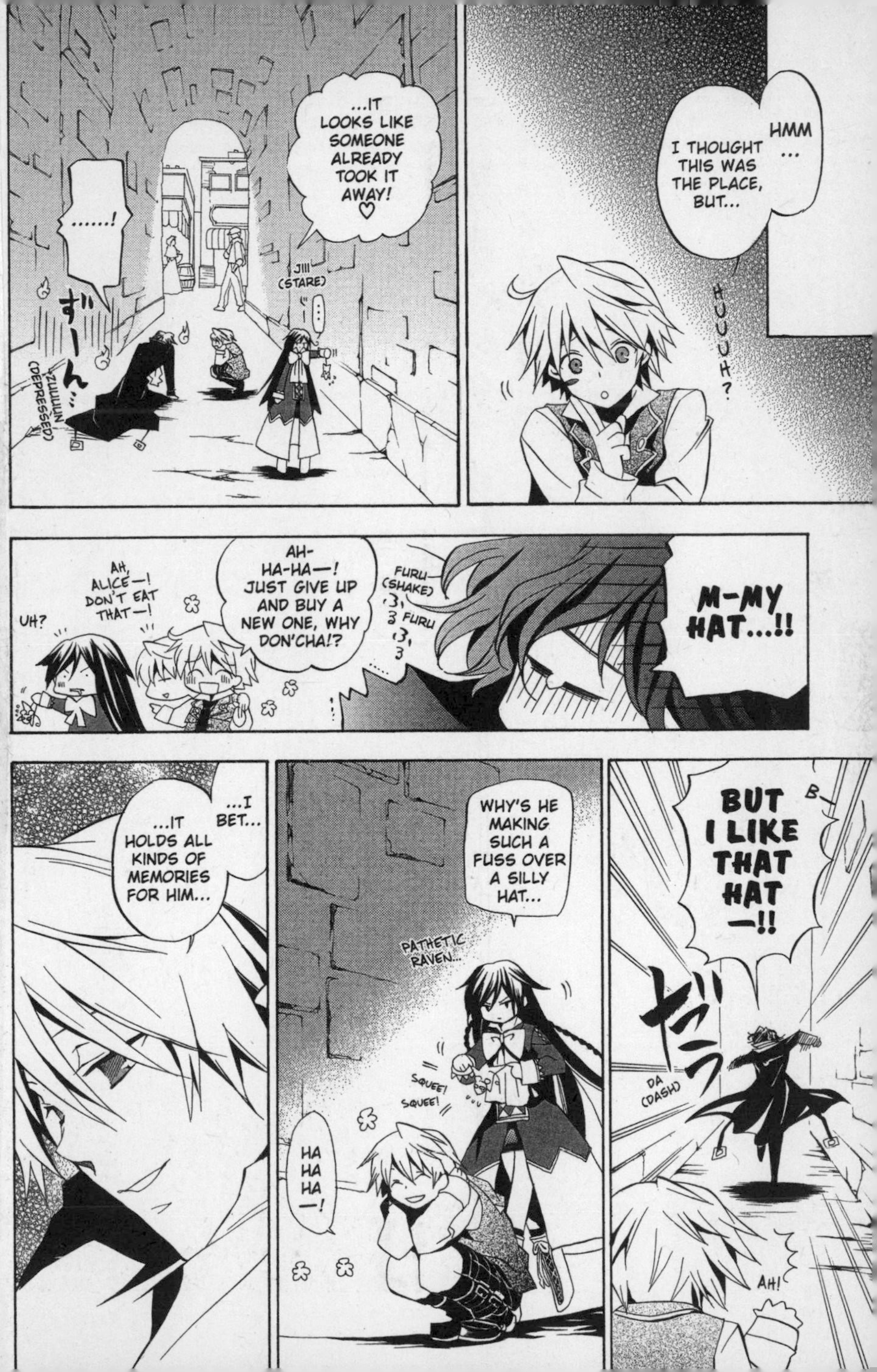
HMM...
I THOUGHT THIS WAS THE PLACE, BUT...
HUUUH?
...IT LOOKS LIKE SOMEONE ALREADY TOOK IT AWAY! ♡
JIII (STARE)
...!
......!
ずーん
ZUUUN (DEPRESSED)
M-MY HAT...!!
FURU (SHAKE)
FURU
AH-HA-HA—! JUST GIVE UP AND BUY A NEW ONE, WHY DON'CHA!?
AH, ALICE—! DON'T EAT THAT—!
UH?
B—
BUT I LIKE THAT HAT—!!
DA (DASH)
AH!
WHY'S HE MAKING SUCH A FUSS OVER A SILLY HAT...
PATHETIC RAVEN...
SQUEE! SQUEE!
HA HA HA HA—!
...I BET...
...IT HOLDS ALL KINDS OF MEMORIES FOR HIM...

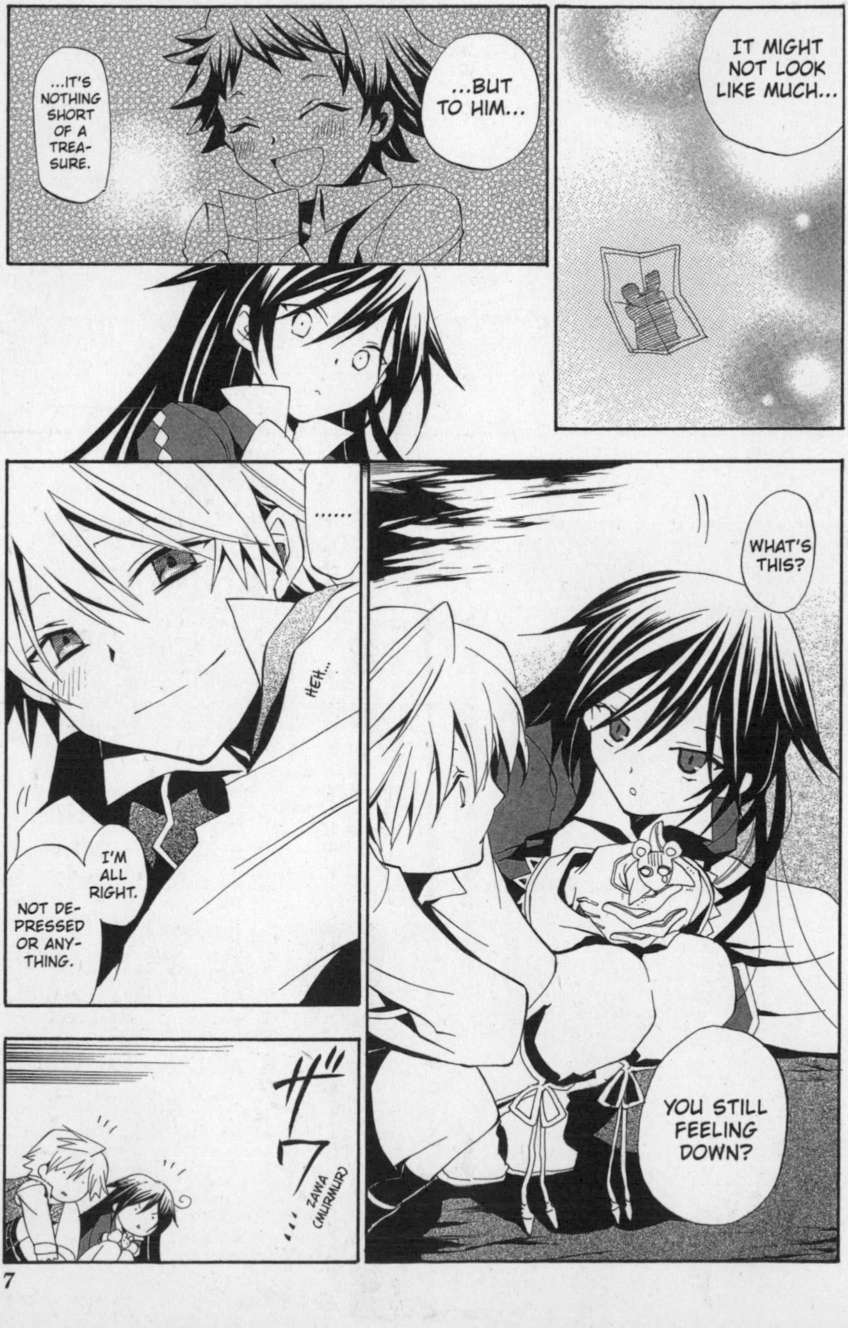
IT MIGHT NOT LOOK LIKE MUCH...
...BUT TO HIM...
...IT'S NOTHING SHORT OF A TREASURE.
WHAT'S THIS?
YOU STILL FEELING DOWN?
......
HEH...
I'M ALL RIGHT.
NOT DEPRESSED OR ANYTHING.
ZAWA (MURMUR)

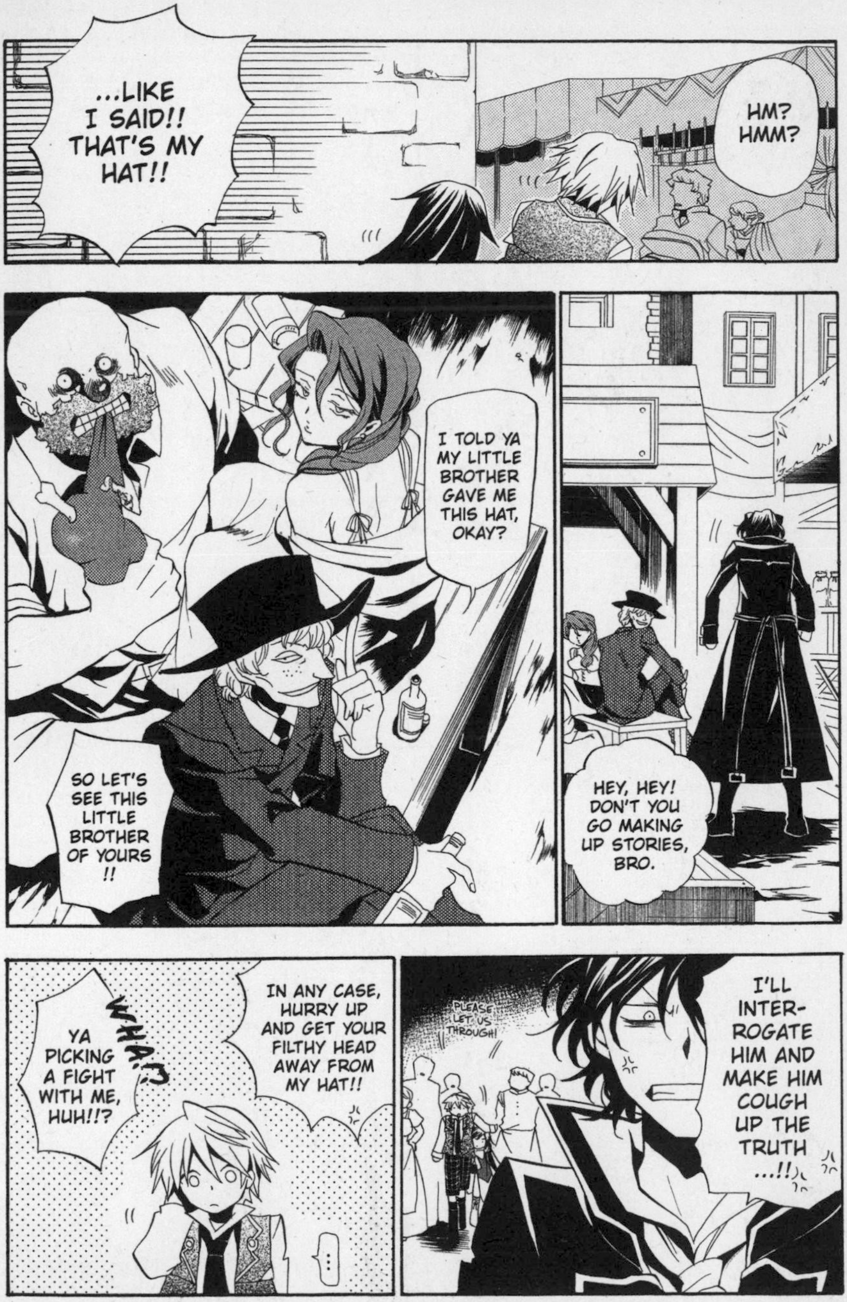
HM? HMM?
...LIKE I SAID!! THAT'S MY HAT!!
HEY, HEY! DON'T YOU GO MAKING UP STORIES, BRO.
I TOLD YA MY LITTLE BROTHER GAVE ME THIS HAT, OKAY?
SO LET'S SEE THIS LITTLE BROTHER OF YOURS!!
I'LL INTERROGATE HIM AND MAKE HIM COUGH UP THE TRUTH...!!
PLEASE LET US THROUGH!
IN ANY CASE, HURRY UP AND GET YOUR FILTHY HEAD AWAY FROM MY HAT!!
WHA!?
YA PICKING A FIGHT WITH ME, HUH!!?
...

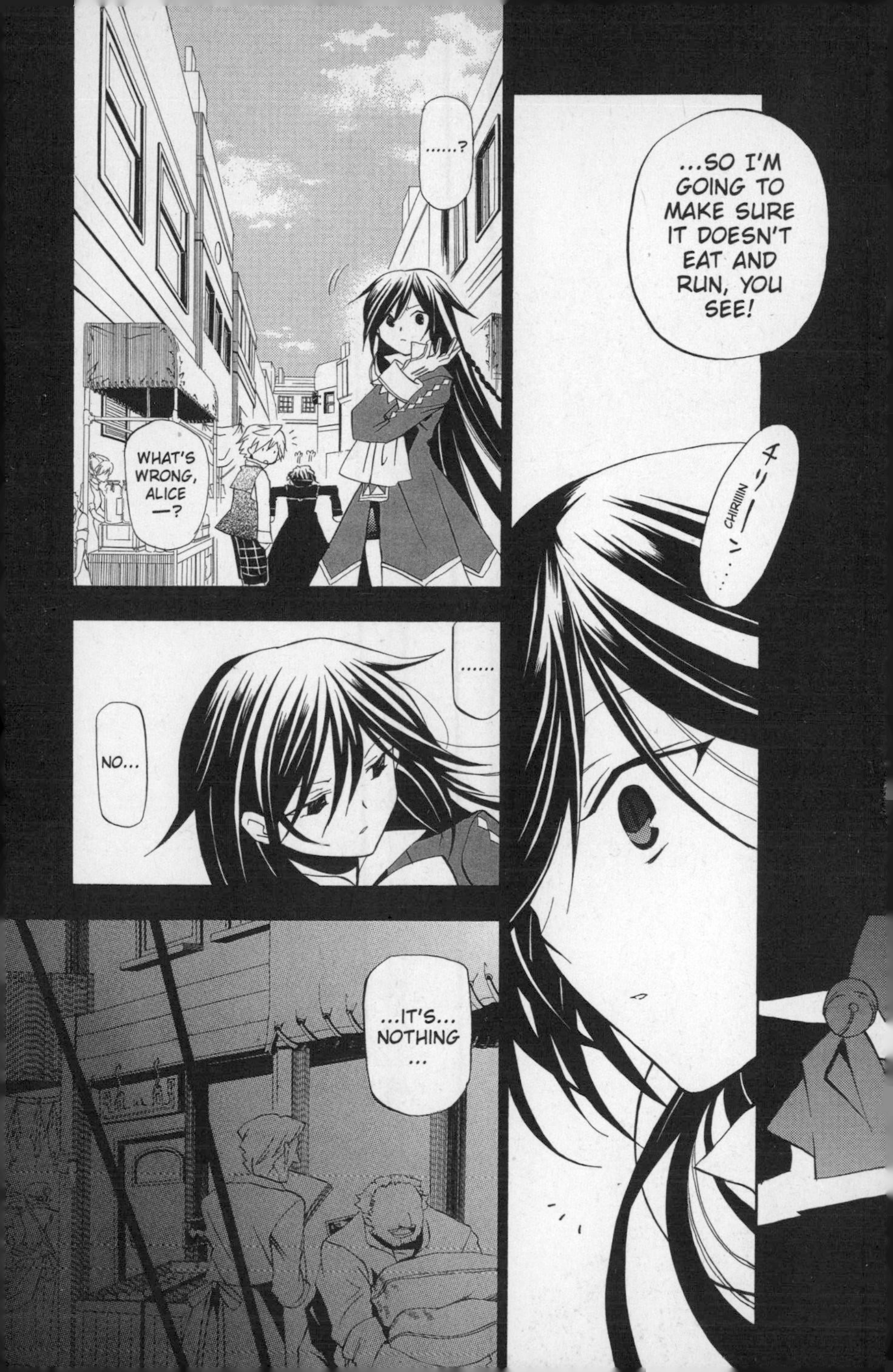

...SO I'M GOING TO MAKE SURE IT DOESN'T EAT AND RUN, YOU SEE!
CHIRIIIN
......?
WHAT'S WRONG, ALICE—?
......
NO...
...IT'S... NOTHING...

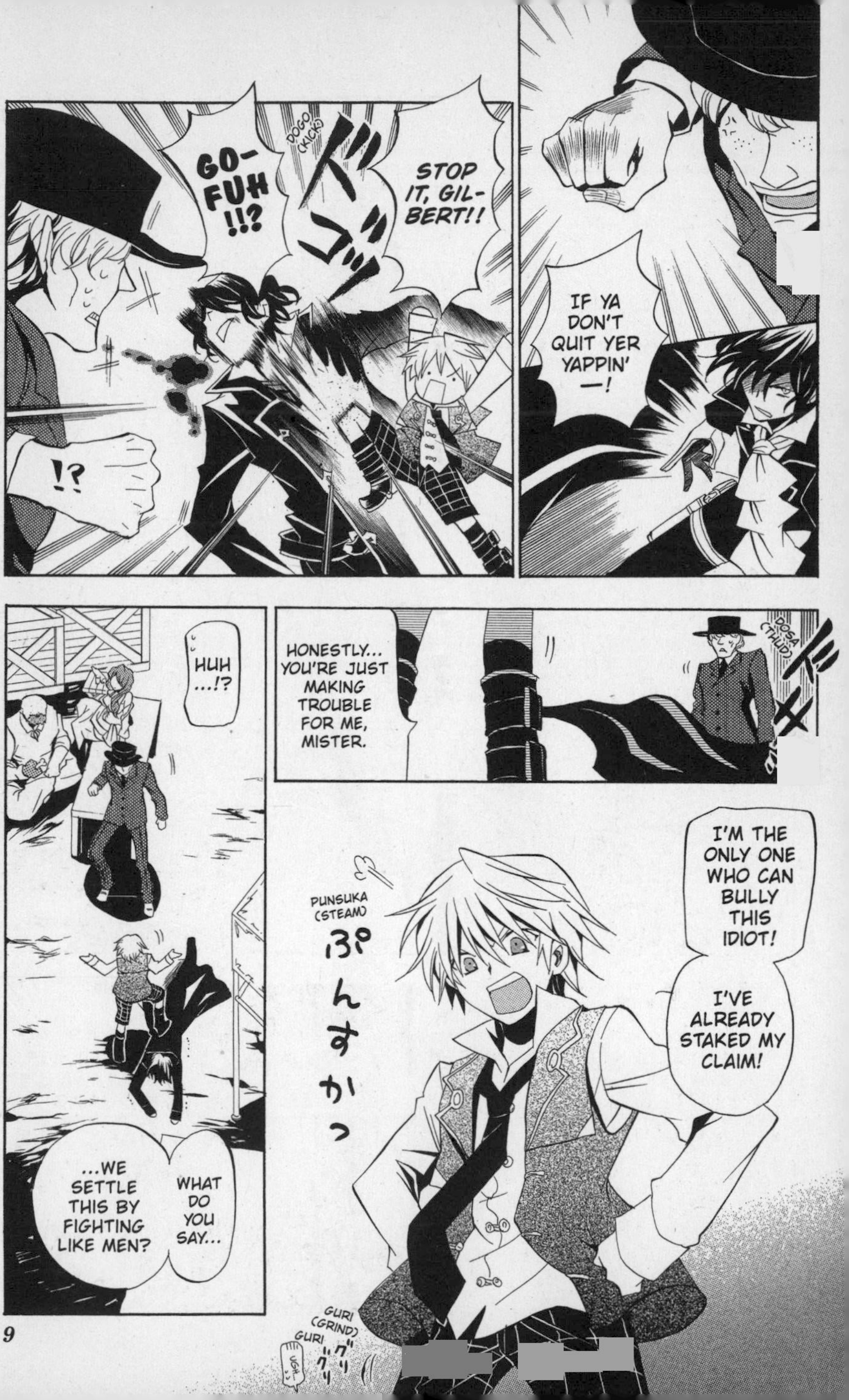
IF YA DON'T QUIT YER YAPPIN' —!
STOP IT, GIL-BERT!!
DOGO (KICK)
ドゴッ
GO-FUH!!?
!?
DOSA (THUD)
ドサッ
HONESTLY... YOU'RE JUST MAKING TROUBLE FOR ME, MISTER.
I'M THE ONLY ONE WHO CAN BULLY THIS IDIOT!
I'VE ALREADY STAKED MY CLAIM!
PUNSUKA (STEAM)
ぷんすかっ
GURI GURI (GRIND)
グリグリ
UGH
HUH ...!?
WHAT DO YOU SAY...
...WE SETTLE THIS BY FIGHTING LIKE MEN?

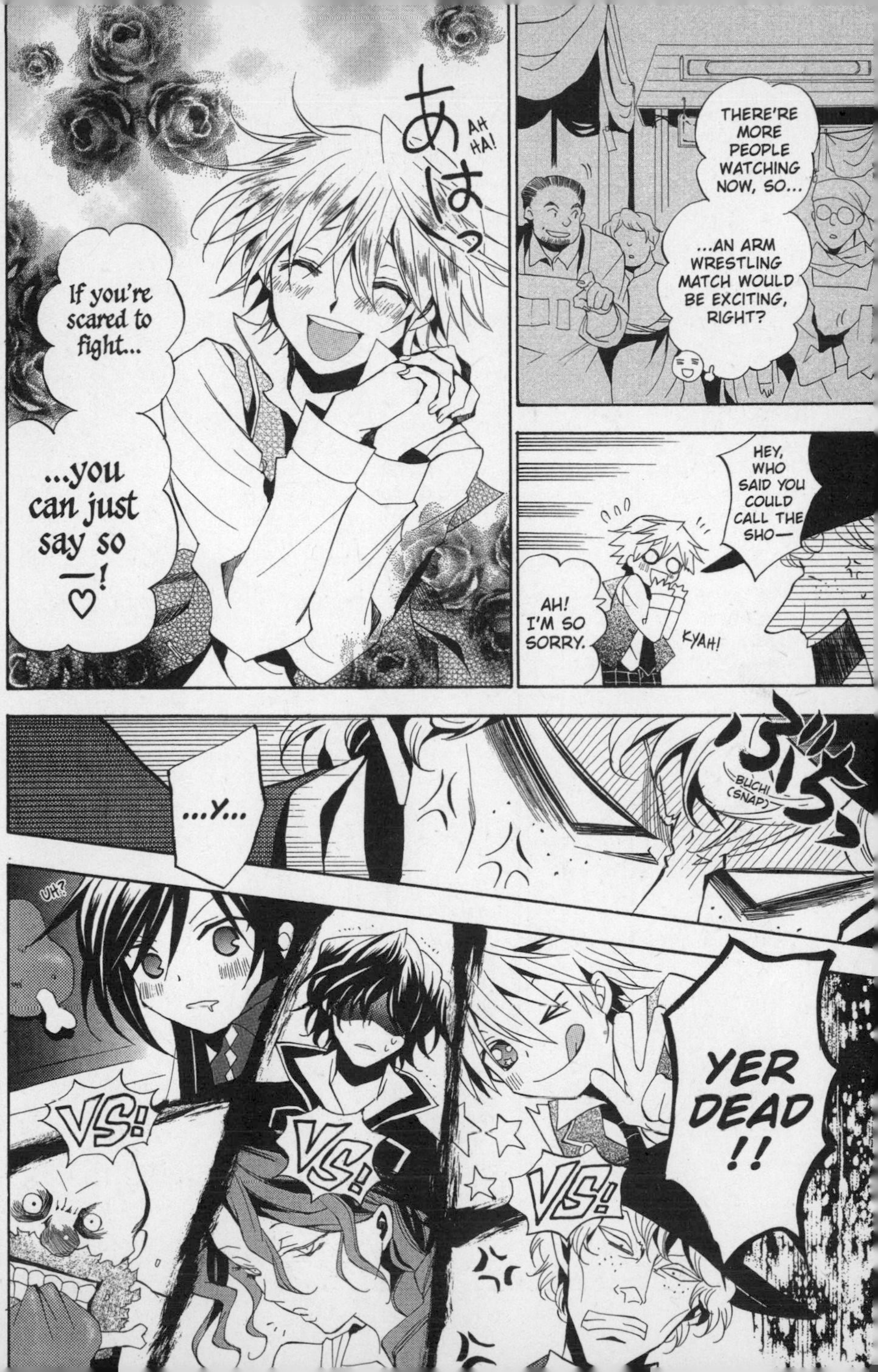
THERE'RE MORE PEOPLE WATCHING NOW, SO...
...AN ARM WRESTLING MATCH WOULD BE EXCITING, RIGHT?
HEY, WHO SAID YOU COULD CALL THE SHO—
KYAH!
AH! I'M SO SORRY.
あはっ
AH HA!
If you're scared to fight...
...you can just say so—! ♡
ぶちっ
BUCHI (SNAP)
...y...
YER DEAD!!
VS!
VS!
UH?
VS!

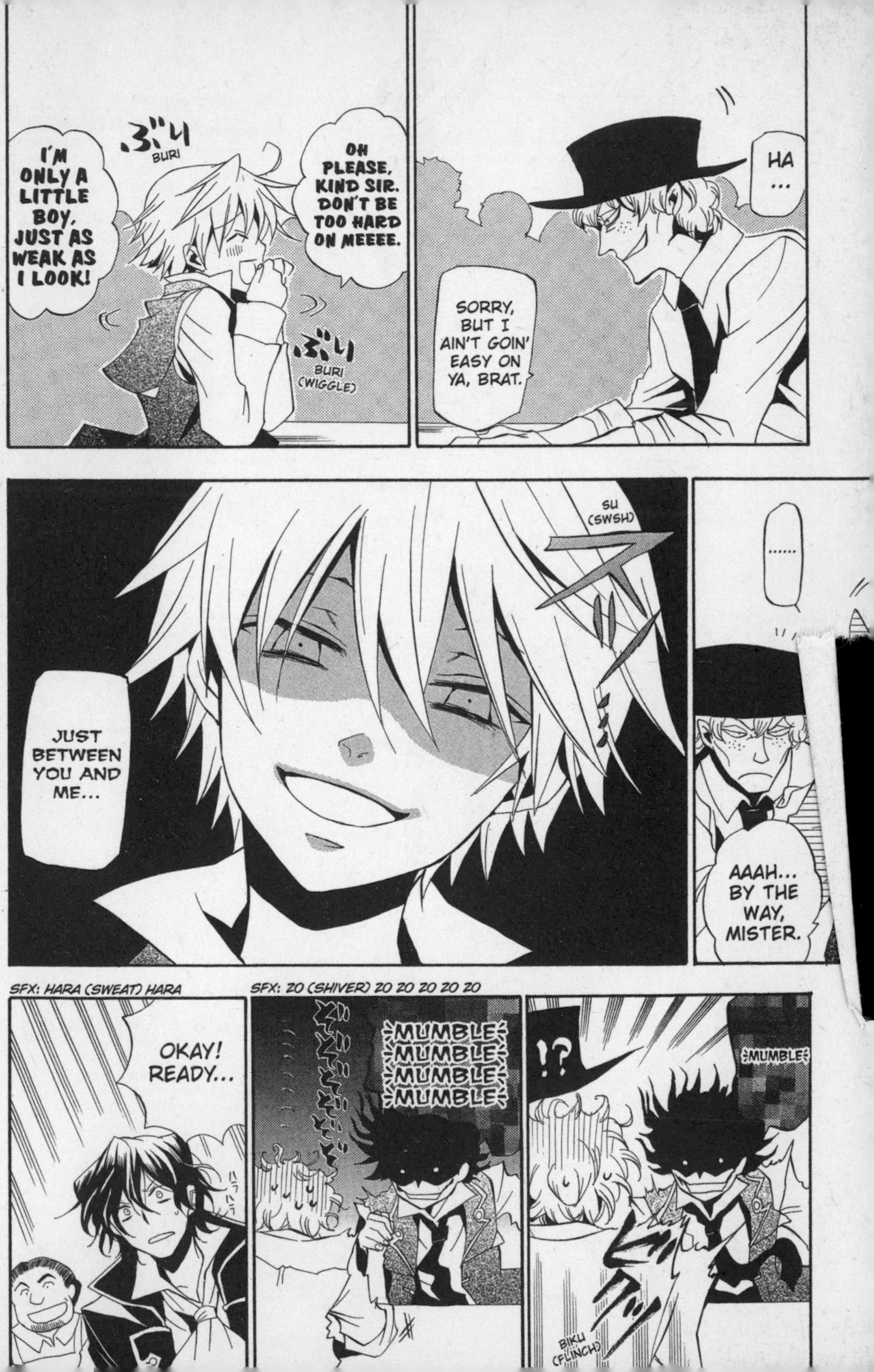
HA ...
SORRY, BUT I AIN'T GOIN' EASY ON YA, BRAT.
OH PLEASE, KIND SIR. DON'T BE TOO HARD ON MEEEE.
ぶり BURI
I'M ONLY A LITTLE BOY, JUST AS WEAK AS I LOOK!
ぶり BURI (WIGGLE)
......
AAAH... BY THE WAY, MISTER.
SU (SWSH)
JUST BETWEEN YOU AND ME...
SFX: HARA (SWEAT) HARA
SFX: ZO (SHIVER) ZO ZO ZO ZO ZO
!?
MUMBLE
BIKU (FLINCH)
MUMBLE MUMBLE MUMBLE MUMBLE
OKAY! READY...

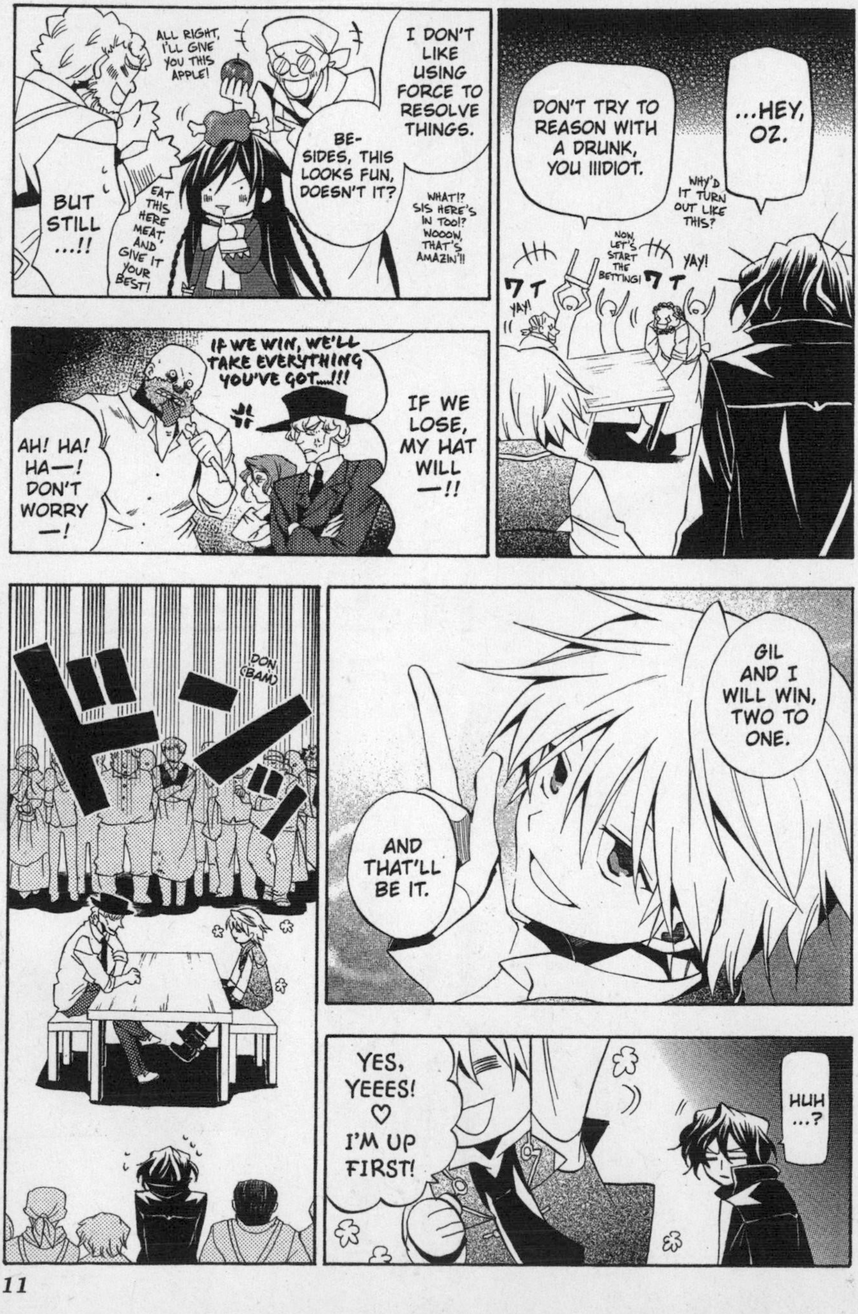
...HEY, OZ.
WHY'D IT TURN OUT LIKE THIS?
DON'T TRY TO REASON WITH A DRUNK, YOU IIIDIOT.
YAY!
NOW, LET'S START THE BETTING!
YAY!
I DON'T LIKE USING FORCE TO RESOLVE THINGS.
BE-SIDES, THIS LOOKS FUN, DOESN'T IT?
WHAT!? SIS HERE'S IN TOO!? WOOOW, THAT'S AMAZIN'!!
ALL RIGHT, I'LL GIVE YOU THIS APPLE!
EAT THIS HERE MEAT, AND GIVE IT YOUR BEST!
BUT STILL ...!!
IF WE LOSE, MY HAT WILL —!!
IF WE WIN, WE'LL TAKE EVERYTHING YOU'VE GOT...!!!
AH! HA! HA—! DON'T WORRY —!
GIL AND I WILL WIN, TWO TO ONE.
AND THAT'LL BE IT.
HUH ...?
YES, YEEES! ♡ I'M UP FIRST!
DON (BAM)

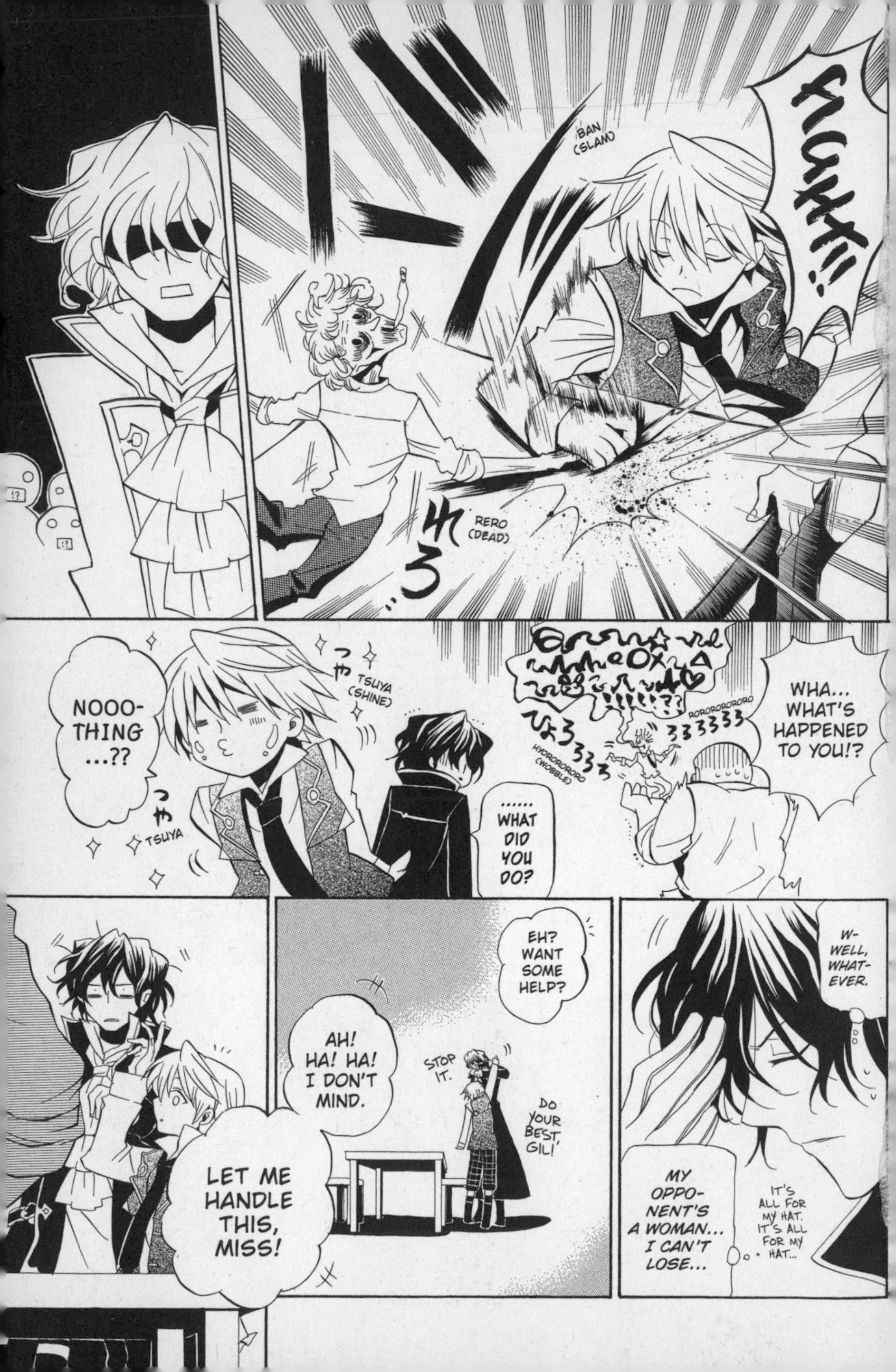
BAN (SLAM)
RERO (DEAD)
WHA... WHAT'S HAPPENED TO YOU!?
RORORORORORO
HYORORORORO (WOBBLE)
...... WHAT DID YOU DO?
TSUYA (SHINE)
NOOO-THING ...??
TSUYA
W-WELL, WHAT-EVER.
MY OPPO-NENT'S A WOMAN... I CAN'T LOSE...
IT'S ALL FOR MY HAT. IT'S ALL FOR MY HAT...
EH? WANT SOME HELP?
DO YOUR BEST, GIL!
STOP IT.
AH! HA! HA! I DON'T MIND.
LET ME HANDLE THIS, MISS!

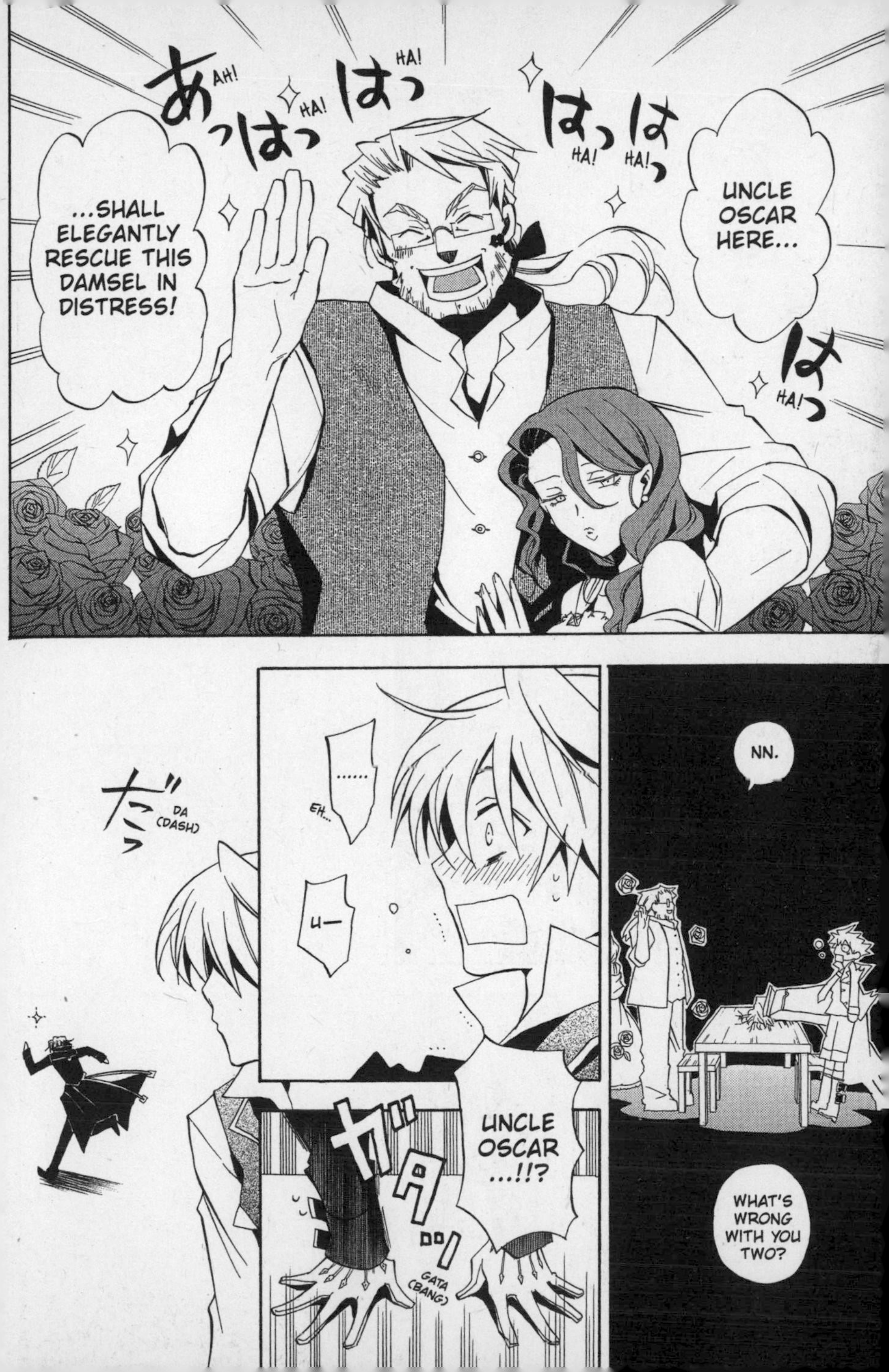
あっはっはっはっはっはっ
AH! HA! HA! HA! HA! HA!
UNCLE OSCAR HERE...
...SHALL ELEGANTLY RESCUE THIS DAMSEL IN DISTRESS!
NN.
WHAT'S WRONG WITH YOU TWO?
......
EH...
U—
UNCLE OSCAR ...!!?
GATA (BANG)
DA (DASH)

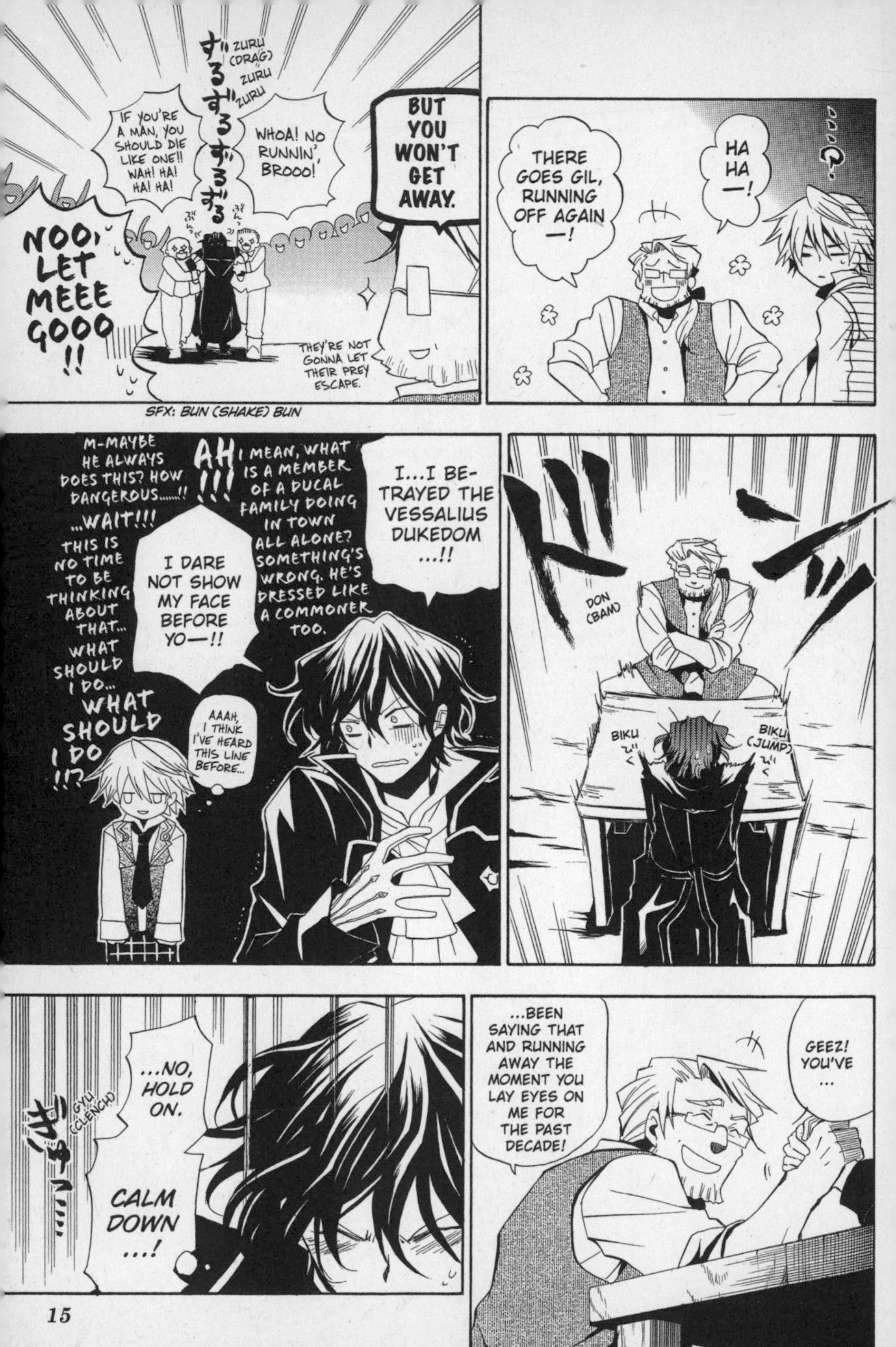
HA HA—!
THERE GOES GIL, RUNNING OFF AGAIN—!
BUT YOU WON'T GET AWAY.
WHOA! NO RUNNIN', BROOO!
ZURU (DRAG) ZURU ZURU
IF YOU'RE A MAN, YOU SHOULD DIE LIKE ONE!! WAH! HA! HA! HA!
NOO, LET MEEE GOOO!!
THEY'RE NOT GONNA LET THEIR PREY ESCAPE.
SFX: BUN (SHAKE) BUN
DON (BAM)
BIKU (JUMP)
BIKU
I...I BETRAYED THE VESSALIUS DUKEDOM ...!!
I DARE NOT SHOW MY FACE BEFORE YO—!!
I MEAN, WHAT IS A MEMBER OF A DUCAL FAMILY DOING IN TOWN ALL ALONE? SOMETHING'S WRONG. HE'S DRESSED LIKE A COMMONER TOO.
AH!!!
M-MAYBE HE ALWAYS DOES THIS? HOW DANGEROUS.......!!
...WAIT!!! THIS IS NO TIME TO BE THINKING ABOUT THAT... WHAT SHOULD I DO... WHAT SHOULD I DO!!?
AAAH, I THINK I'VE HEARD THIS LINE BEFORE...
GEEZ! YOU'VE ...
...BEEN SAYING THAT AND RUNNING AWAY THE MOMENT YOU LAY EYES ON ME FOR THE PAST DECADE!
...NO, HOLD ON.
GYU (CLENCH)
CALM DOWN ...!

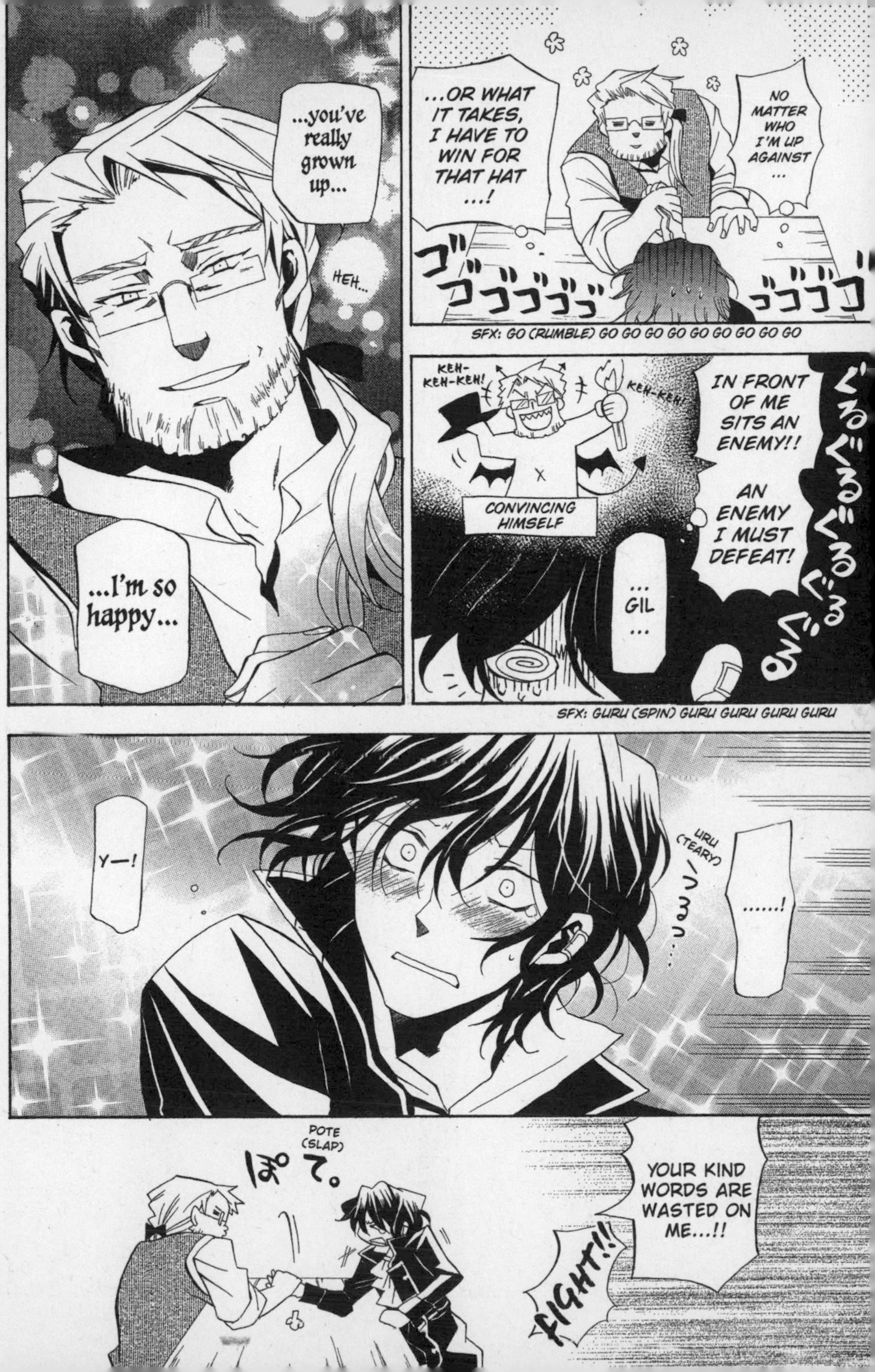
NO MATTER WHO I'M UP AGAINST ...
...OR WHAT IT TAKES, I HAVE TO WIN FOR THAT HAT ...!
SFX: GO (RUMBLE) GO GO GO GO GO GO GO GO GO
IN FRONT OF ME SITS AN ENEMY!!
AN ENEMY I MUST DEFEAT!
KEH-KEH!
KEH-KEH-KEH!
CONVINCING HIMSELF
... GIL ...
SFX: GURU (SPIN) GURU GURU GURU GURU
...you've really grown up...
HEH...
...I'm so happy...
......!
URU (TEARY)
Y—!
YOUR KIND WORDS ARE WASTED ON ME...!!
FIGHT!!
POTE (SLAP)

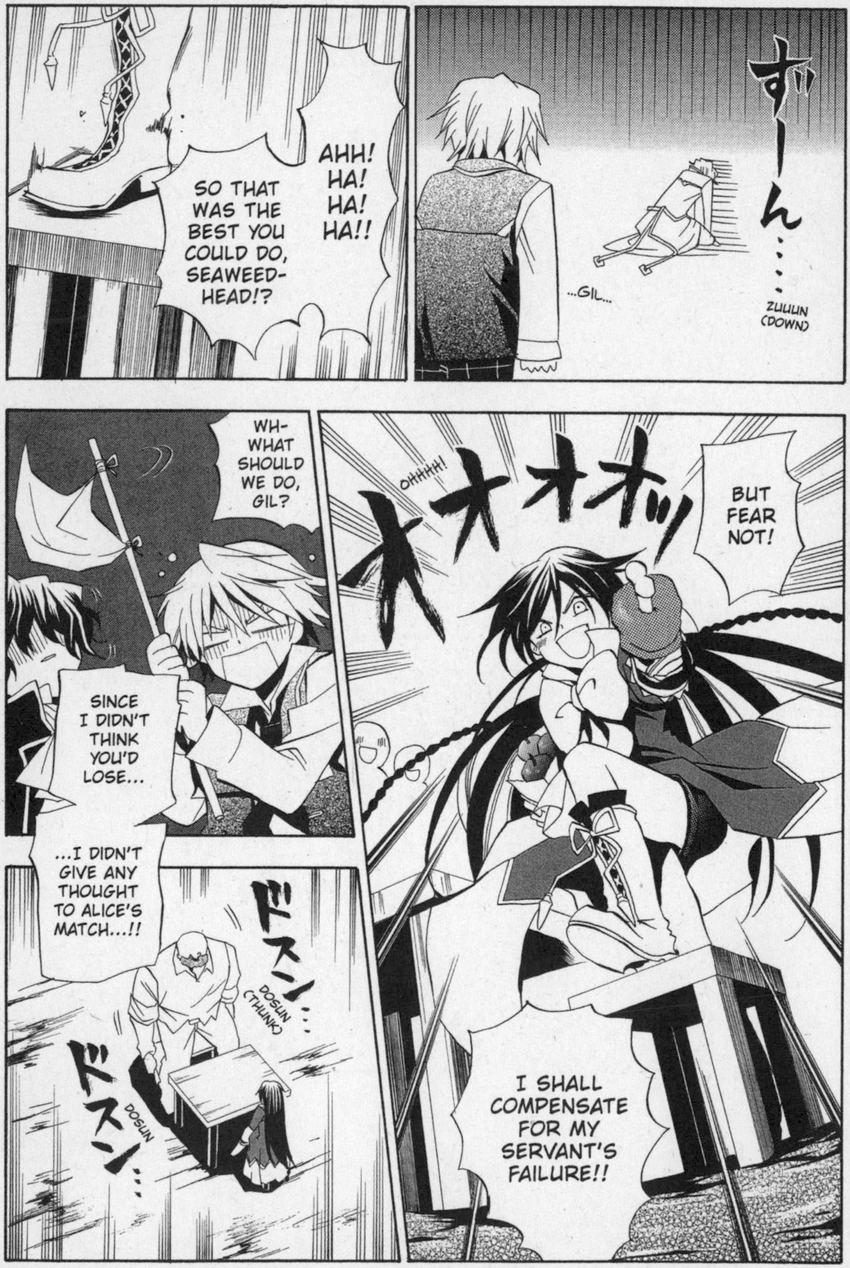
ずーん…
ZUUUN (DOWN)
...GIL...
AHH! HA! HA! HA!!
SO THAT WAS THE BEST YOU COULD DO, SEAWEED-HEAD!?
BUT FEAR NOT!
オオオオッ
OHHHH!
I SHALL COMPENSATE FOR MY SERVANT'S FAILURE!!
WH-WHAT SHOULD WE DO, GIL?
SINCE I DIDN'T THINK YOU'D LOSE...
...I DIDN'T GIVE ANY THOUGHT TO ALICE'S MATCH...!!
ドスン…
DOSUN (THUNK)
ドスン…
DOSUN

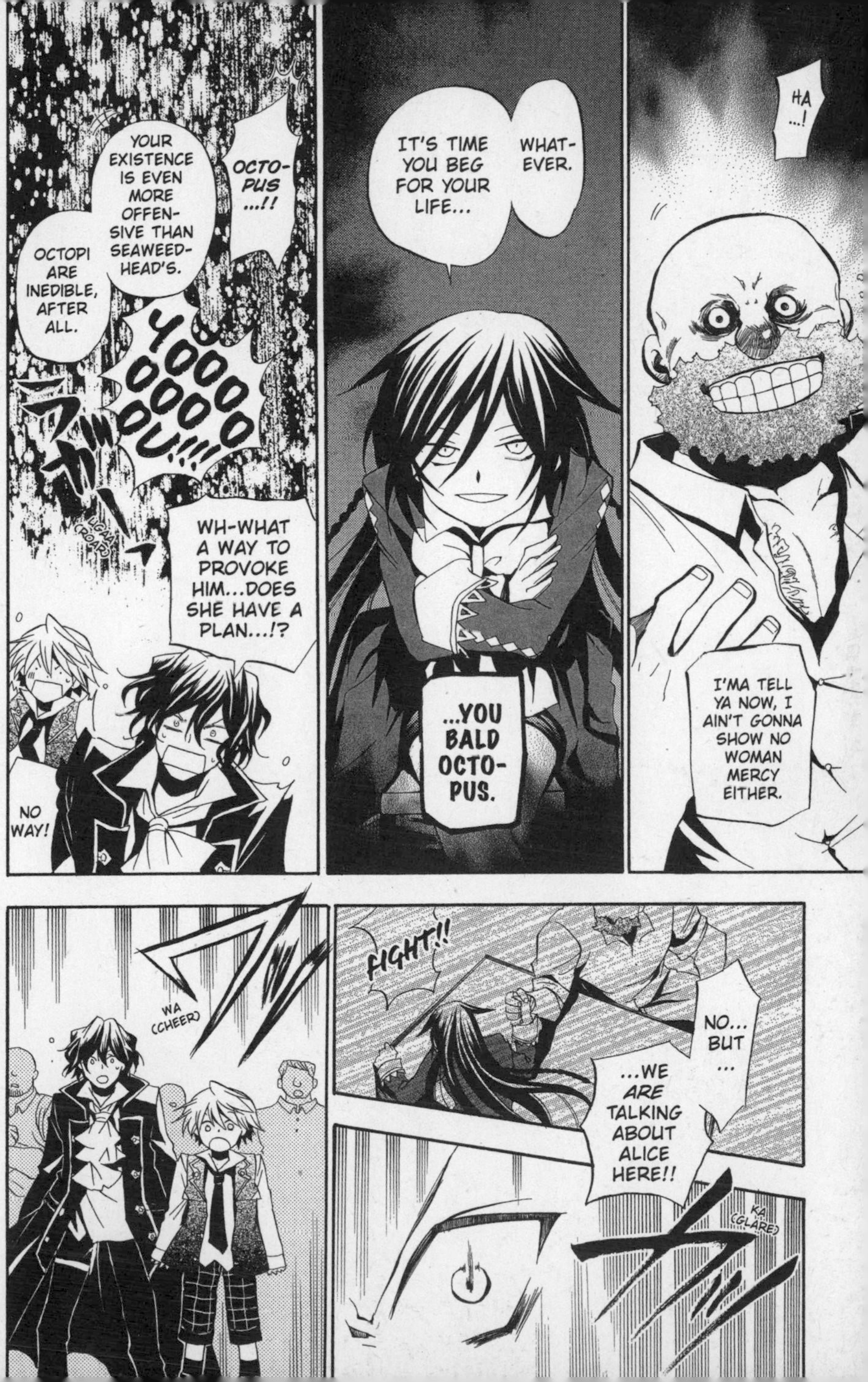
HA ...!
I'MA TELL YA NOW, I AIN'T GONNA SHOW NO WOMAN MERCY EITHER.
WHAT-EVER.
IT'S TIME YOU BEG FOR YOUR LIFE...
...YOU BALD OCTO-PUS.
OCTO-PUS ...!!
YOUR EXISTENCE IS EVEN MORE OFFEN-SIVE THAN SEAWEED-HEAD'S.
OCTOPI ARE INEDIBLE, AFTER ALL.
YOOOOOOOOOOOU!!!!
LIGAA (ROAR)
WH-WHAT A WAY TO PROVOKE HIM...DOES SHE HAVE A PLAN...!?
NO WAY!
FIGHT!!
NO... BUT ...
...WE ARE TALKING ABOUT ALICE HERE!!
KA (GLARE)
WA (CHEER)

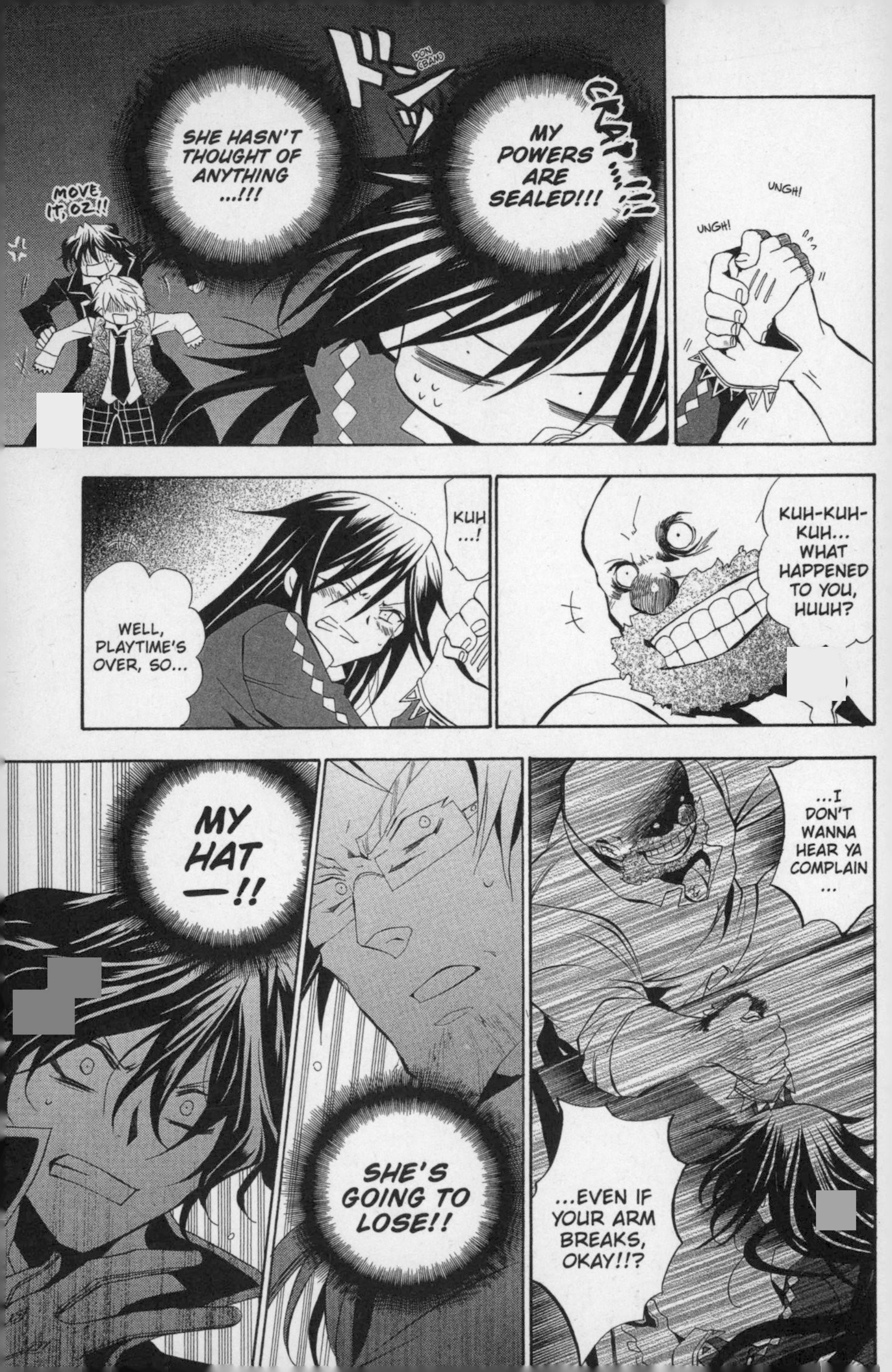
UNGH!
UNGH!
DON (BAM)
CRAP...!!!
MY POWERS ARE SEALED!!!
SHE HASN'T THOUGHT OF ANYTHING ...!!!
MOVE IT, OZ!!
KUH-KUH-KUH... WHAT HAPPENED TO YOU, HUUH?
KUH ...!
WELL, PLAYTIME'S OVER, SO...
...I DON'T WANNA HEAR YA COMPLAIN ...
...EVEN IF YOUR ARM BREAKS, OKAY!!?
SHE'S GOING TO LOSE!!
MY HAT—!!

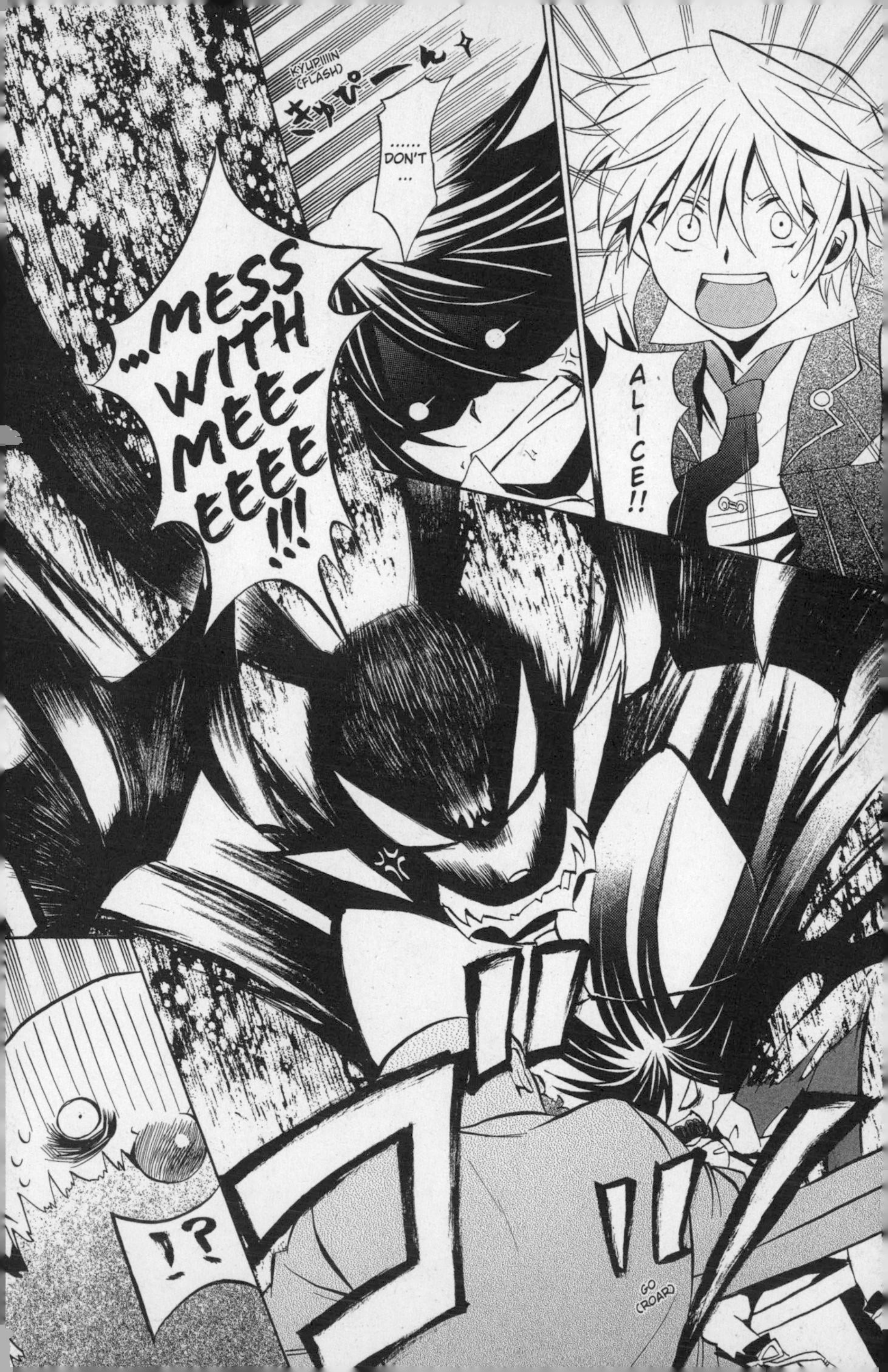
ALICE!!
KYUPIIIIN (FLASH)
きゅぴーん
......DON'T...
...MESS WITH MEEEEEEE!!!
GO (ROAR)
!?

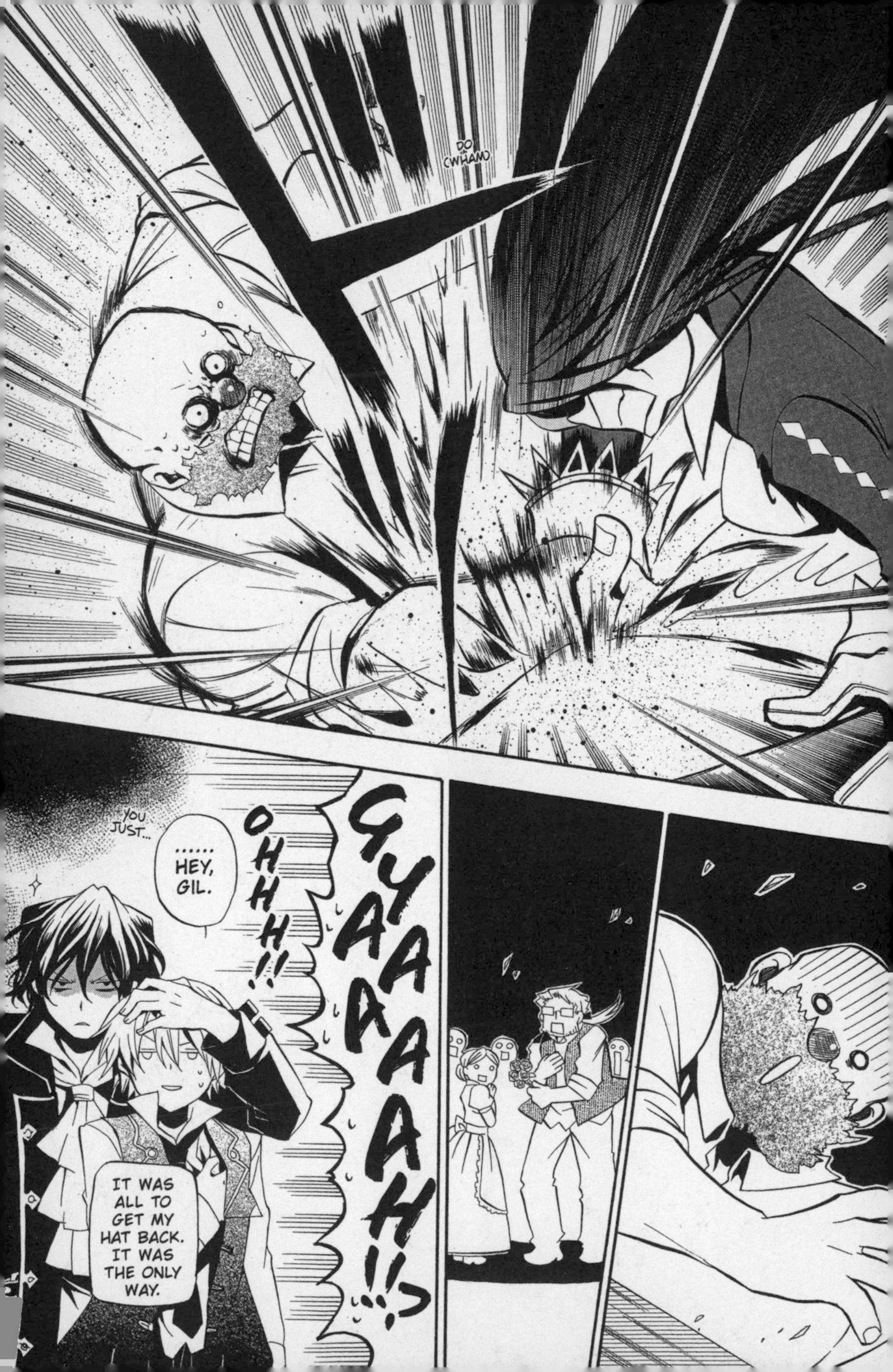
DO (WHAM)
GYAAAAAAAH!!?
OHHHH!!
...... HEY, GIL.
YOU JUST...
IT WAS ALL TO GET MY HAT BACK. IT WAS THE ONLY WAY.

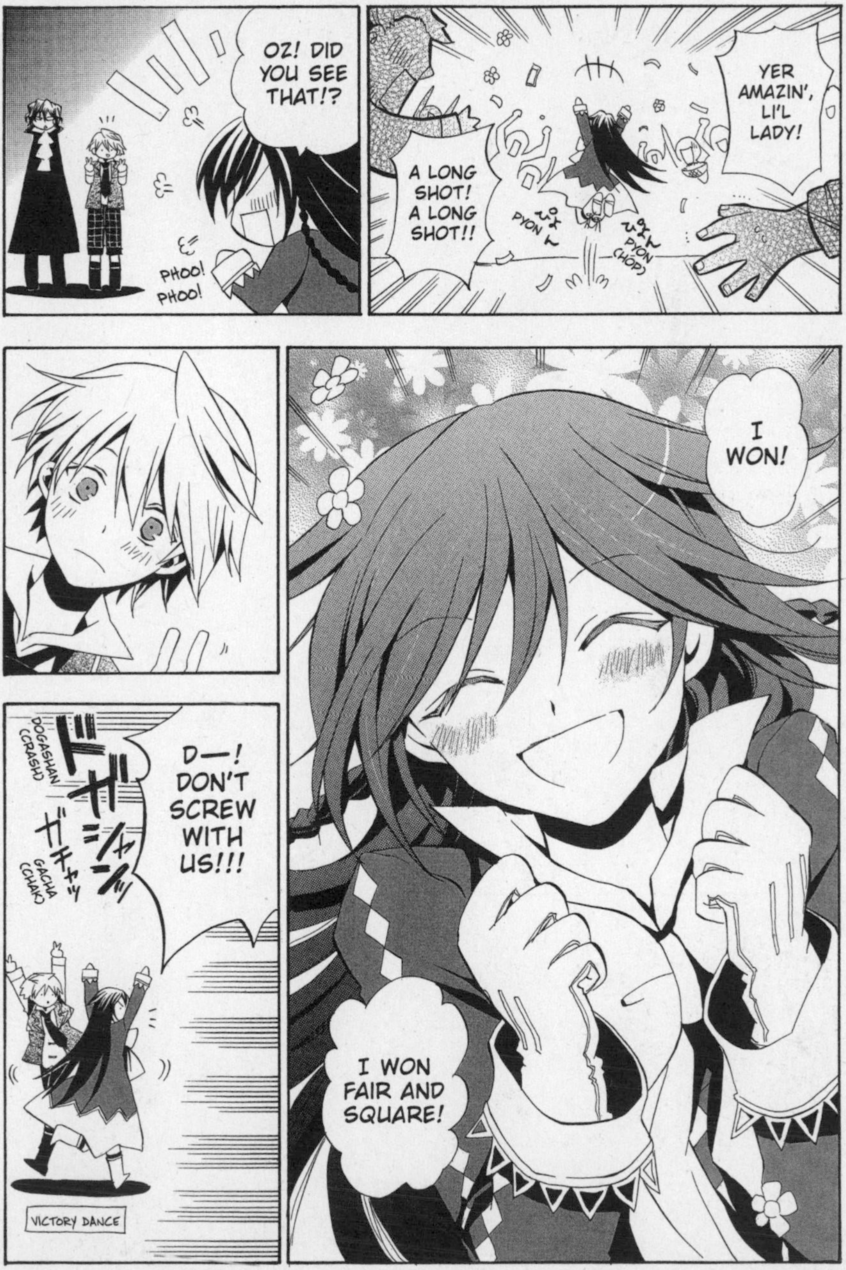
YER AMAZIN', LI'L LADY!
A LONG SHOT! A LONG SHOT!!
ぴょん PYON
ぴょん PYON (HOP)
OZ! DID YOU SEE THAT!?
PHOO! PHOO!
I WON!
I WON FAIR AND SQUARE!
D—! DON'T SCREW WITH US!!!
ドガシャン DOGASHAN (CRASH)
ガチャッ GACHA (CHAK)
VICTORY DANCE

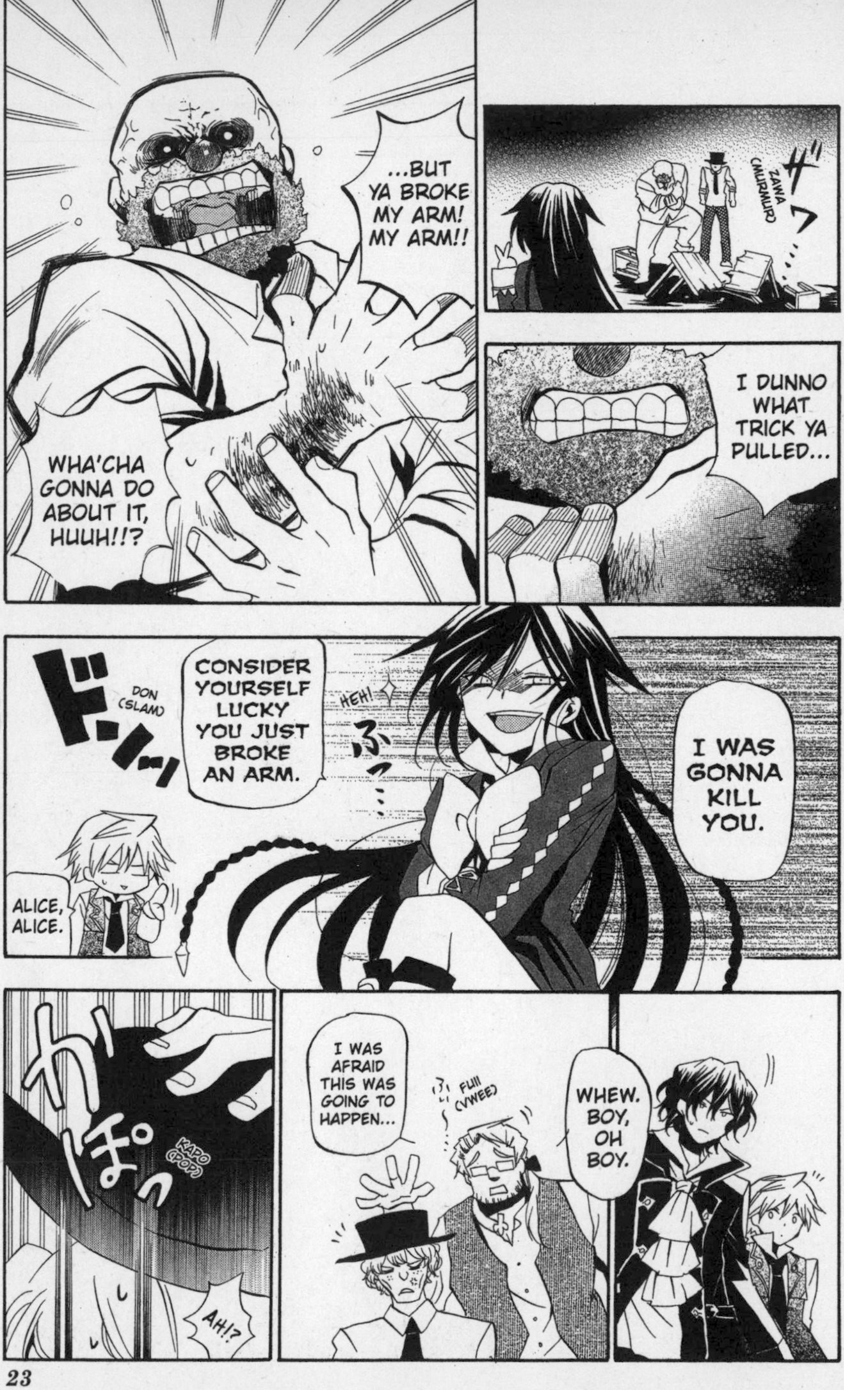
ZAWA (MURMUR)
I DUNNO WHAT TRICK YA PULLED...
...BUT YA BROKE MY ARM! MY ARM!!
WHA'CHA GONNA DO ABOUT IT, HUUH!!?
I WAS GONNA KILL YOU.
HEH!
CONSIDER YOURSELF LUCKY YOU JUST BROKE AN ARM.
DON (SLAM)
ALICE, ALICE.
WHEW. BOY, OH BOY.
FUII (VWEE)
I WAS AFRAID THIS WAS GOING TO HAPPEN...
KAPO (POP)
AH!?

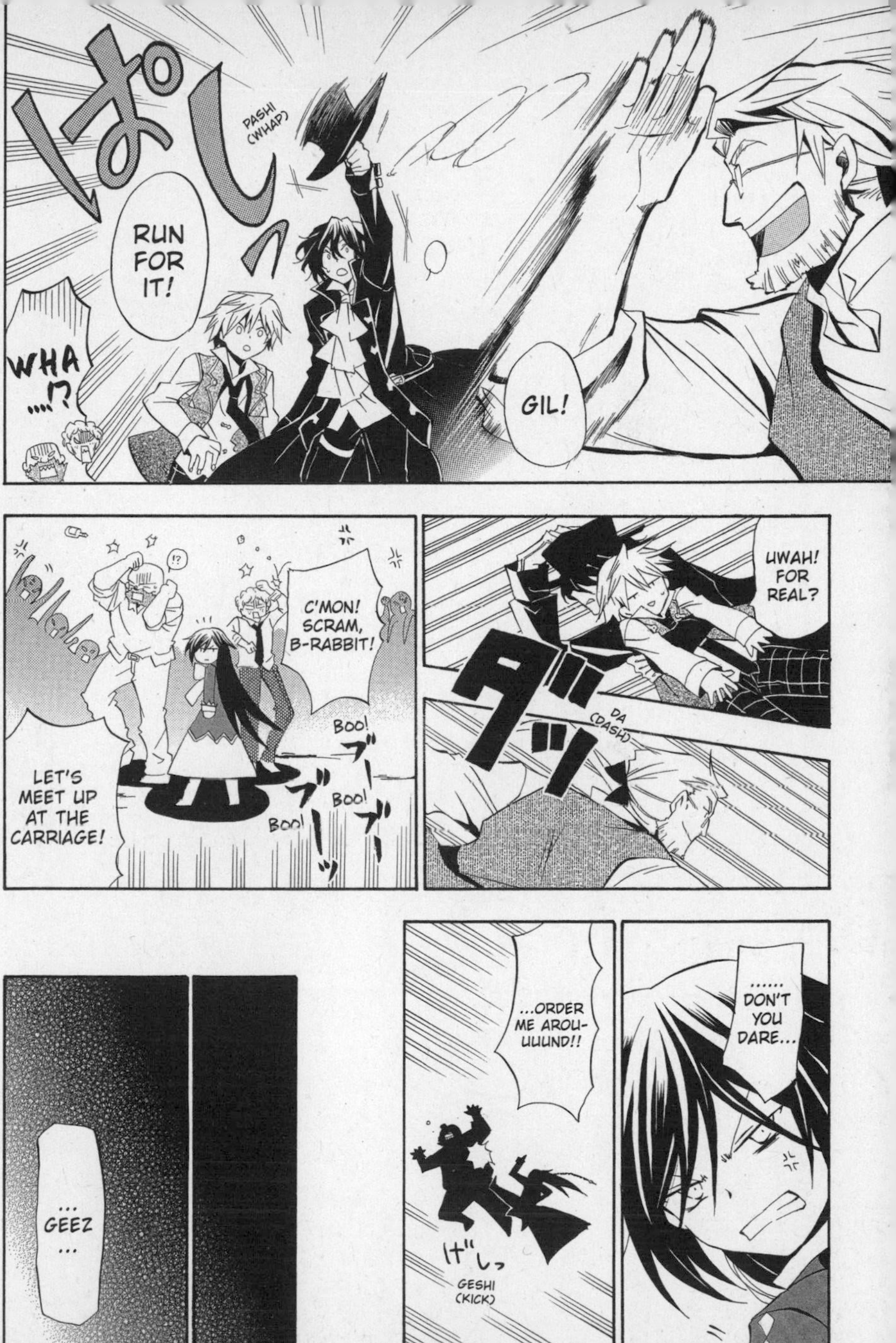
GIL!
RUN FOR IT!
ぱしっ
PASHI (WHAP)
WHA ....!?
UWAH! FOR REAL?
ダッ
DA (DASH)
C'MON! SCRAM, B-RABBIT!
LET'S MEET UP AT THE CARRIAGE!
BOO!
BOO!
BOO!
ブーブーブー
...... DON'T YOU DARE...
...ORDER ME AROU-UUUND!!
げしっ
GESHI (KICK)
... GEEZ ...

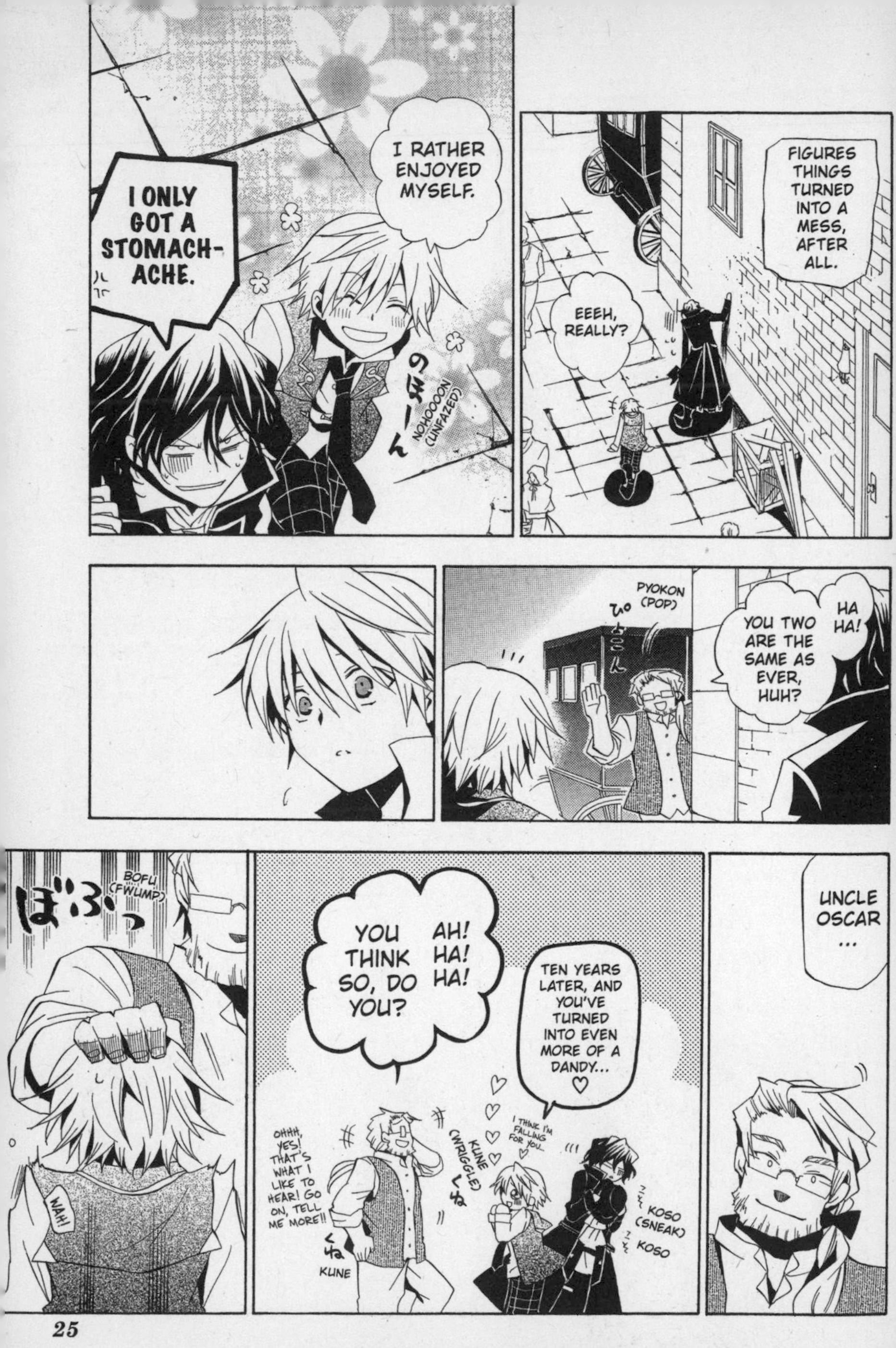

FIGURES THINGS TURNED INTO A MESS, AFTER ALL.
EEEH, REALLY?
I RATHER ENJOYED MYSELF.
I ONLY GOT A STOMACH-ACHE.
のほーん
NOHOOOON (UNFAZED)
HA HA!
YOU TWO ARE THE SAME AS EVER, HUH?
PYOKON (POP)
UNCLE OSCAR ...
TEN YEARS LATER, AND YOU'VE TURNED INTO EVEN MORE OF A DANDY...
I THINK I'M FALLING FOR YOU...
AH! HA! HA!
YOU THINK SO, DO YOU?
OHHH, YES! THAT'S WHAT I LIKE TO HEAR! GO ON, TELL ME MORE!!
KUNE (WRIGGLE)
KUNE
KOSO (SNEAK)
KOSO
BOFU (FWLUMP)
ぼふっ
WAH!

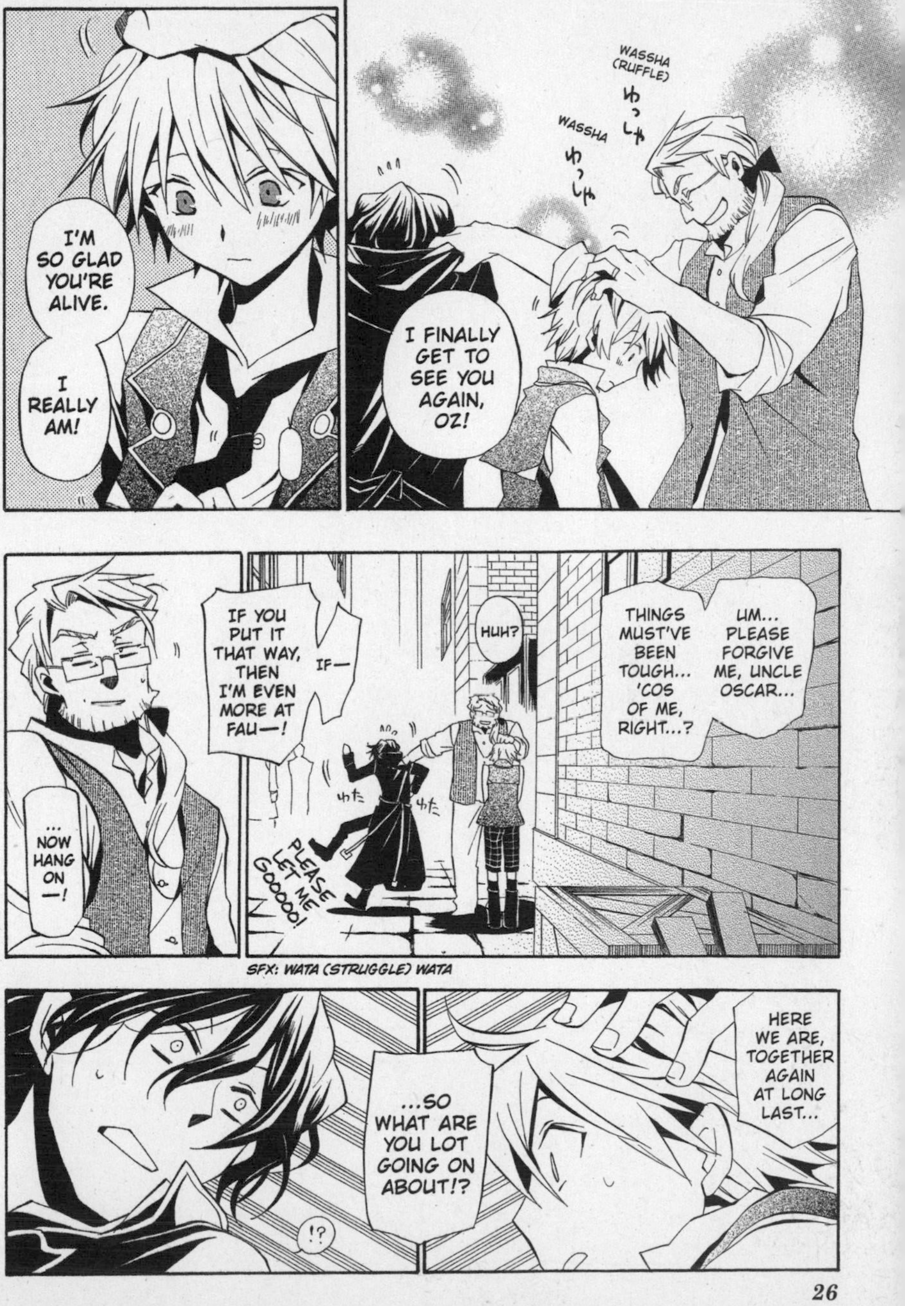
WASSHA (RUFFLE)
わっしゃ
WASSHA
わっしゃ
I FINALLY GET TO SEE YOU AGAIN, OZ!
I'M SO GLAD YOU'RE ALIVE.
I REALLY AM!
UM... PLEASE FORGIVE ME, UNCLE OSCAR...
THINGS MUST'VE BEEN TOUGH... 'COS OF ME, RIGHT...?
HUH?
IF YOU PUT IT THAT WAY, THEN I'M EVEN MORE AT FAU—!
IF—
わた
わた
PLEASE LET ME GOOOOO!
...NOW HANG ON—!
SFX: WATA (STRUGGLE) WATA
HERE WE ARE, TOGETHER AGAIN AT LONG LAST...
...SO WHAT ARE YOU LOT GOING ON ABOUT!?
!?

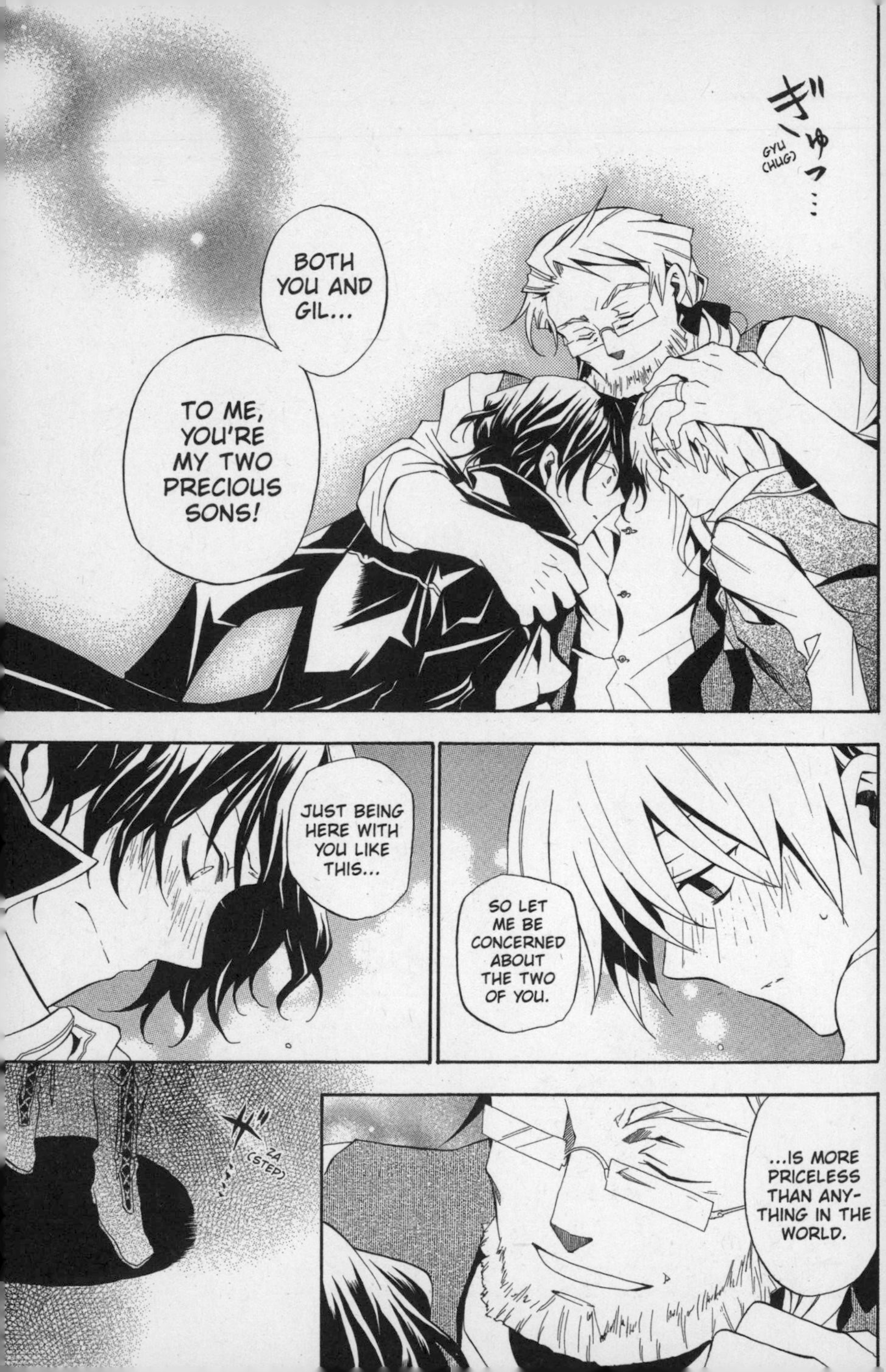
ぎゅっ
GYU (HUG)
BOTH YOU AND GIL...
TO ME, YOU'RE MY TWO PRECIOUS SONS!
SO LET ME BE CONCERNED ABOUT THE TWO OF YOU.
JUST BEING HERE WITH YOU LIKE THIS...
...IS MORE PRICELESS THAN ANY-THING IN THE WORLD.
ザッ
ZA (STEP)

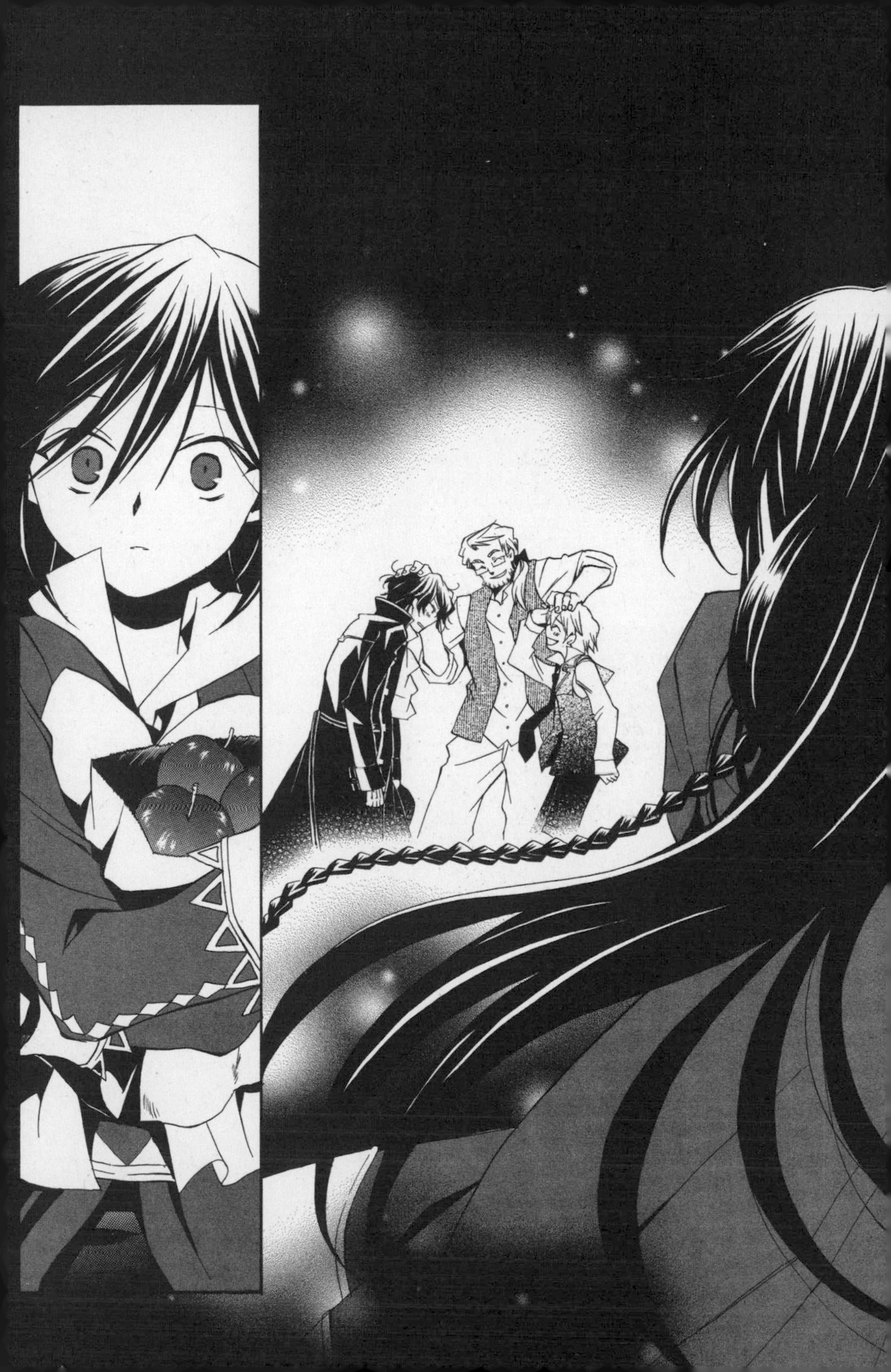

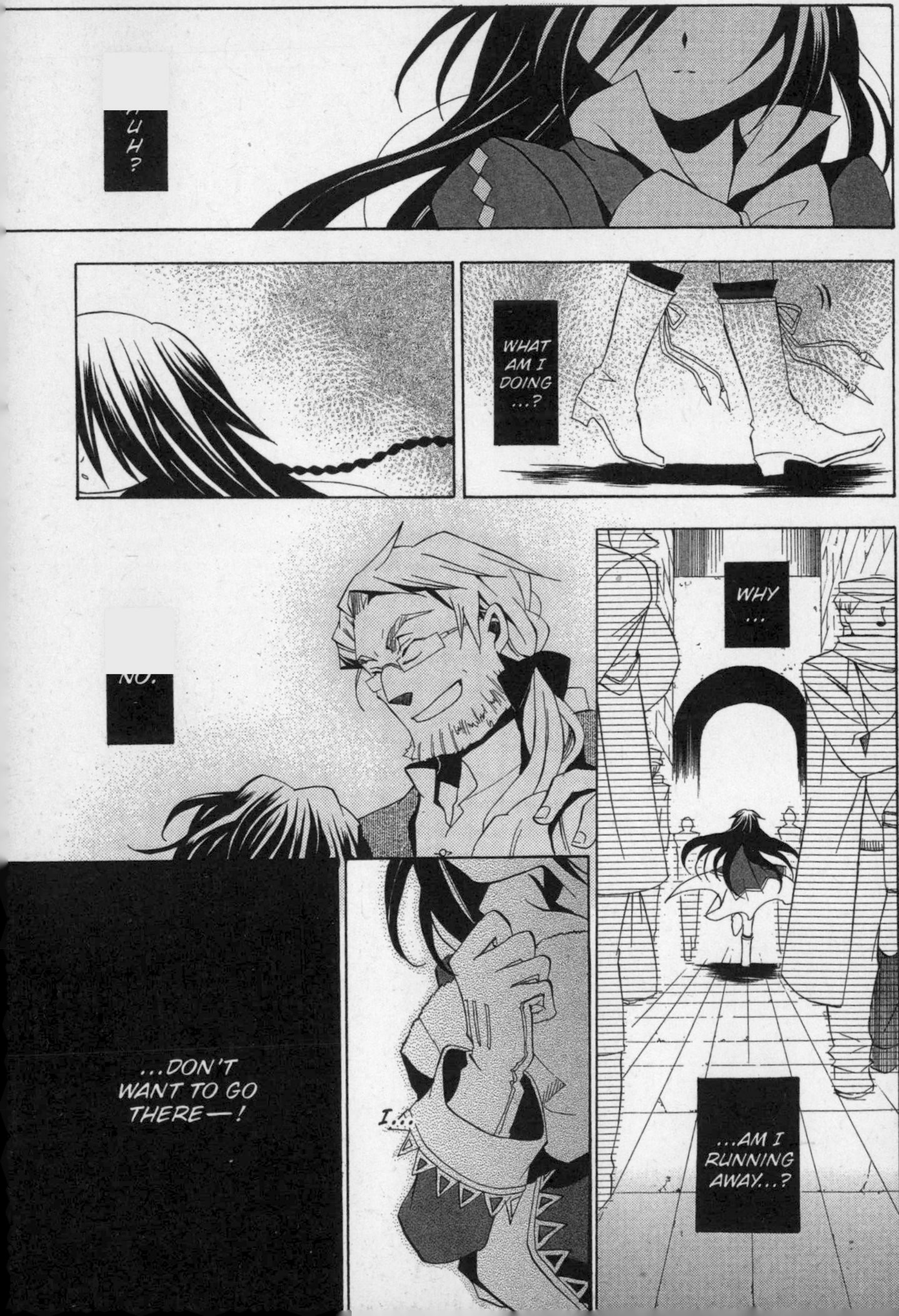
UH?
WHAT AM I DOING...?
WHY...
...AM I RUNNING AWAY...?
NO.
I...
...DON'T WANT TO GO THERE—!

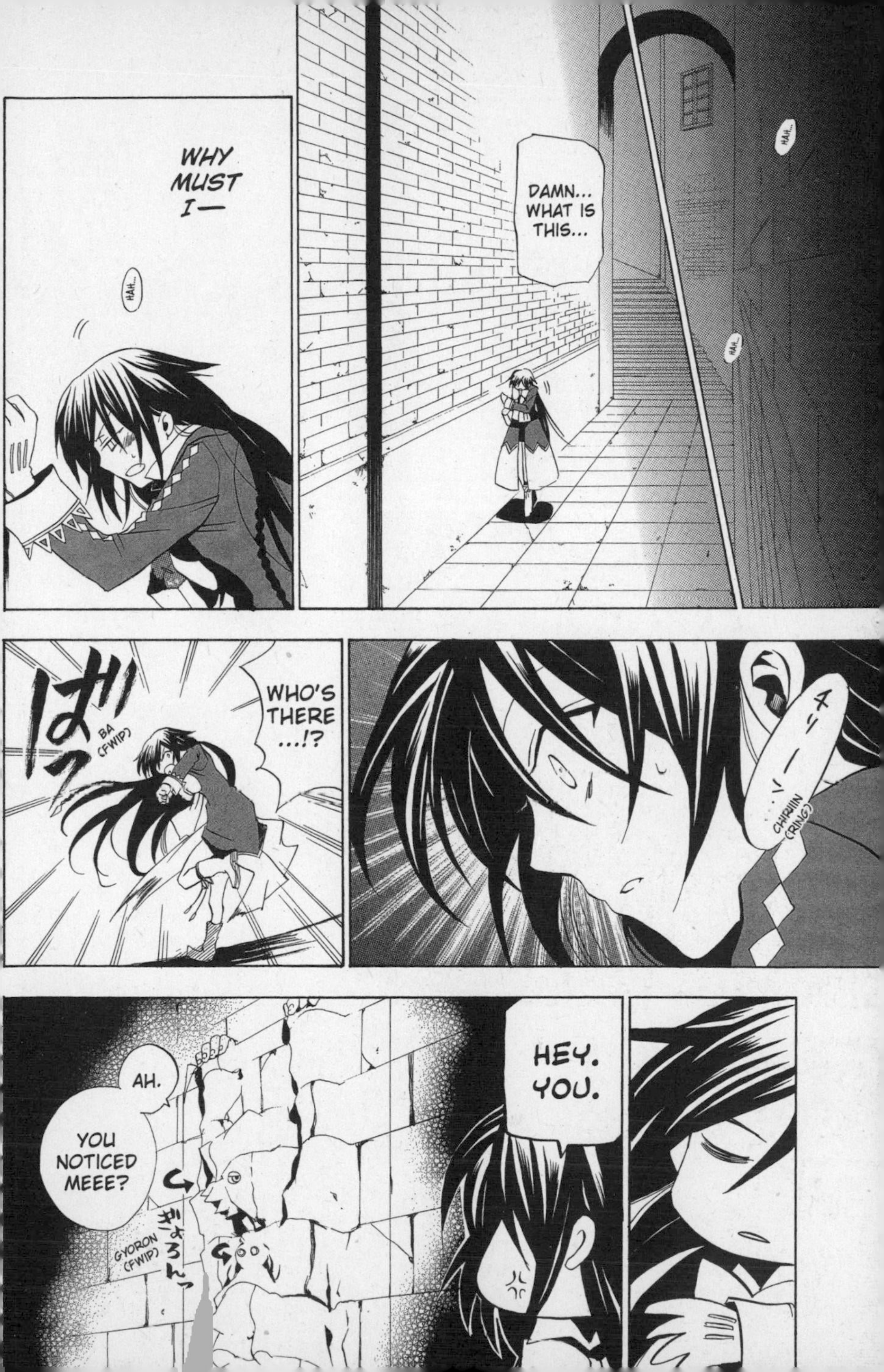
DAMN... WHAT IS THIS...
HAH...
HAH...
WHY MUST I—
HAH...
チリーン
CHIRIIN (RING)
WHO'S THERE ...!?
ばっ
BA (FWIP)
HEY. YOU.
AH.
YOU NOTICED MEEE?
ぎょろんっ
GYORON (FWIP)

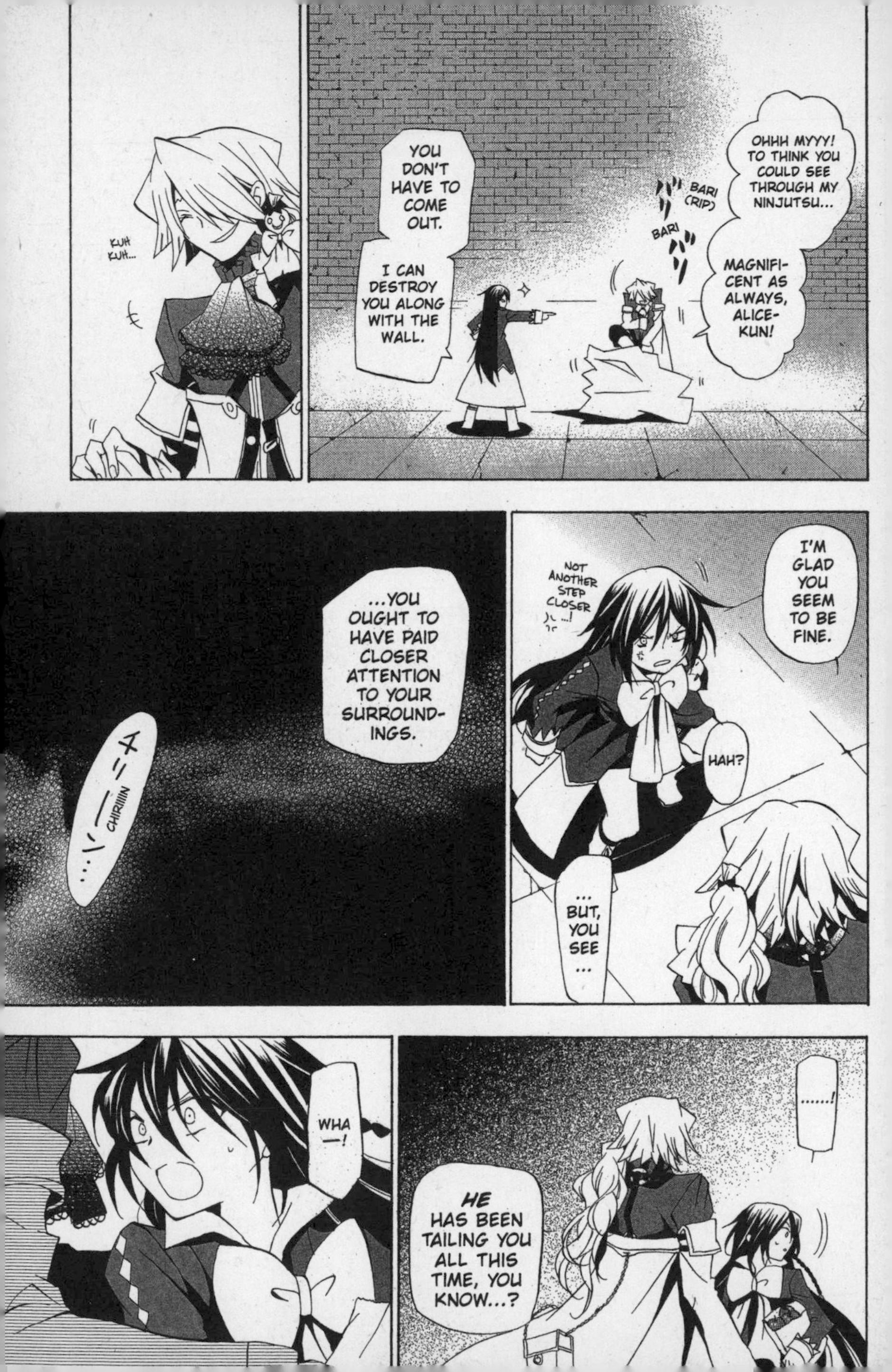
OHHH MYYY! TO THINK YOU COULD SEE THROUGH MY NINJUTSU...
MAGNIFICENT AS ALWAYS, ALICE-KUN!
BARI (RIP)
BARI
YOU DON'T HAVE TO COME OUT.
I CAN DESTROY YOU ALONG WITH THE WALL.
KUH KUH...
I'M GLAD YOU SEEM TO BE FINE.
NOT ANOTHER STEP CLOSER...!
HAH?
...BUT, YOU SEE...
...YOU OUGHT TO HAVE PAID CLOSER ATTENTION TO YOUR SURROUNDINGS.
CHIRIIIIN
......!
HE HAS BEEN TAILING YOU ALL THIS TIME, YOU KNOW...?
WHA—!

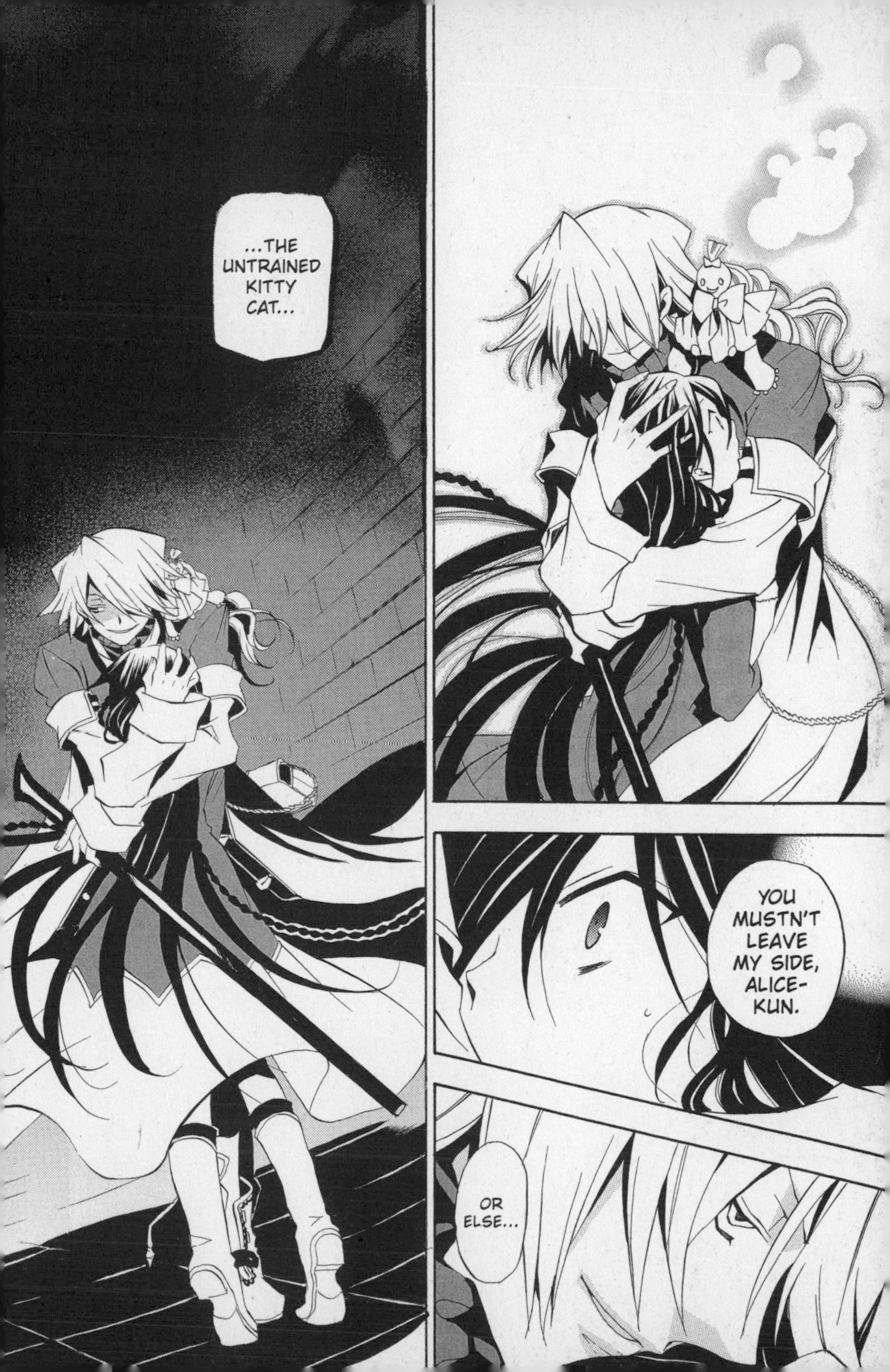
YOU MUSTN'T LEAVE MY SIDE, ALICE-KUN.
OR ELSE...
...THE UNTRAINED KITTY CAT...

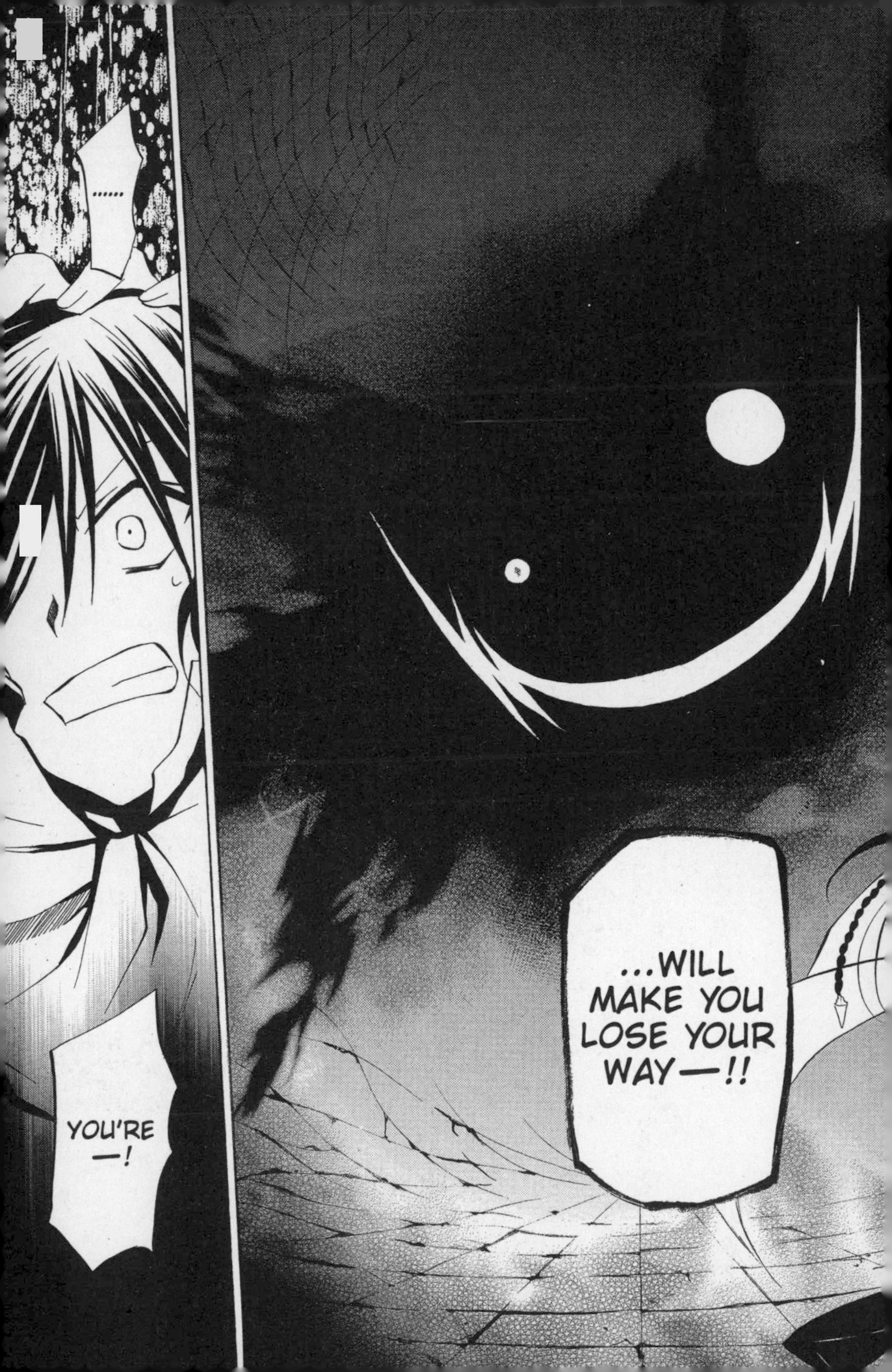
...WILL MAKE YOU LOSE YOUR WAY—!!
......
YOU'RE —!

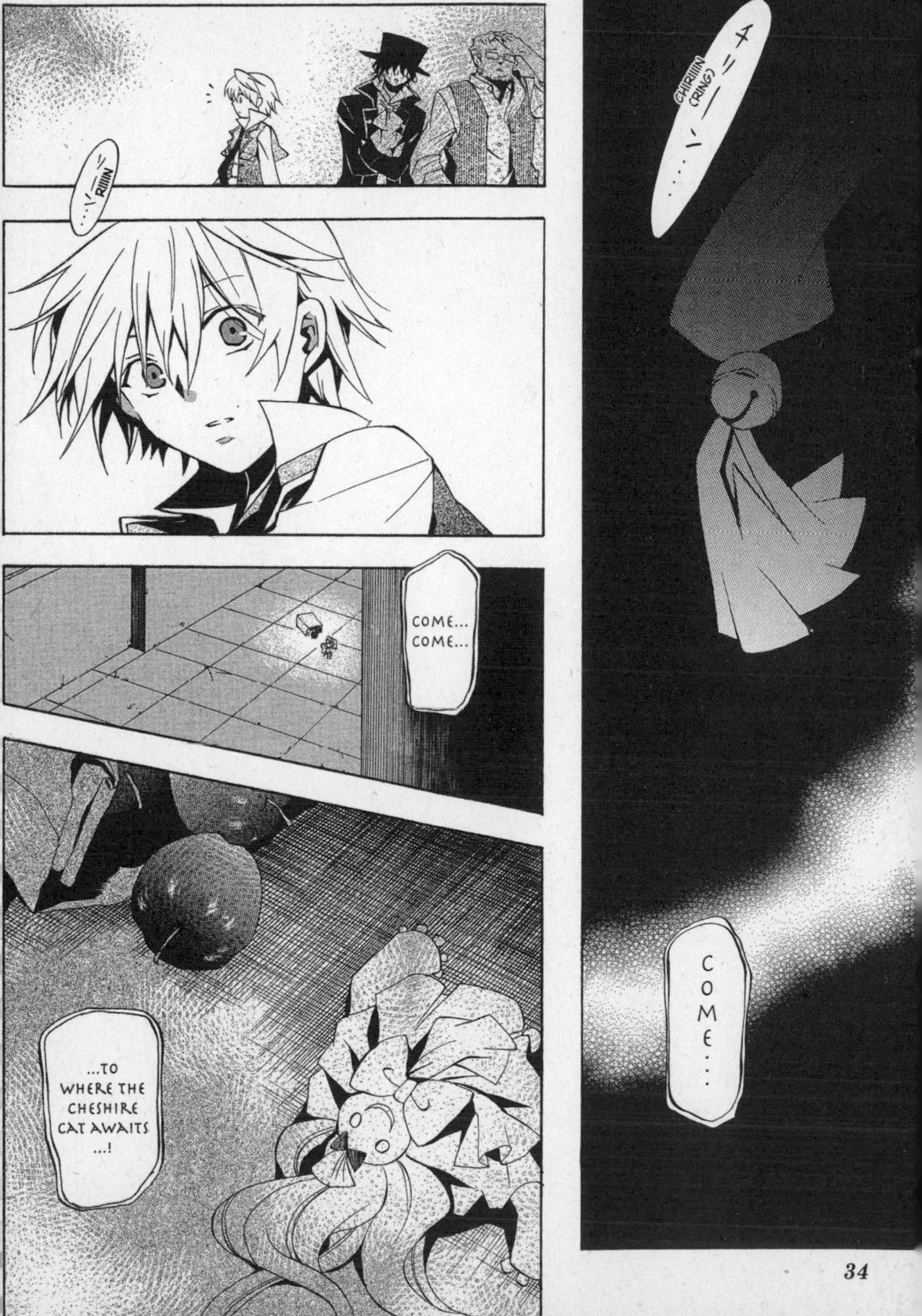
CHIRIIIN (RING)
COME...
RIIIN
COME... COME...
...TO WHERE THE CHESHIRE CAT AWAITS ...!

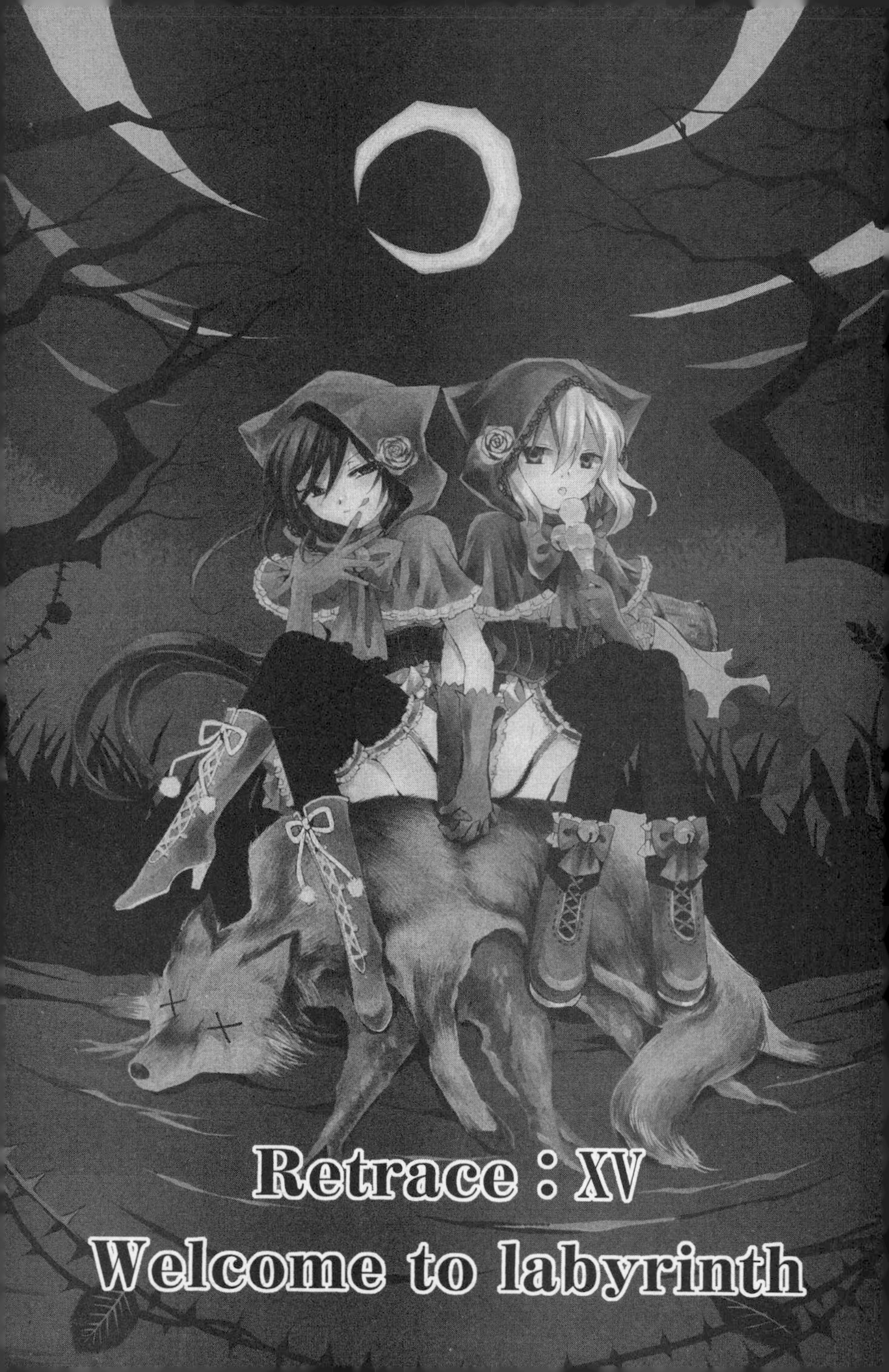
Retrace : XV
Welcome to labyrinth

BONUS: IF OSCAR WERE BREAK IN THAT SCENE....!!? MANGA

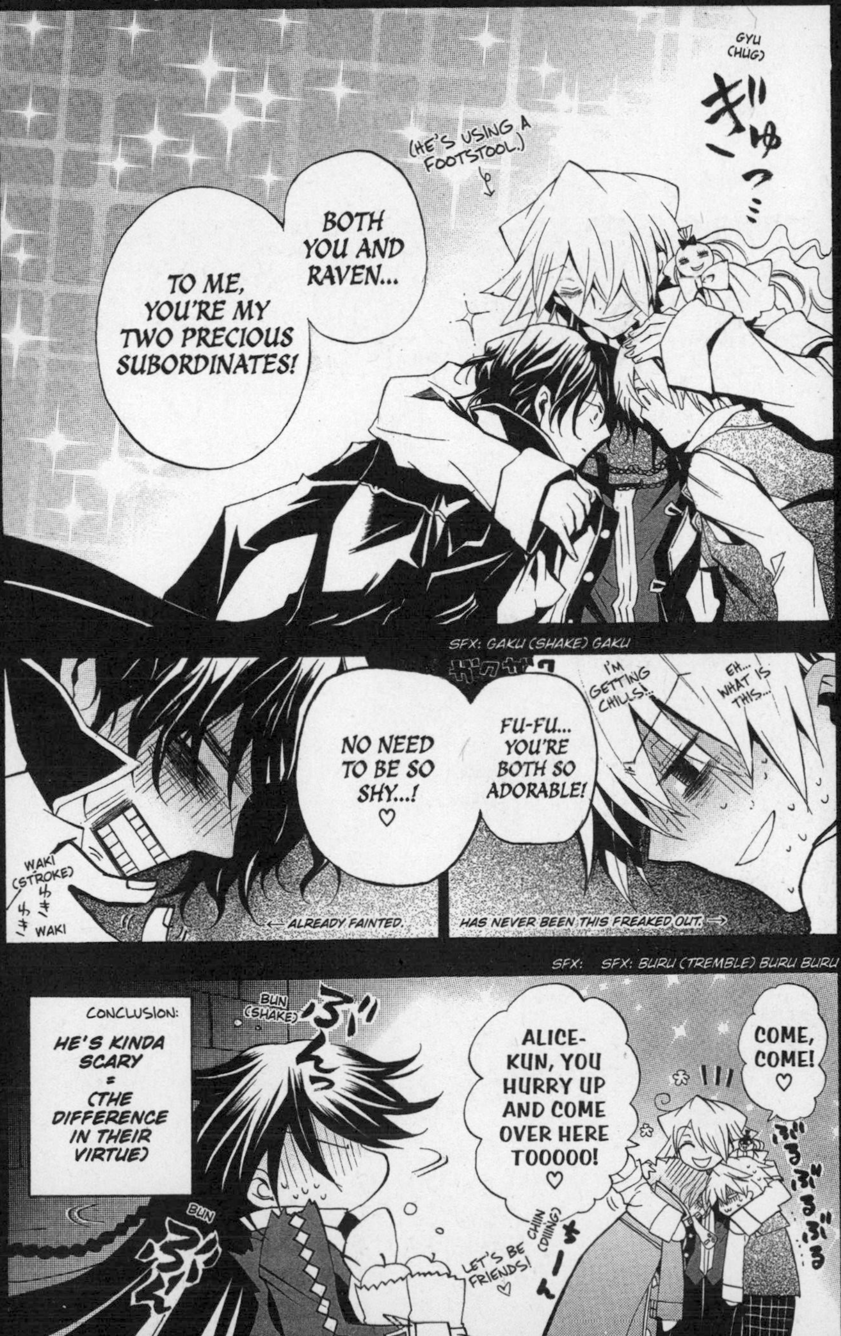
GYU (HUG)
(HE'S USING A FOOTSTOOL.)
BOTH YOU AND RAVEN...
TO ME, YOU'RE MY TWO PRECIOUS SUBORDINATES!
SFX: GAKU (SHAKE) GAKU
EH... WHAT IS THIS...
I'M GETTING CHILLS!...
HAS NEVER BEEN THIS FREAKED OUT.
FU-FU... YOU'RE BOTH SO ADORABLE!
NO NEED TO BE SO SHY...! ♡
WAKI (STROKE) WAKI
ALREADY FAINTED.
SFX: SFX: BURU (TREMBLE) BURU BURU
COME, COME! ♡
ALICE-KUN, YOU HURRY UP AND COME OVER HERE TOOOOO! ♡
CHIIN (DIIING)
LET'S BE FRIENDS! ♡
BUN (SHAKE)
BUN
CONCLUSION:
HE'S KINDA SCARY = (THE DIFFERENCE IN THEIR VIRTUE)

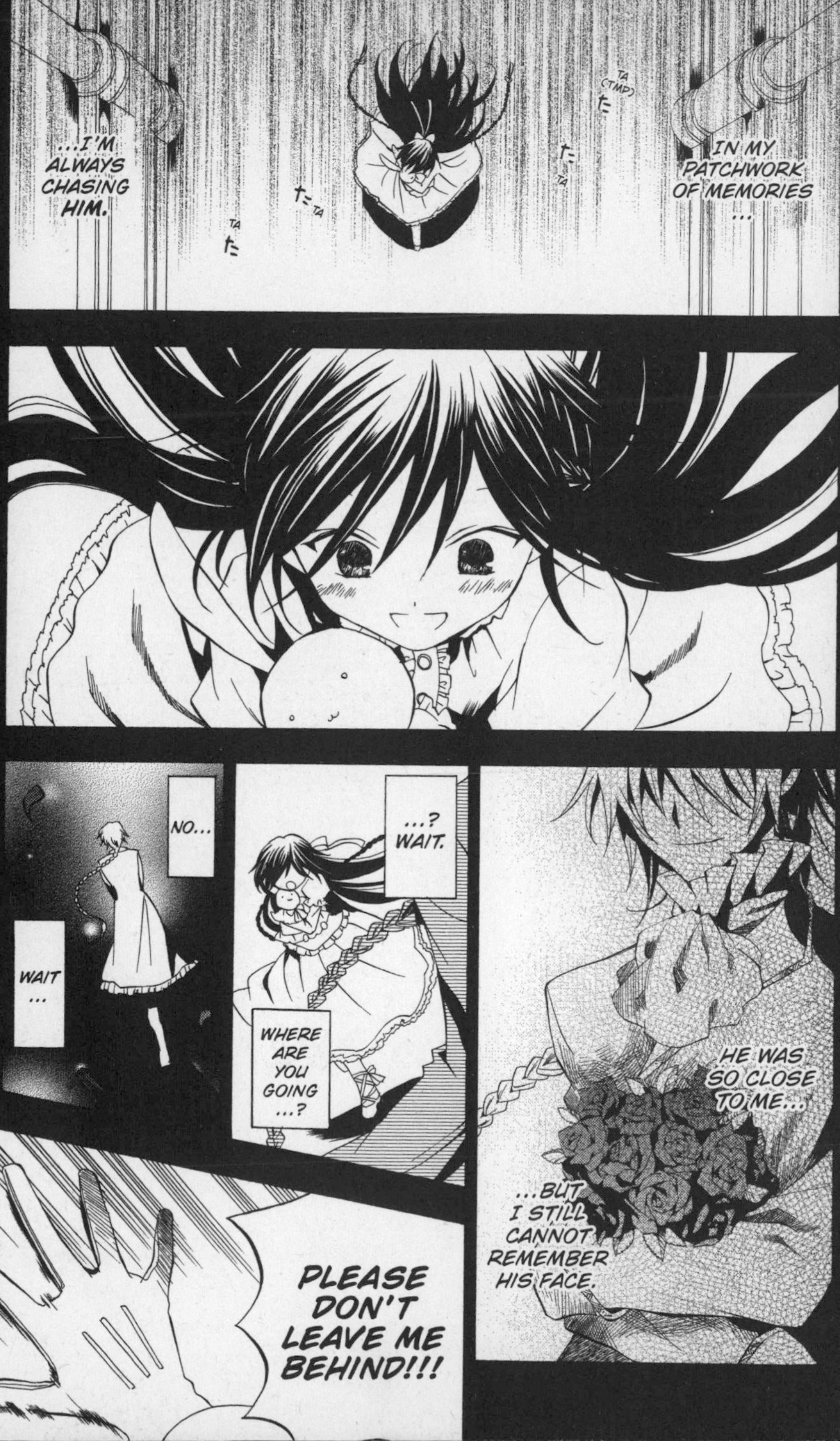
IN MY PATCHWORK OF MEMORIES ...
TA (TMP)
TA
TA
TA
...I'M ALWAYS CHASING HIM.
HE WAS SO CLOSE TO ME...
...BUT I STILL CANNOT REMEMBER HIS FACE.
...? WAIT.
WHERE ARE YOU GOING ...?
NO...
WAIT ...
PLEASE DON'T LEAVE ME BEHIND!!!

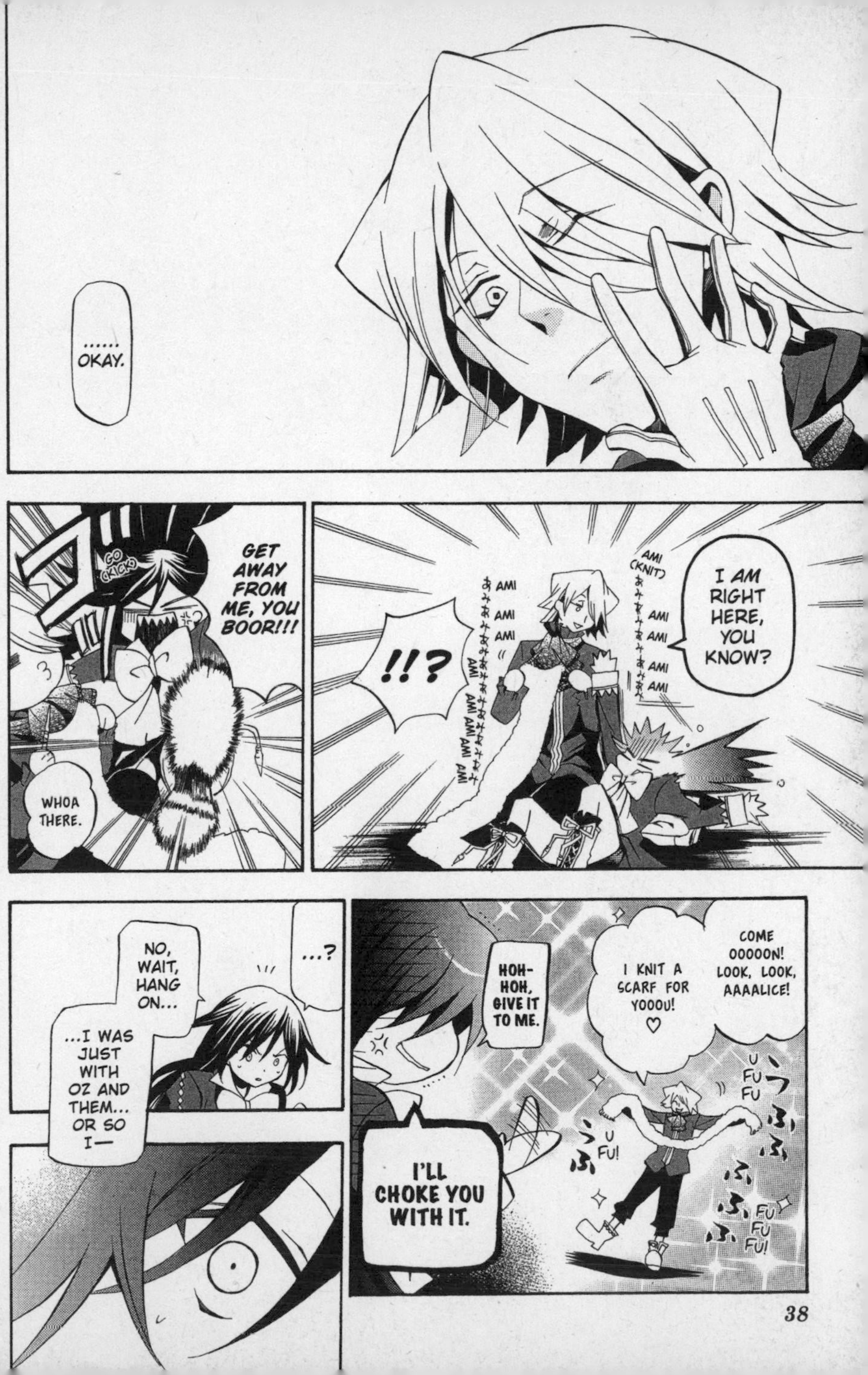

......OKAY.
I AM RIGHT HERE, YOU KNOW?
AMI (KNIT)
AMI AMI AMI AMI
AMI AMI AMI
AMI AMI AMI AMI
!!?
GET AWAY FROM ME, YOU BOOR!!!
GO (KICK)
WHOA THERE.
COME OOOOON! LOOK, LOOK, AAAALICE!
I KNIT A SCARF FOR YOOOU! ♡
HOH-HOH, GIVE IT TO ME.
U FU FU
U FU!
FU FU FU!
I'LL CHOKE YOU WITH IT.
...?
NO, WAIT, HANG ON...
...I WAS JUST WITH OZ AND THEM... OR SO I—

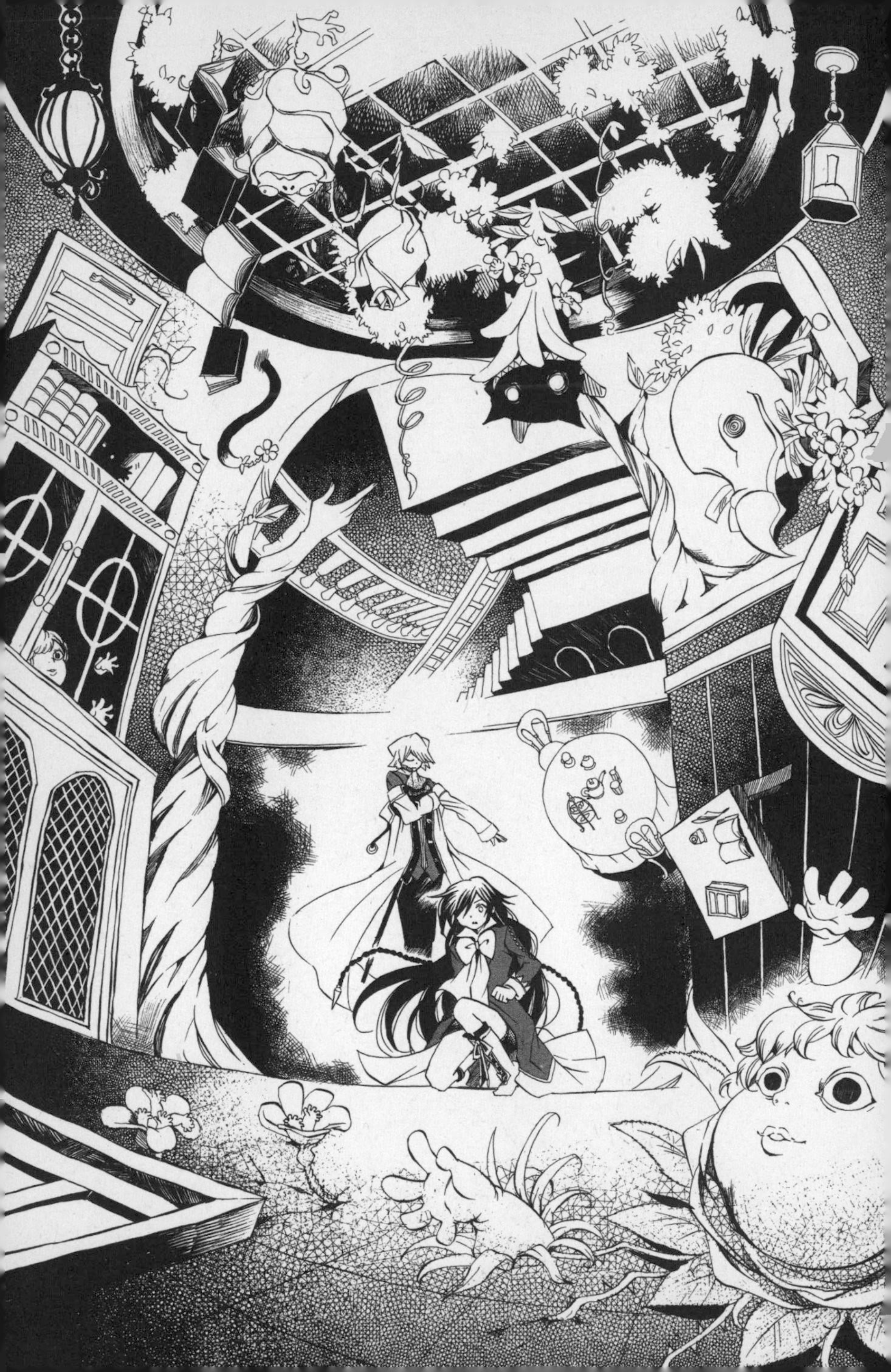

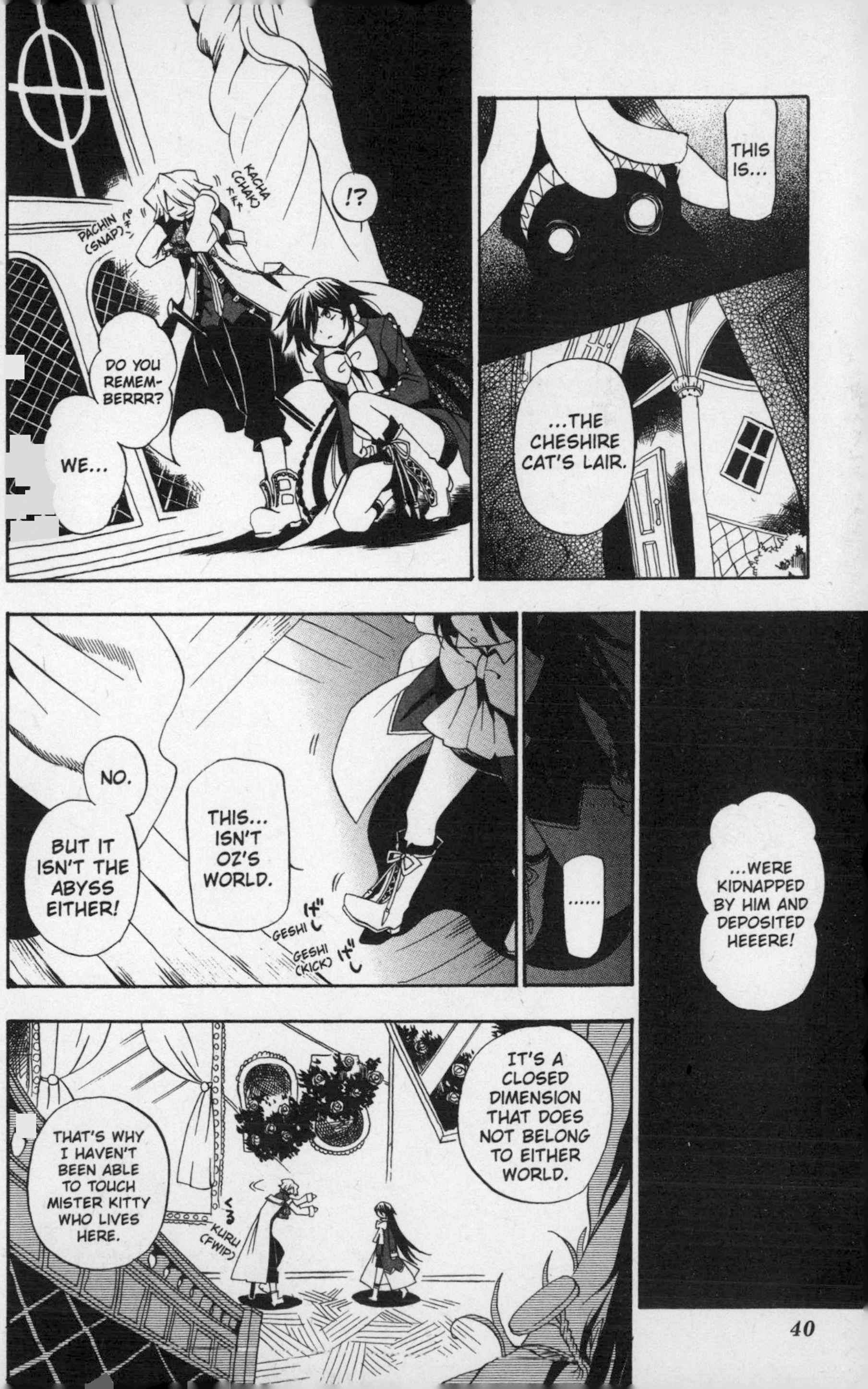
THIS IS...
...THE CHESHIRE CAT'S LAIR.
KACHA (CHAK) カチャ
!?
PACHIN (SNAP) パチン
DO YOU REMEMBERRR?
WE...
...WERE KIDNAPPED BY HIM AND DEPOSITED HEEERE!
......
GESHI げし
GESHI (KICK) げし
THIS... ISN'T OZ'S WORLD.
NO.
BUT IT ISN'T THE ABYSS EITHER!
IT'S A CLOSED DIMENSION THAT DOES NOT BELONG TO EITHER WORLD.
KURU (FWIP) くる
THAT'S WHY I HAVEN'T BEEN ABLE TO TOUCH MISTER KITTY WHO LIVES HERE.

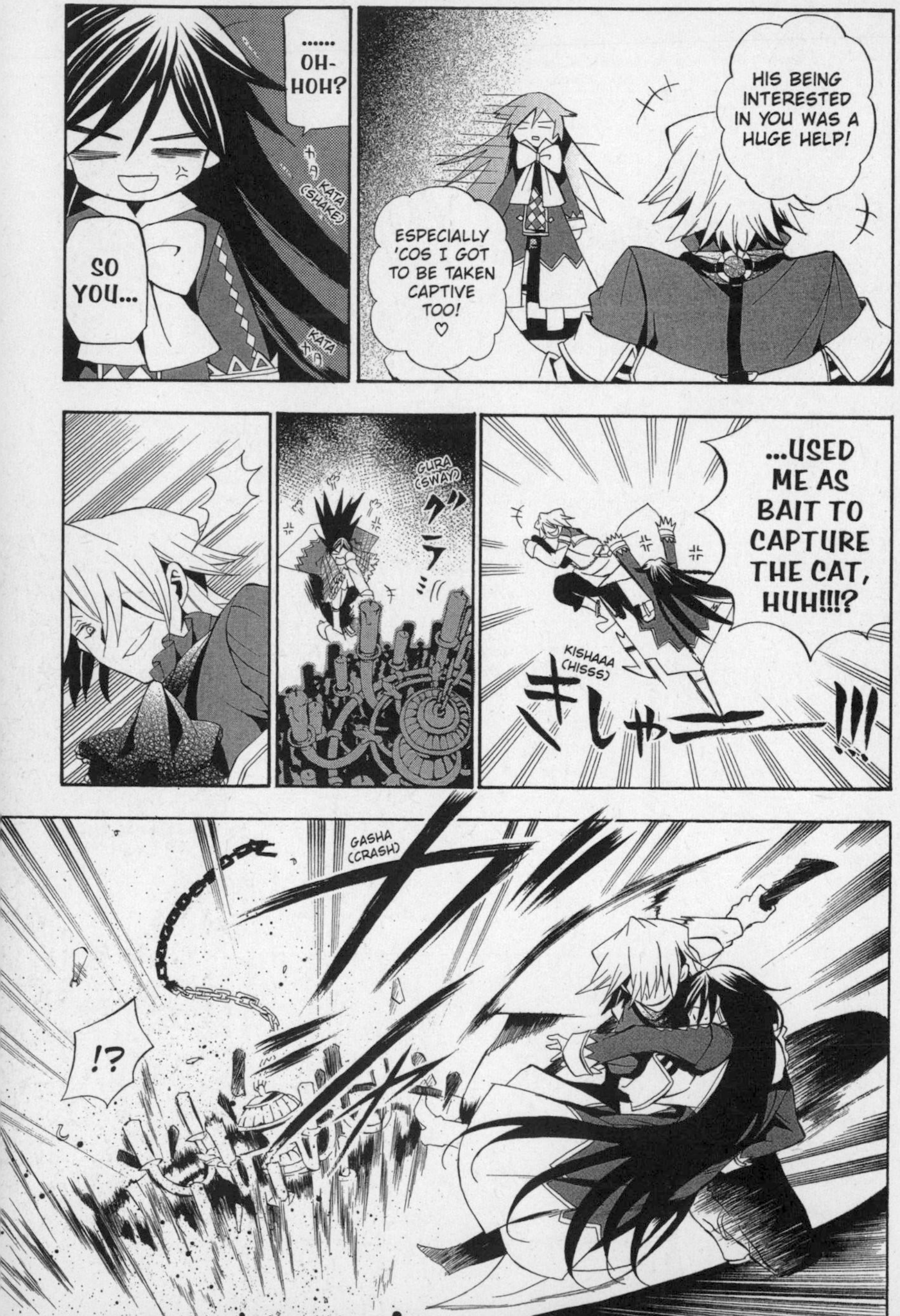
HIS BEING INTERESTED IN YOU WAS A HUGE HELP!
ESPECIALLY 'COS I GOT TO BE TAKEN CAPTIVE TOO! ♡
...... OH-HOH?
KATA (SHAKE)
SO YOU...
KATA
...USED ME AS BAIT TO CAPTURE THE CAT, HUH!!!?
KISHAAA (HISSS)
きしゃー!!!
GURA (SWAY)
グラ
GASHA (CRASH)
!?

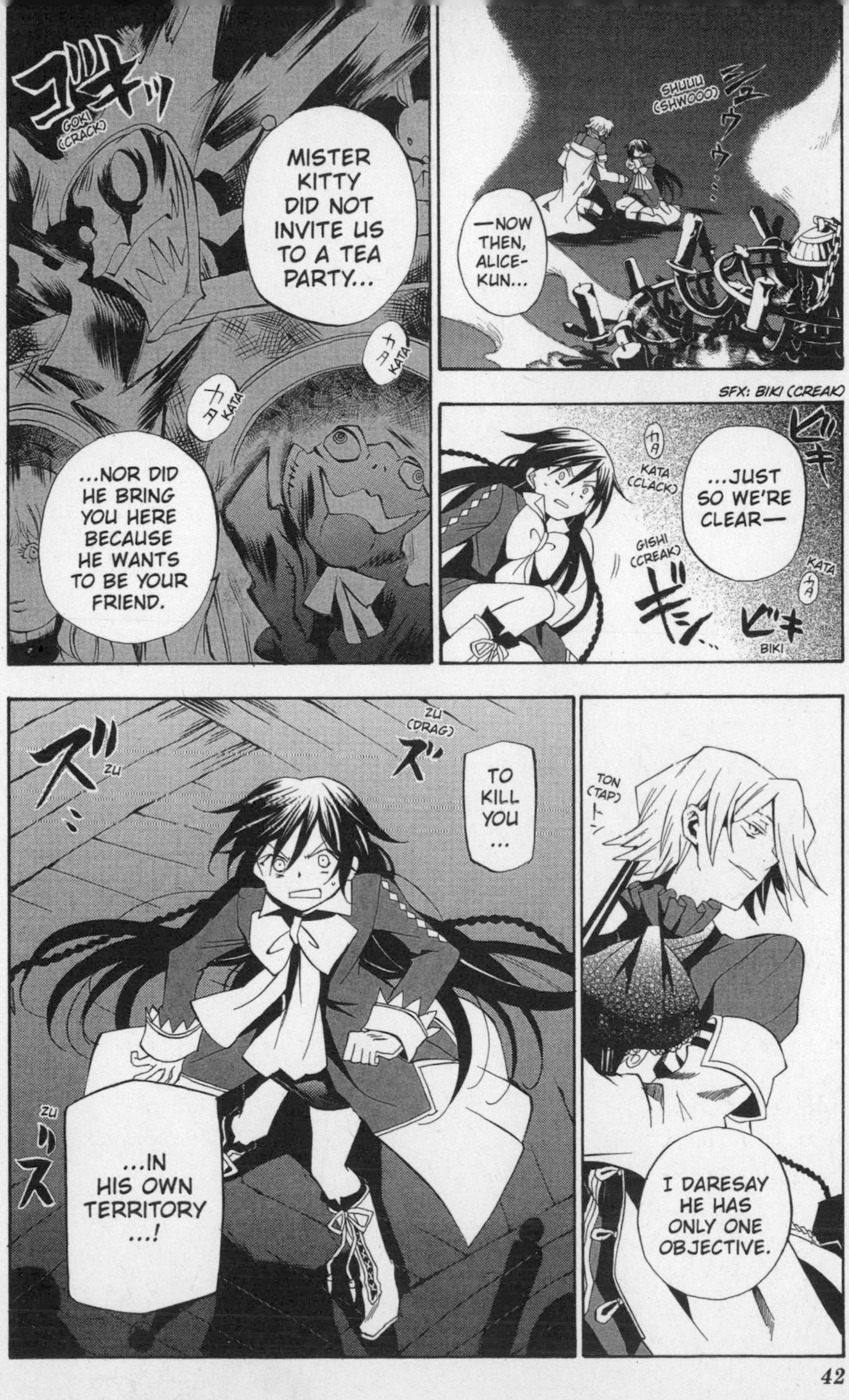
SHUUU (SHWOOO)
—NOW THEN, ALICE-KUN...
SFX: BIKI (CREAK)
KATA (CLACK)
...JUST SO WE'RE CLEAR—
GISHI (CREAK)
KATA
BIKI
GOKI (CRACK)
MISTER KITTY DID NOT INVITE US TO A TEA PARTY...
KATA
KATA
...NOR DID HE BRING YOU HERE BECAUSE HE WANTS TO BE YOUR FRIEND.
TON (TAP)
I DARESAY HE HAS ONLY ONE OBJECTIVE.
ZU (DRAG)
TO KILL YOU...
ZU
ZU
...IN HIS OWN TERRITORY...!

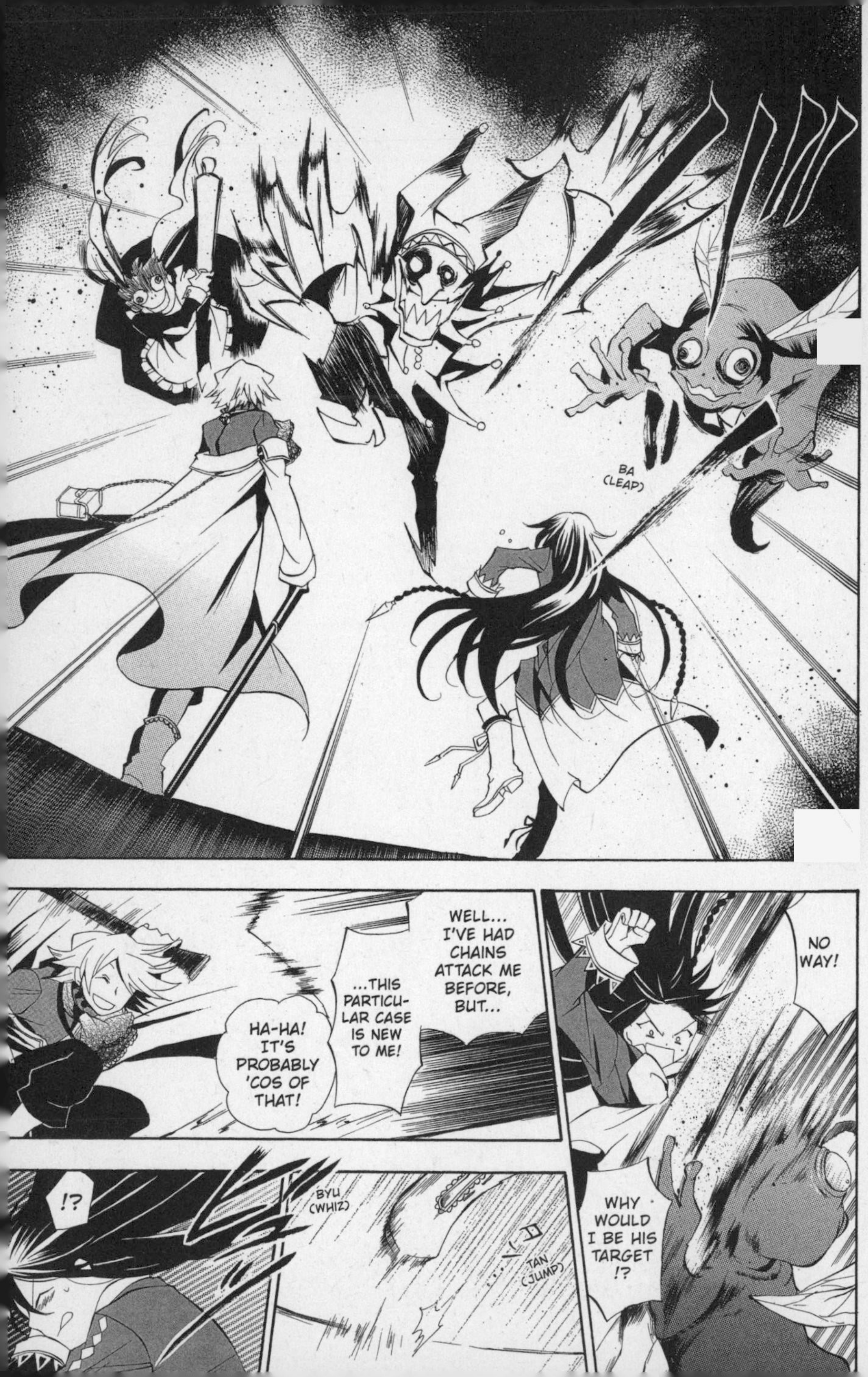
BA
(LEAP)
NO WAY!
WELL... I'VE HAD CHAINS ATTACK ME BEFORE, BUT...
...THIS PARTICULAR CASE IS NEW TO ME!
HA-HA! IT'S PROBABLY 'COS OF THAT!
WHY WOULD I BE HIS TARGET !?
BYU
(WHIZ)
TAN
(JUMP)
!?

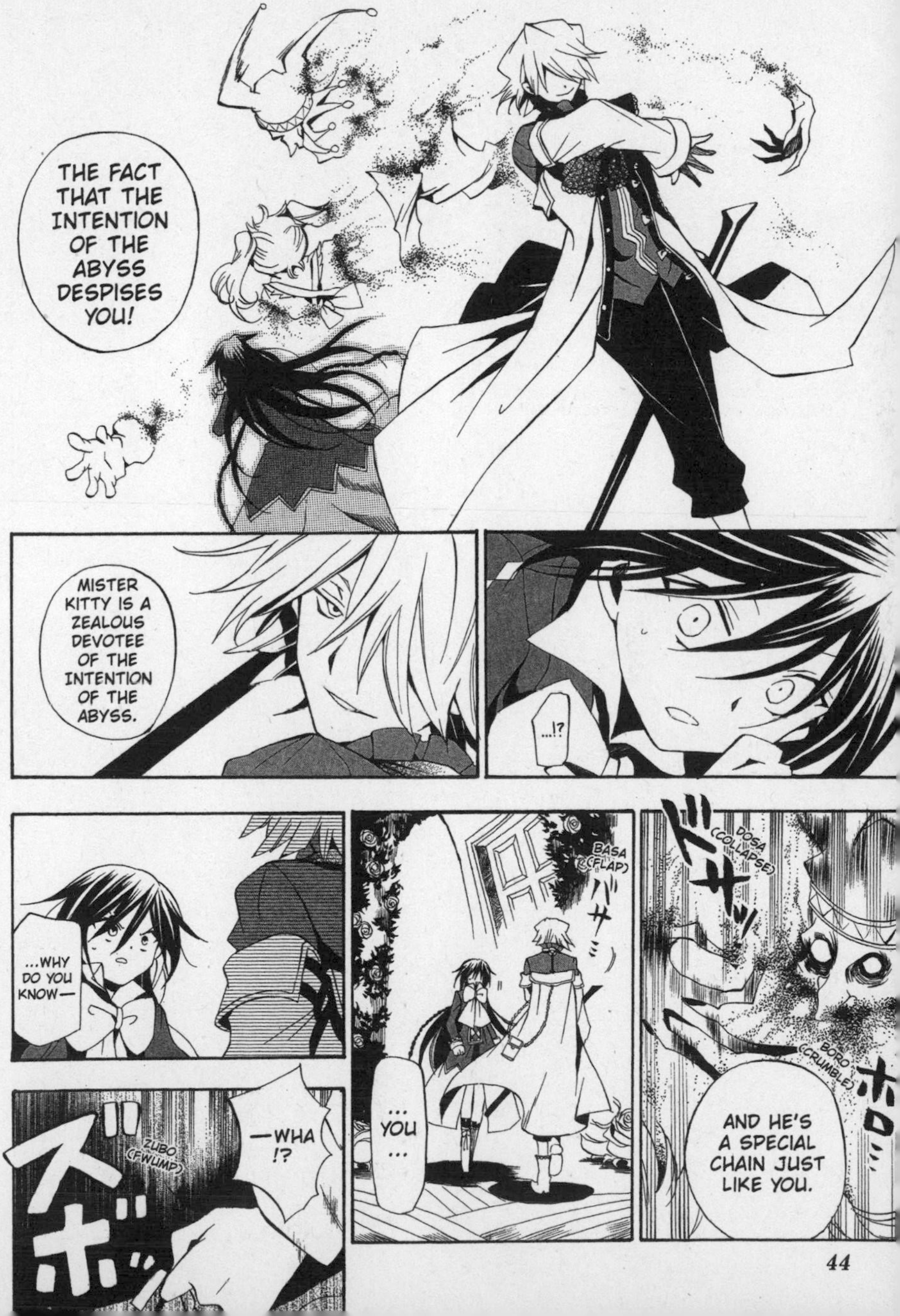
THE FACT THAT THE INTENTION OF THE ABYSS DESPISES YOU!
...!?
MISTER KITTY IS A ZEALOUS DEVOTEE OF THE INTENTION OF THE ABYSS.
DOSA (COLLAPSE)
BORO (CRUMBLE)
AND HE'S A SPECIAL CHAIN JUST LIKE YOU.
BASA (FLAP)
... YOU ...
...WHY DO YOU KNOW—
ZUBO (FWUMP)
—WHA !?

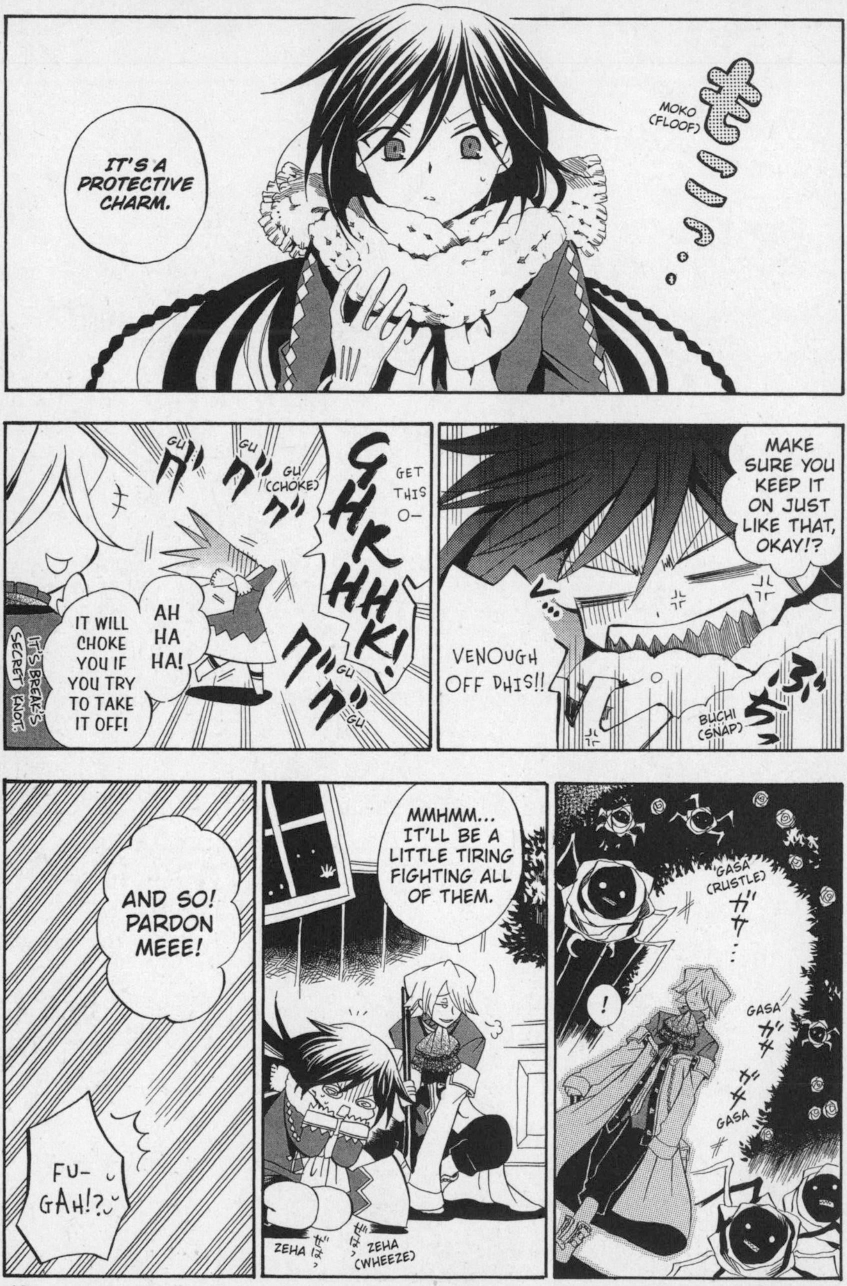
MOKO (FLOOF)
IT'S A PROTECTIVE CHARM.
MAKE SURE YOU KEEP IT ON JUST LIKE THAT, OKAY!?
VENOUGH OFF DHIS!!
BUCHI (SNAP)
GHRRHHK!
GET THIS O—
GU
GU
GU (CHOKE)
AH HA HA!
IT WILL CHOKE YOU IF YOU TRY TO TAKE IT OFF!
IT'S BREAK'S SECRET KNOT.
GU
GU
GASA (RUSTLE)
!
GASA
GASA
MMHMM... IT'LL BE A LITTLE TIRING FIGHTING ALL OF THEM.
ZEHA
ZEHA (WHEEZE)
AND SO! PARDON MEEE!
FU-GAH!?

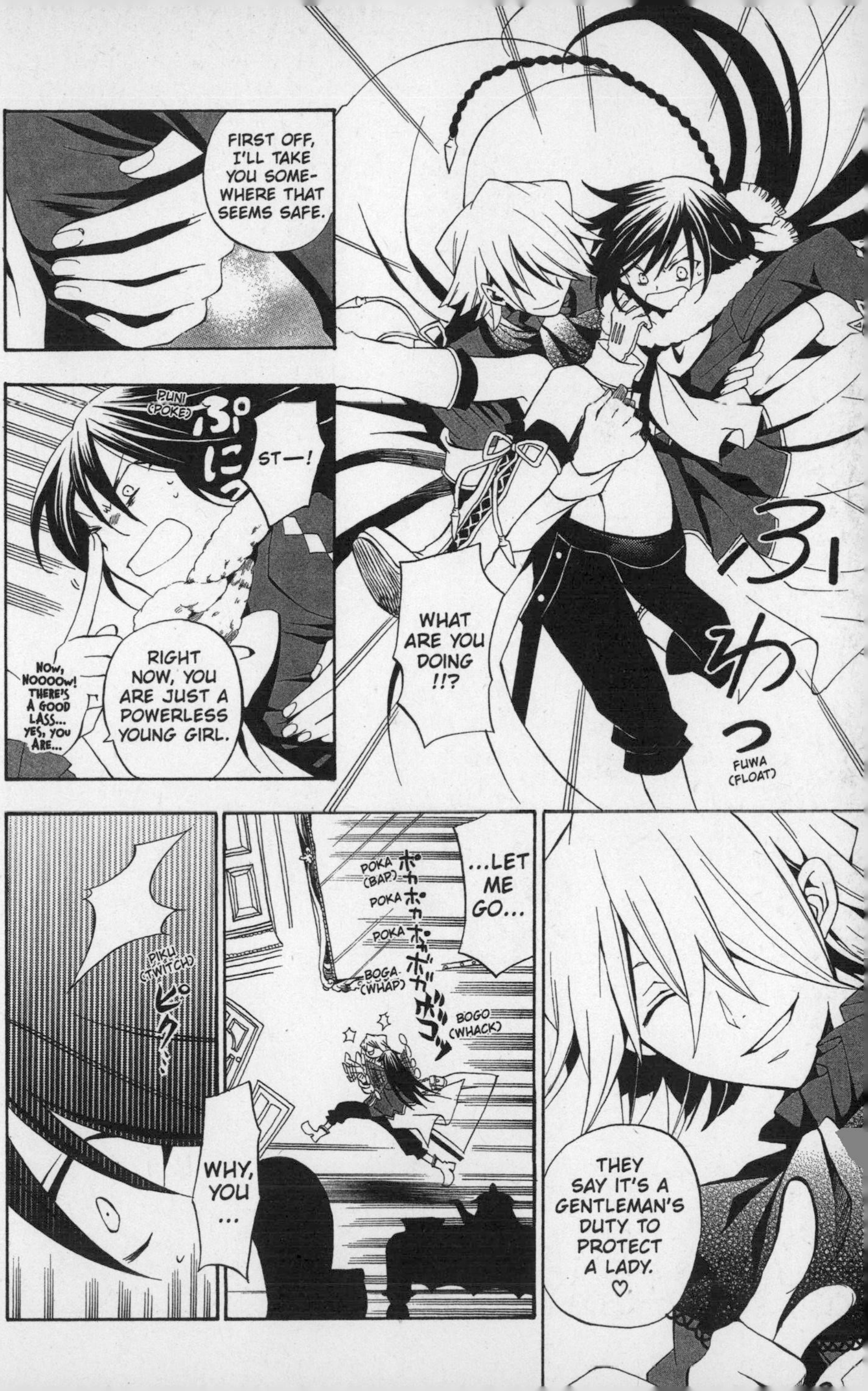
WHAT ARE YOU DOING !!?
ふわっ
FUWA (FLOAT)
FIRST OFF, I'LL TAKE YOU SOME-WHERE THAT SEEMS SAFE.
ぷにっ
PUNI (POKE)
ST—!
RIGHT NOW, YOU ARE JUST A POWERLESS YOUNG GIRL.
NOW, NOOOOW! THERE'S A GOOD LASS... YES, YOU ARE...
THEY SAY IT'S A GENTLEMAN'S DUTY TO PROTECT A LADY. ♡
...LET ME GO...
POKA (BAP)
POKA
POKA
BOGA (WHAP)
BOGO (WHACK)
PIKU (TWITCH)
WHY, YOU ...

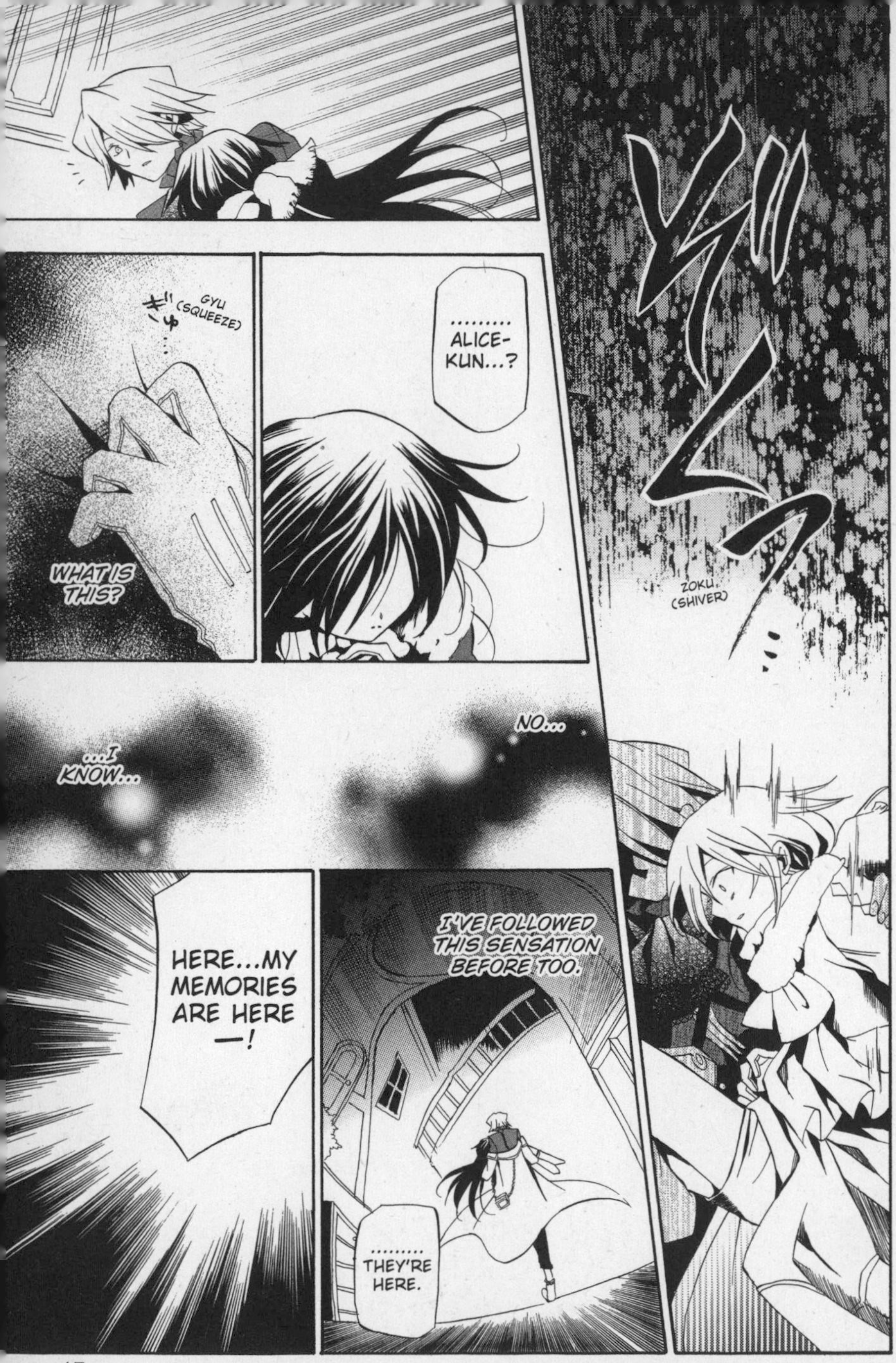
ZOKU (SHIVER)
....
ALICE-KUN...?
GYU (SQUEEZE)
WHAT IS THIS?
NO...
...I KNOW...
I'VE FOLLOWED THIS SENSATION BEFORE TOO.
....
THEY'RE HERE.
HERE...MY MEMORIES ARE HERE—!

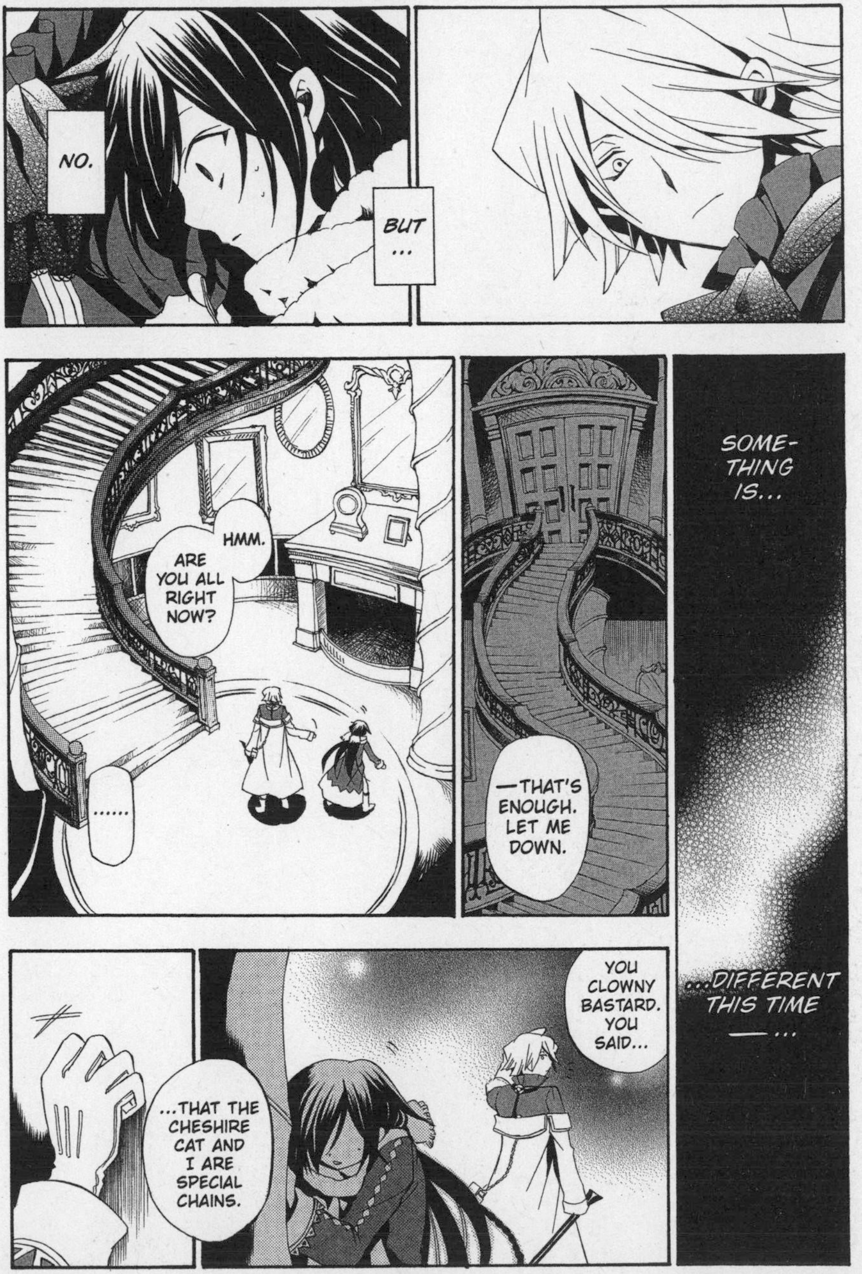
NO.
BUT ...
SOME-THING IS...
—THAT'S ENOUGH. LET ME DOWN.
HMM.
ARE YOU ALL RIGHT NOW?
......
...DIFFERENT THIS TIME —...
YOU CLOWNY BASTARD. YOU SAID...
...THAT THE CHESHIRE CAT AND I ARE SPECIAL CHAINS.

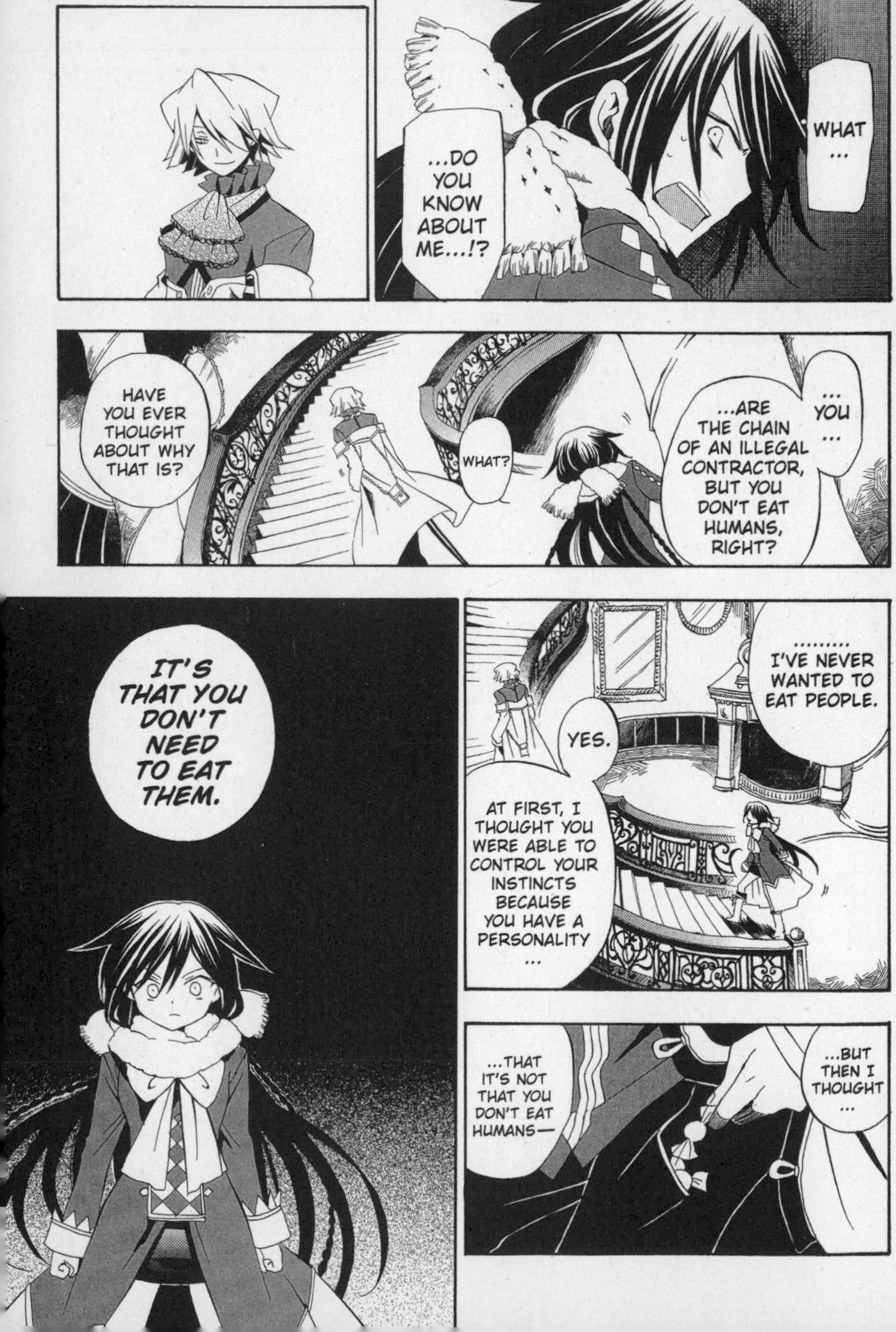
WHAT ...
...DO YOU KNOW ABOUT ME...!?
... YOU ...
...ARE THE CHAIN OF AN ILLEGAL CONTRACTOR, BUT YOU DON'T EAT HUMANS, RIGHT?
WHAT?
HAVE YOU EVER THOUGHT ABOUT WHY THAT IS?
.... I'VE NEVER WANTED TO EAT PEOPLE.
YES.
AT FIRST, I THOUGHT YOU WERE ABLE TO CONTROL YOUR INSTINCTS BECAUSE YOU HAVE A PERSONALITY ...
...BUT THEN I THOUGHT ...
...THAT IT'S NOT THAT YOU DON'T EAT HUMANS—
IT'S THAT YOU DON'T NEED TO EAT THEM.

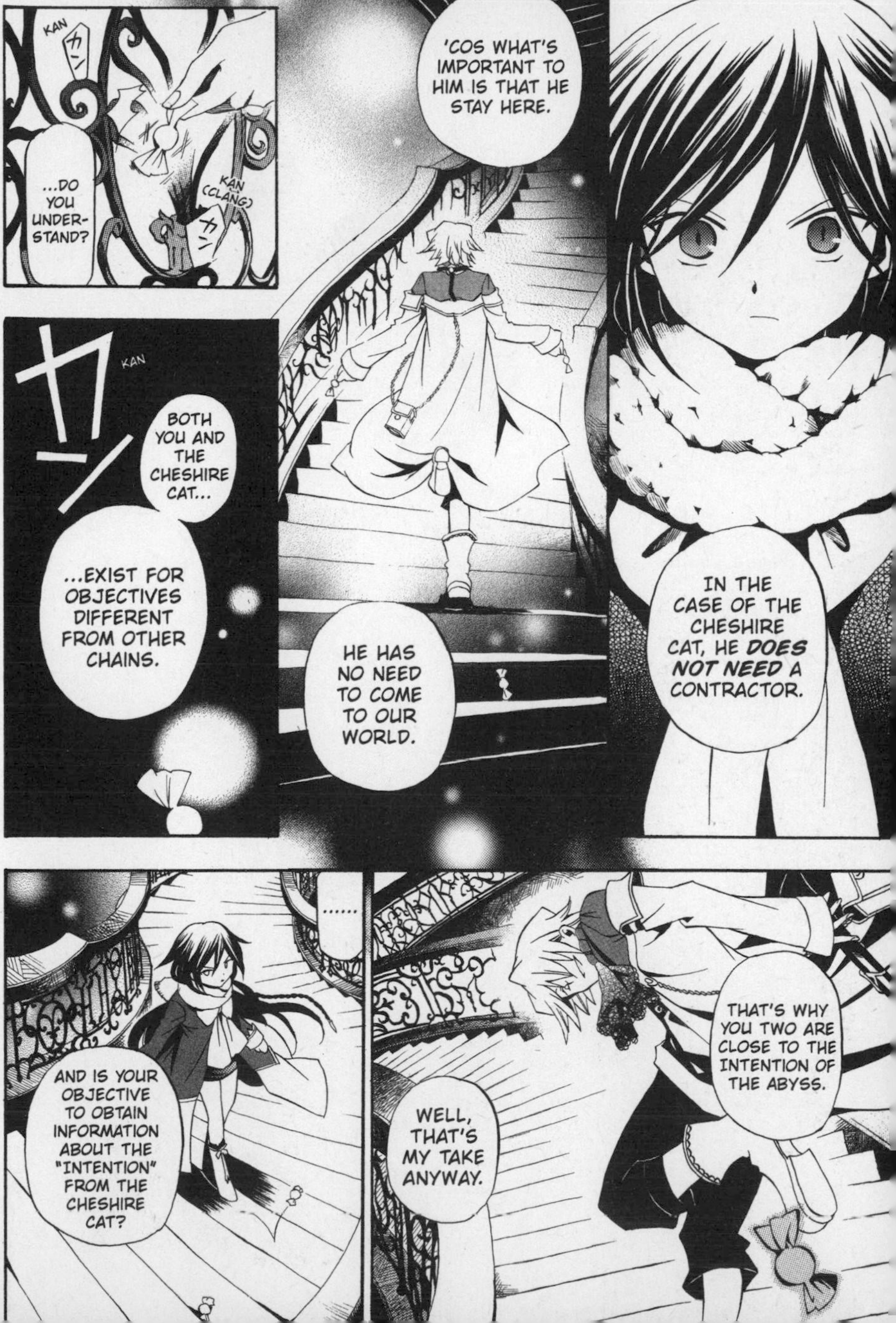
IN THE CASE OF THE CHESHIRE CAT, HE **DOES NOT NEED** A CONTRACTOR.
'COS WHAT'S IMPORTANT TO HIM IS THAT HE STAY HERE.
HE HAS NO NEED TO COME TO OUR WORLD.
KAN
...DO YOU UNDER-STAND?
KAN (CLANG)
KAN
BOTH YOU AND THE CHESHIRE CAT...
...EXIST FOR OBJECTIVES DIFFERENT FROM OTHER CHAINS.
THAT'S WHY YOU TWO ARE CLOSE TO THE INTENTION OF THE ABYSS.
WELL, THAT'S MY TAKE ANYWAY.
......
AND IS YOUR OBJECTIVE TO OBTAIN INFORMATION ABOUT THE "INTENTION" FROM THE CHESHIRE CAT?

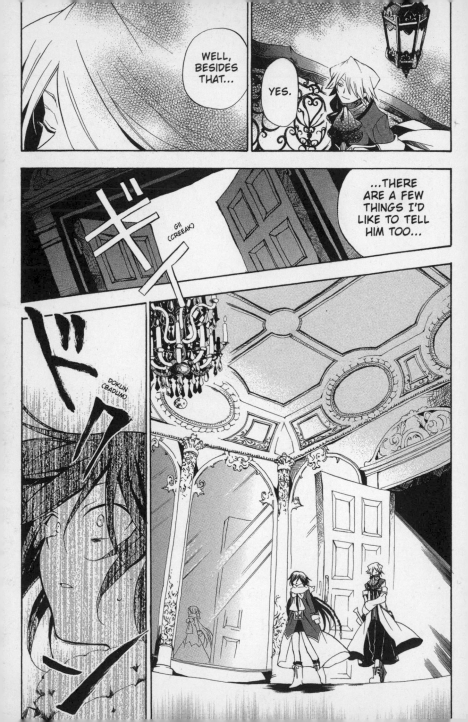

WELL, BESIDES THAT...

YES.

...THERE ARE A FEW THINGS I'D LIKE TO TELL HIM TOO...

GII (CREAK)

DOKUN (BADUMP)

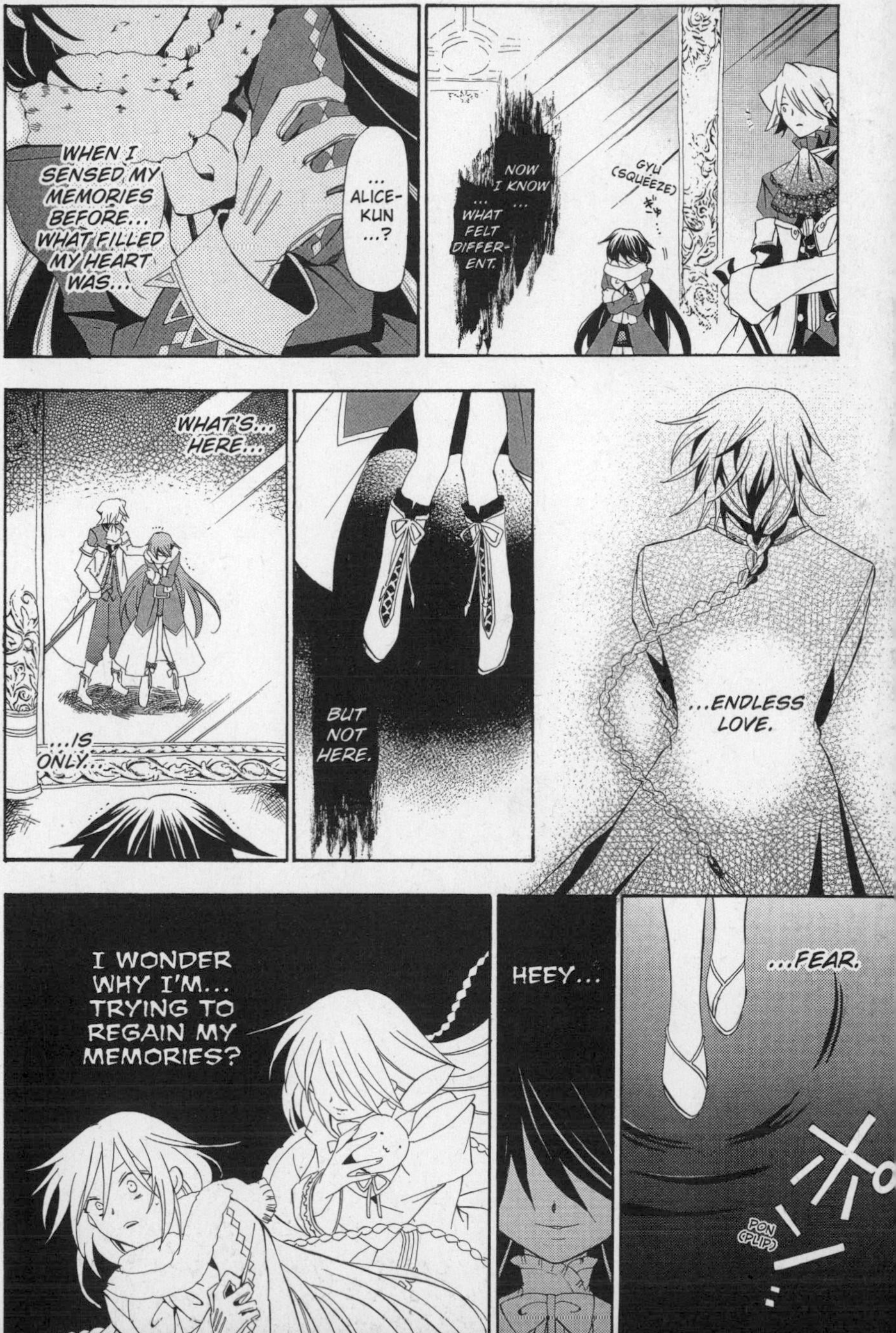
GYU (SQUEEZE)
NOW I KNOW... ...WHAT FELT DIFFERENT.
... ALICE-KUN ...?
WHEN I SENSED MY MEMORIES BEFORE... WHAT FILLED MY HEART WAS...
...ENDLESS LOVE.
BUT NOT HERE.
WHAT'S... HERE...
...IS ONLY...
...FEAR.
PON (PLIP)
HEEY...
I WONDER WHY I'M... TRYING TO REGAIN MY MEMORIES?

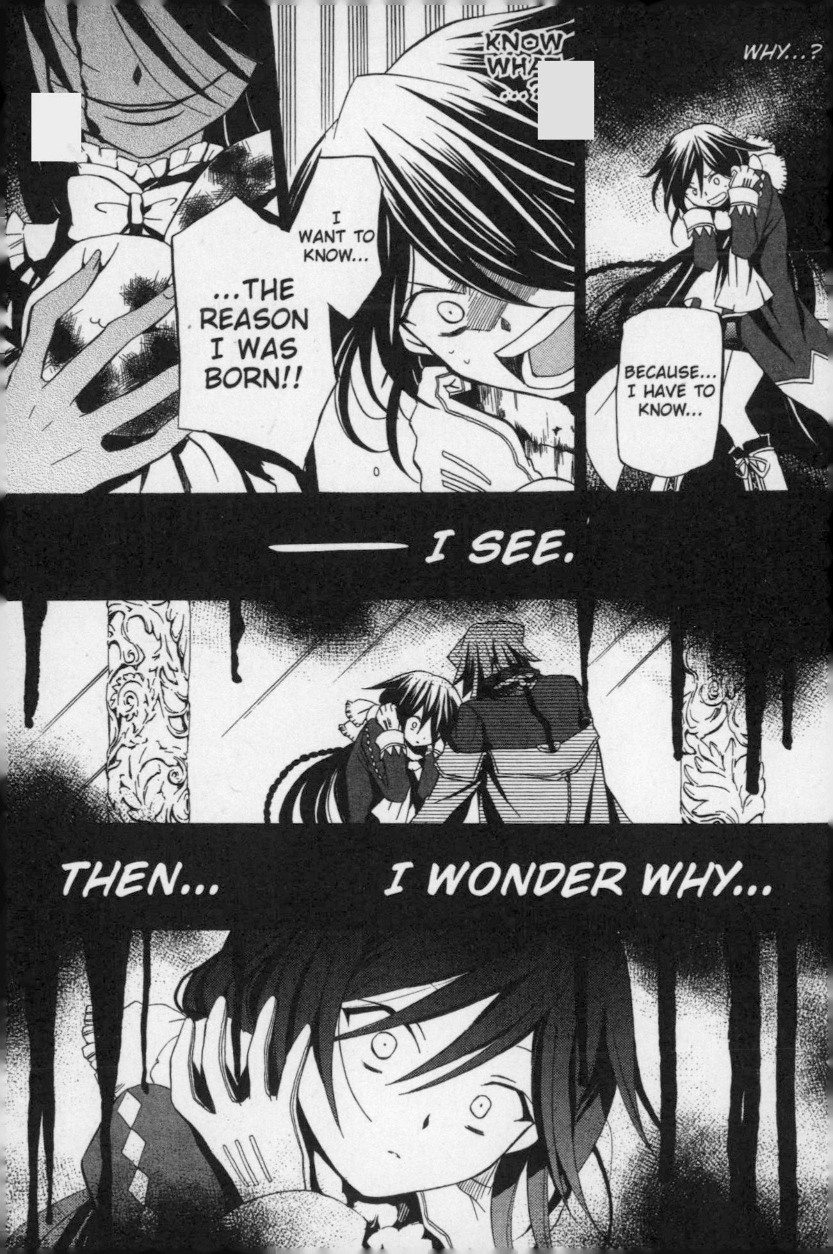

WHY...?
BECAUSE... I HAVE TO KNOW...
KNOW WHA
I WANT TO KNOW...
...THE REASON I WAS BORN!!
——— I SEE.
THEN... I WONDER WHY...

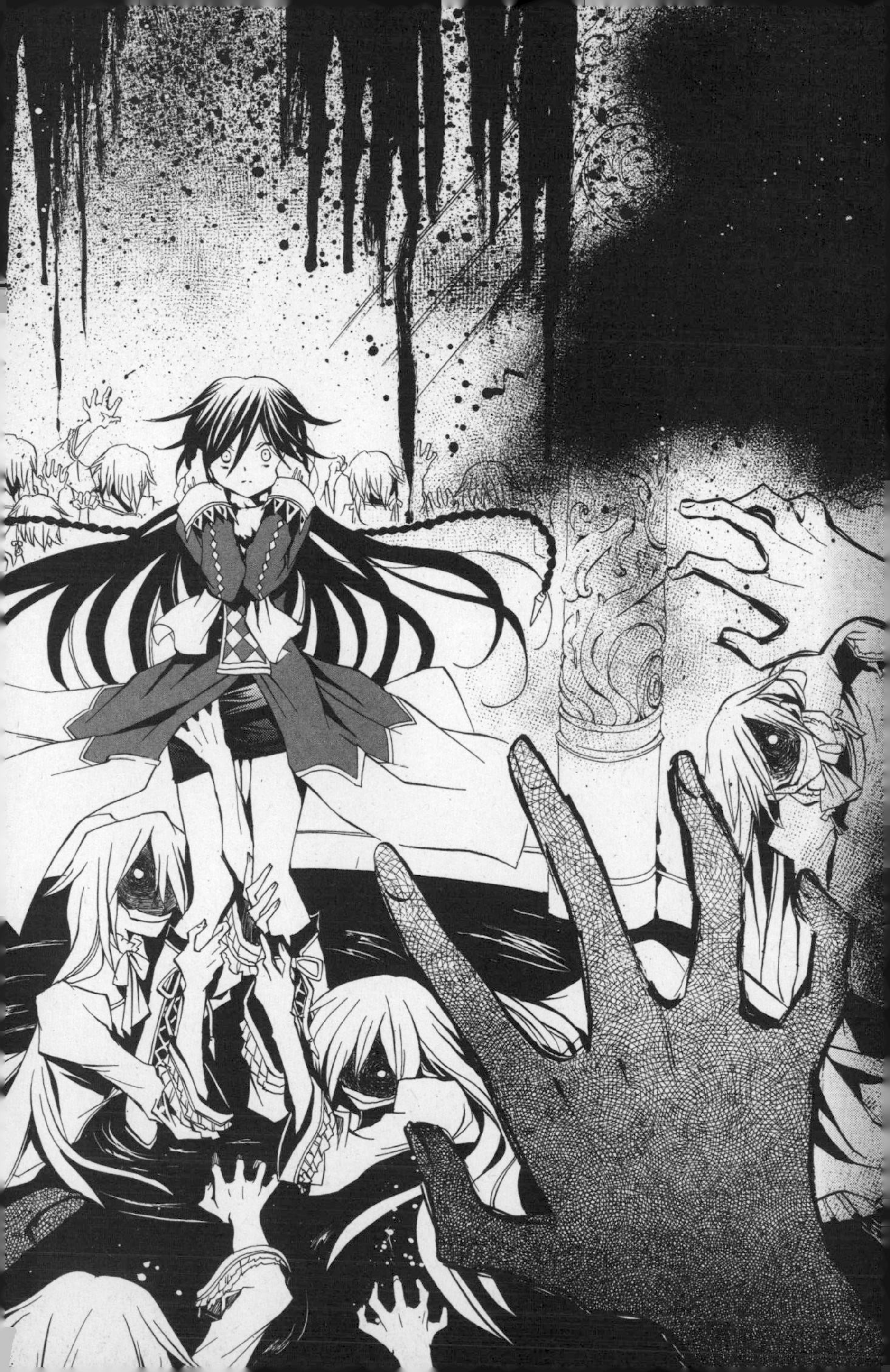

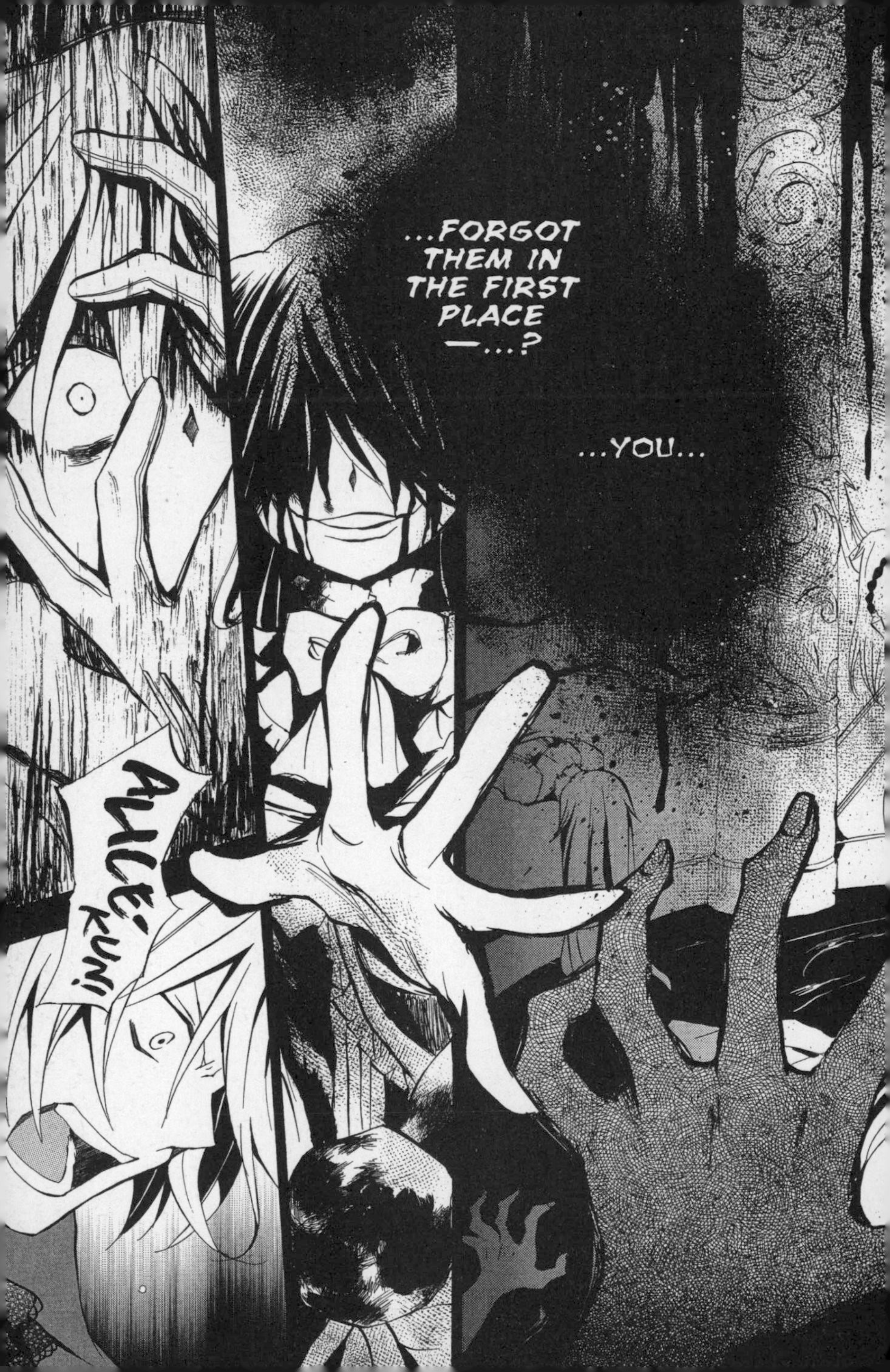
...YOU...
...FORGOT THEM IN THE FIRST PLACE —...?
ALICE-KUN!

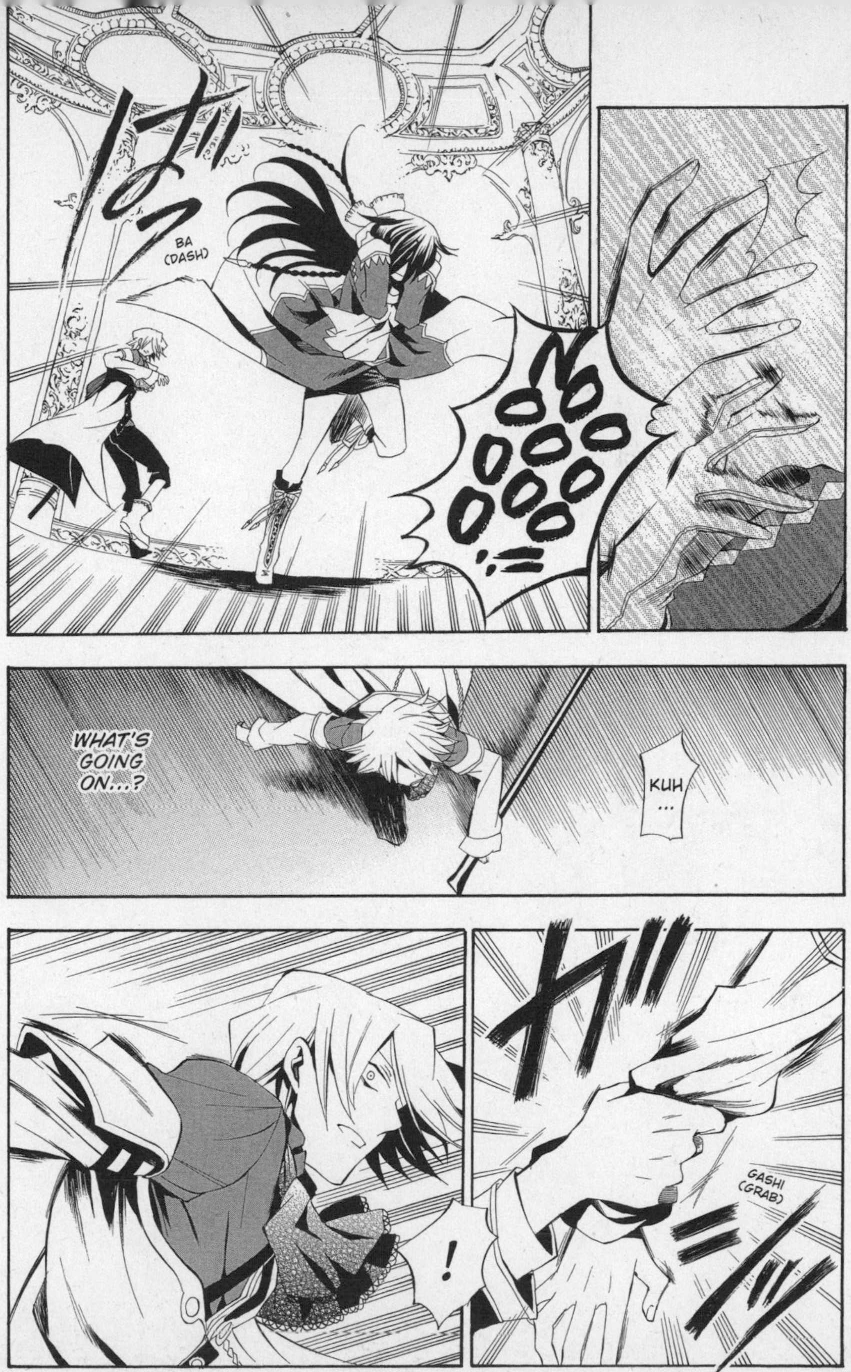
BA (DASH)
NOOOOOOOOOOOOOOO...!!
KUH...
WHAT'S GOING ON...?
GASHI (GRAB)
!

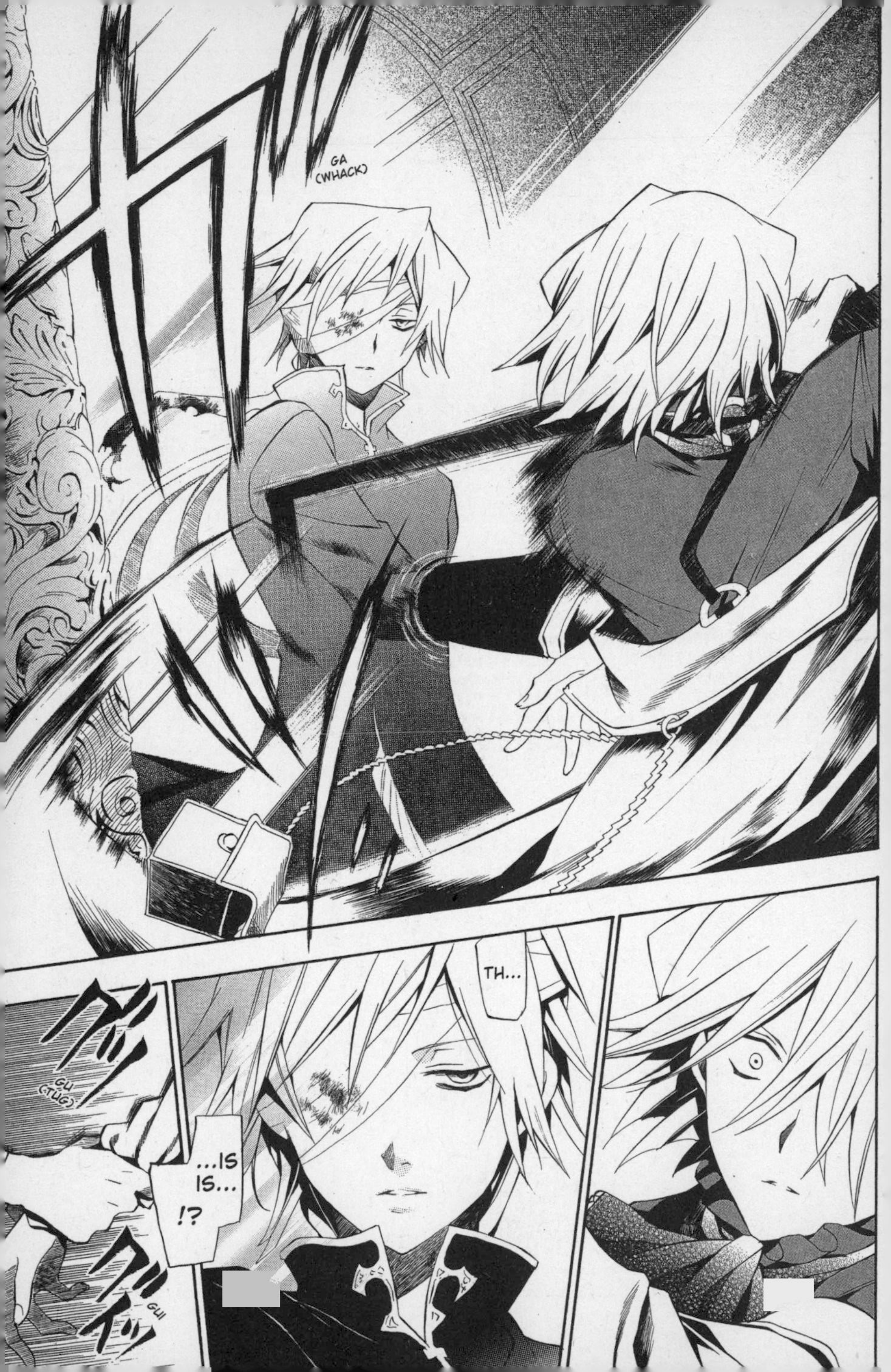
GA
(WHACK)
TH...
...IS
IS...
!?
GU
(TUG)
GUI

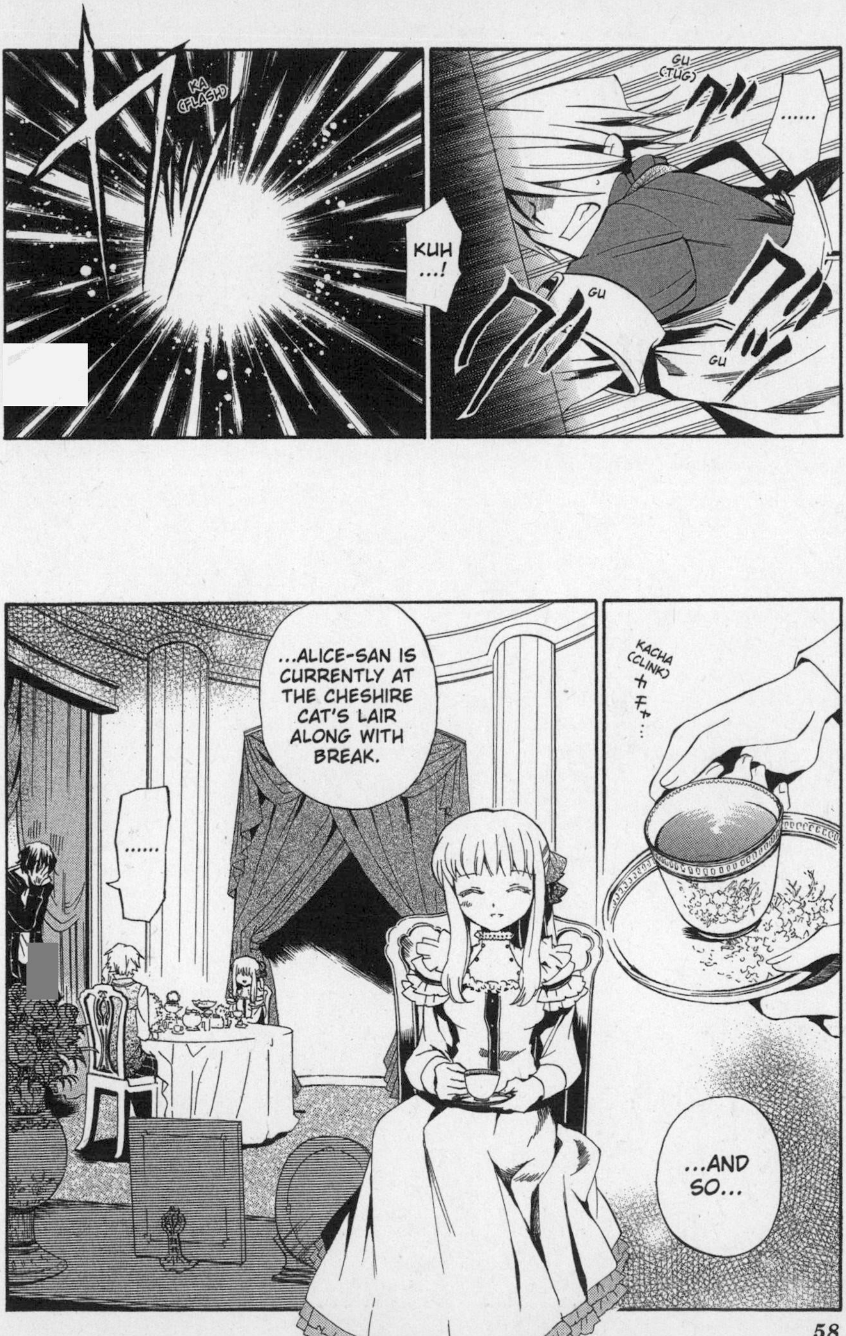
GU (TUG)
......
KUH ...!
GU
GU
KA (FLASH)
KACHA (CLINK)
...AND SO...
...ALICE-SAN IS CURRENTLY AT THE CHESHIRE CAT'S LAIR ALONG WITH BREAK.
......

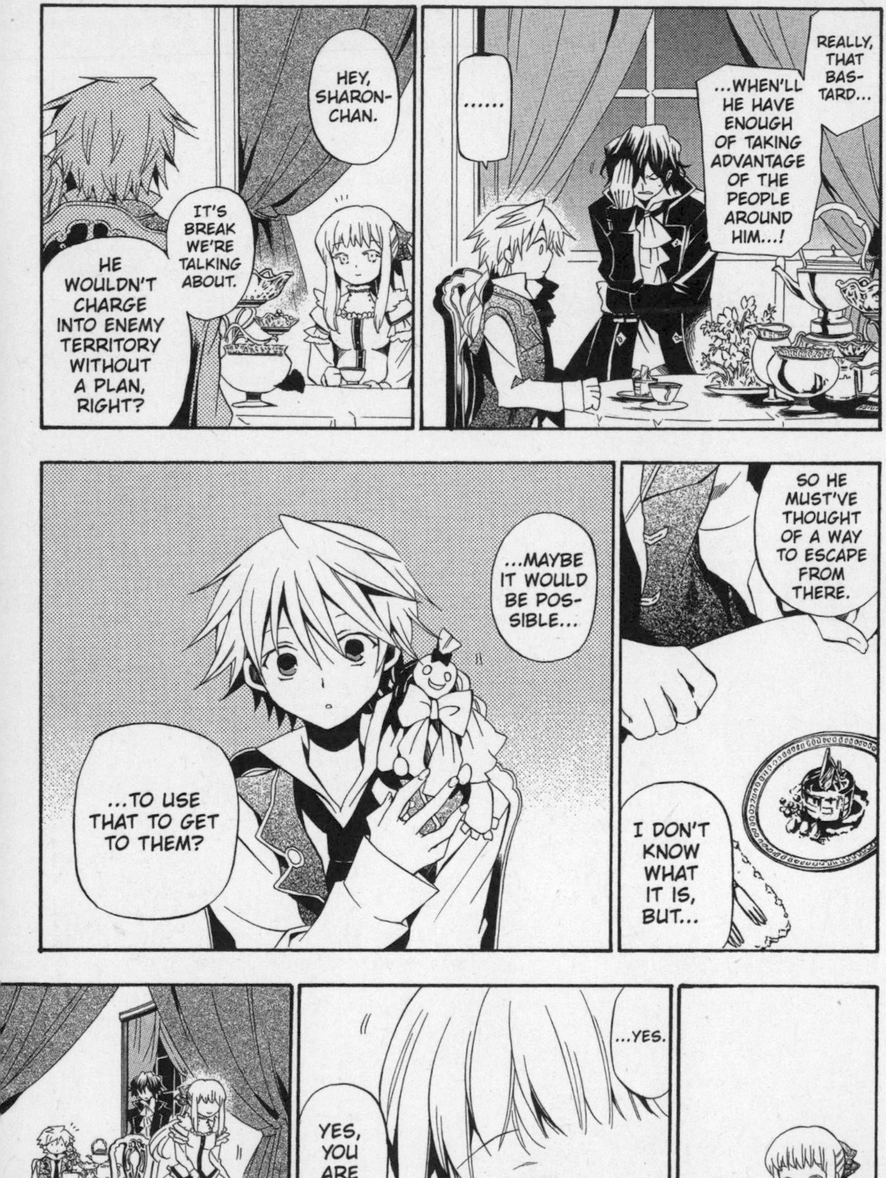
REALLY, THAT BAS- TARD...
...WHEN'LL HE HAVE ENOUGH OF TAKING ADVANTAGE OF THE PEOPLE AROUND HIM...!
......
HEY, SHARON- CHAN.
IT'S BREAK WE'RE TALKING ABOUT.
HE WOULDN'T CHARGE INTO ENEMY TERRITORY WITHOUT A PLAN, RIGHT?
SO HE MUST'VE THOUGHT OF A WAY TO ESCAPE FROM THERE.
I DON'T KNOW WHAT IT IS, BUT...
...MAYBE IT WOULD BE POS- SIBLE...
...TO USE THAT TO GET TO THEM?
...YES.
YES, YOU ARE RIGHT.

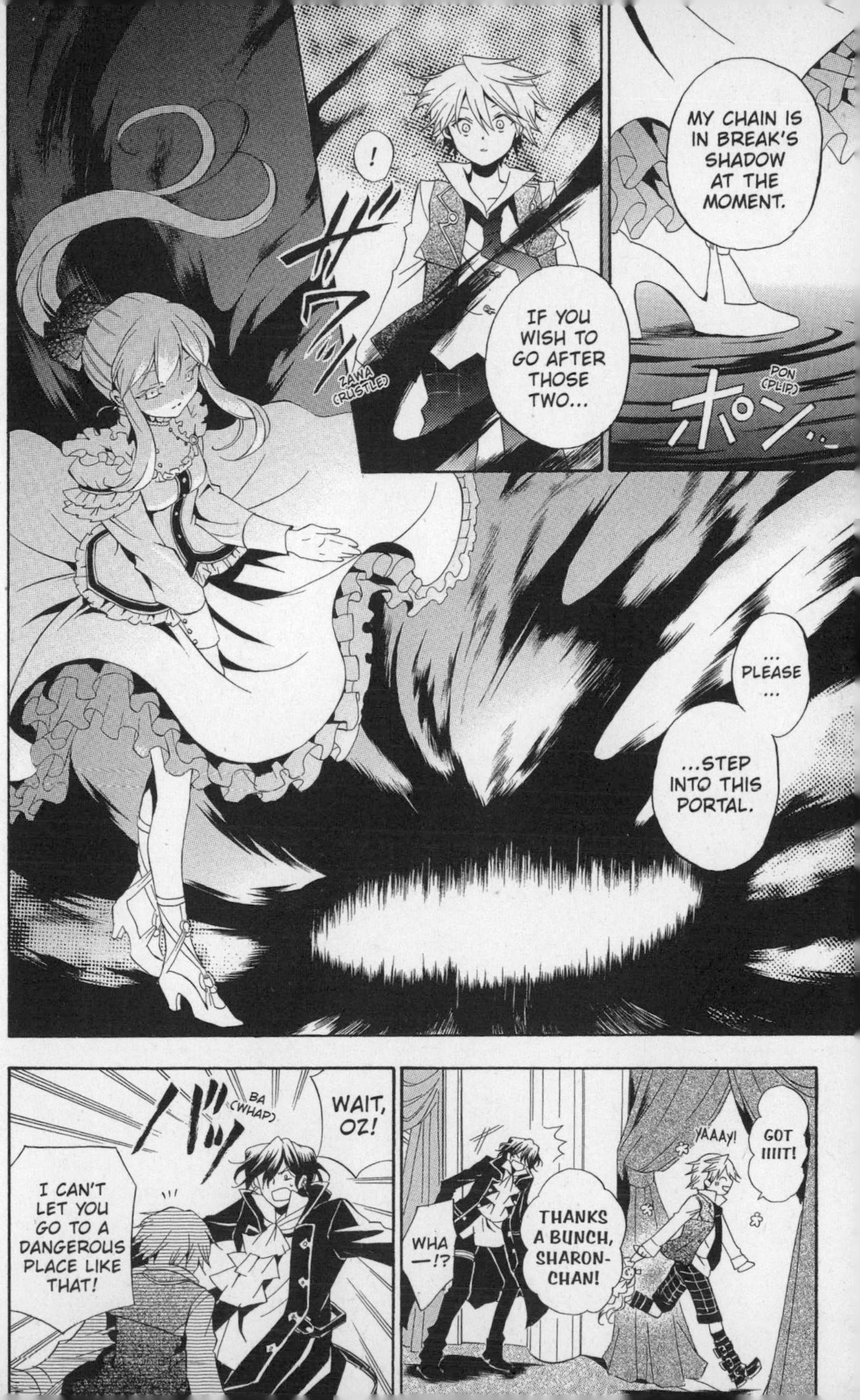
MY CHAIN IS IN BREAK'S SHADOW AT THE MOMENT.
PON (PLIP)
!
ZAWA (RUSTLE)
IF YOU WISH TO GO AFTER THOSE TWO...
...PLEASE...
...STEP INTO THIS PORTAL.
GOT IIIIT!
YAAAY!
THANKS A BUNCH, SHARON-CHAN!
WHA—!?
WAIT, OZ!
BA (WHAP)
I CAN'T LET YOU GO TO A DANGEROUS PLACE LIKE THAT!

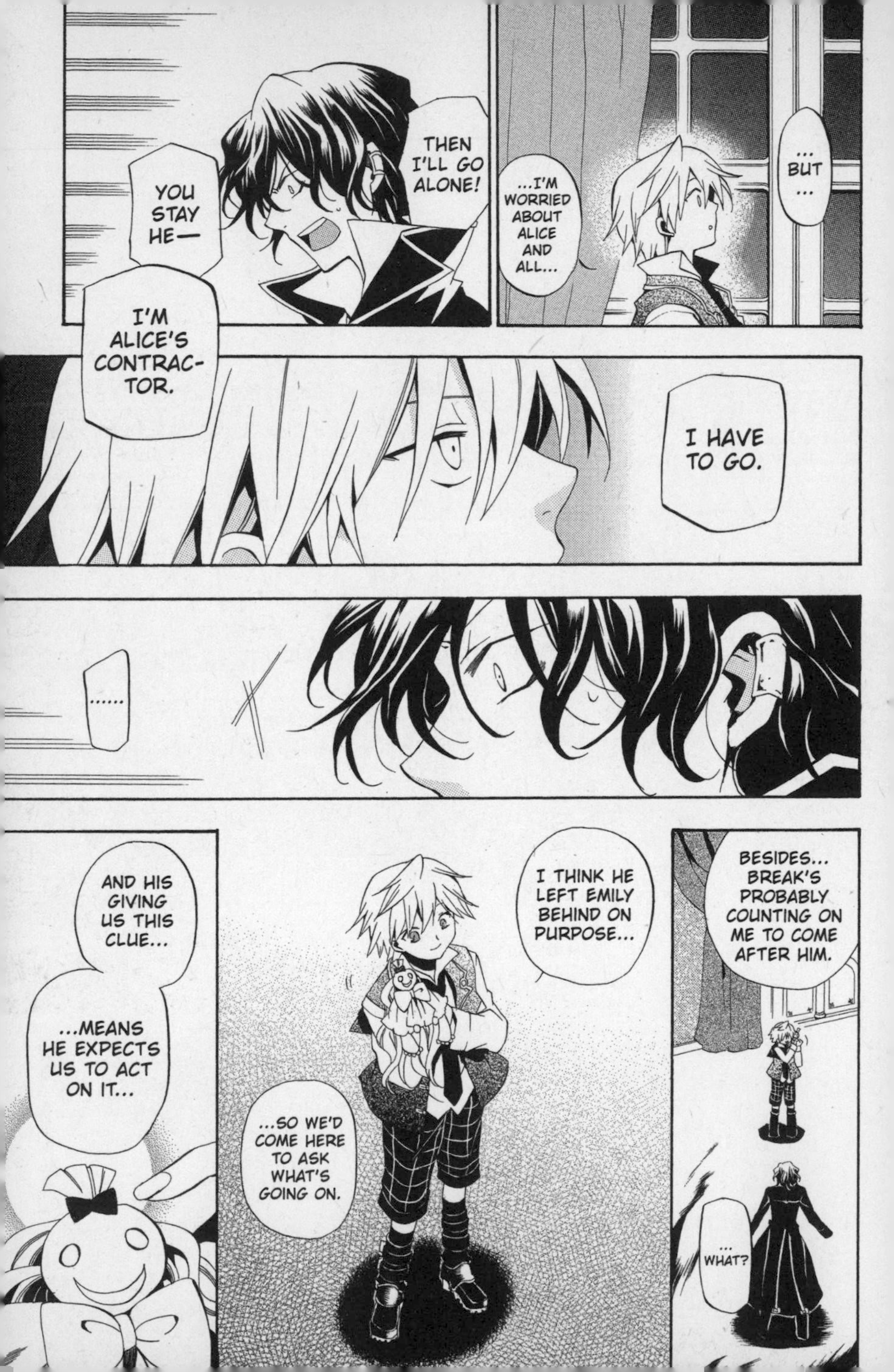
... BUT ...
...I'M WORRIED ABOUT ALICE AND ALL...
THEN I'LL GO ALONE!
YOU STAY HE—
I'M ALICE'S CONTRAC-TOR.
I HAVE TO GO.
......
BESIDES... BREAK'S PROBABLY COUNTING ON ME TO COME AFTER HIM.
... WHAT?
I THINK HE LEFT EMILY BEHIND ON PURPOSE...
...SO WE'D COME HERE TO ASK WHAT'S GOING ON.
AND HIS GIVING US THIS CLUE...
...MEANS HE EXPECTS US TO ACT ON IT...

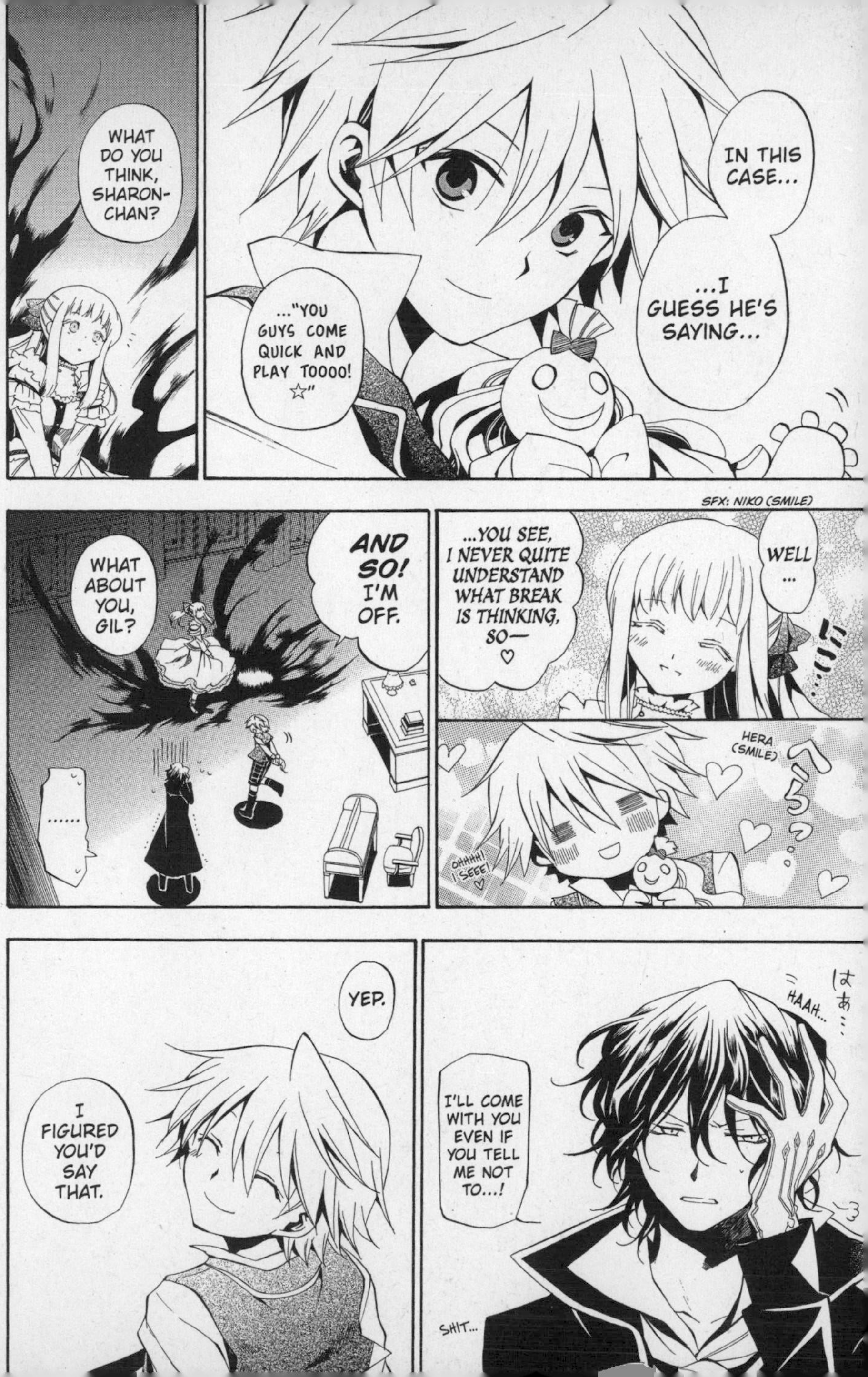
IN THIS CASE...
...I GUESS HE'S SAYING...
..."YOU GUYS COME QUICK AND PLAY TOOOO! ☆"
WHAT DO YOU THINK, SHARON-CHAN?
SFX: NIKO (SMILE)
WELL...
...YOU SEE, I NEVER QUITE UNDERSTAND WHAT BREAK IS THINKING, SO—♡
HERA (SMILE)
OHHHH! I SEEE! ♡
AND SO! I'M OFF.
WHAT ABOUT YOU, GIL?
......
HAAH...
I'LL COME WITH YOU EVEN IF YOU TELL ME NOT TO...!
SHIT...
YEP.
I FIGURED YOU'D SAY THAT.

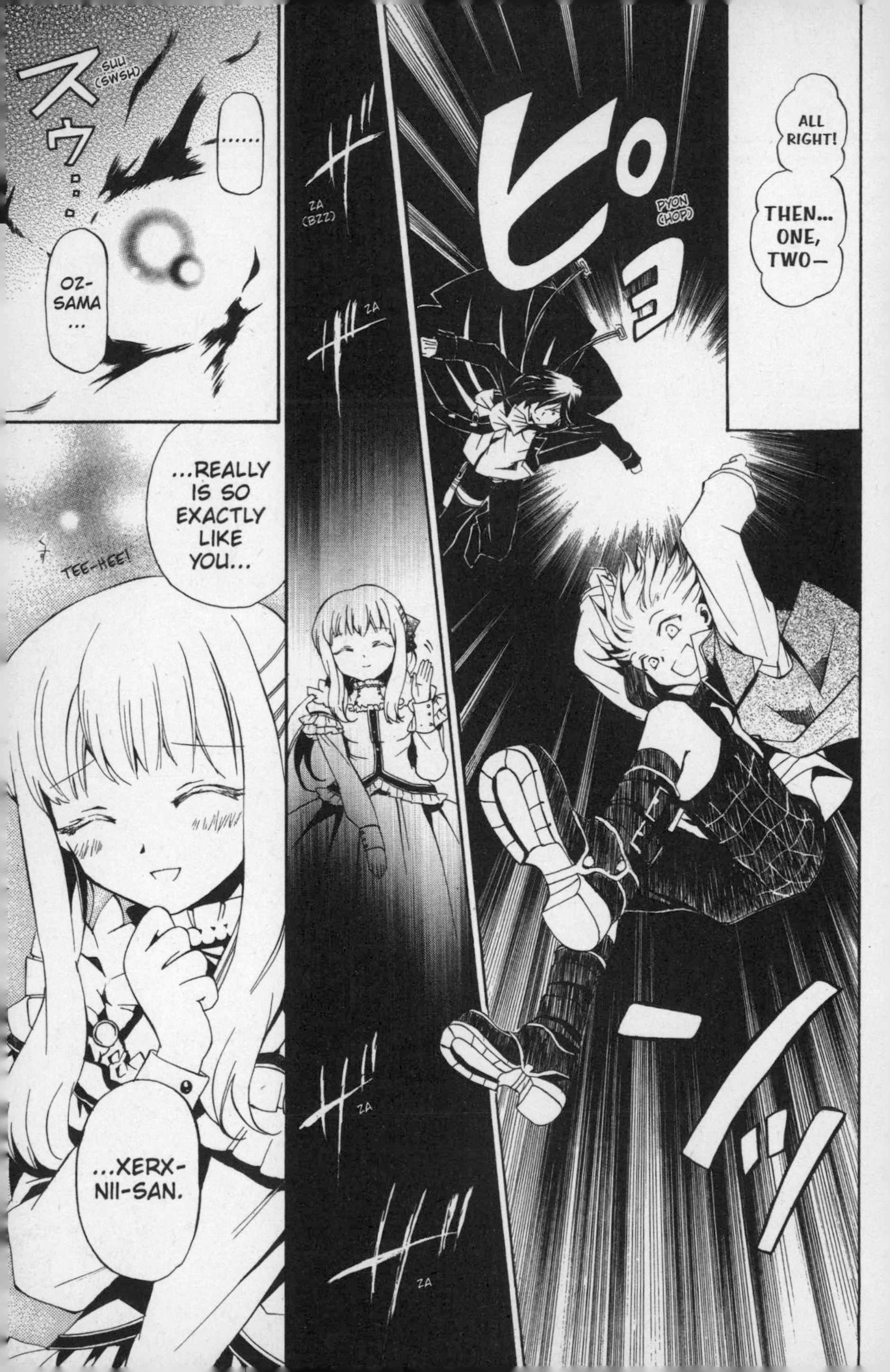
ALL RIGHT!
THEN... ONE, TWO—
ピョ
PYON (HOP)
ー
ッ
ZA (BZZ)
ZA
ZA
ZA
スゥ...
SUU (SWSH)
......
OZ-SAMA...
...REALLY IS SO EXACTLY LIKE YOU...
TEE-HEE!
...XERX-NII-SAN.

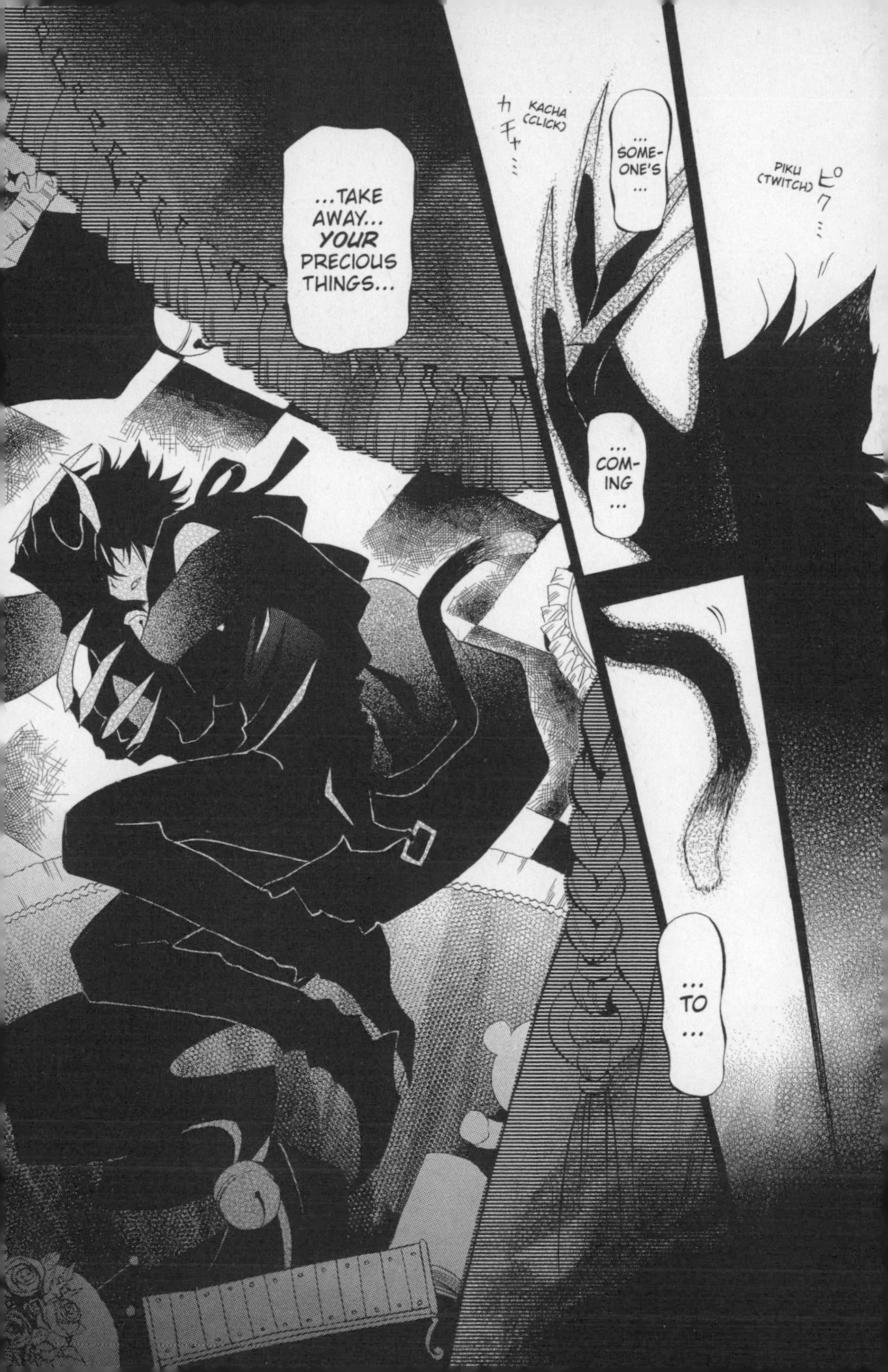

ピク
PIKU (TWITCH)
カチャ
KACHA (CLICK)
...SOME-ONE'S...
...COM-ING...
...TO...
...TAKE AWAY... YOUR PRECIOUS THINGS...

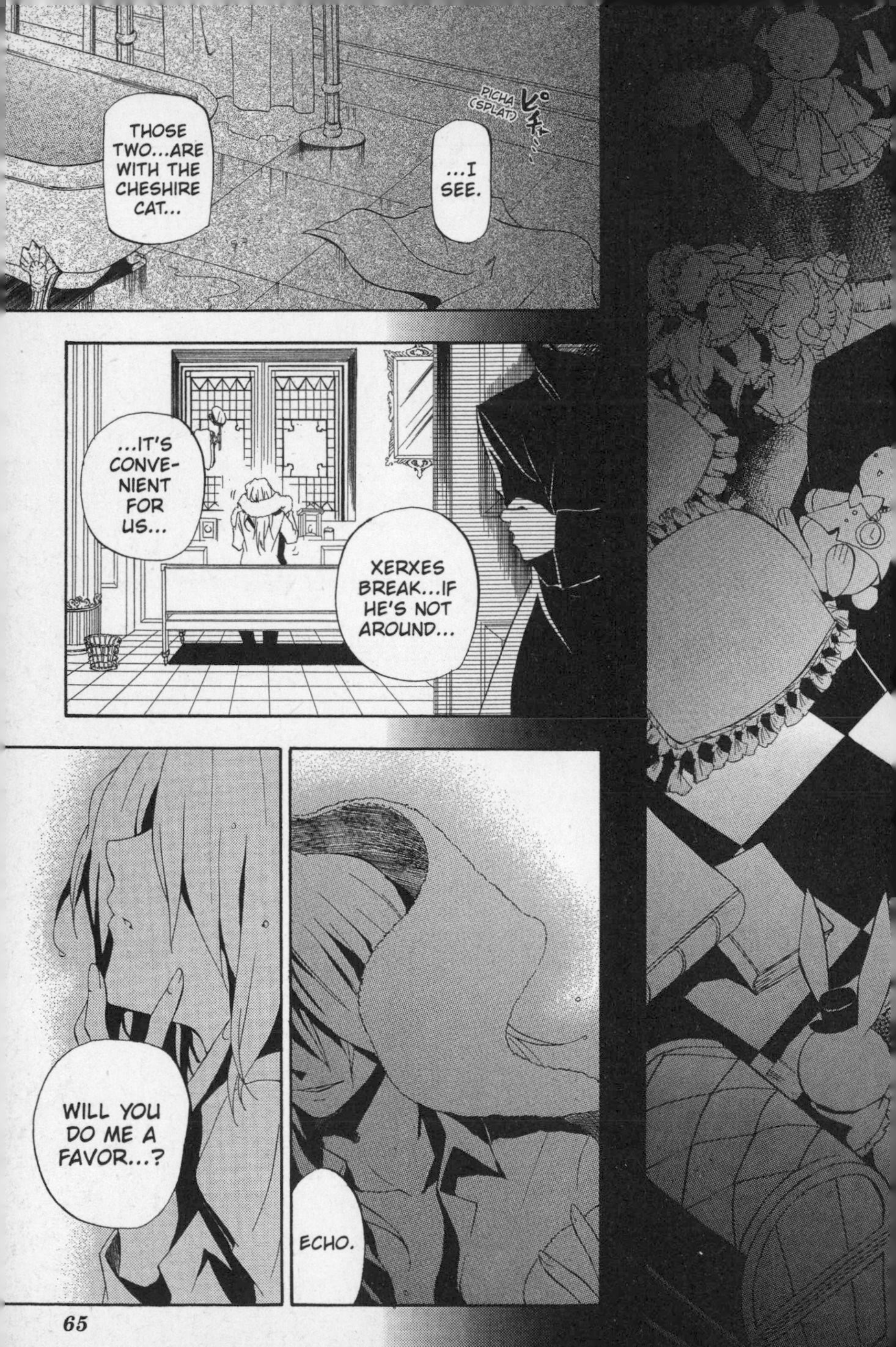
PICHA (SPLAT)
ピチャ…
...I SEE.
THOSE TWO...ARE WITH THE CHESHIRE CAT...
XERXES BREAK...IF HE'S NOT AROUND...
...IT'S CONVENIENT FOR US...
ECHO.
WILL YOU DO ME A FAVOR...?

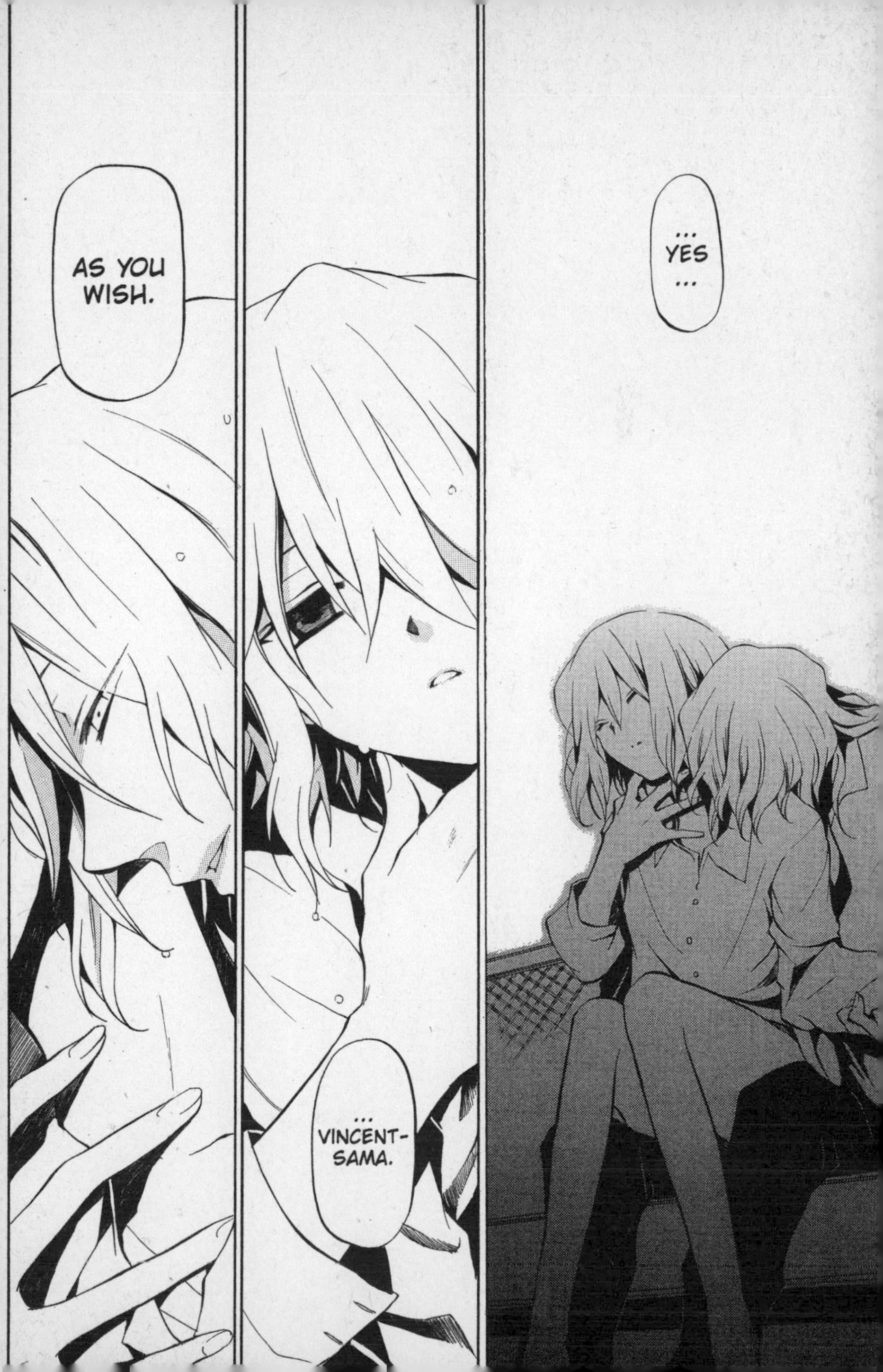
... YES ...
... VINCENT-SAMA.
AS YOU WISH.

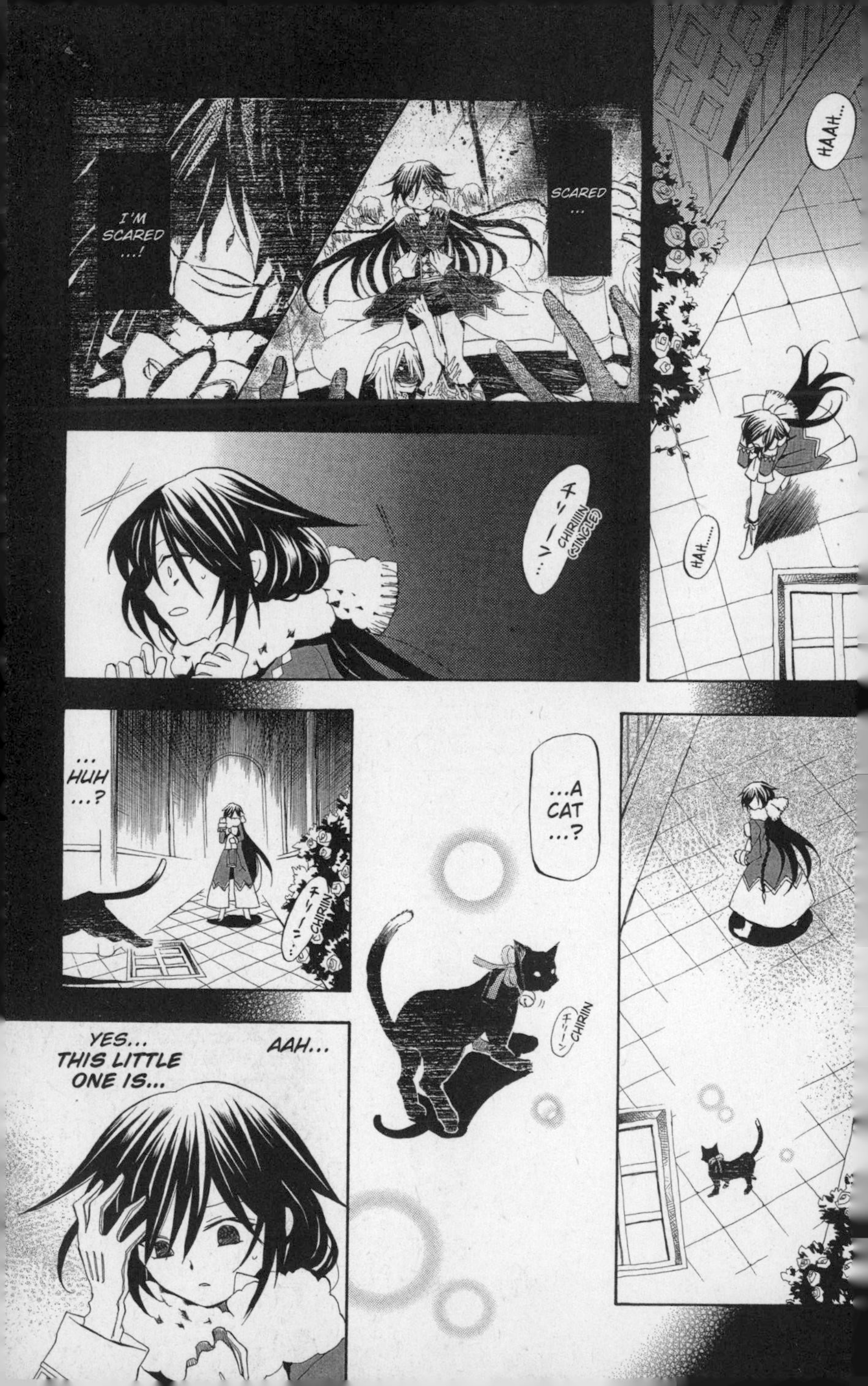
HAAH...
HAH......
SCARED...
I'M SCARED...!
チリーン...
CHIRIIIN (JINGLE)
...A CAT...?
チリーン
CHIRIIN
...HUH...?
チリーン...
CHIRIIN
AAH...
YES... THIS LITTLE ONE IS...

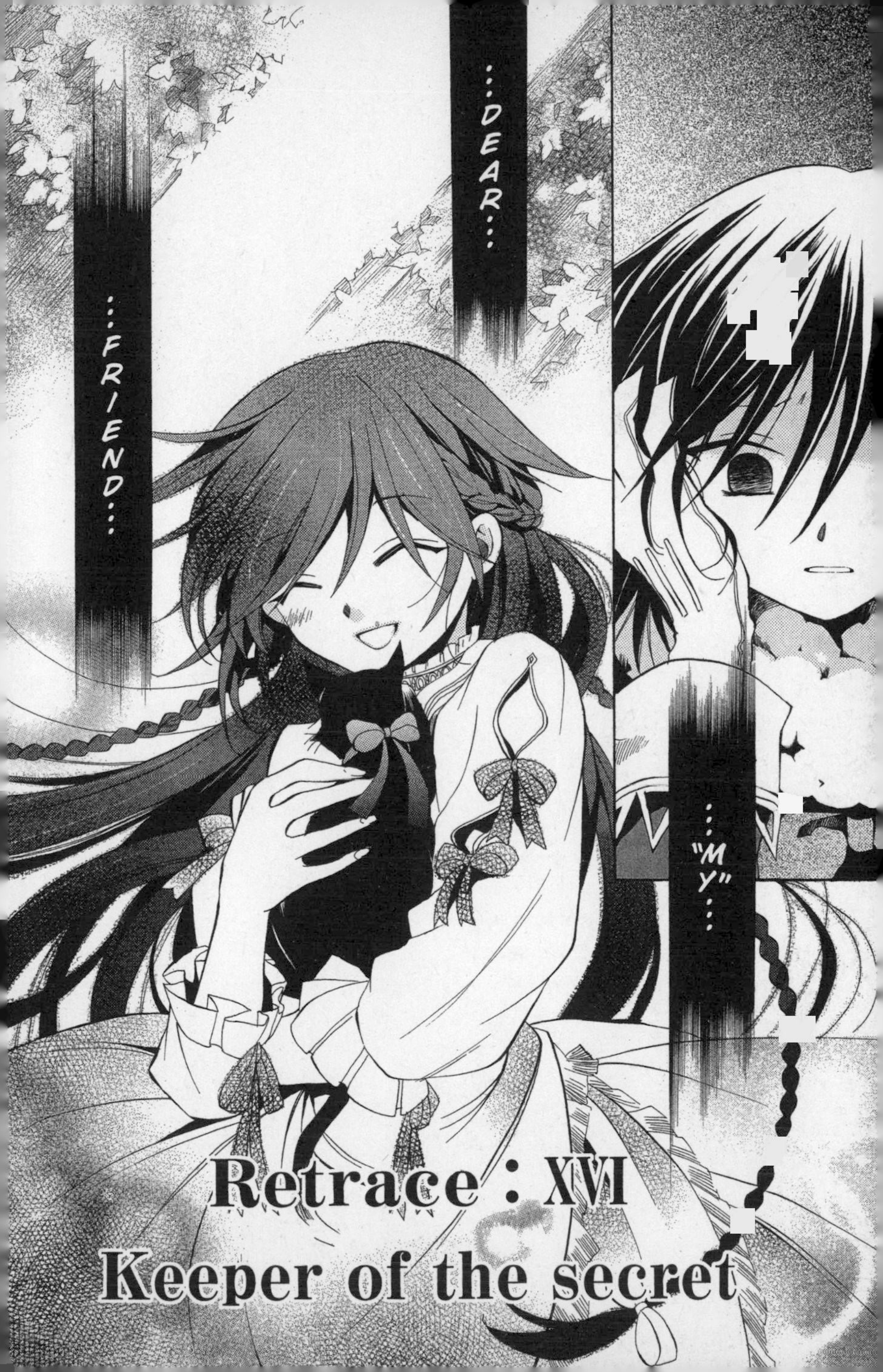
..."MY"...
...DEAR...
...FRIEND...

Retrace : XVI
Keeper of the secret

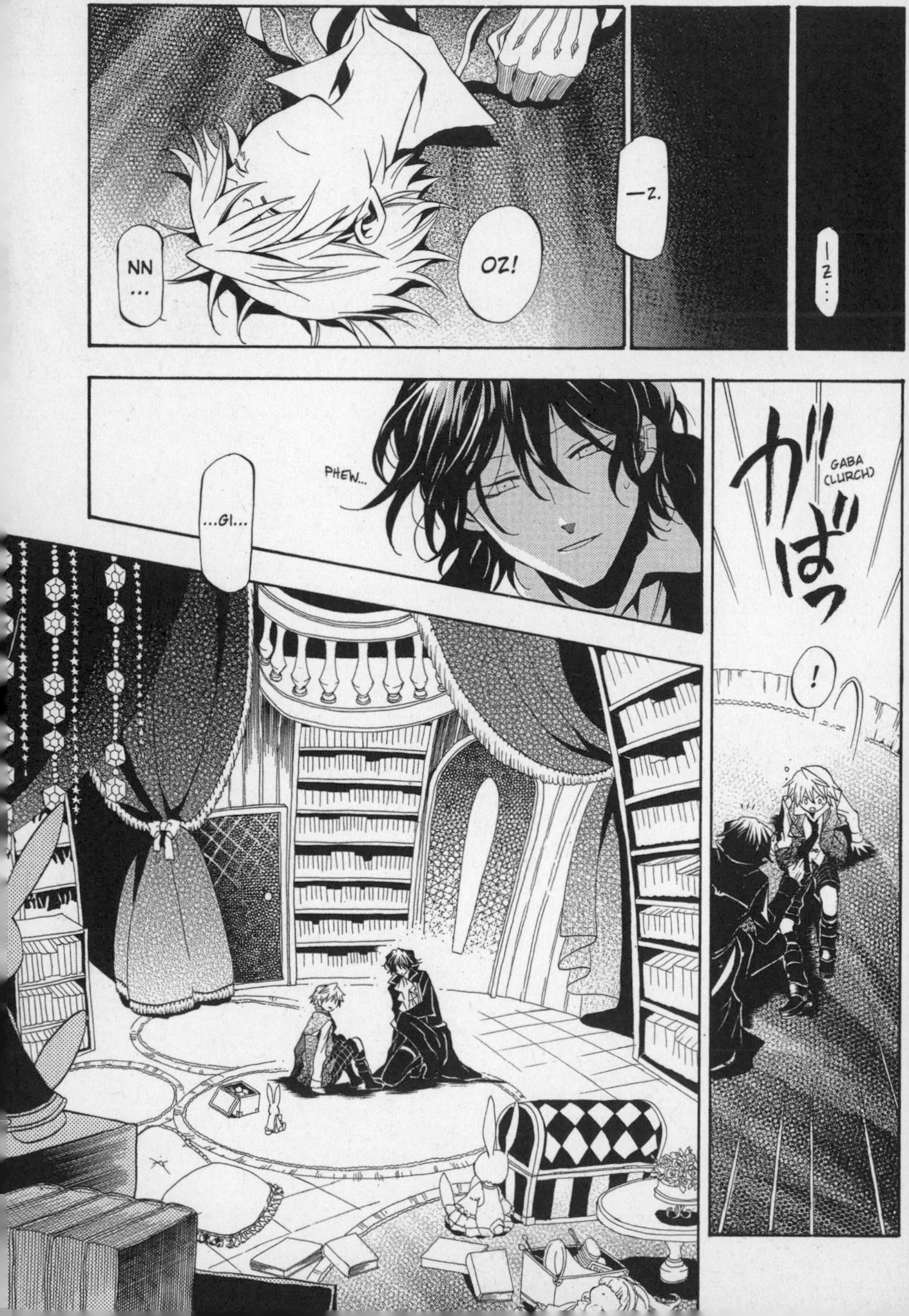

—Z...
—Z.
OZ!
NN...
がばっ
GABA (LURCH)
!
PHEW...
...GI...

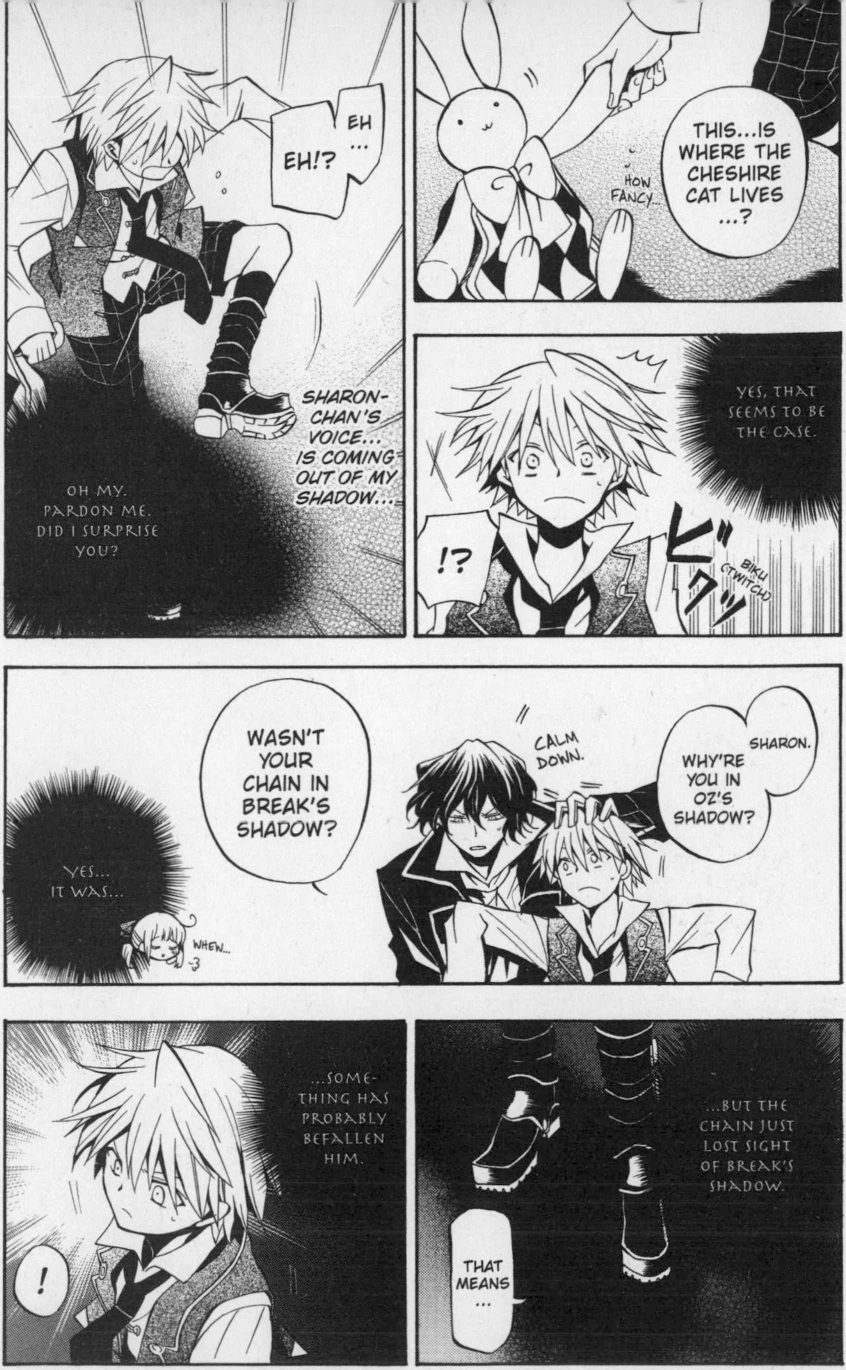
THIS...IS WHERE THE CHESHIRE CAT LIVES ...?
HOW FANCY...
YES, THAT SEEMS TO BE THE CASE.
ビクッ
BIKU (TWITCH)
!?
EH ... EH!?
SHARON-CHAN'S VOICE... IS COMING OUT OF MY SHADOW...
OH MY. PARDON ME. DID I SURPRISE YOU?
SHARON. WHY'RE YOU IN OZ'S SHADOW?
CALM DOWN.
WASN'T YOUR CHAIN IN BREAK'S SHADOW?
YES... IT WAS...
WHEW...
...BUT THE CHAIN JUST LOST SIGHT OF BREAK'S SHADOW.
THAT MEANS ...
...SOME-THING HAS PROBABLY BEFALLEN HIM.
!

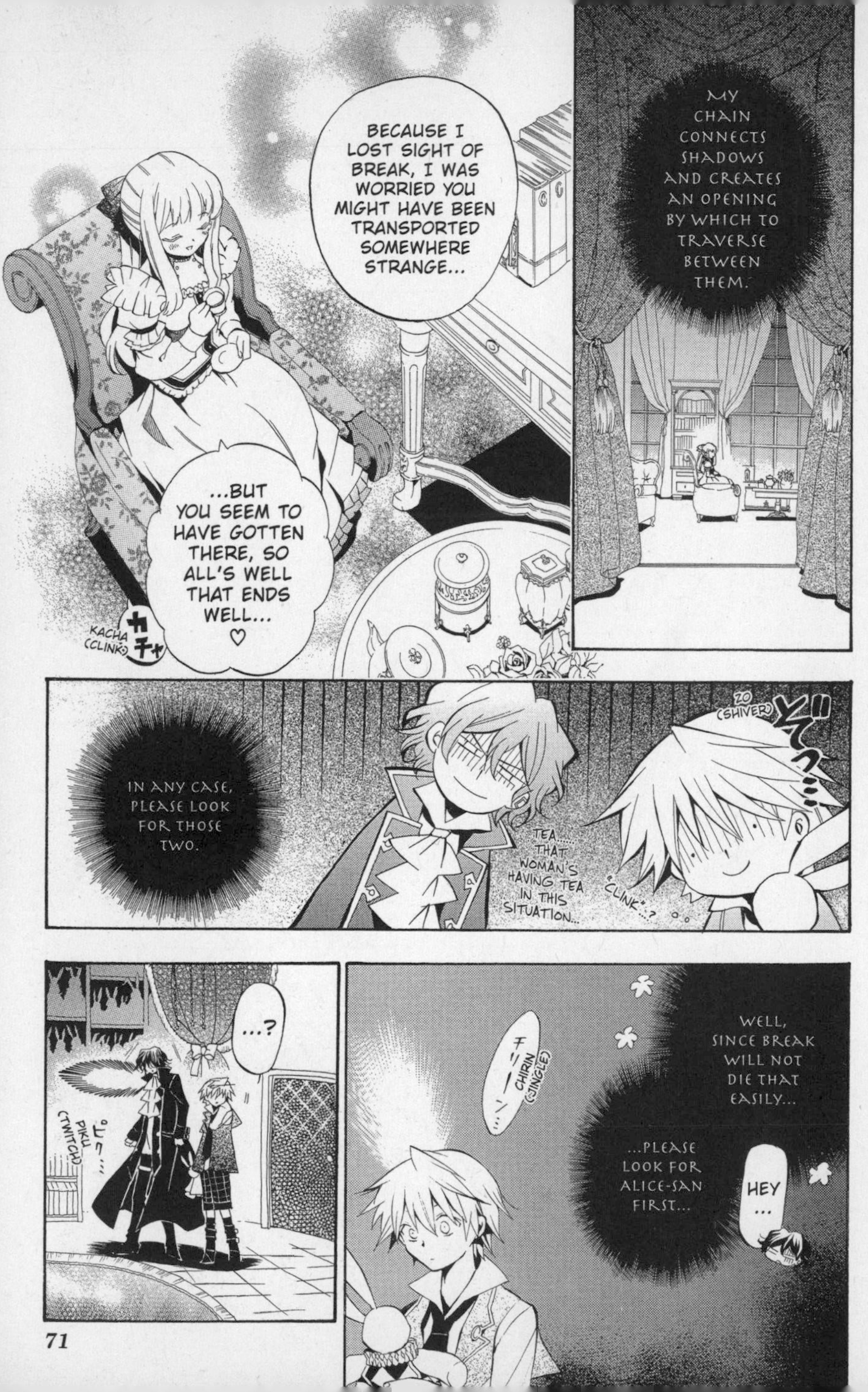
MY CHAIN CONNECTS SHADOWS AND CREATES AN OPENING BY WHICH TO TRAVERSE BETWEEN THEM.
BECAUSE I LOST SIGHT OF BREAK, I WAS WORRIED YOU MIGHT HAVE BEEN TRANSPORTED SOMEWHERE STRANGE...
...BUT YOU SEEM TO HAVE GOTTEN THERE, SO ALL'S WELL THAT ENDS WELL... ♡
カチャ
KACHA (CLINK)
ZO (SHIVER)
"CLINK"...?
TEA...... THAT WOMAN'S HAVING TEA IN THIS SITUATION...
IN ANY CASE, PLEASE LOOK FOR THOSE TWO.
WELL, SINCE BREAK WILL NOT DIE THAT EASILY...
チリーン...
CHIRIN (JINGLE)
...PLEASE LOOK FOR ALICE-SAN FIRST...
HEY ...
...?
ピクッ...
PIKU (TWITCH)

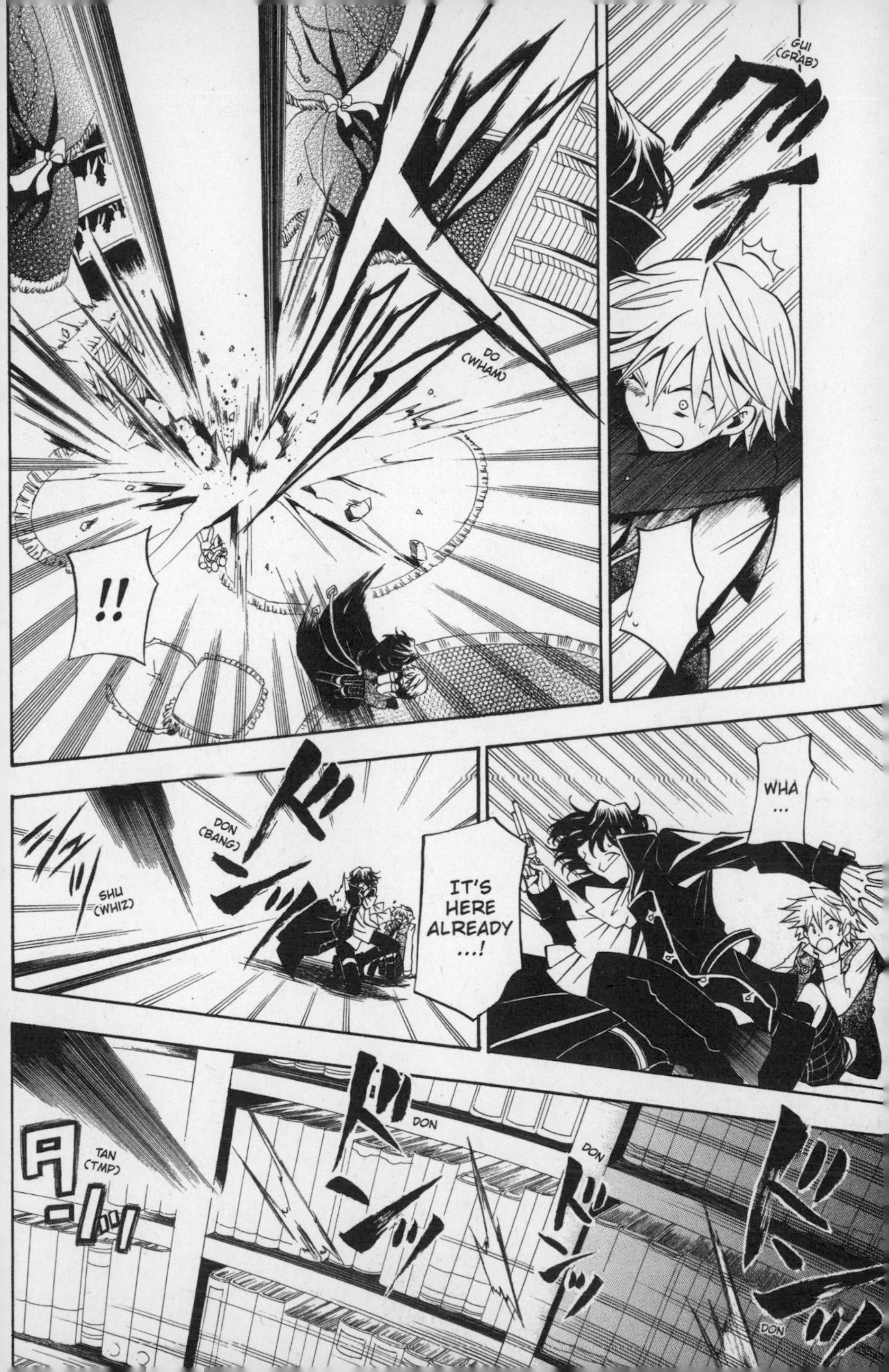
GUI (GRAB)
DO (WHAM)
!!
WHA ...
IT'S HERE ALREADY ...!
DON (BANG)
SHU (WHIZ)
DON
DON
DON
TAN (TMP)

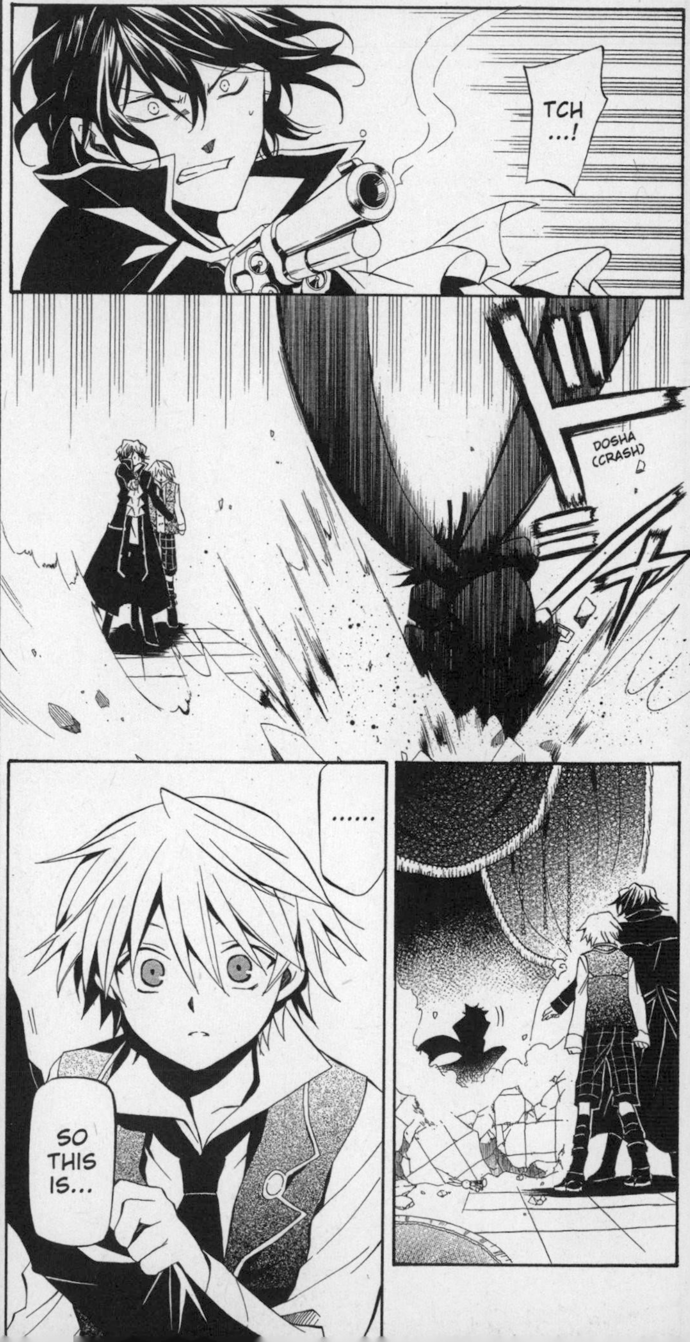
TCH ...!
DOSHA (CRASH)
......
SO THIS IS...
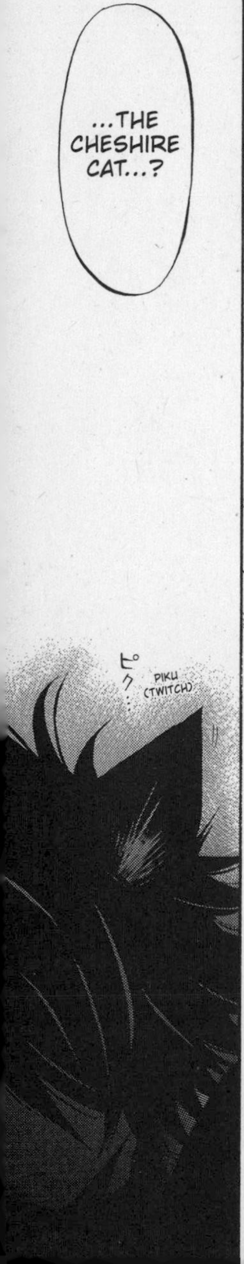
...THE CHESHIRE CAT...?
ピク...
PIKU (TWITCH)

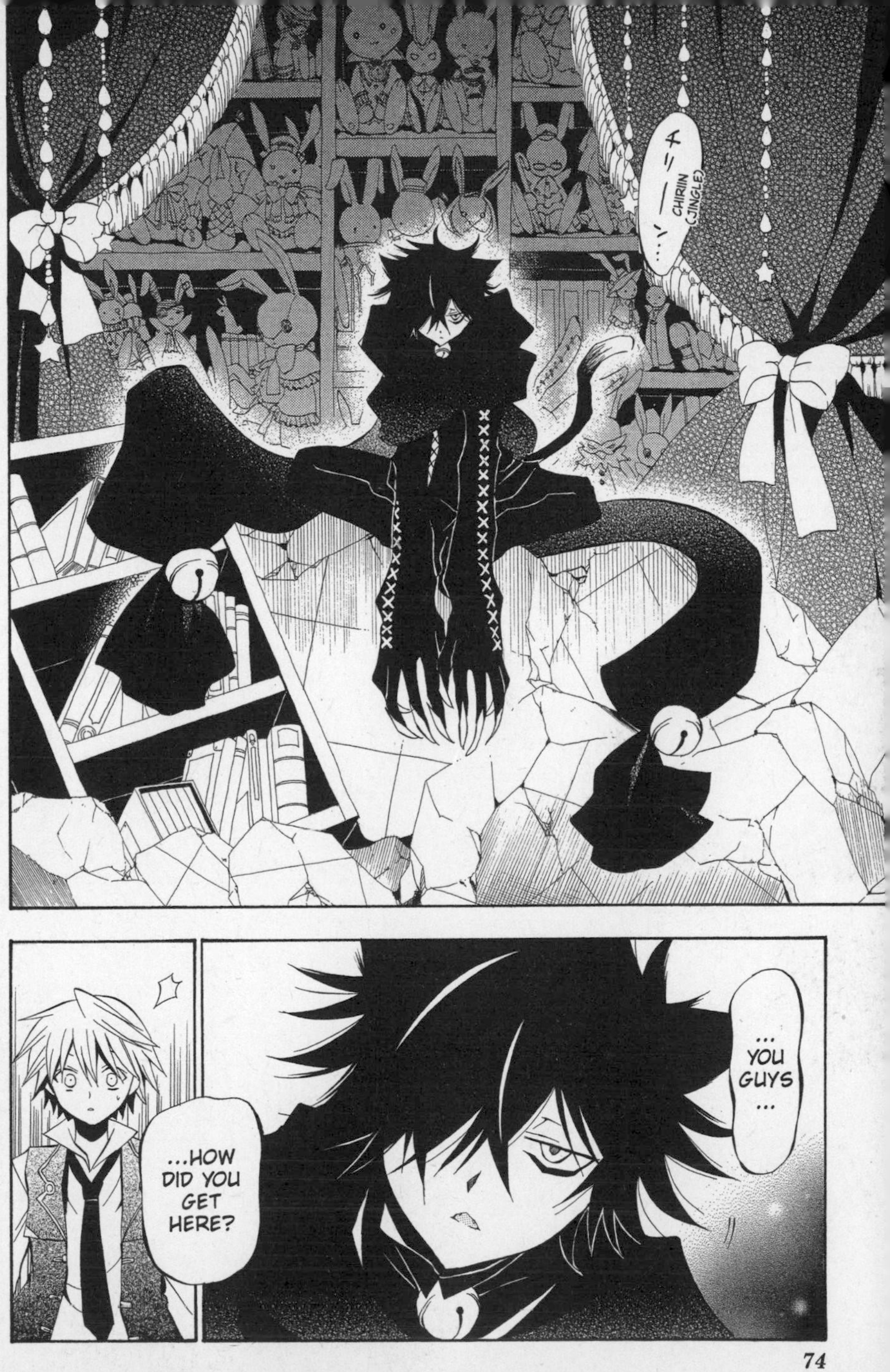

チリーーン…
CHIRIIN (JINGLE)
...YOU GUYS...
...HOW DID YOU GET HERE?

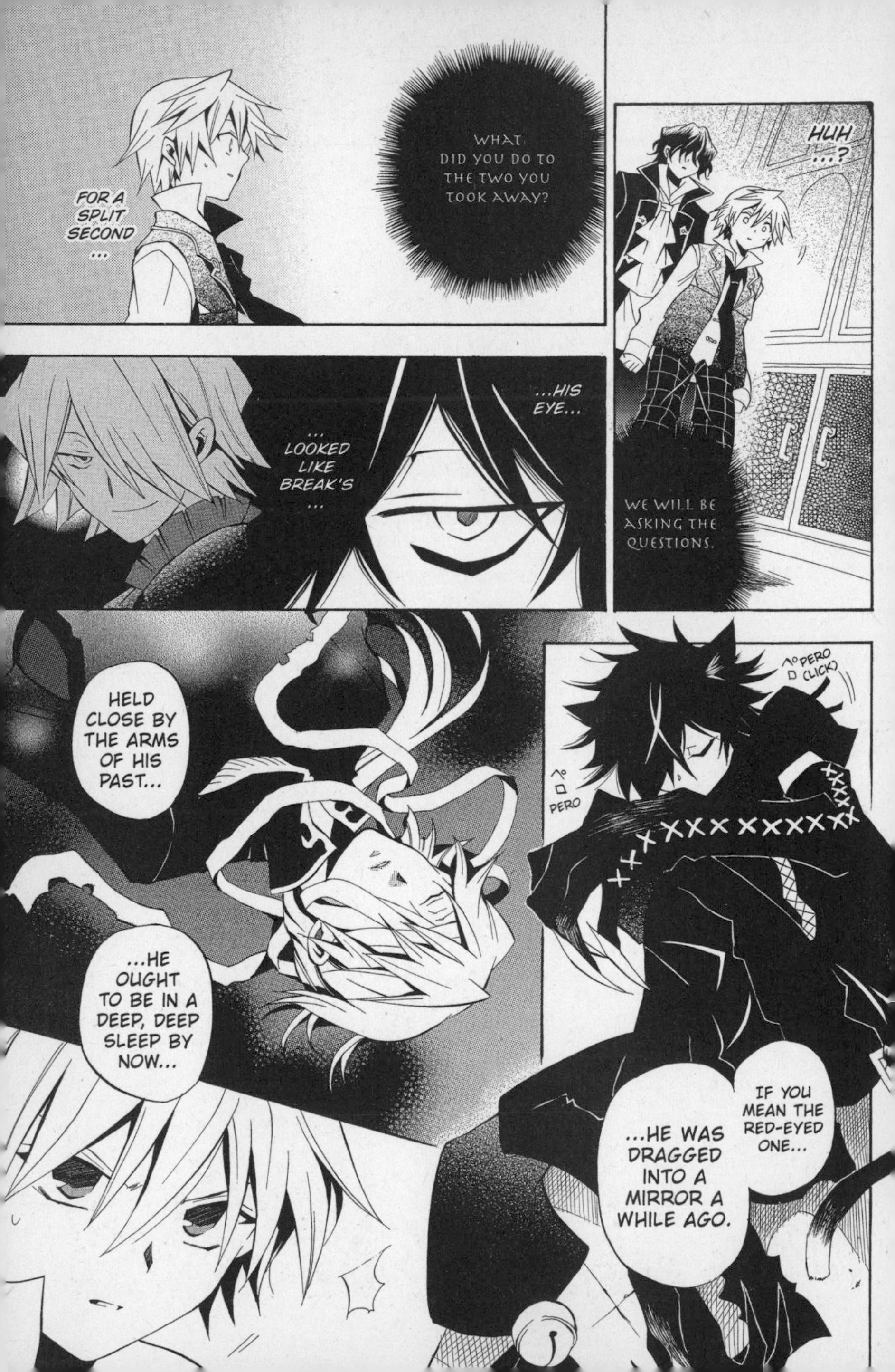
HUH ...?
WE WILL BE ASKING THE QUESTIONS.
WHAT DID YOU DO TO THE TWO YOU TOOK AWAY?
FOR A SPLIT SECOND ...
...HIS EYE...
...LOOKED LIKE BREAK'S ...
PERO (CLICK)
PERO
IF YOU MEAN THE RED-EYED ONE...
...HE WAS DRAGGED INTO A MIRROR A WHILE AGO.
HELD CLOSE BY THE ARMS OF HIS PAST...
...HE OUGHT TO BE IN A DEEP, DEEP SLEEP BY NOW...

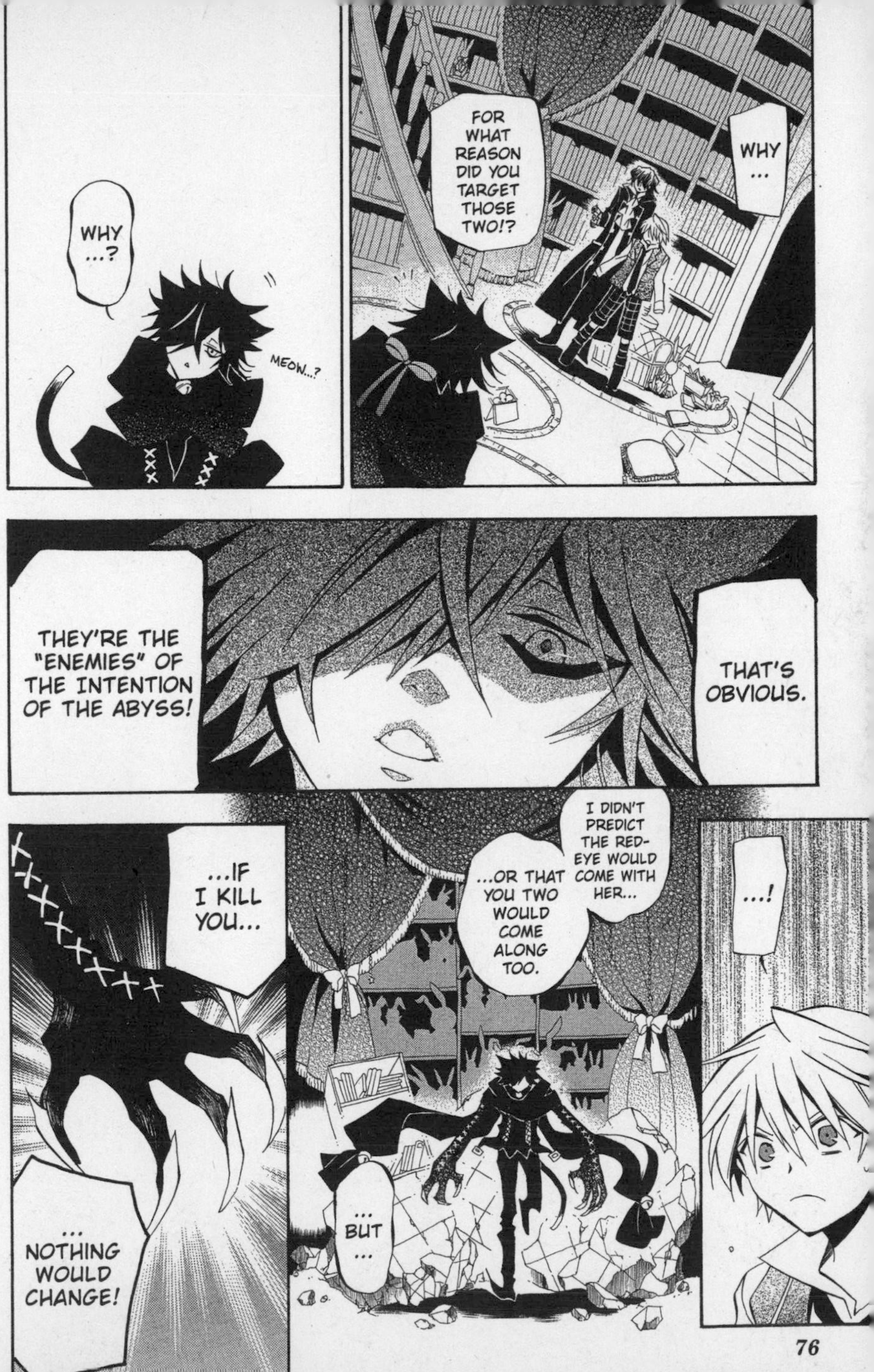
WHY ...
FOR WHAT REASON DID YOU TARGET THOSE TWO!?
WHY ...?
MEOW...?
THAT'S OBVIOUS.
THEY'RE THE "ENEMIES" OF THE INTENTION OF THE ABYSS!
...!
I DIDN'T PREDICT THE RED-EYE WOULD COME WITH HER...
...OR THAT YOU TWO WOULD COME ALONG TOO.
... BUT ...
...IF I KILL YOU...
... NOTHING WOULD CHANGE!

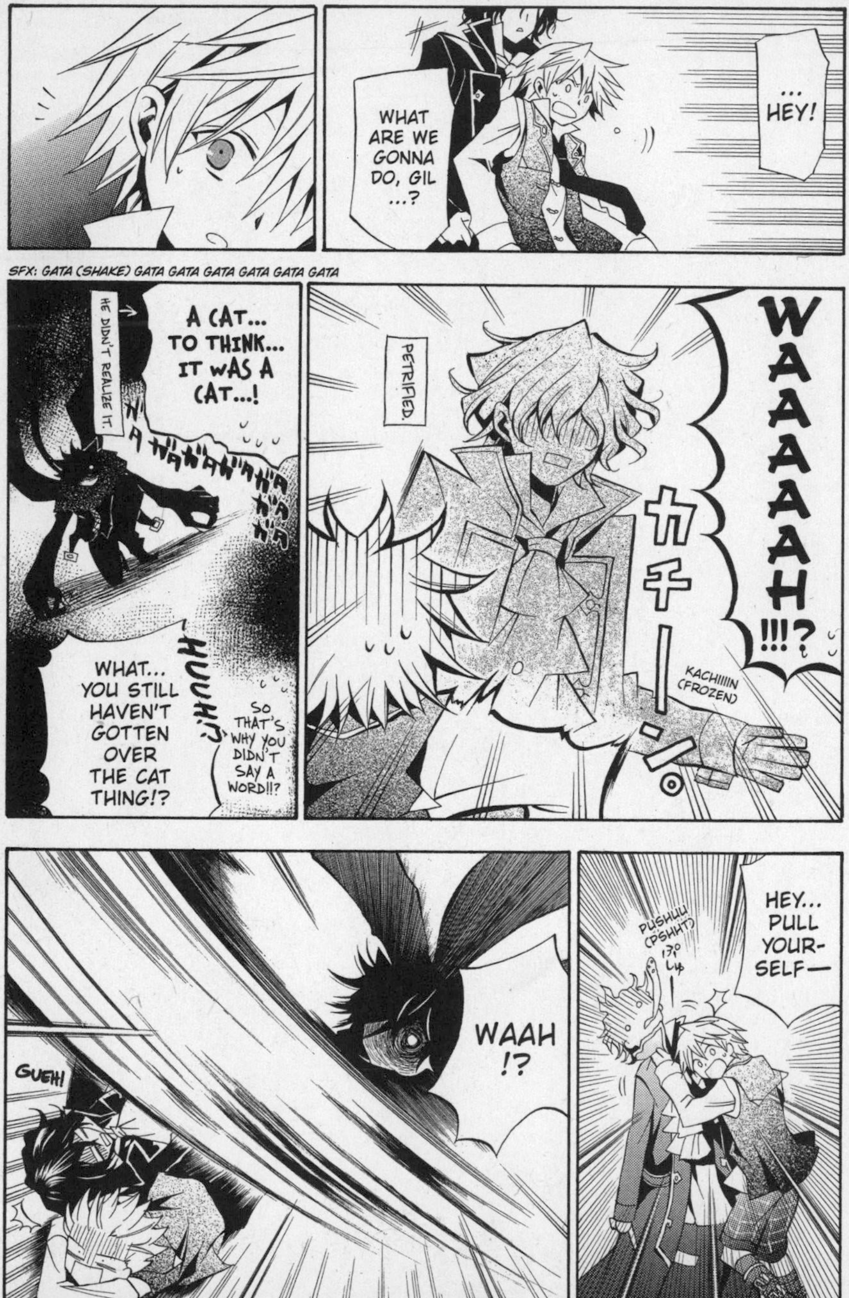
...HEY!
WHAT ARE WE GONNA DO, GIL ...?
SFX: GATA (SHAKE) GATA GATA GATA GATA GATA GATA
WAAAAAAH!!!?
PETRIFIED.
KACHIIIIN (FROZEN)
A CAT... TO THINK... IT WAS A CAT...!
HE DIDN'T REALIZE IT.
HUUH!?
SO THAT'S WHY YOU DIDN'T SAY A WORD!!?
WHAT... YOU STILL HAVEN'T GOTTEN OVER THE CAT THING!?
HEY... PULL YOURSELF—
PUSHUU (PSHHT)
WAAH!?
GUEH!

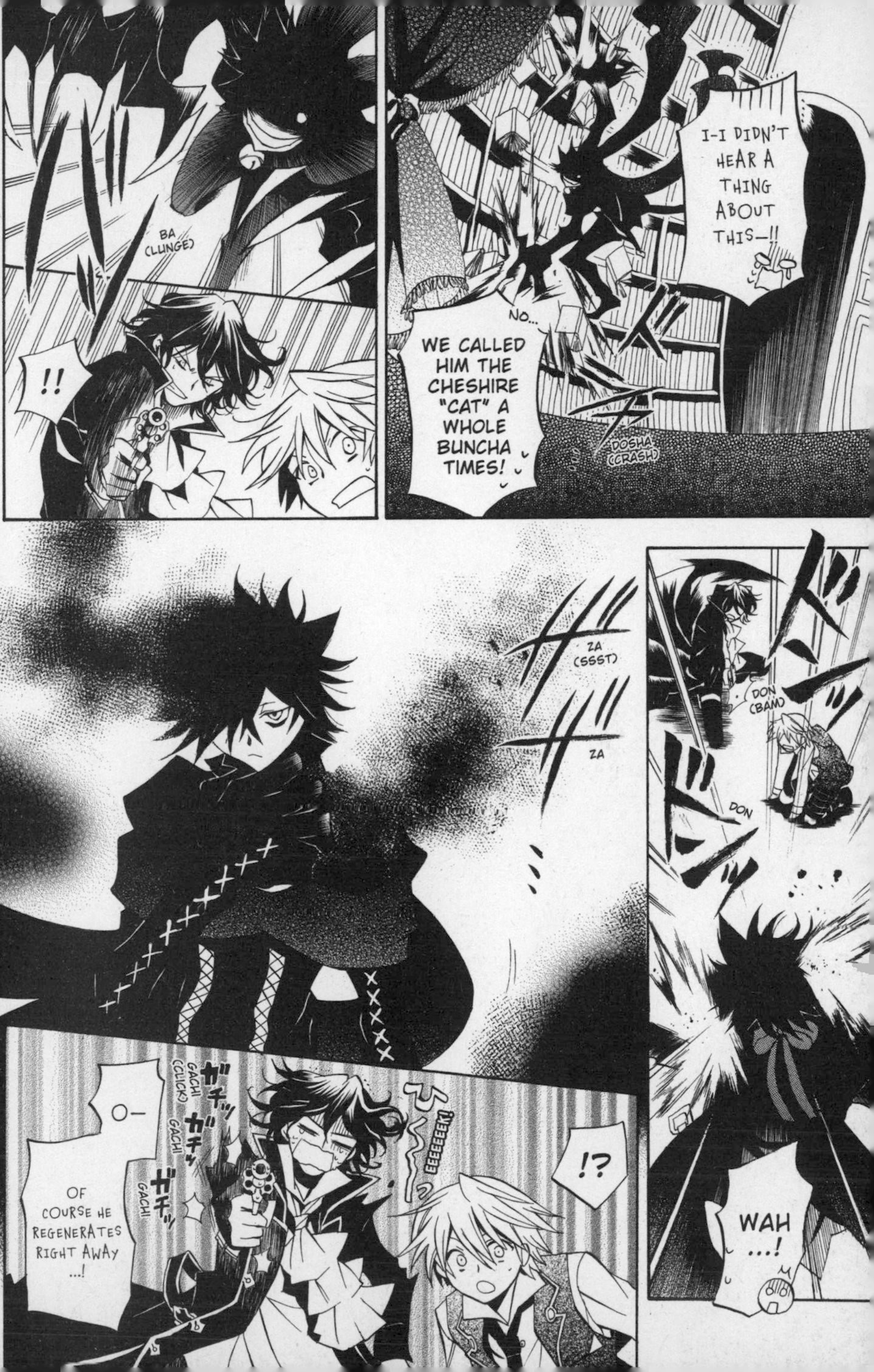
I-I DIDN'T HEAR A THING ABOUT THIS—!!
NO...
WE CALLED HIM THE CHESHIRE "CAT" A WHOLE BUNCHA TIMES!
DOSHA (CRASH)
BA (LUNGE)
!!
DON (BAM)
DON
WAH ...!
ZA (SSST)
ZA
!?
EEEEEEK!
GACHI (CLICK)
GACHI
GACHI
O–
OF COURSE HE REGENERATES RIGHT AWAY ...!

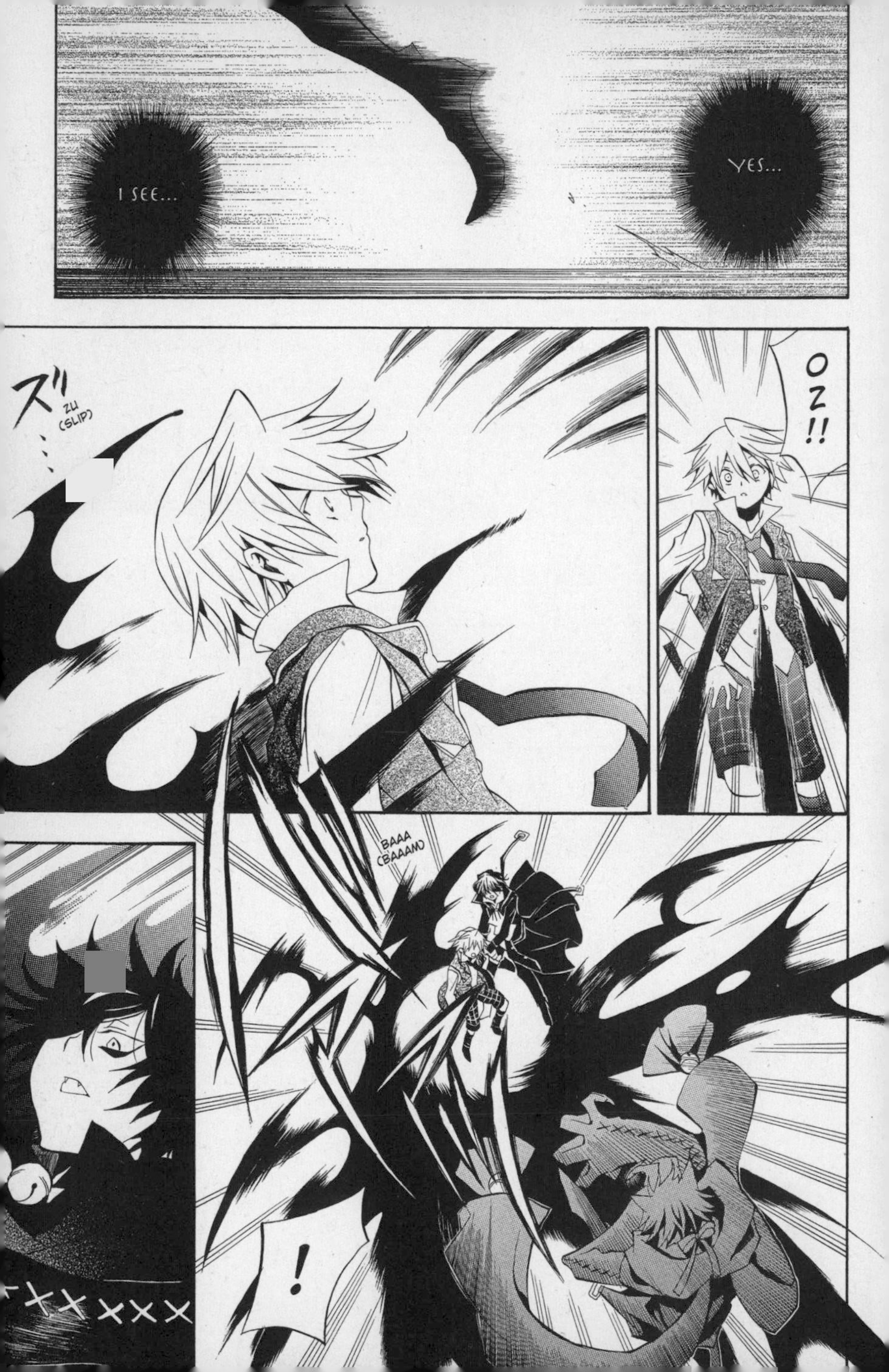
YES...
I SEE...
OZ!!
ズリ
ZU (SLIP)
BAAA (BAAAM)
!

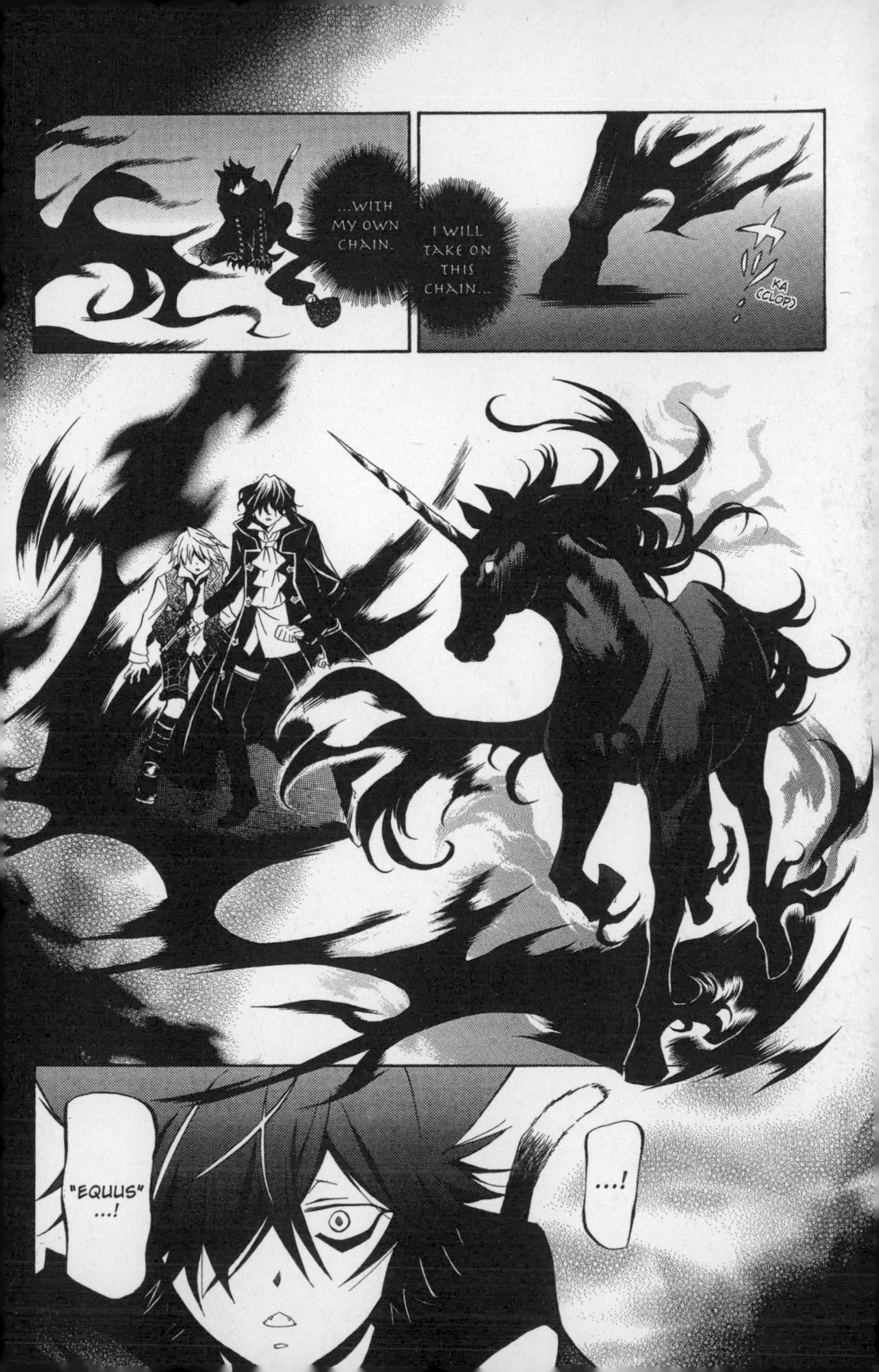
KA (CLOP)
I WILL TAKE ON THIS CHAIN...
...WITH MY OWN CHAIN.
...!
"EQUUS" ...!

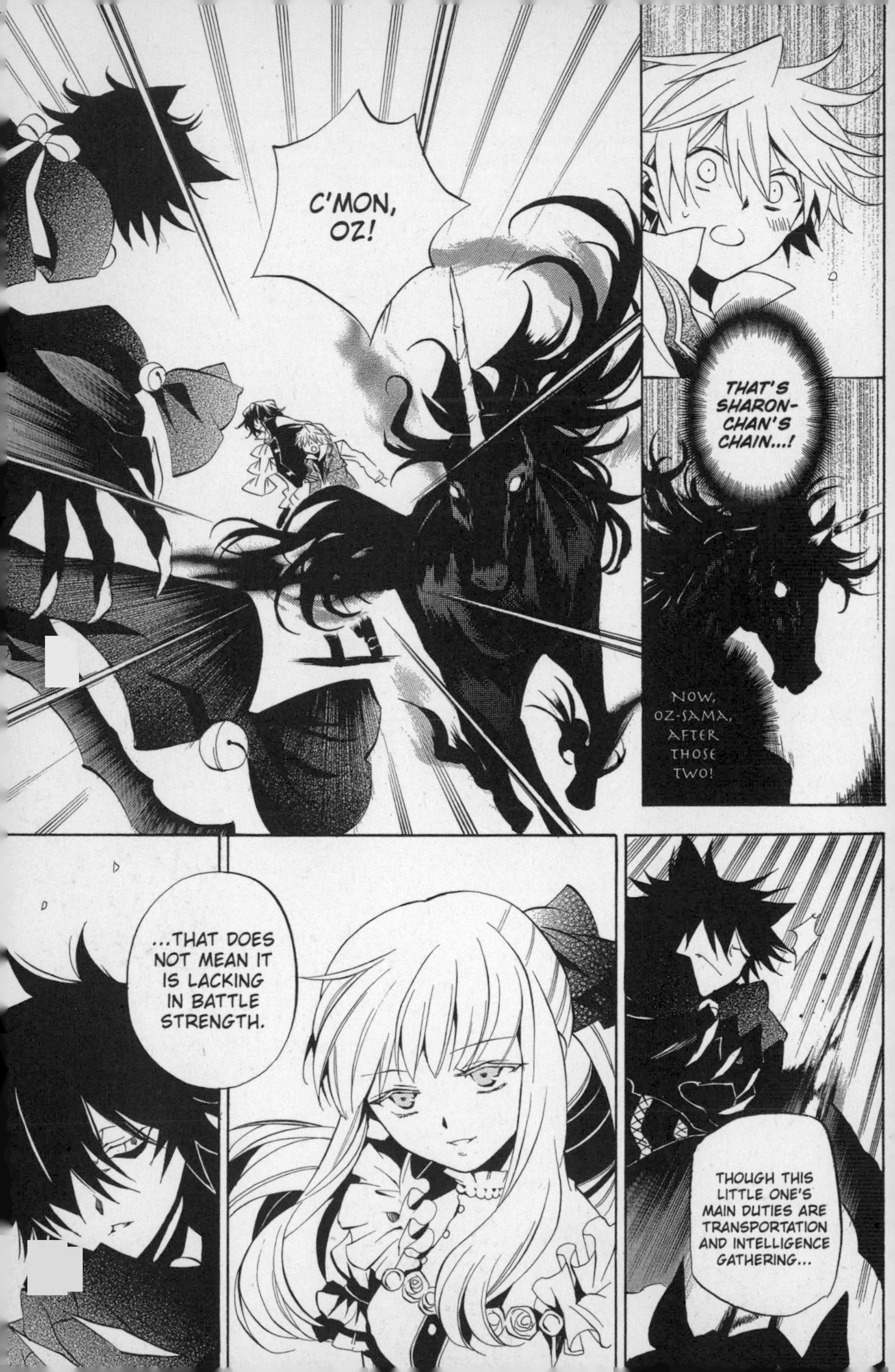
THAT'S SHARON-CHAN'S CHAIN...!
NOW, OZ-SAMA, AFTER THOSE TWO!
C'MON, OZ!
THOUGH THIS LITTLE ONE'S MAIN DUTIES ARE TRANSPORTATION AND INTELLIGENCE GATHERING...
...THAT DOES NOT MEAN IT IS LACKING IN BATTLE STRENGTH.

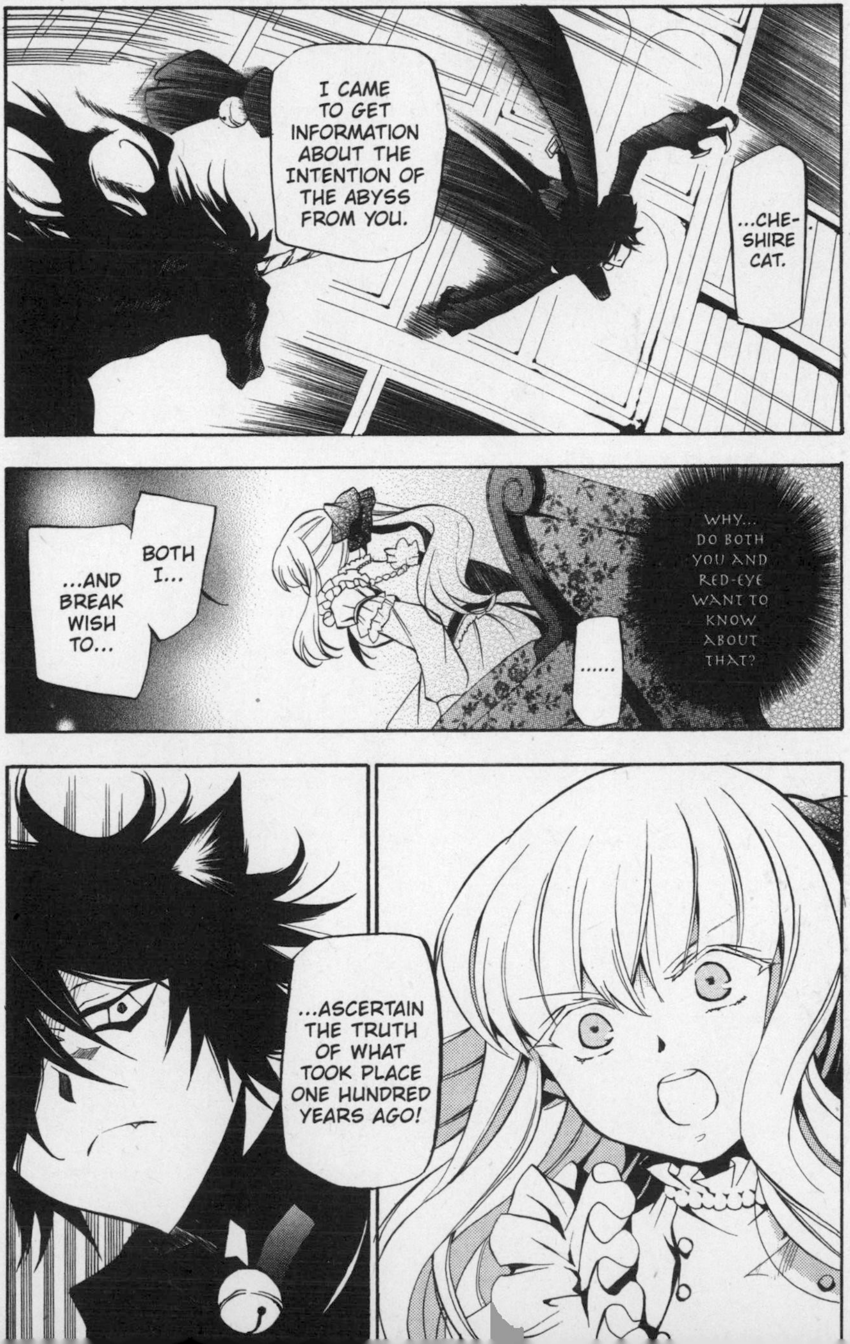
...CHE-SHIRE CAT.
I CAME TO GET INFORMATION ABOUT THE INTENTION OF THE ABYSS FROM YOU.
WHY... DO BOTH YOU AND RED-EYE WANT TO KNOW ABOUT THAT?
......
BOTH I...
...AND BREAK WISH TO...
...ASCERTAIN THE TRUTH OF WHAT TOOK PLACE ONE HUNDRED YEARS AGO!

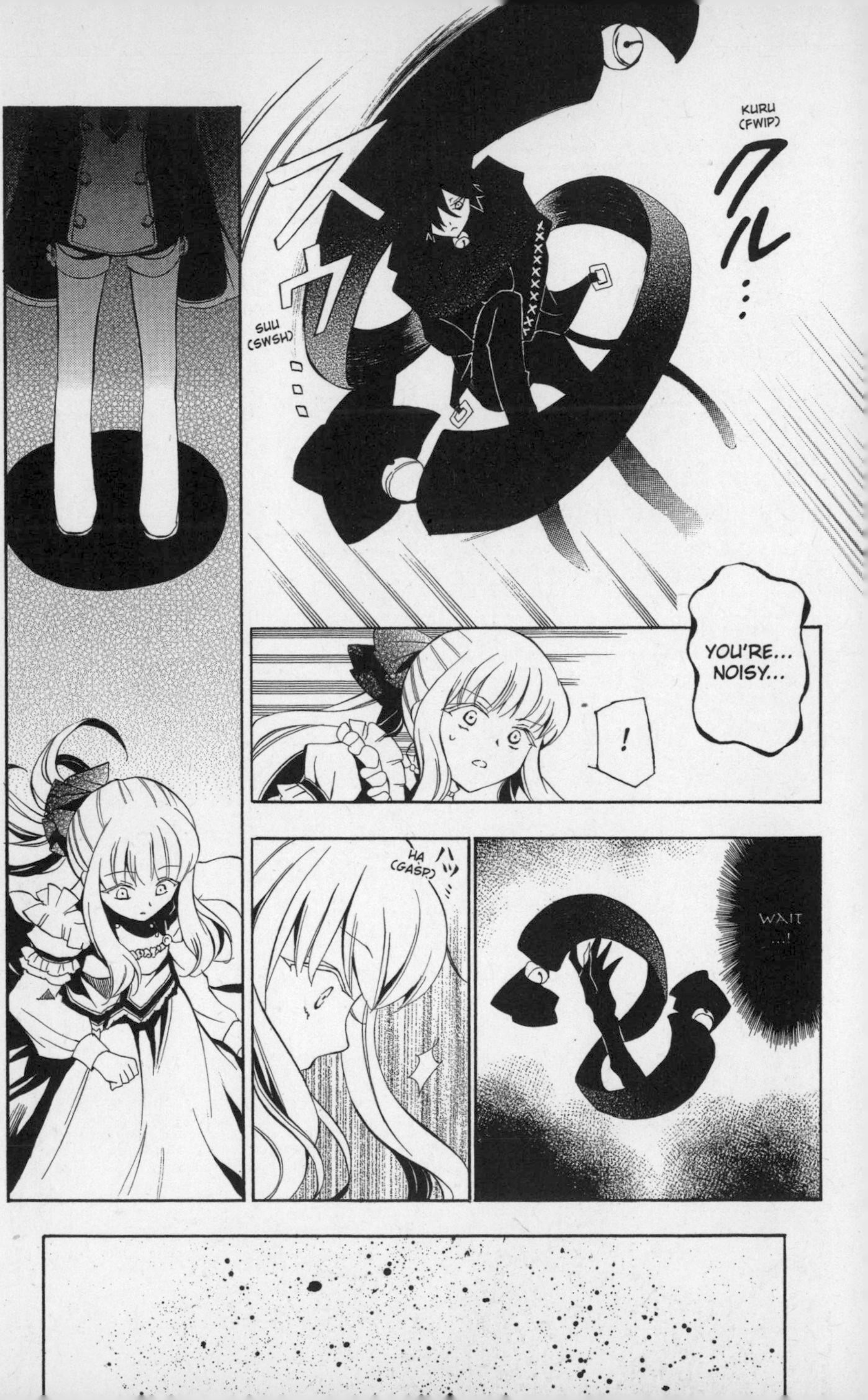
KURU (FWIP)
クル…
SUU (SWSH)
スゥ
YOU'RE... NOISY...
!
WAIT ...!
HA (GASP)
ハッ

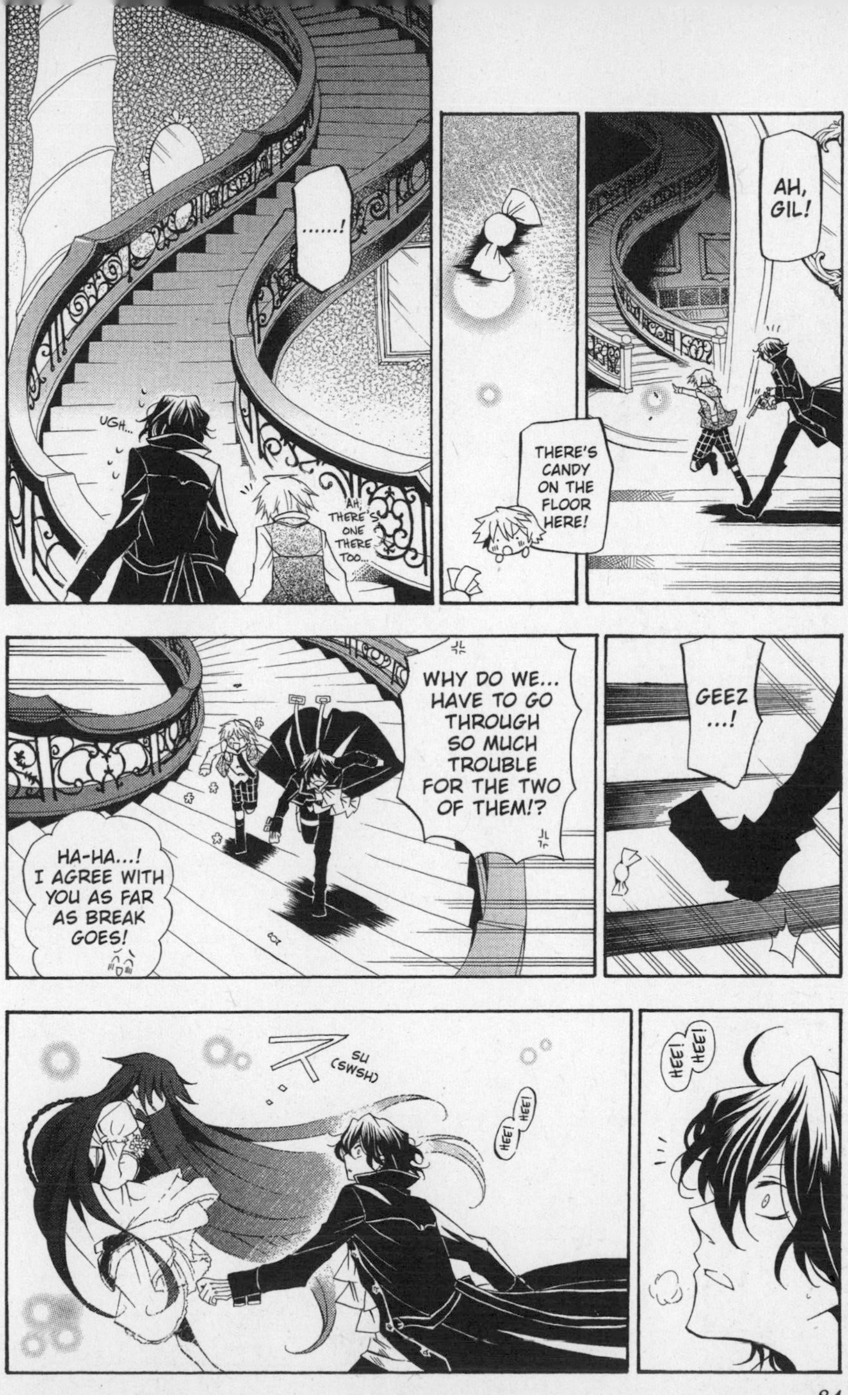
AH, GIL!
THERE'S CANDY ON THE FLOOR HERE!
......!
UGH...
AH, THERE'S ONE THERE TOO...
GEEZ ...!
WHY DO WE... HAVE TO GO THROUGH SO MUCH TROUBLE FOR THE TWO OF THEM!?
HA-HA...! I AGREE WITH YOU AS FAR AS BREAK GOES!
HEE! HEE!
SU (SWSH)
HEE! HEE!

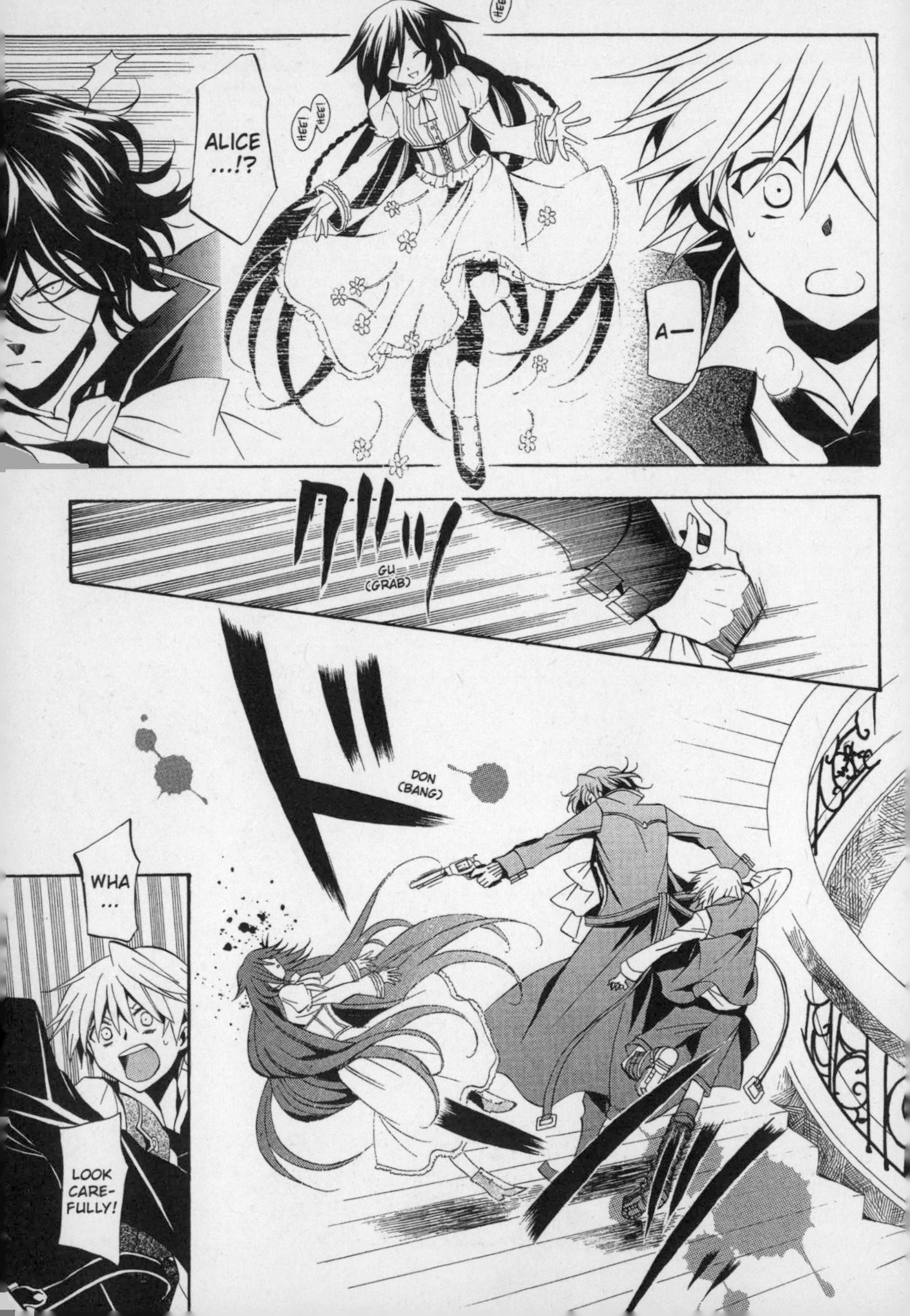
HEE!
HEE! HEE!
A—
ALICE ...!?
GU (GRAB)
DON (BANG)
WHA ...
LOOK CARE-FULLY!

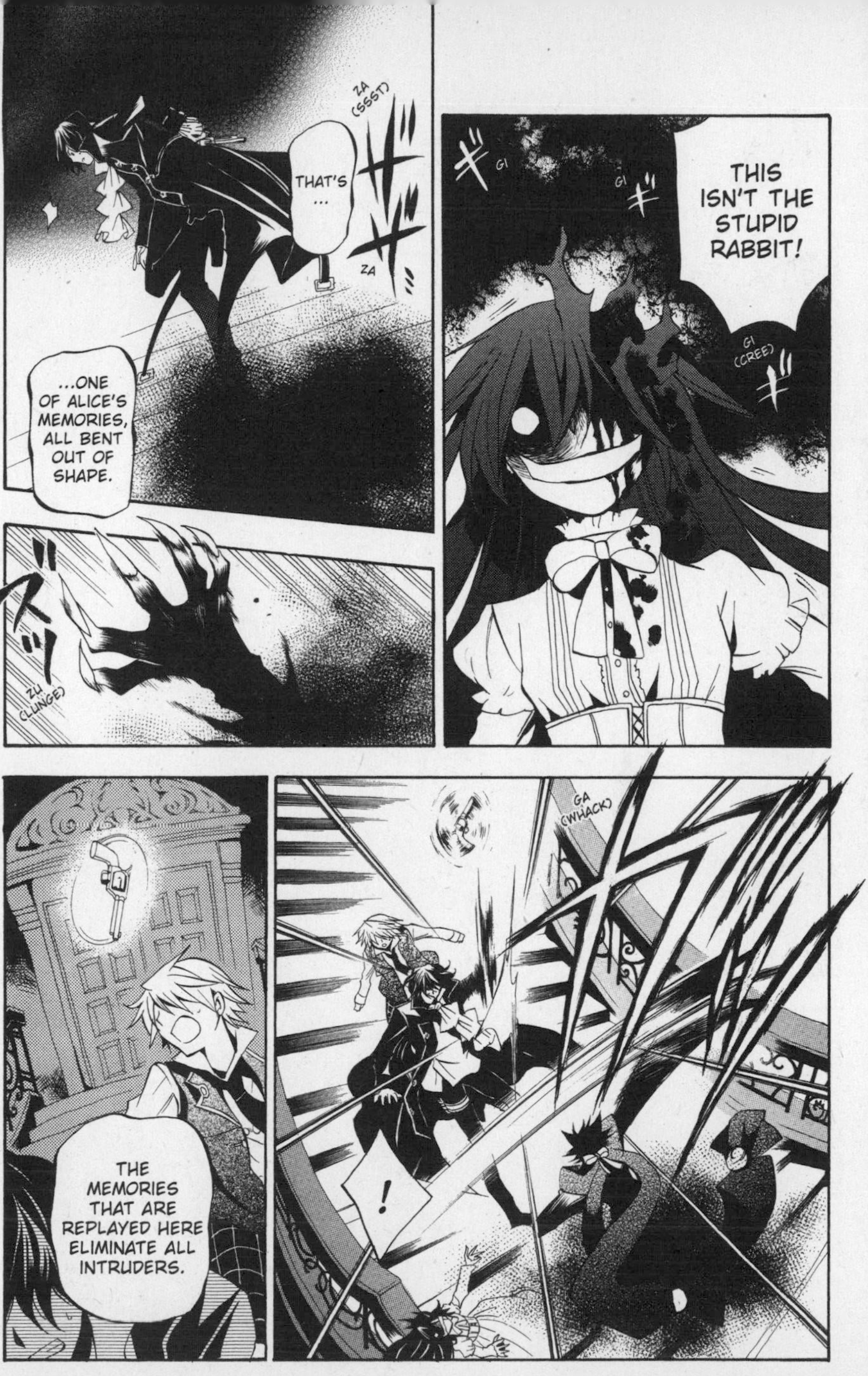
GI
GI
THIS ISN'T THE STUPID RABBIT!
GI (CREE)
ZA (SSST)
THAT'S ...
ZA
...ONE OF ALICE'S MEMORIES, ALL BENT OUT OF SHAPE.
ZU (LUNGE)
GA (WHACK)
!
THE MEMORIES THAT ARE REPLAYED HERE ELIMINATE ALL INTRUDERS.

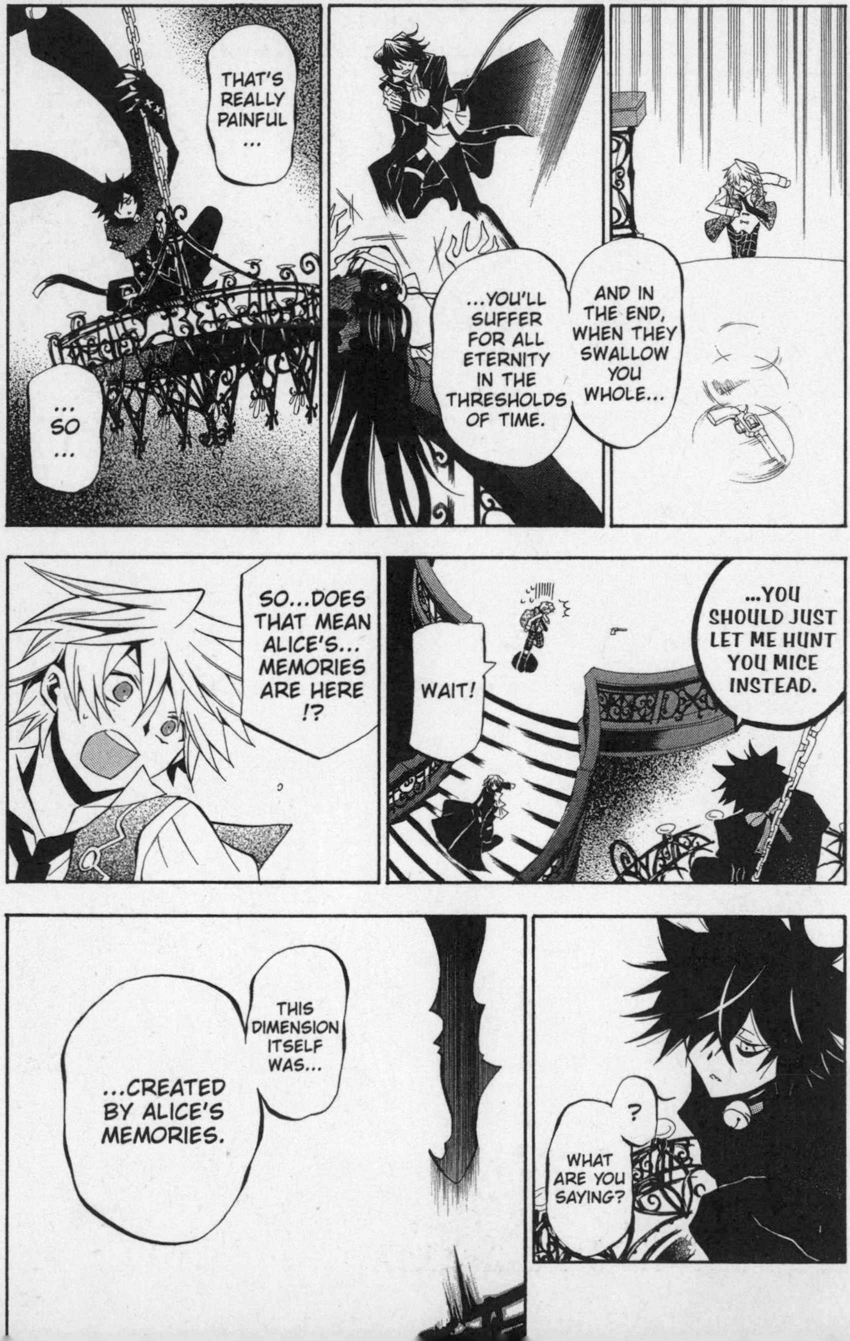
AND IN THE END, WHEN THEY SWALLOW YOU WHOLE...
...YOU'LL SUFFER FOR ALL ETERNITY IN THE THRESHOLDS OF TIME.
THAT'S REALLY PAINFUL ...
... SO ...
...YOU SHOULD JUST LET ME HUNT YOU MICE INSTEAD.
WAIT!
SO...DOES THAT MEAN ALICE'S... MEMORIES ARE HERE!?
?
WHAT ARE YOU SAYING?
THIS DIMENSION ITSELF WAS...
...CREATED BY ALICE'S MEMORIES.

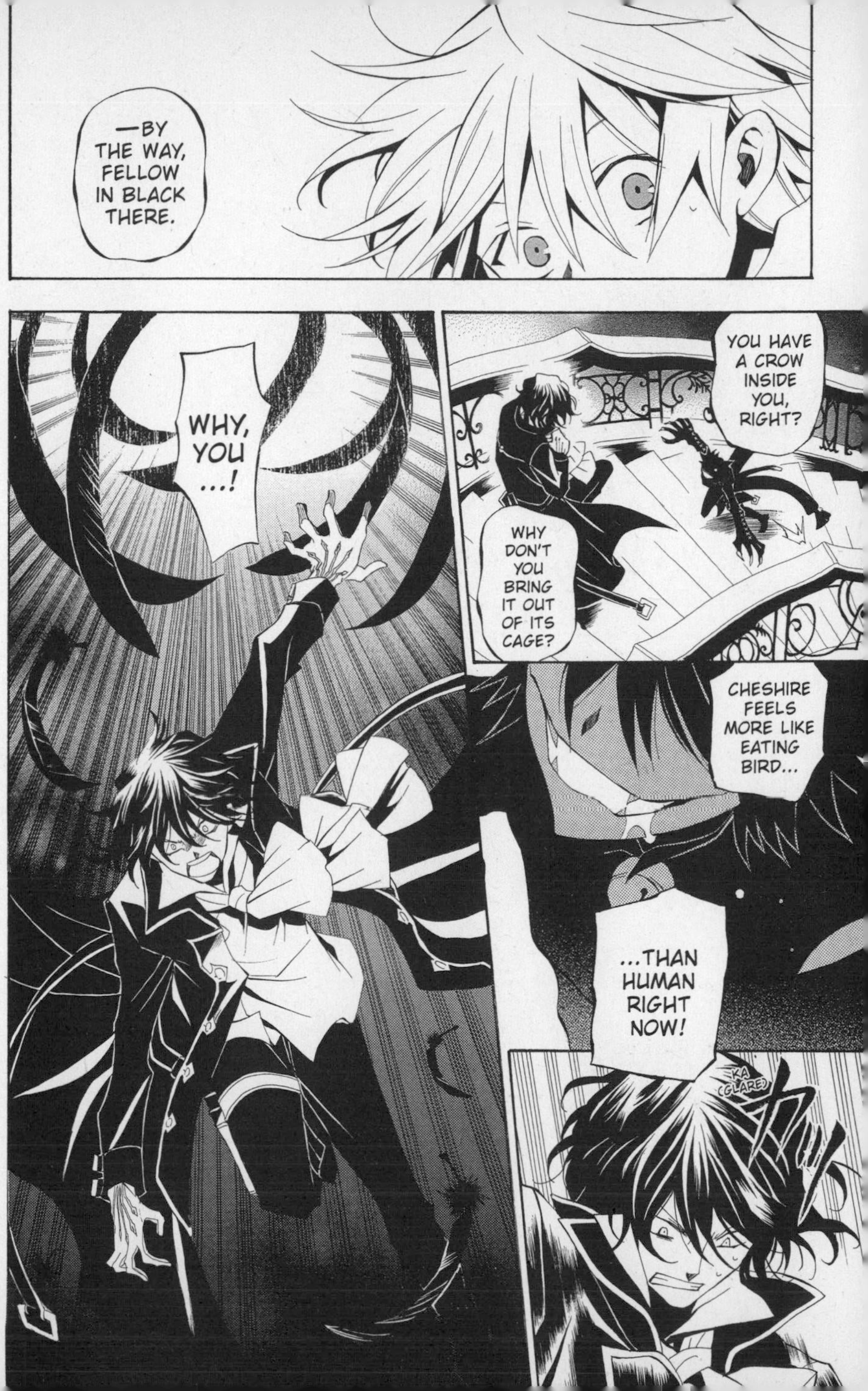
—BY THE WAY, FELLOW IN BLACK THERE.
YOU HAVE A CROW INSIDE YOU, RIGHT?
WHY DON'T YOU BRING IT OUT OF ITS CAGE?
CHESHIRE FEELS MORE LIKE EATING BIRD...
...THAN HUMAN RIGHT NOW!
KA (GLARE)
WHY, YOU ...!

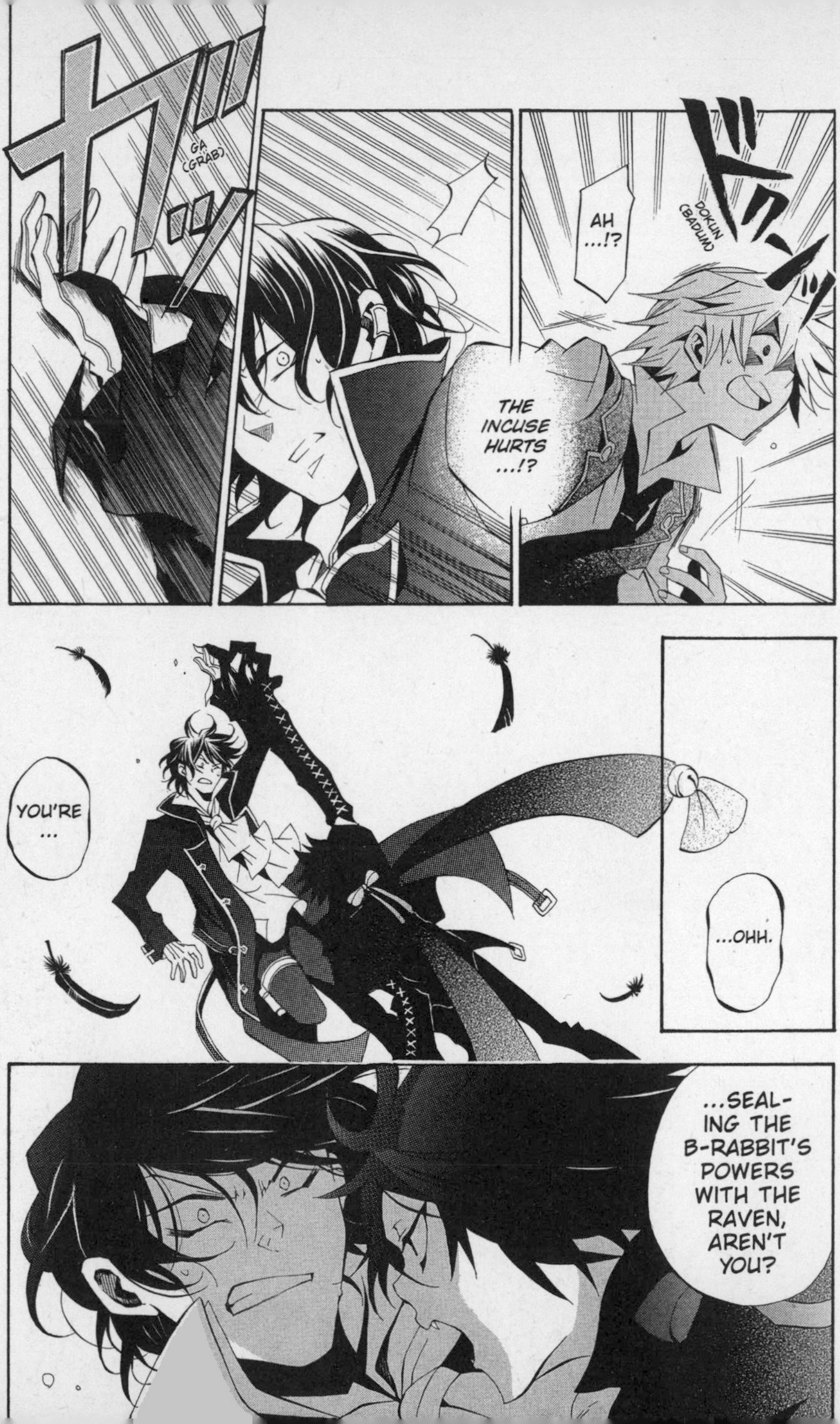
DOKUN (BADUM)
AH ...!?
THE INCUSE HURTS ...!?
GA (GRAB)
...OHH.
YOU'RE ...
...SEAL-ING THE B-RABBIT'S POWERS WITH THE RAVEN, AREN'T YOU?

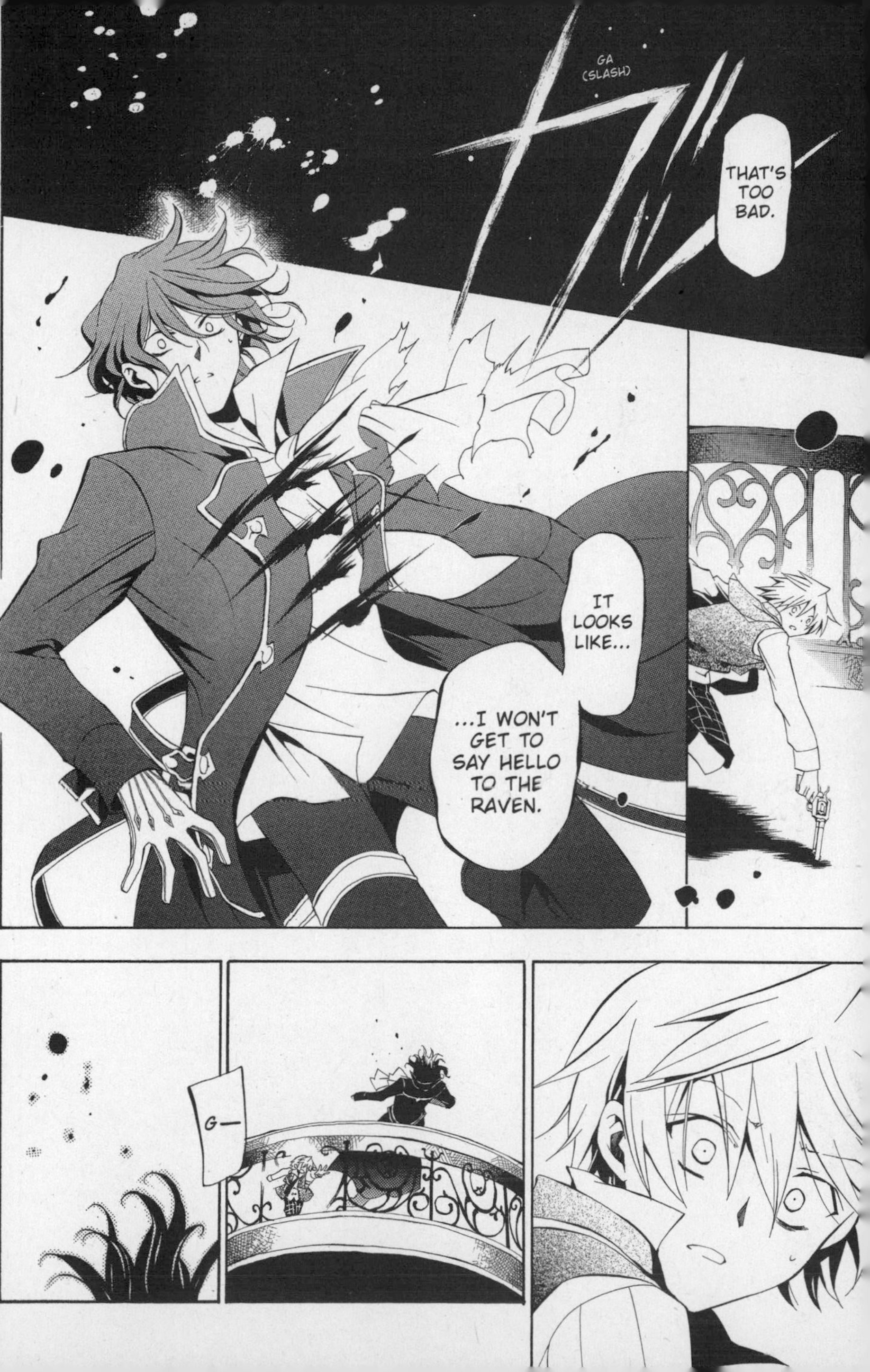
GA (SLASH)
THAT'S TOO BAD.
IT LOOKS LIKE...
...I WON'T GET TO SAY HELLO TO THE RAVEN.
G—

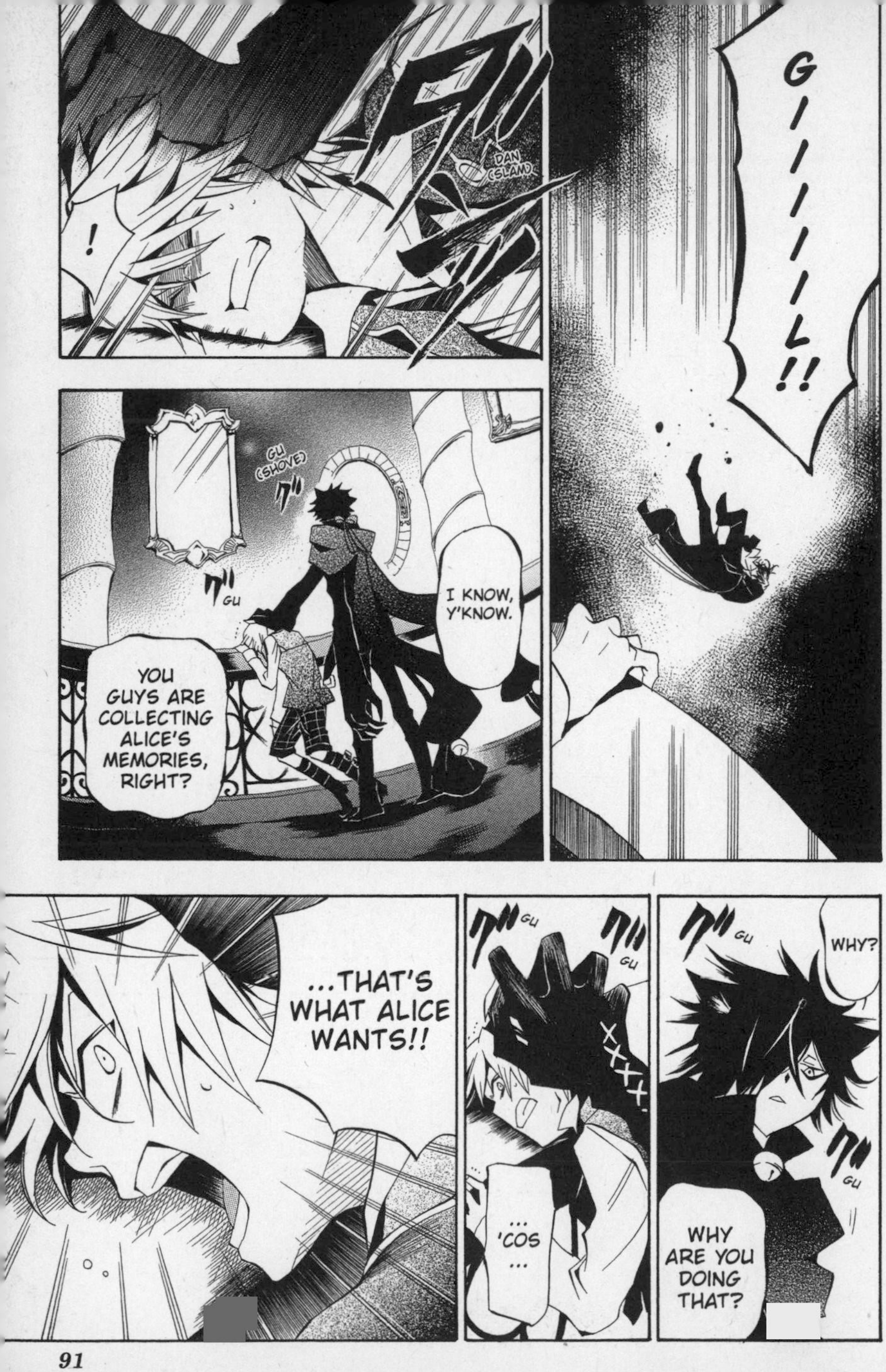
G I I I I I L!!
DAN (SLAM)
!
GU (SHOVE)
GU
I KNOW, Y'KNOW.
YOU GUYS ARE COLLECTING ALICE'S MEMORIES, RIGHT?
GU
WHY?
GU
WHY ARE YOU DOING THAT?
GU
GU
...'COS...
...THAT'S WHAT ALICE WANTS!!

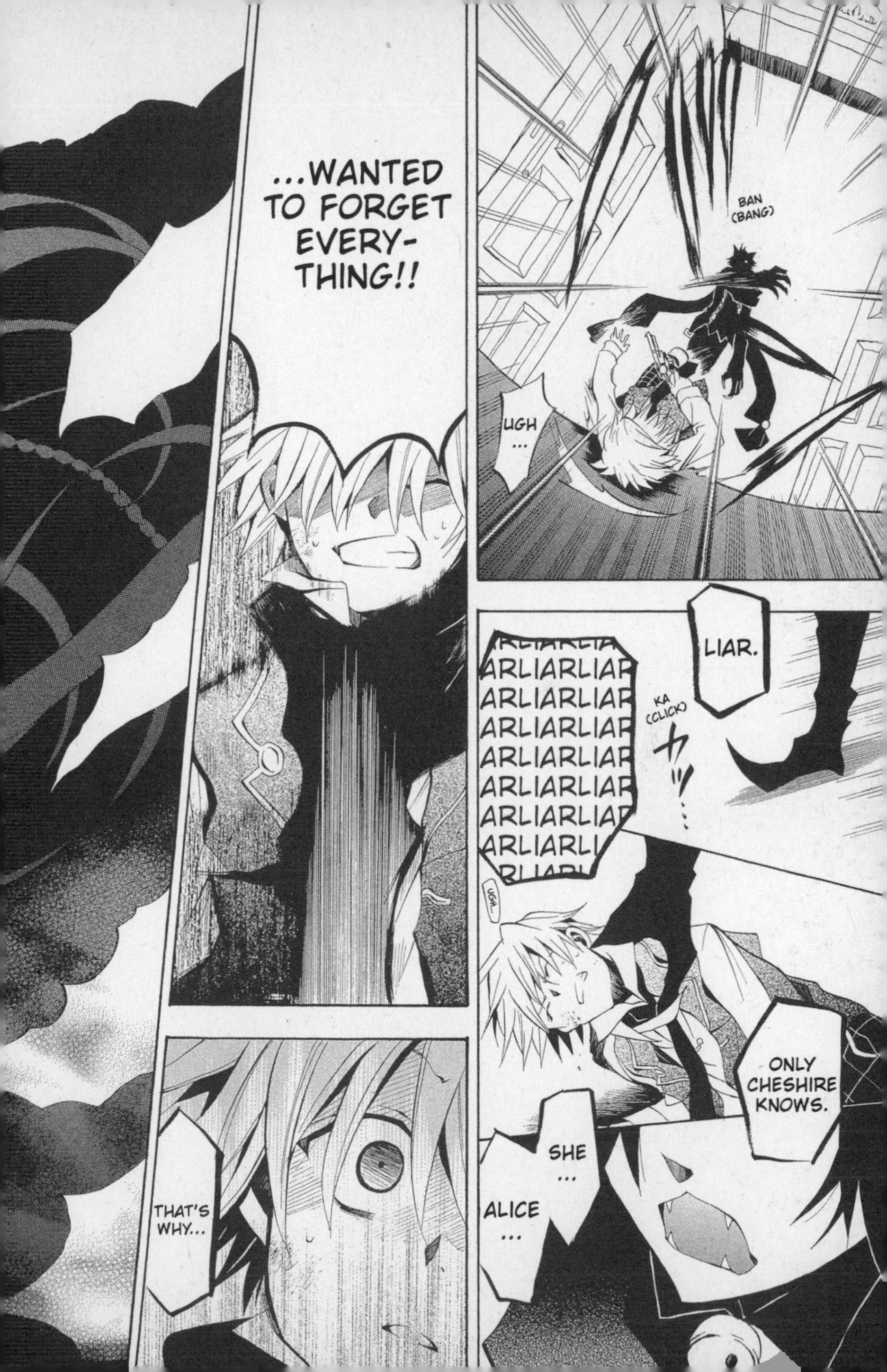

BAN (BANG)
UGH ...
LIAR.
ARLIARLIAR
ARLIARLIAR
ARLIARLIAR
ARLIARLIAR
ARLIARLIAR
ARLIARLIAR
ARLIARLI
KA (CLICK)
UGH...
ONLY CHESHIRE KNOWS.
SHE ...
ALICE ...
...WANTED TO FORGET EVERY-THING!!
THAT'S WHY...

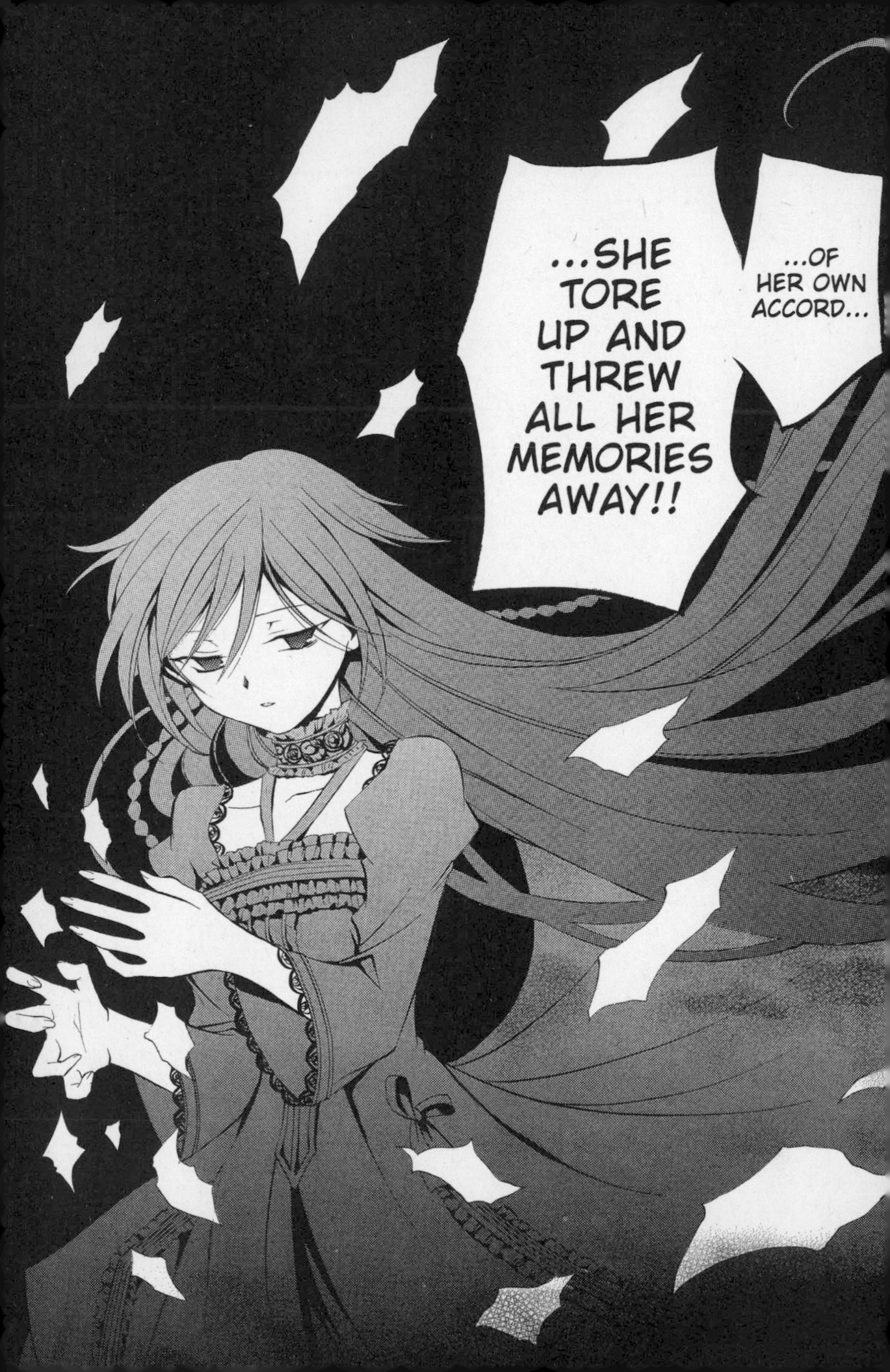
...OF HER OWN ACCORD...
...SHE TORE UP AND THREW ALL HER MEMORIES AWAY!!

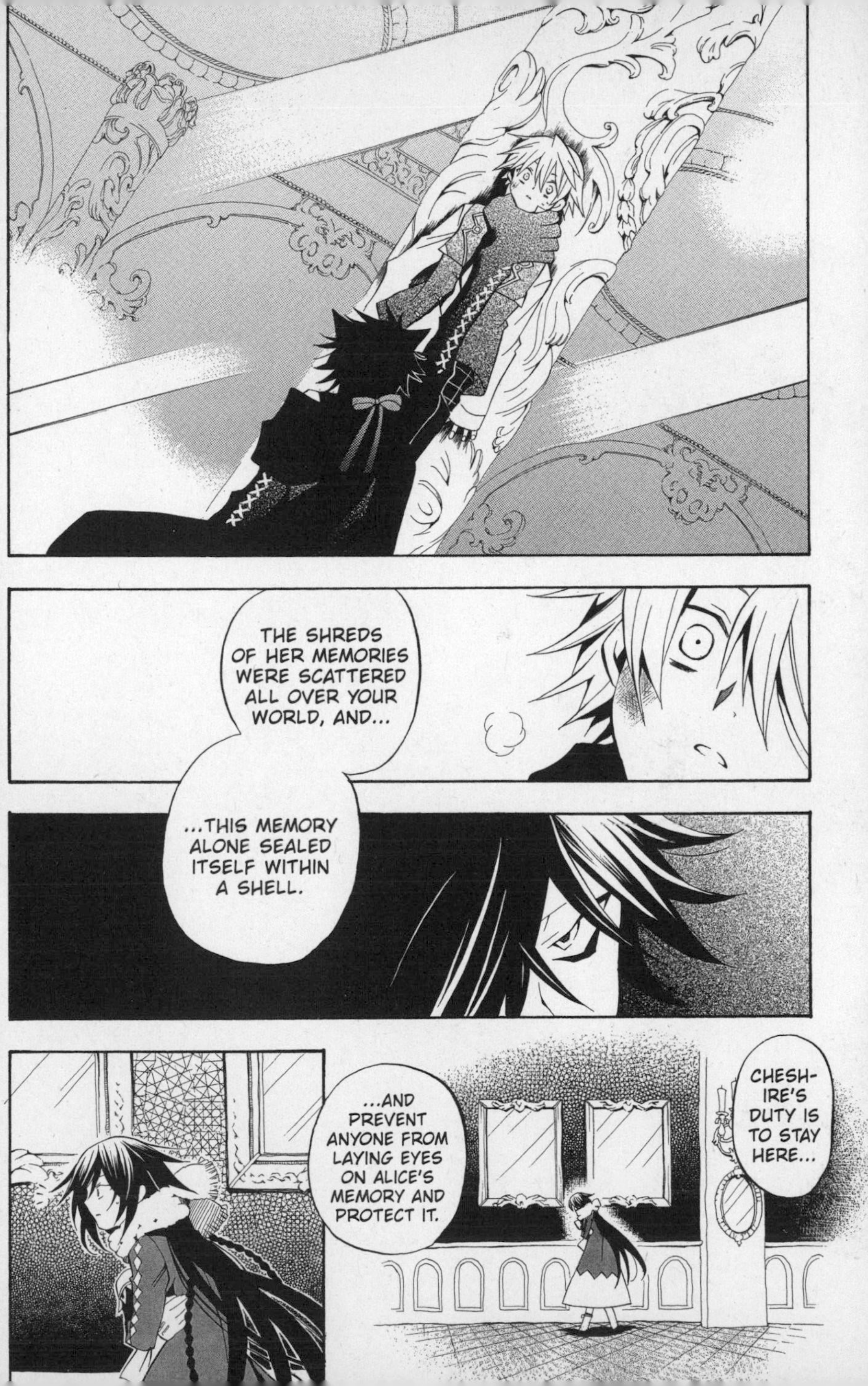
THE SHREDS OF HER MEMORIES WERE SCATTERED ALL OVER YOUR WORLD, AND...
...THIS MEMORY ALONE SEALED ITSELF WITHIN A SHELL.
CHESH-IRE'S DUTY IS TO STAY HERE...
...AND PREVENT ANYONE FROM LAYING EYES ON ALICE'S MEMORY AND PROTECT IT.

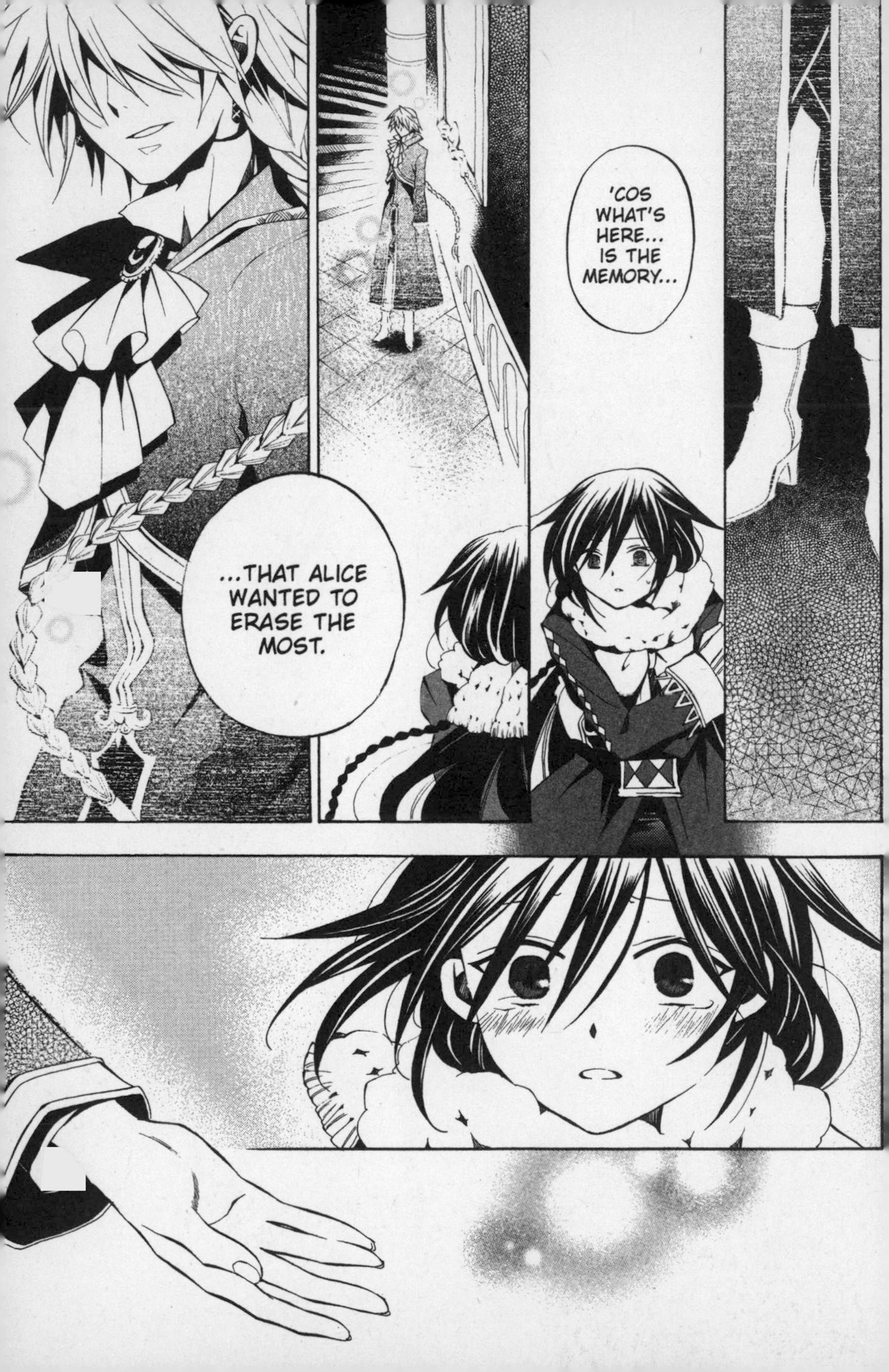
'COS WHAT'S HERE... IS THE MEMORY...
...THAT ALICE WANTED TO ERASE THE MOST.

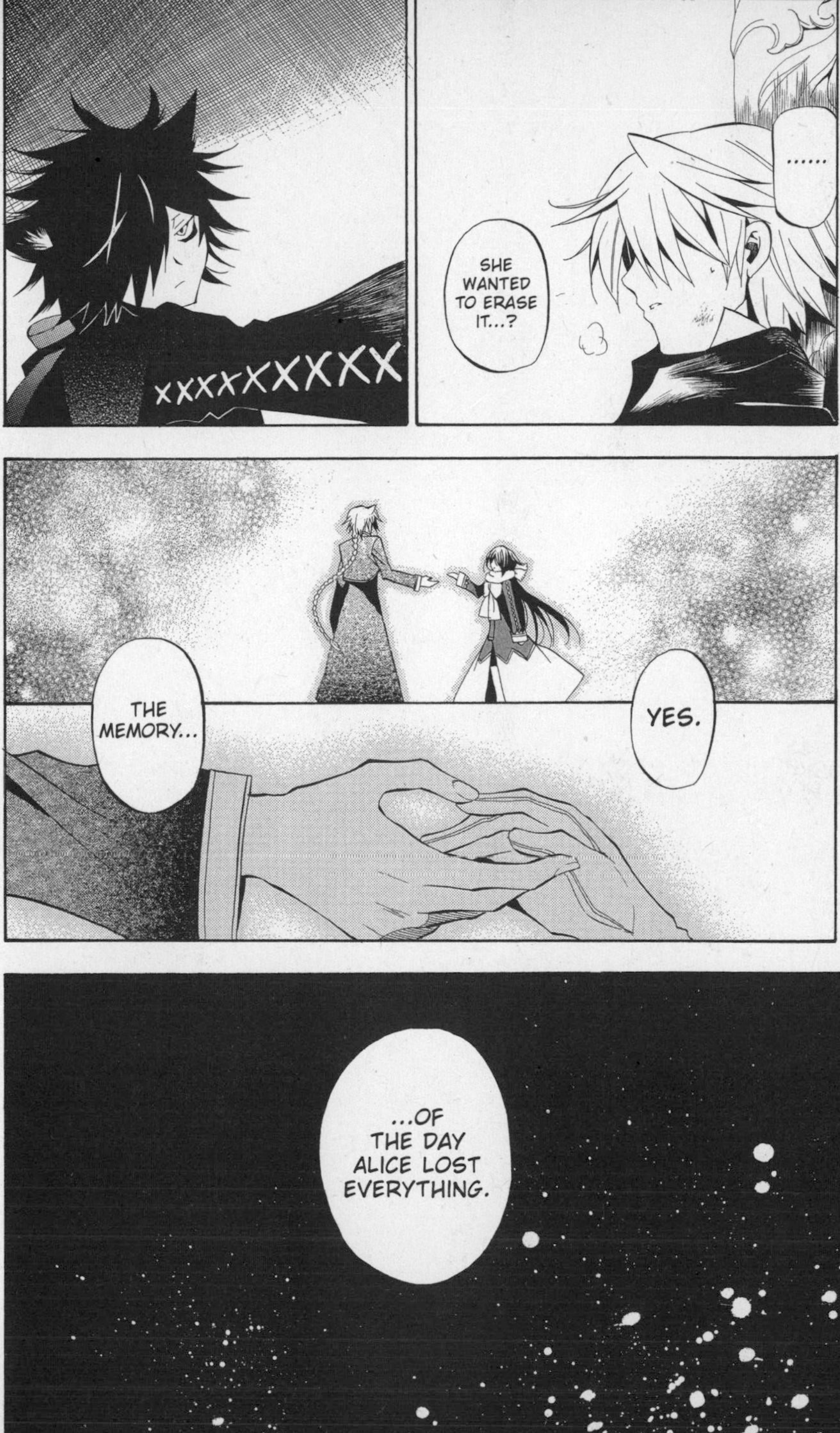
......
SHE WANTED TO ERASE IT...?
xxxxXXXXXX
YES.
THE MEMORY...
...OF THE DAY ALICE LOST EVERYTHING.

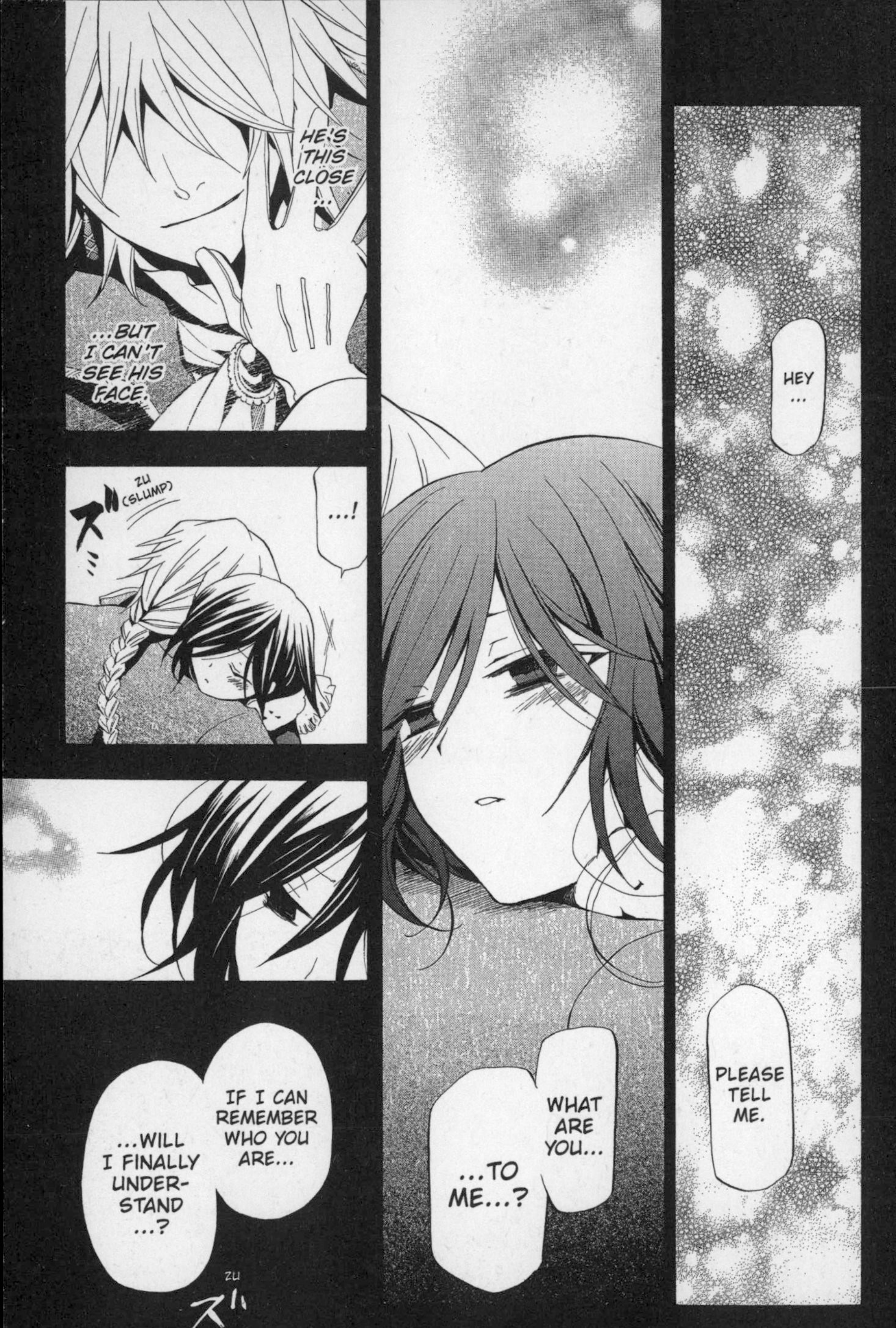
HEY...
PLEASE TELL ME.
WHAT ARE YOU...
...TO ME...?
HE'S THIS CLOSE...
...BUT I CAN'T SEE HIS FACE.
...!
ZU (SLUMP)
IF I CAN REMEMBER WHO YOU ARE...
...WILL I FINALLY UNDERSTAND...?
ZU

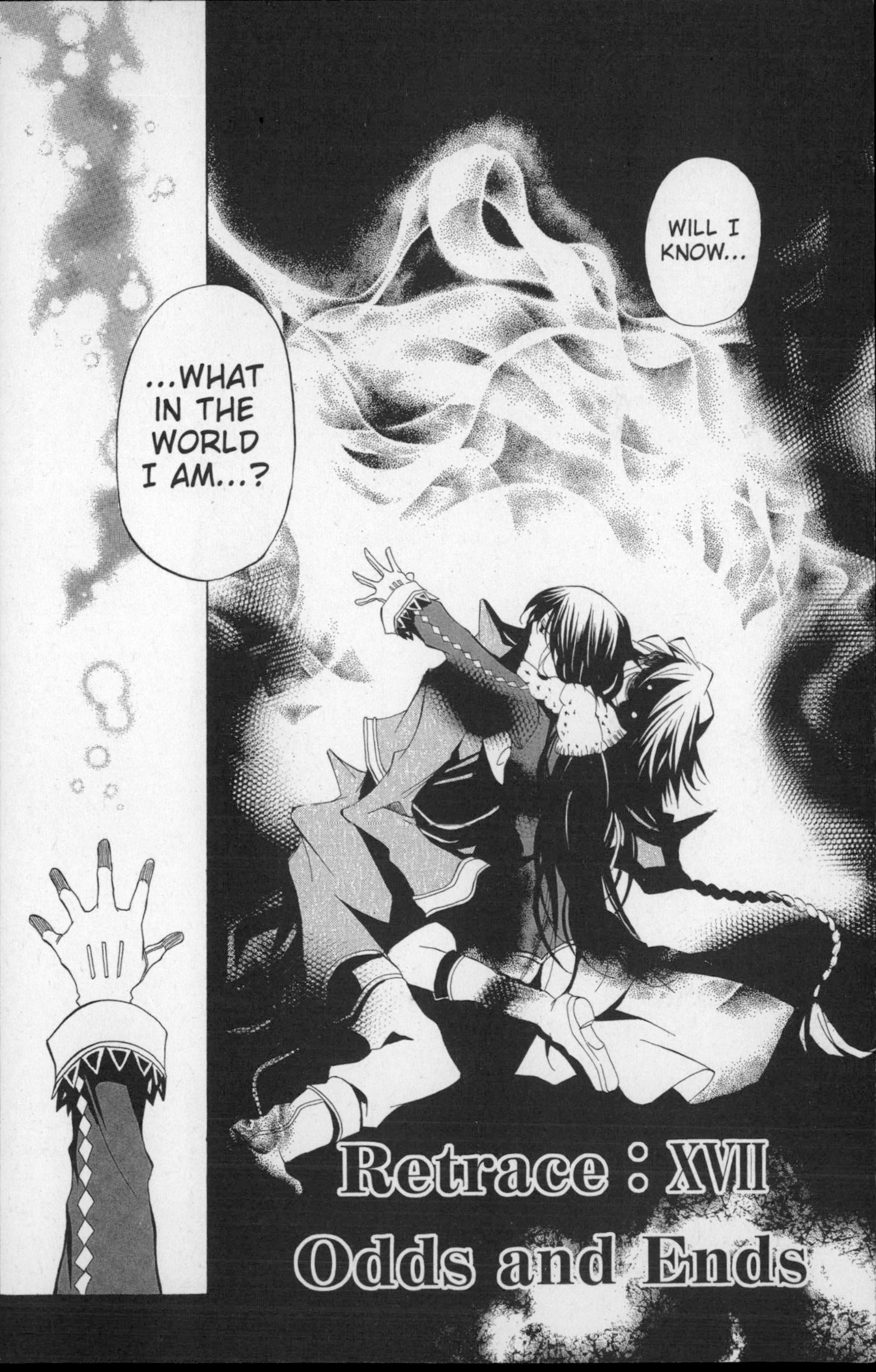
WILL I KNOW...
...WHAT IN THE WORLD I AM...?
Retrace : XVII
Odds and Ends

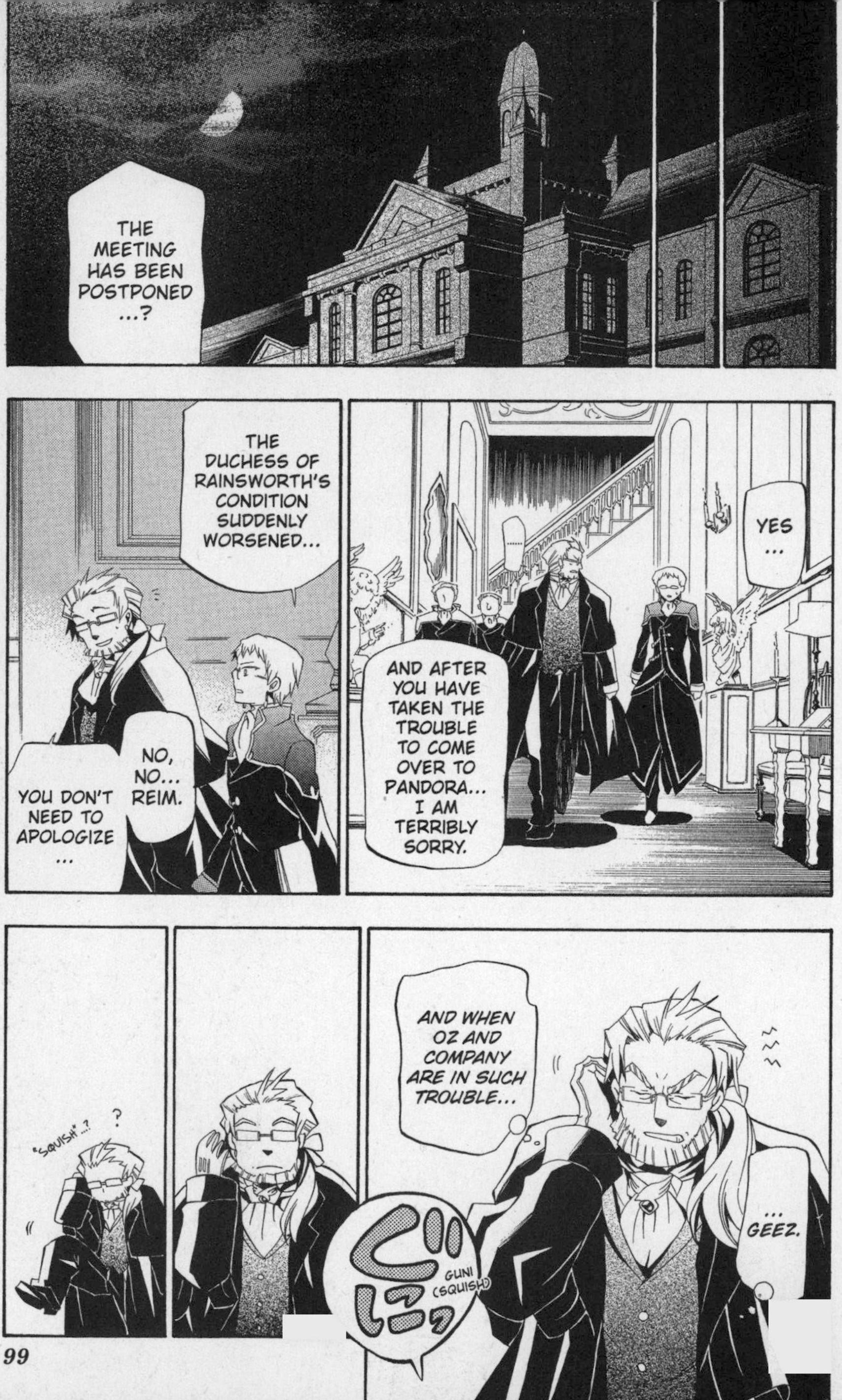
THE MEETING HAS BEEN POSTPONED ...?
YES ...
......
AND AFTER YOU HAVE TAKEN THE TROUBLE TO COME OVER TO PANDORA... I AM TERRIBLY SORRY.
THE DUCHESS OF RAINSWORTH'S CONDITION SUDDENLY WORSENED...
NO, NO... REIM.
YOU DON'T NEED TO APOLOGIZE ...
AND WHEN OZ AND COMPANY ARE IN SUCH TROUBLE...
... GEEZ.
GUNI (SQUISH)
"SQUISH"...?
?

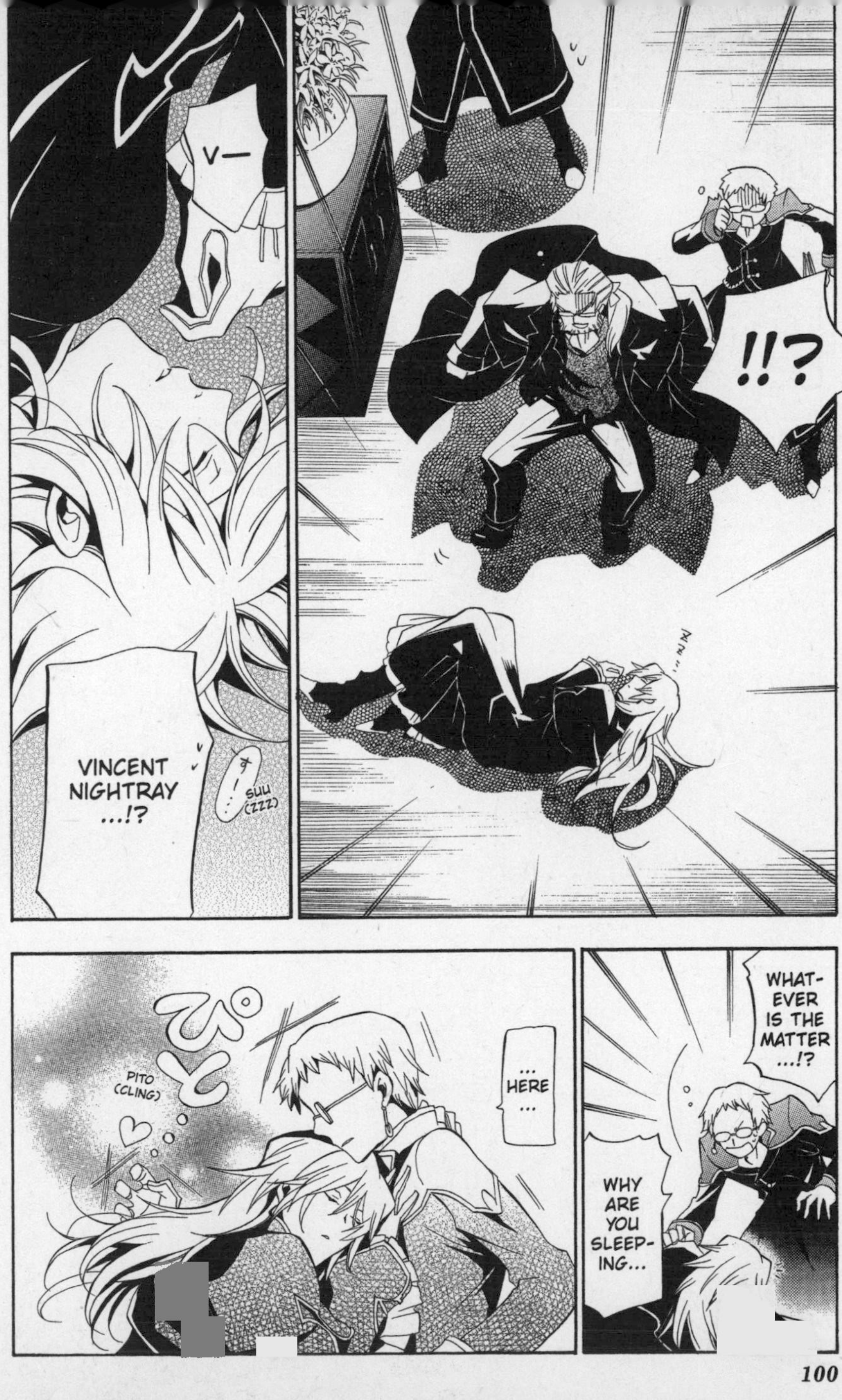
!!?
V—
VINCENT NIGHTRAY ...!?
す
SUU (ZZZ)
WHAT-EVER IS THE MATTER ...!?
WHY ARE YOU SLEEP-ING...
... HERE ...
ぴと
PITO (CLING)

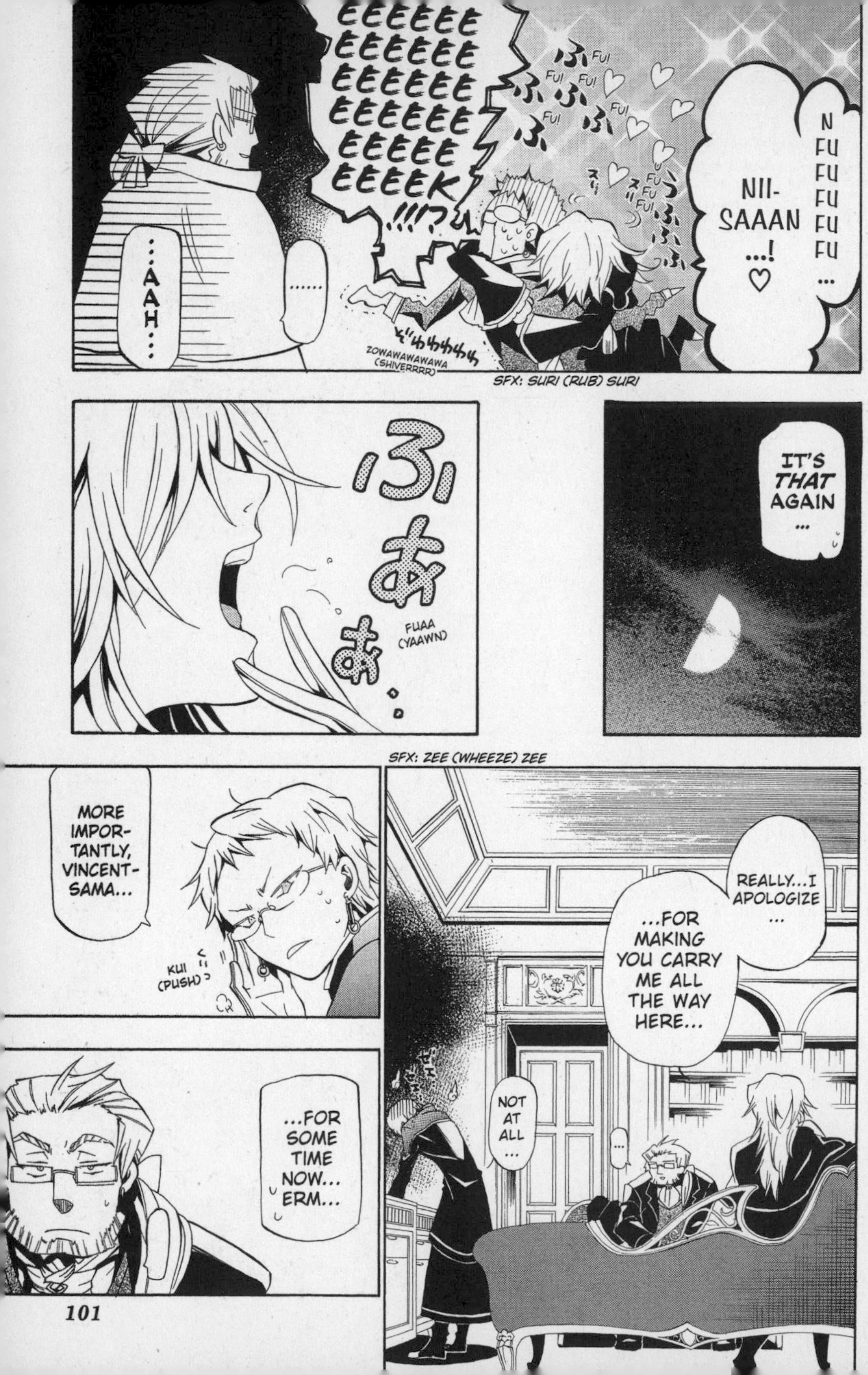
N FU FU FU FU FU...
NII-SAAAN...! ♡
FU! FU! FU! FU! FU! FU! FU! FU!
EEEEEEEEEEEEEEEEEEEEEEEEEEEEEEEEEEEEEEEEEK!!!?
......
...AAH...
ZOWAWAWAWAWA (SHIVERRRR)
SFX: SURI (RUB) SURI
IT'S *THAT* AGAIN...
FUAA (YAAWN)
SFX: ZEE (WHEEZE) ZEE
REALLY...I APOLOGIZE...
...FOR MAKING YOU CARRY ME ALL THE WAY HERE...
NOT AT ALL...
...
MORE IMPORTANTLY, VINCENT-SAMA...
KUI (PUSH)
...FOR SOME TIME NOW... ERM...

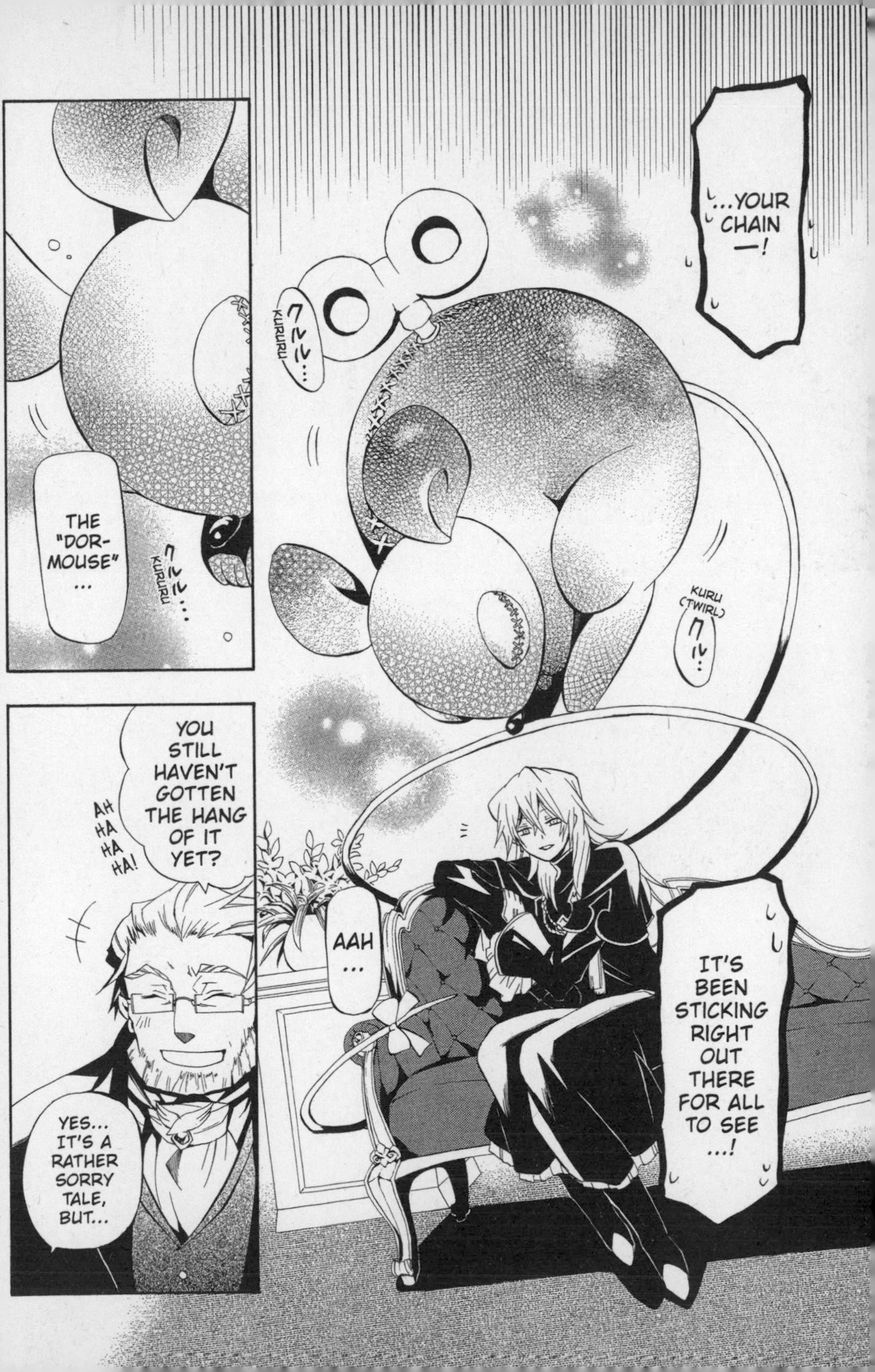
...YOUR CHAIN—!
クルル... KURURU
KURU (TWIRL) クル!
THE "DOR-MOUSE" ...
クルル... KURURU
YOU STILL HAVEN'T GOTTEN THE HANG OF IT YET?
AH HA HA HA!
AAH ...
IT'S BEEN STICKING RIGHT OUT THERE FOR ALL TO SEE ...!
YES... IT'S A RATHER SORRY TALE, BUT...

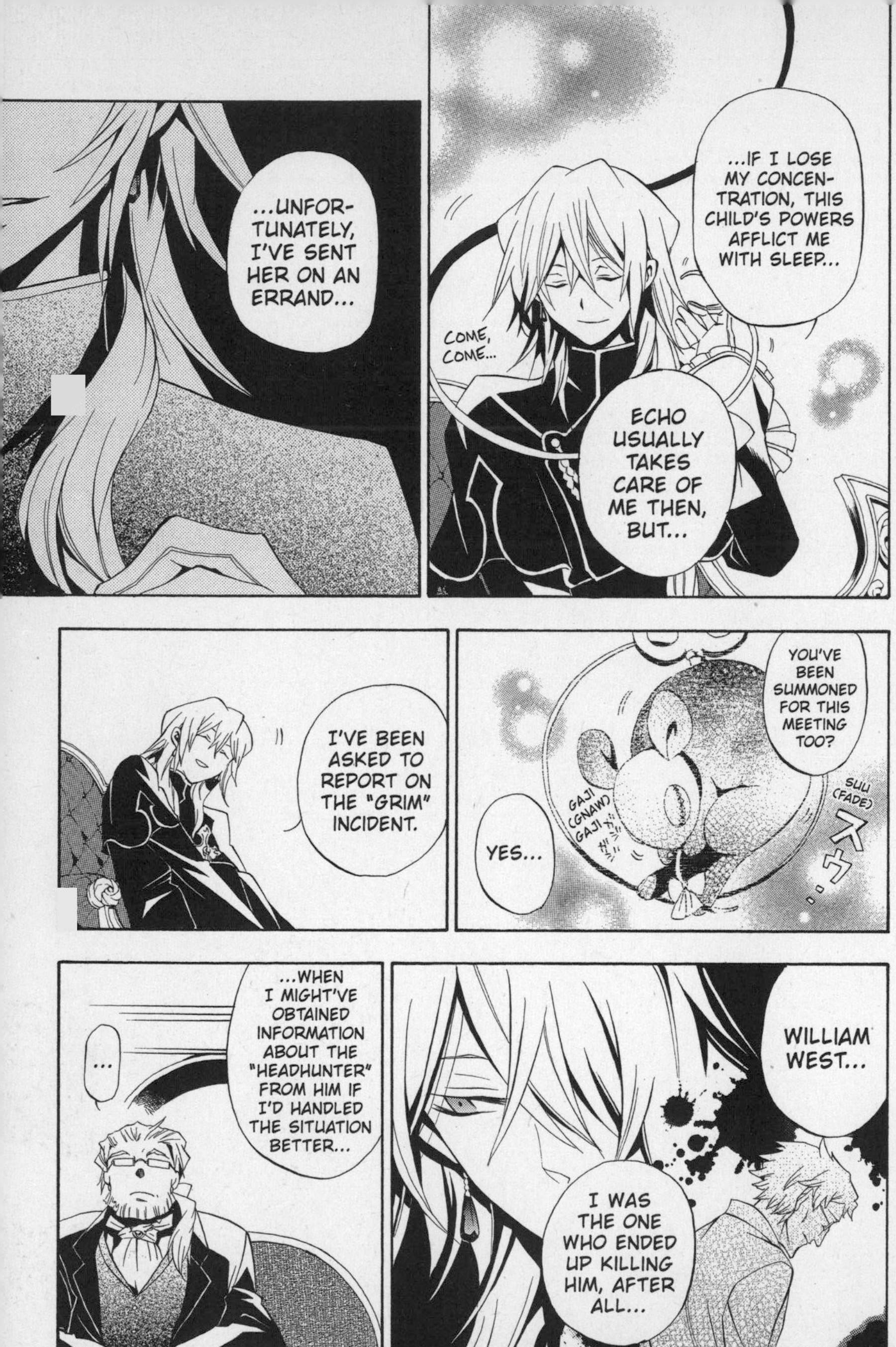
...IF I LOSE MY CONCEN-TRATION, THIS CHILD'S POWERS AFFLICT ME WITH SLEEP...
COME, COME...
ECHO USUALLY TAKES CARE OF ME THEN, BUT...
...UNFOR-TUNATELY, I'VE SENT HER ON AN ERRAND...
YOU'VE BEEN SUMMONED FOR THIS MEETING TOO?
SUU (FADE)
GAJI (GNAW) GAJI
YES...
I'VE BEEN ASKED TO REPORT ON THE "GRIM" INCIDENT.
WILLIAM WEST...
I WAS THE ONE WHO ENDED UP KILLING HIM, AFTER ALL...
...WHEN I MIGHT'VE OBTAINED INFORMATION ABOUT THE "HEADHUNTER" FROM HIM IF I'D HANDLED THE SITUATION BETTER...
...

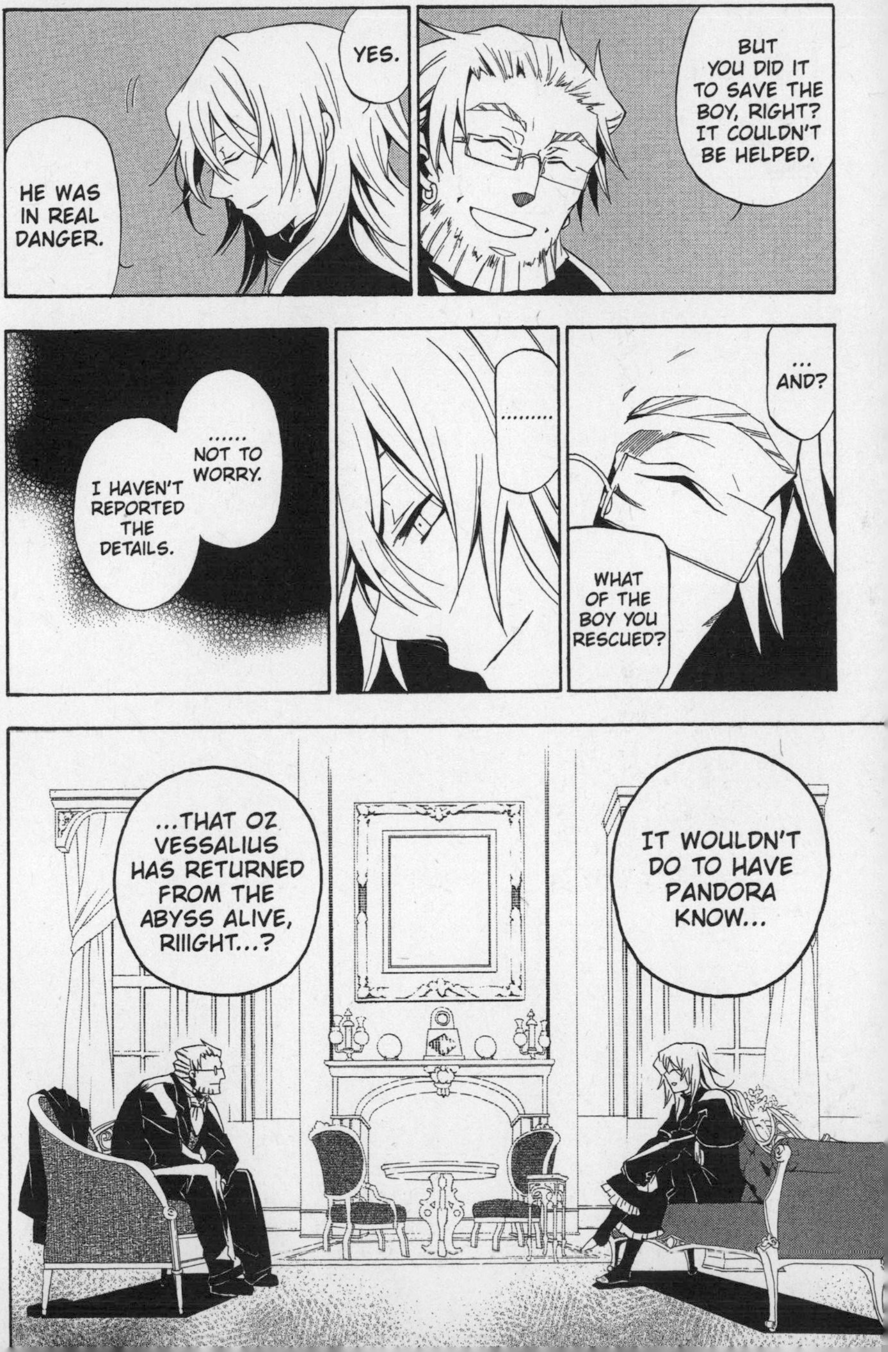
BUT YOU DID IT TO SAVE THE BOY, RIGHT? IT COULDN'T BE HELPED.
YES.
HE WAS IN REAL DANGER.
... AND?
WHAT OF THE BOY YOU RESCUED?
....
...... NOT TO WORRY.
I HAVEN'T REPORTED THE DETAILS.
IT WOULDN'T DO TO HAVE PANDORA KNOW...
...THAT OZ VESSALIUS HAS RETURNED FROM THE ABYSS ALIVE, RIIIGHT...?

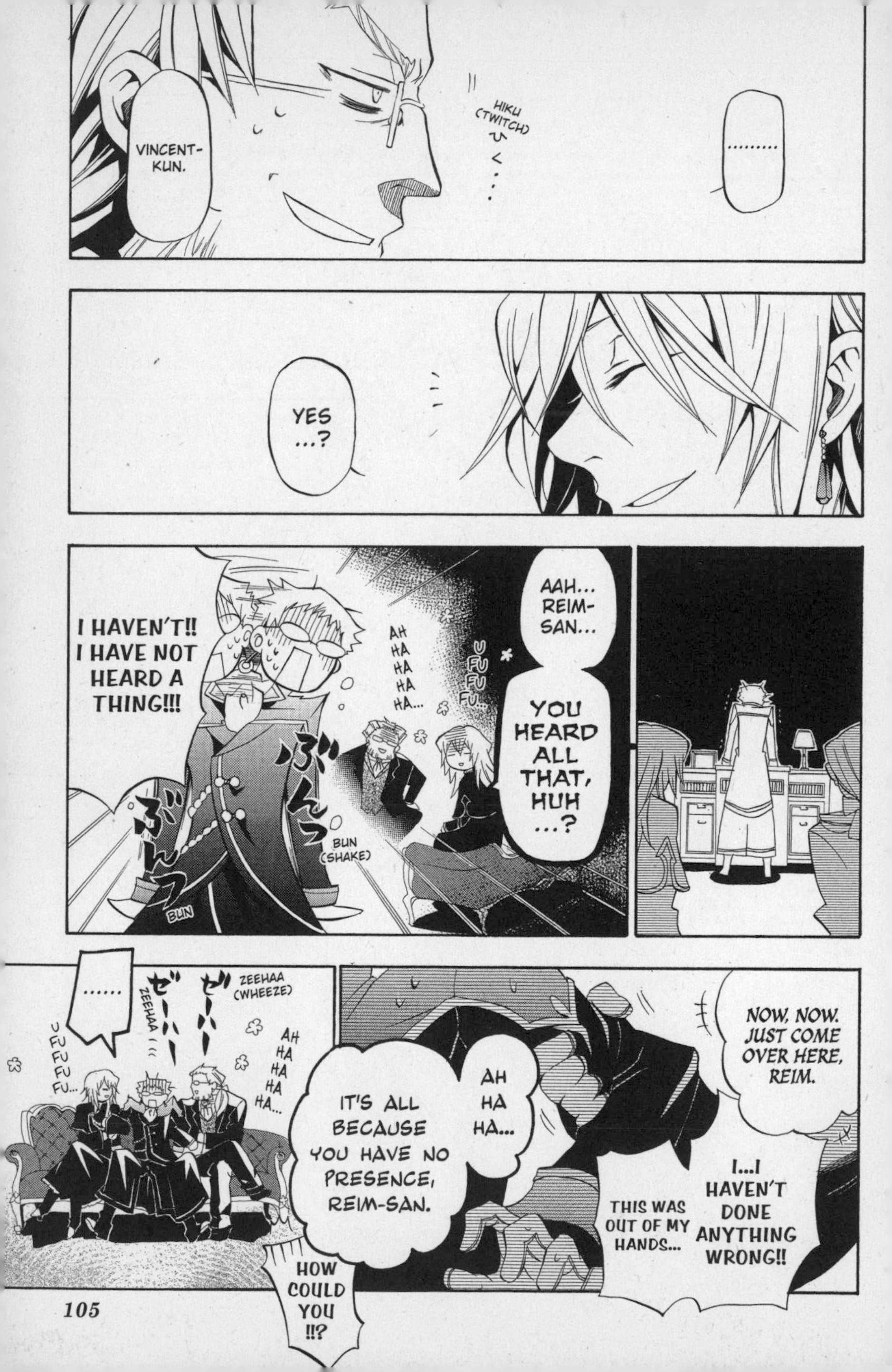
....
HIKU (TWITCH)
VINCENT-KUN.
YES ...?
AAH... REIM-SAN...
YOU HEARD ALL THAT, HUH ...?
U FU FU FU...
AH HA HA HA HA...
I HAVEN'T!! I HAVE NOT HEARD A THING!!!
BUN (SHAKE)
BUN
NOW, NOW. JUST COME OVER HERE, REIM.
I...I HAVEN'T DONE ANYTHING WRONG!!
THIS WAS OUT OF MY HANDS...
AH HA HA...
IT'S ALL BECAUSE YOU HAVE NO PRESENCE, REIM-SAN.
HOW COULD YOU !!?
ZEEHAA (WHEEZE)
ZEEHAA
......
AH HA HA HA HA HA...
U FU FU FU FU...

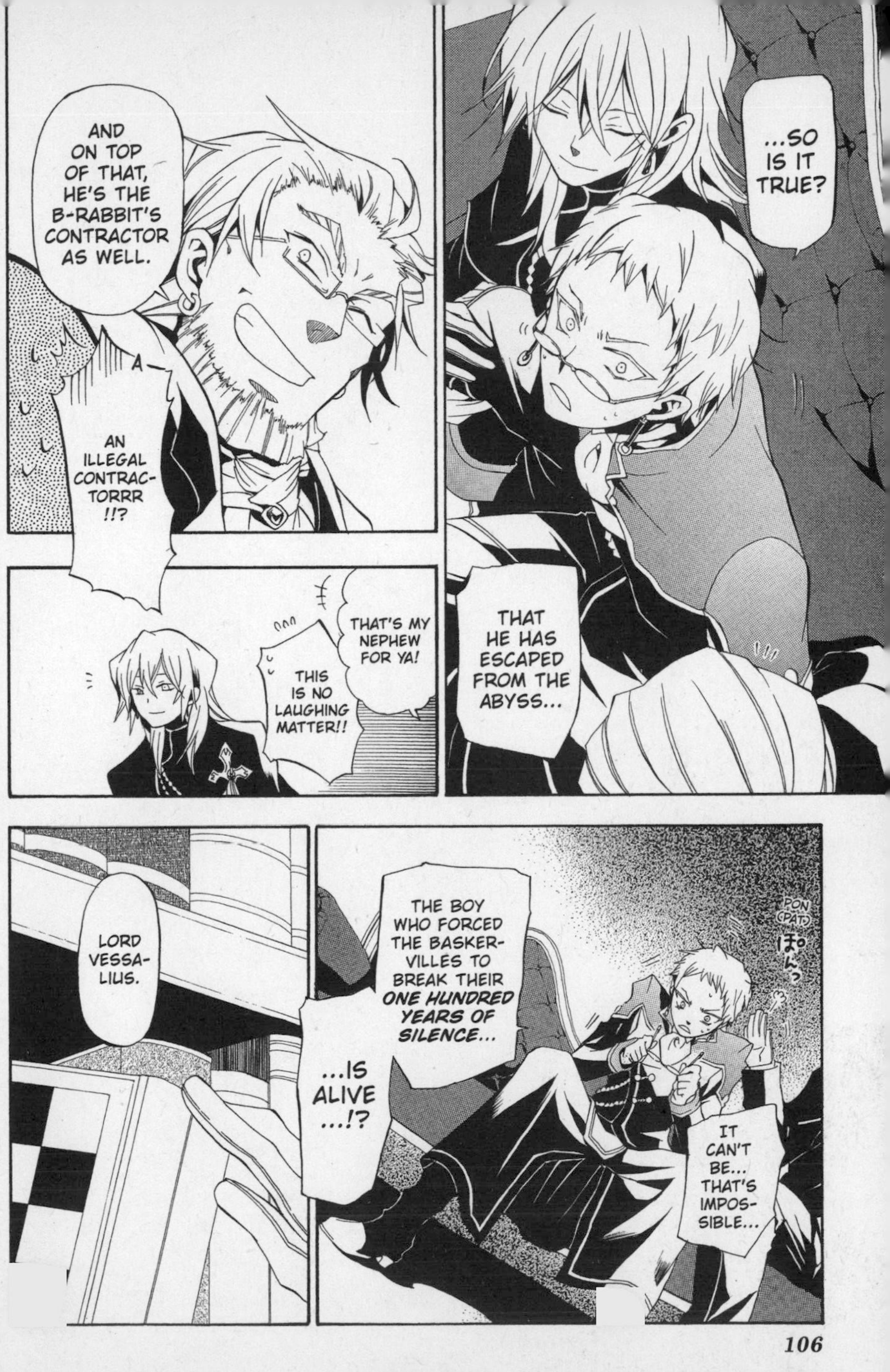
...SO IS IT TRUE?
THAT HE HAS ESCAPED FROM THE ABYSS...
AND ON TOP OF THAT, HE'S THE B-RABBIT'S CONTRACTOR AS WELL.
A—
AN ILLEGAL CONTRACTORRR!!?
THAT'S MY NEPHEW FOR YA!
THIS IS NO LAUGHING MATTER!!
THE BOY WHO FORCED THE BASKERVILLES TO BREAK THEIR ONE HUNDRED YEARS OF SILENCE...
...IS ALIVE...!?
PON (PAT)
ぽんっ
IT CAN'T BE... THAT'S IMPOSSIBLE...
LORD VESSALIUS.

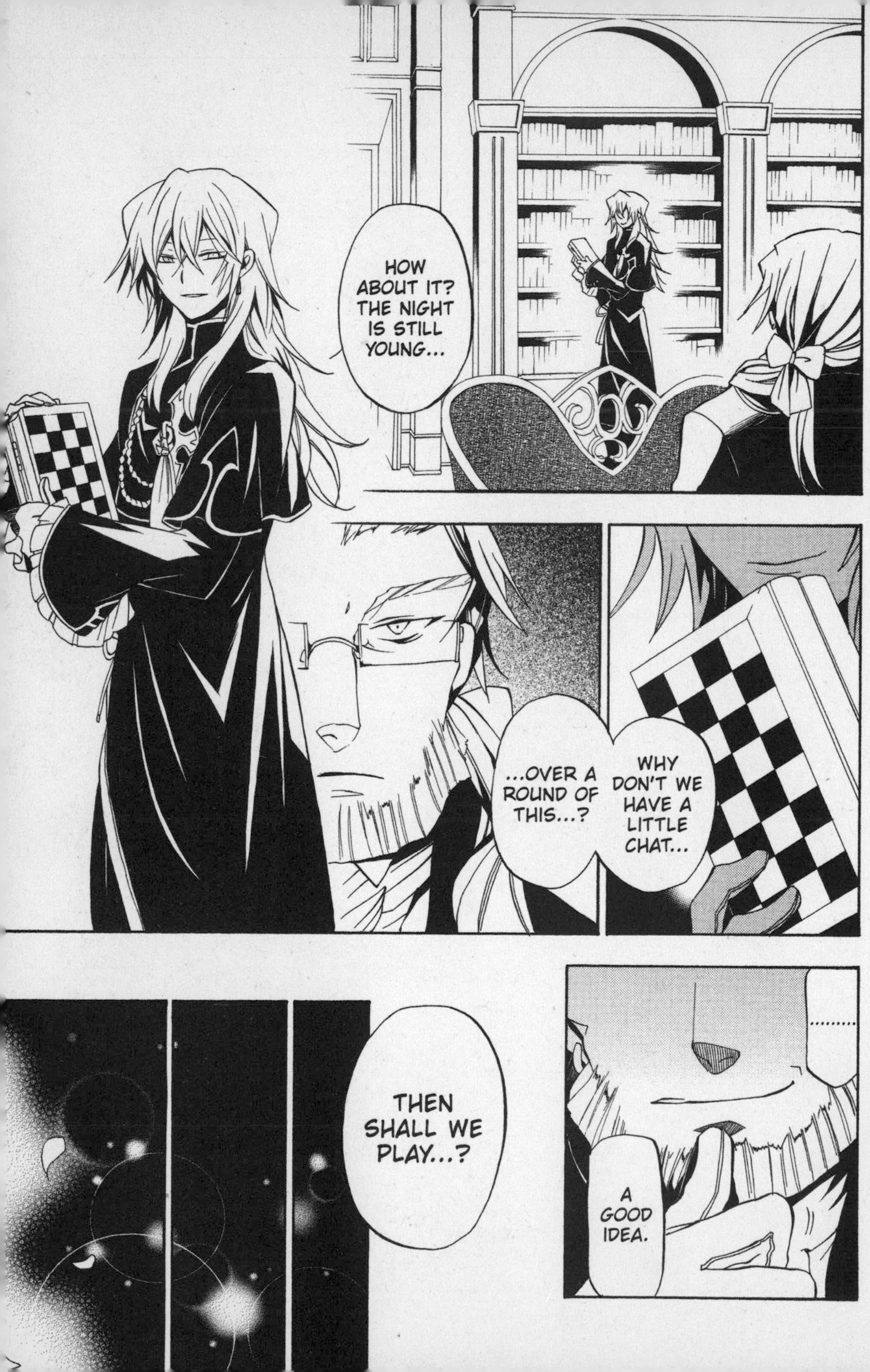

HOW ABOUT IT? THE NIGHT IS STILL YOUNG...
WHY DON'T WE HAVE A LITTLE CHAT...
...OVER A ROUND OF THIS...?
....
A GOOD IDEA.
THEN SHALL WE PLAY...?

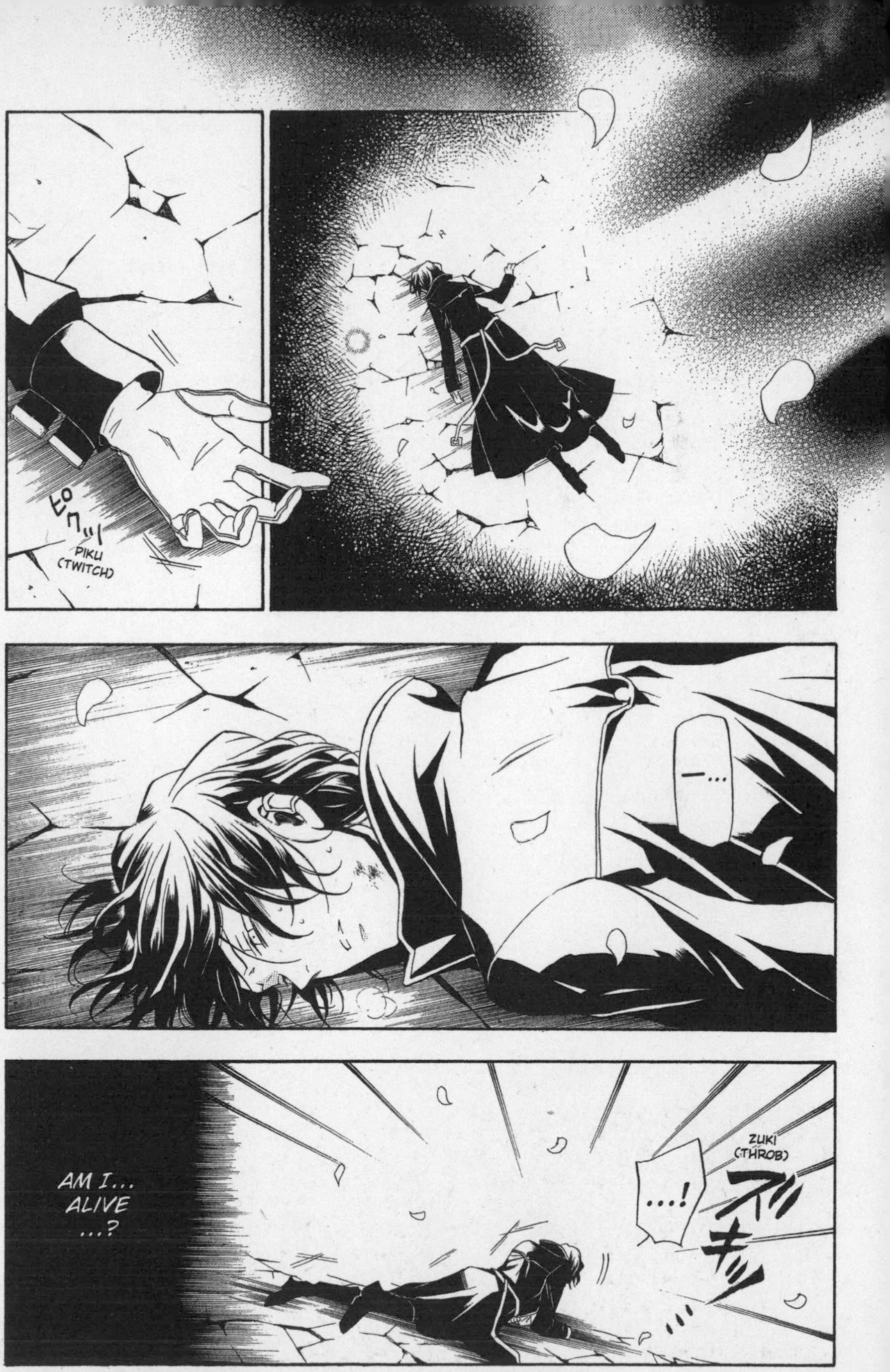
ピクッ
PIKU (TWITCH)
—...
ZUKI (THROB)
ズキッ
...!
AM I... ALIVE ...?

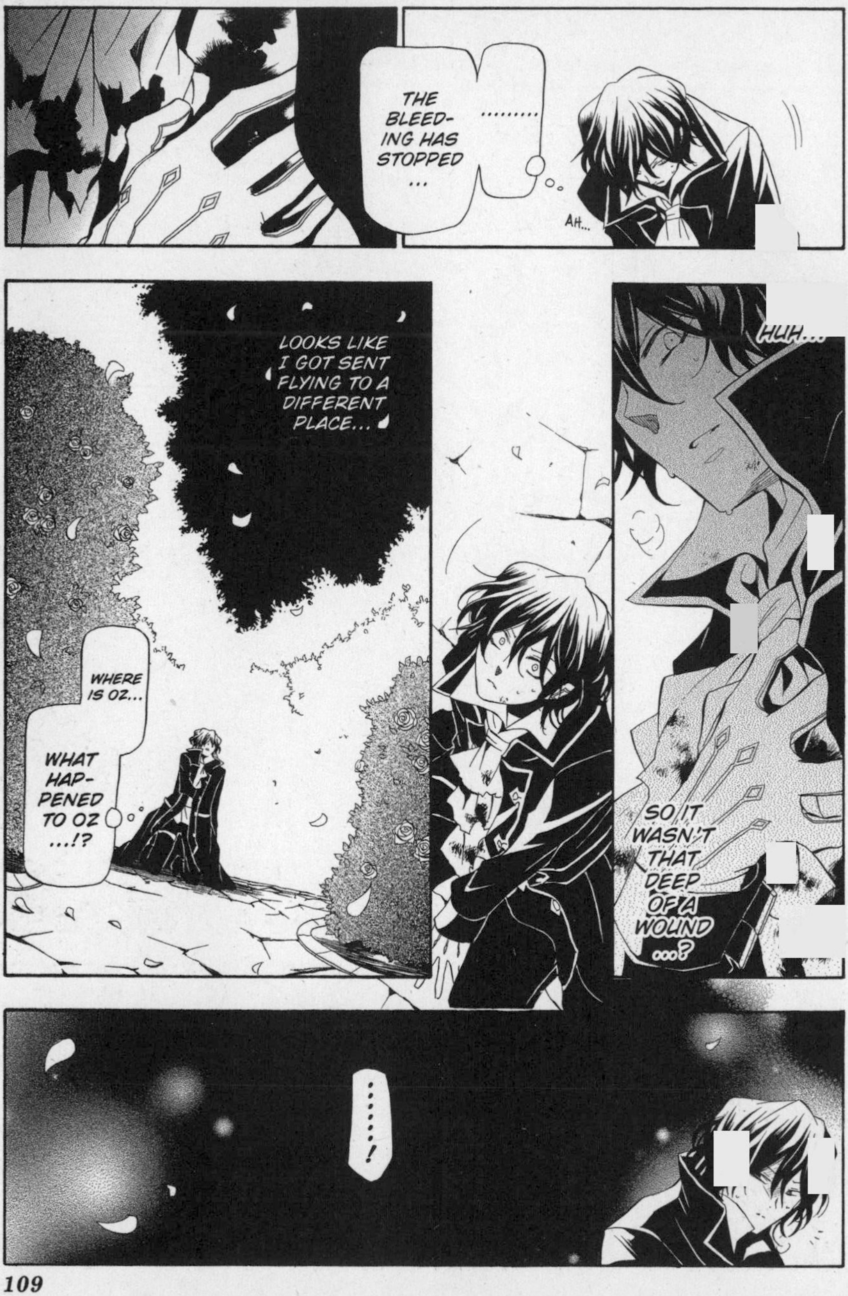

....
THE BLEEDING HAS STOPPED ...
AH...
HUH...
SO IT WASN'T THAT DEEP OF A WOUND ...?
LOOKS LIKE I GOT SENT FLYING TO A DIFFERENT PLACE...
WHERE IS OZ...
WHAT HAPPENED TO OZ ...!?
......!

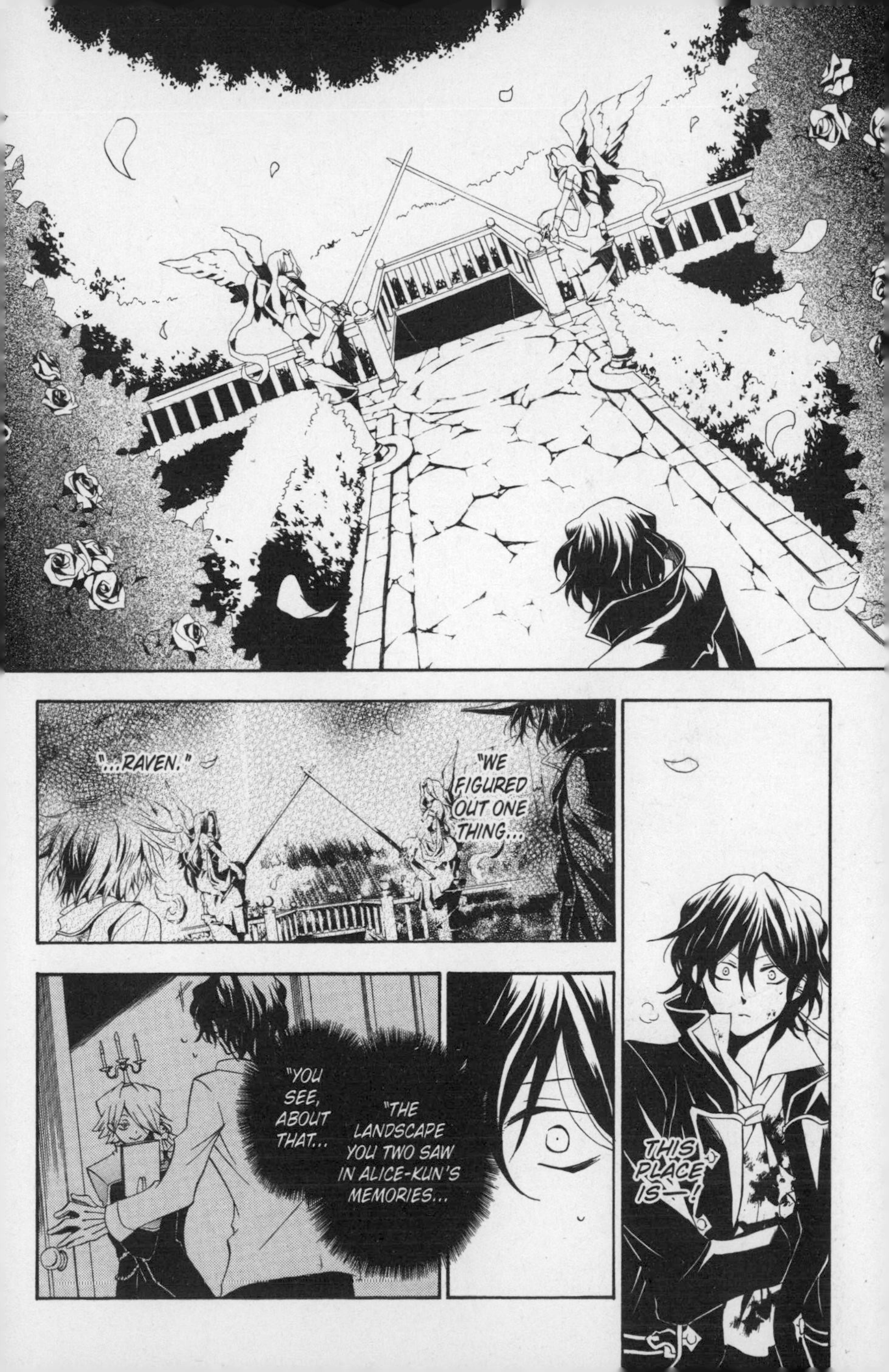
THIS PLACE IS—!
"WE FIGURED OUT ONE THING...
"...RAVEN."
"THE LANDSCAPE YOU TWO SAW IN ALICE-KUN'S MEMORIES...
"YOU SEE, ABOUT THAT...

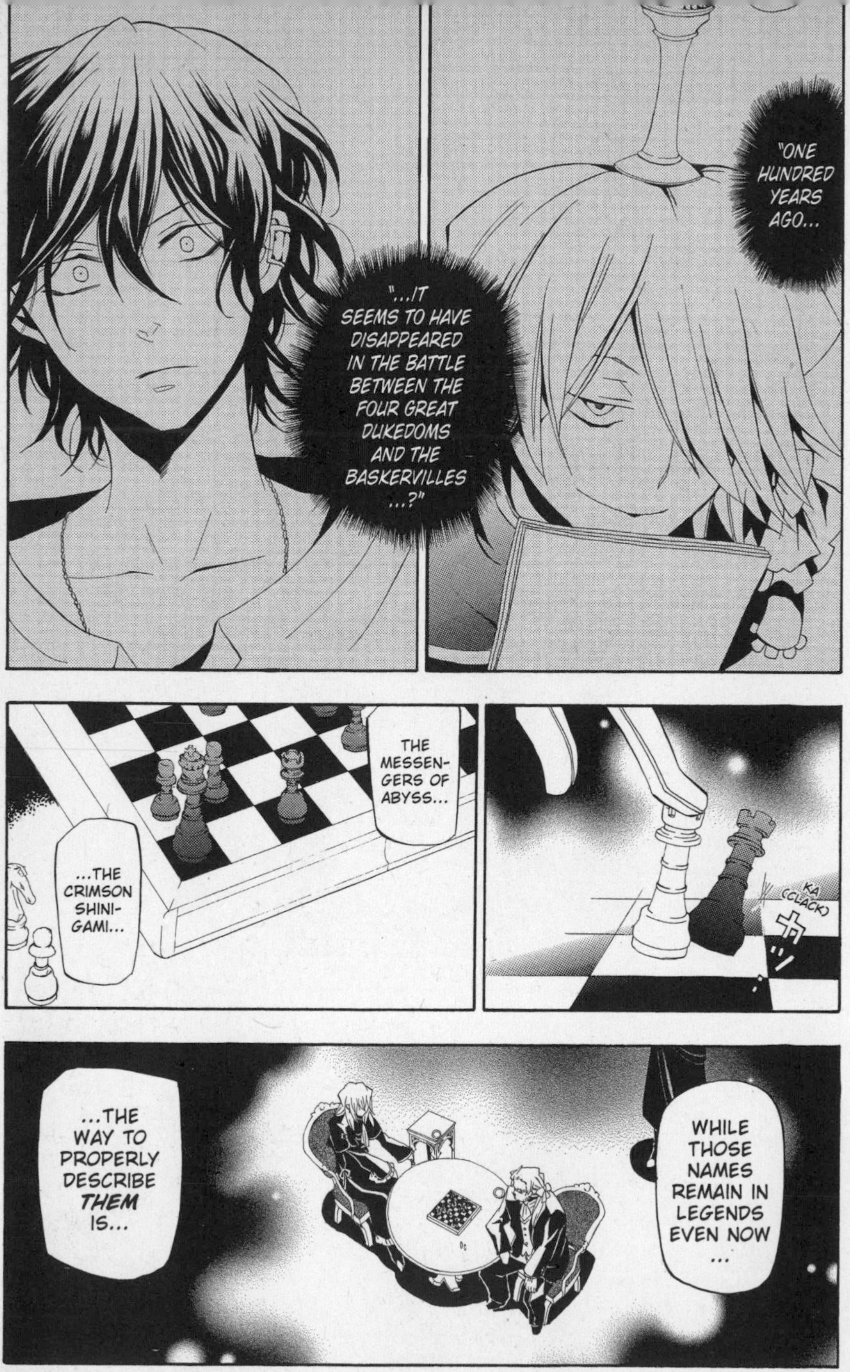
"ONE HUNDRED YEARS AGO...
"...IT SEEMS TO HAVE DISAPPEARED IN THE BATTLE BETWEEN THE FOUR GREAT DUKEDOMS AND THE BASKERVILLES ...?"
KA (CLACK)
THE MESSENGERS OF ABYSS...
...THE CRIMSON SHINIGAMI...
WHILE THOSE NAMES REMAIN IN LEGENDS EVEN NOW ...
...THE WAY TO PROPERLY DESCRIBE *THEM* IS...

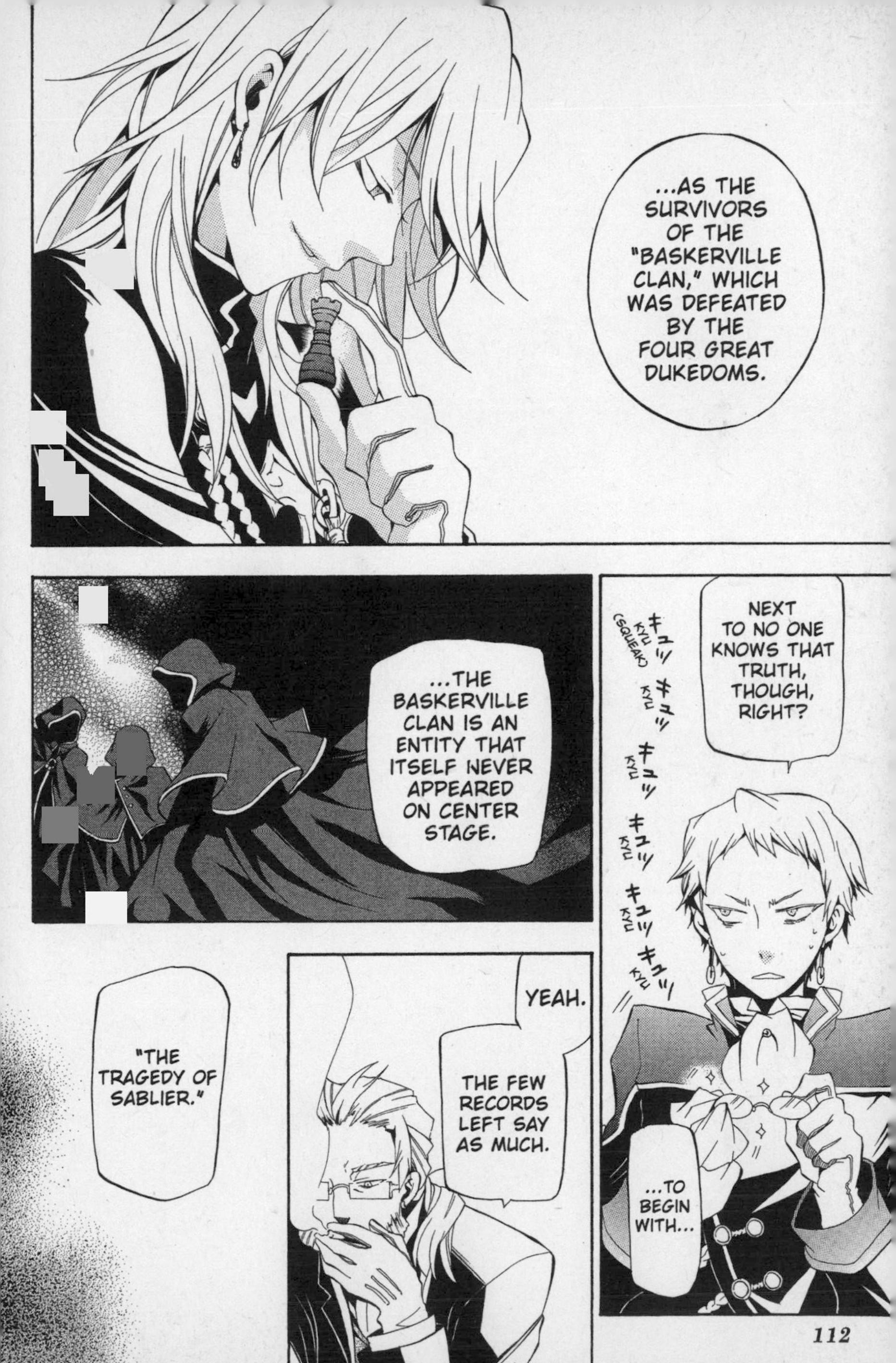
...AS THE SURVIVORS OF THE "BASKERVILLE CLAN," WHICH WAS DEFEATED BY THE FOUR GREAT DUKEDOMS.
NEXT TO NO ONE KNOWS THAT TRUTH, THOUGH, RIGHT?
キュッ KYU (SQUEAK)
キュッ KYU
キュッ KYU
キュッ KYU
キュッ KYU
キュッ KYU
...TO BEGIN WITH...
...THE BASKERVILLE CLAN IS AN ENTITY THAT ITSELF NEVER APPEARED ON CENTER STAGE.
YEAH.
THE FEW RECORDS LEFT SAY AS MUCH.
"THE TRAGEDY OF SABLIER."

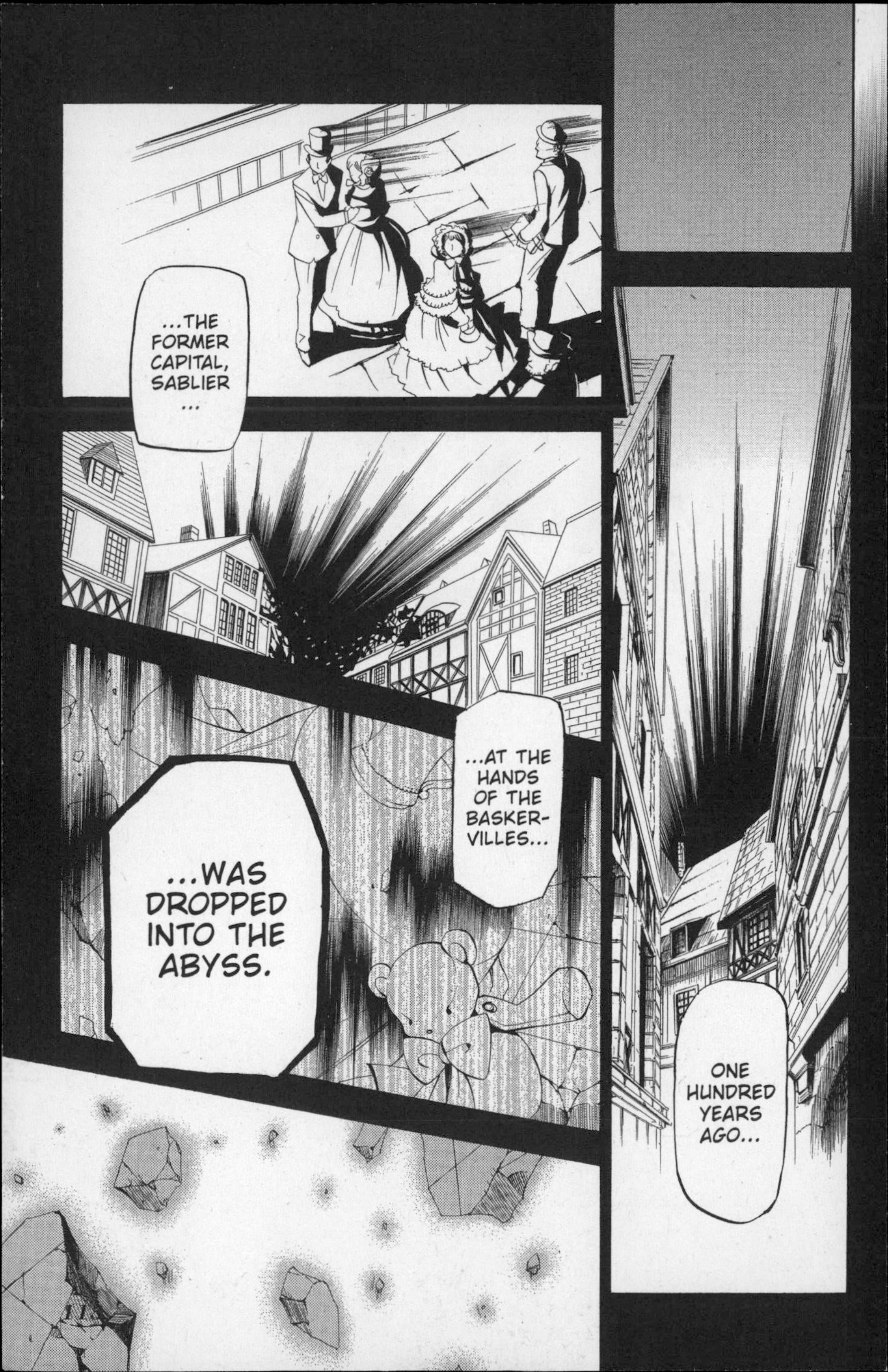
ONE HUNDRED YEARS AGO...
...THE FORMER CAPITAL, SABLIER...
...AT THE HANDS OF THE BASKER-VILLES...
...WAS DROPPED INTO THE ABYSS.

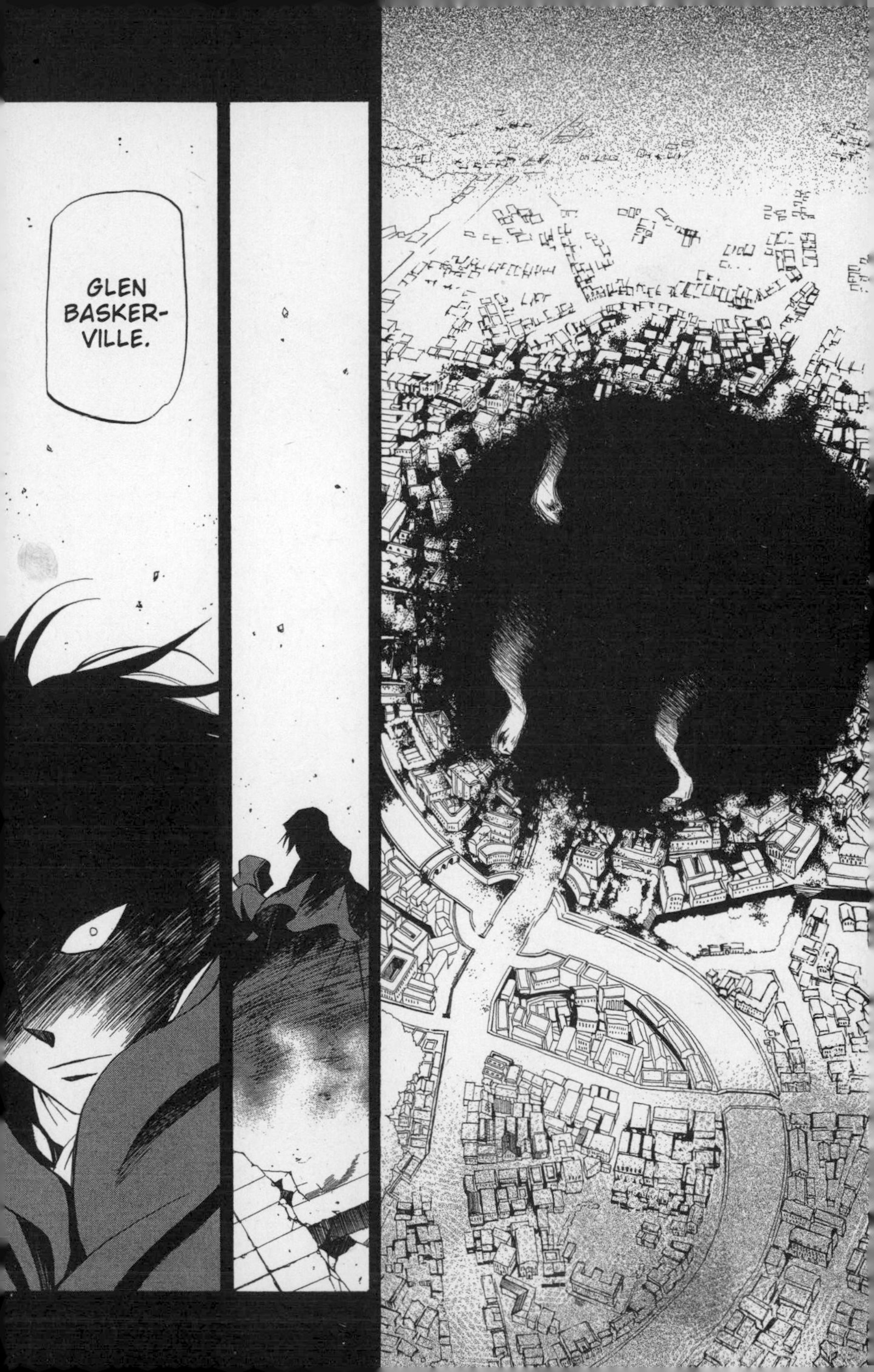
GLEN BASKER-VILLE.

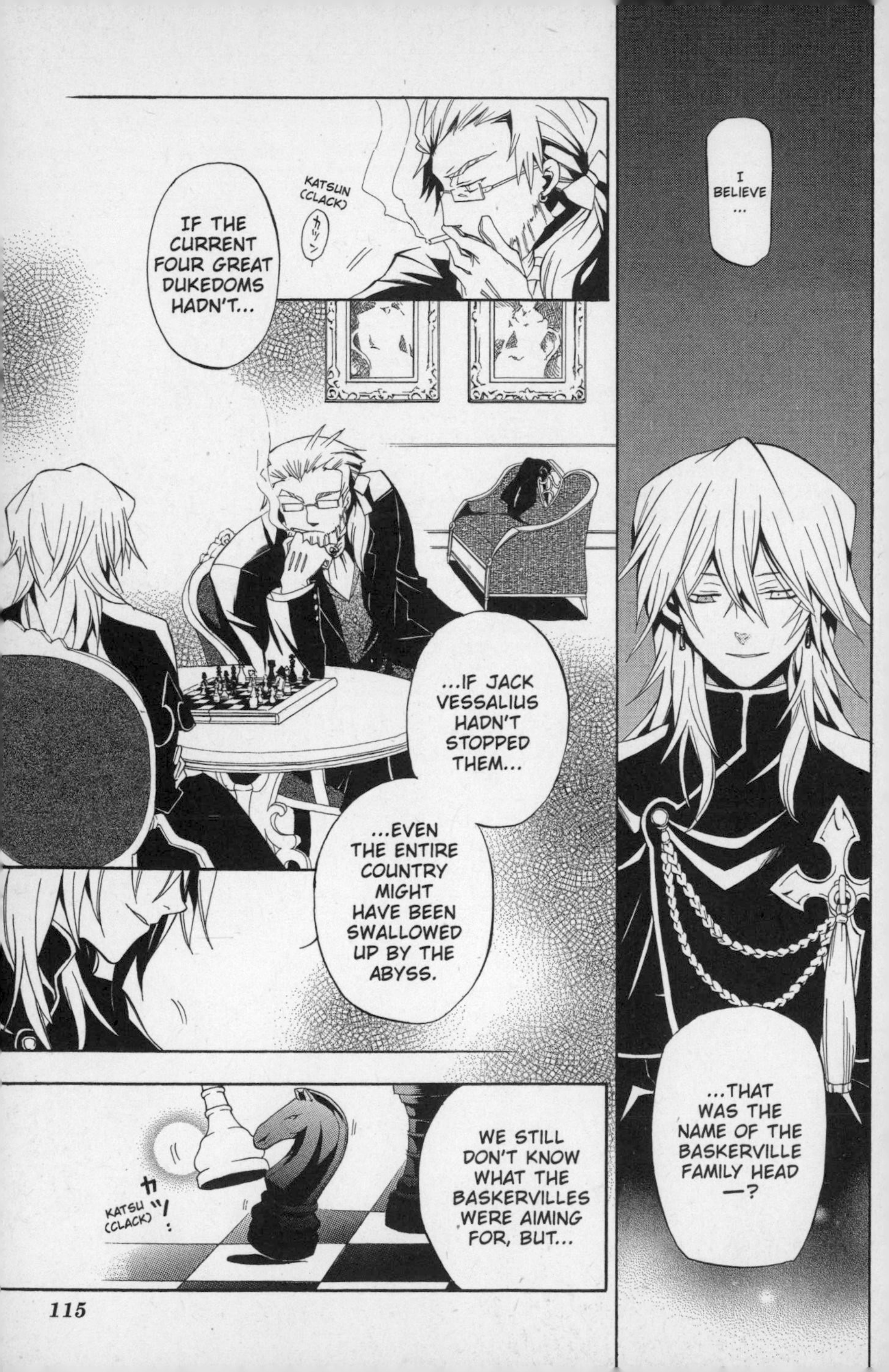

I BELIEVE ...
...THAT WAS THE NAME OF THE BASKERVILLE FAMILY HEAD —?
KATSUN (CLACK)
カッン
IF THE CURRENT FOUR GREAT DUKEDOMS HADN'T...
...IF JACK VESSALIUS HADN'T STOPPED THEM...
...EVEN THE ENTIRE COUNTRY MIGHT HAVE BEEN SWALLOWED UP BY THE ABYSS.
WE STILL DON'T KNOW WHAT THE BASKERVILLES WERE AIMING FOR, BUT...
KATSU (CLACK)
カッ!

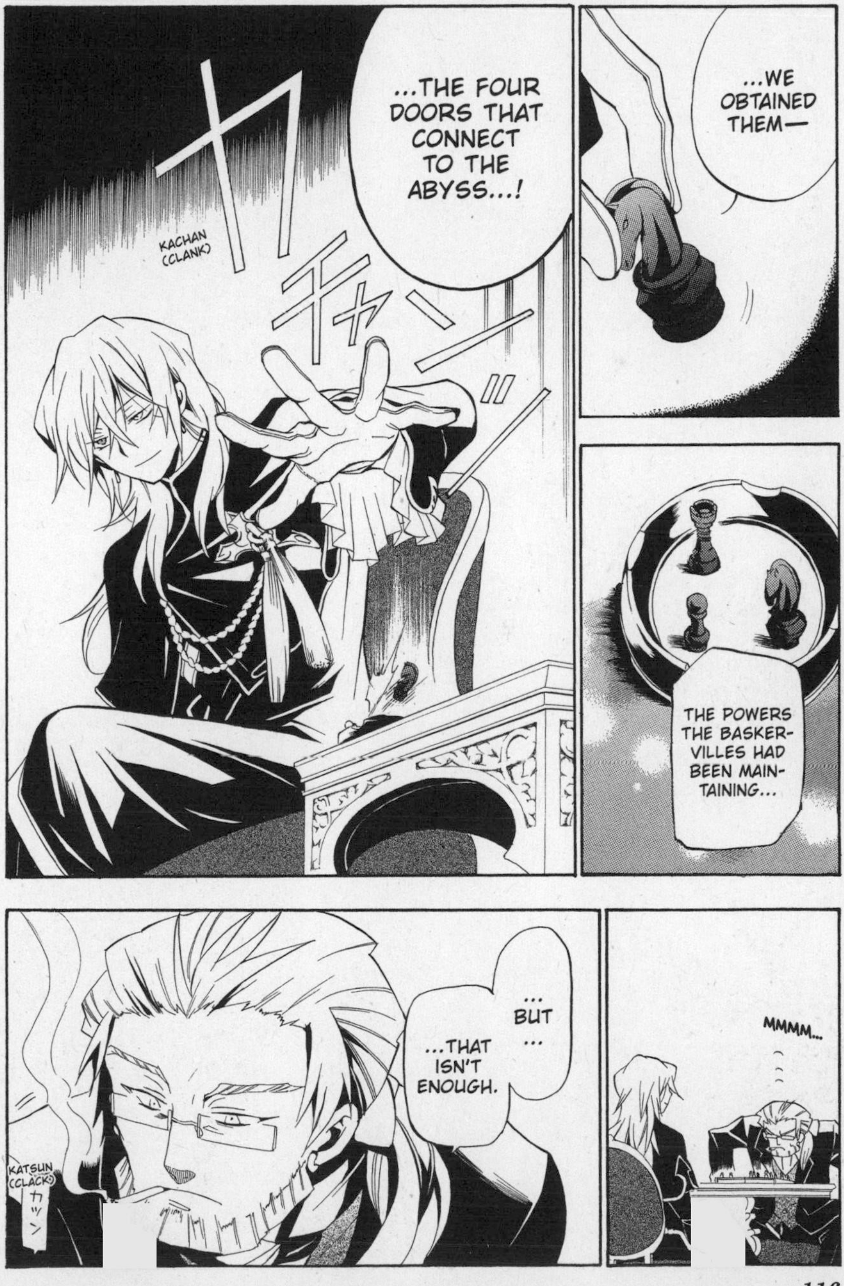
...WE OBTAINED THEM—
THE POWERS THE BASKER-VILLES HAD BEEN MAIN-TAINING...
...THE FOUR DOORS THAT CONNECT TO THE ABYSS...!
KACHAN (CLANK)
MMMM...
... BUT ...
...THAT ISN'T ENOUGH.
KATSUN (CLACK)
カツン

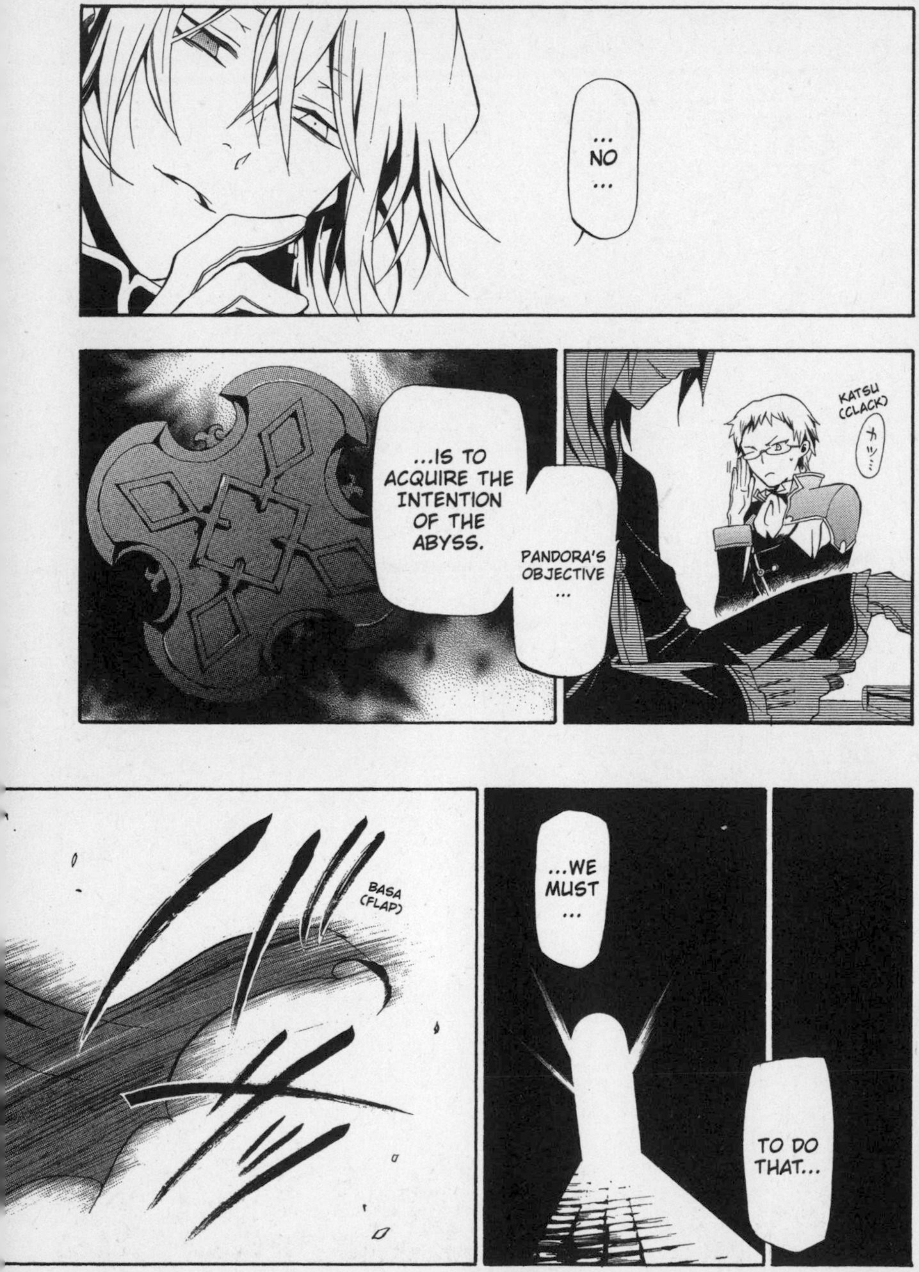

... NO ...
KATSU (CLACK)
カッ…
PANDORA'S OBJECTIVE ...
...IS TO ACQUIRE THE INTENTION OF THE ABYSS.
TO DO THAT...
...WE MUST ...
BASA (FLAP)

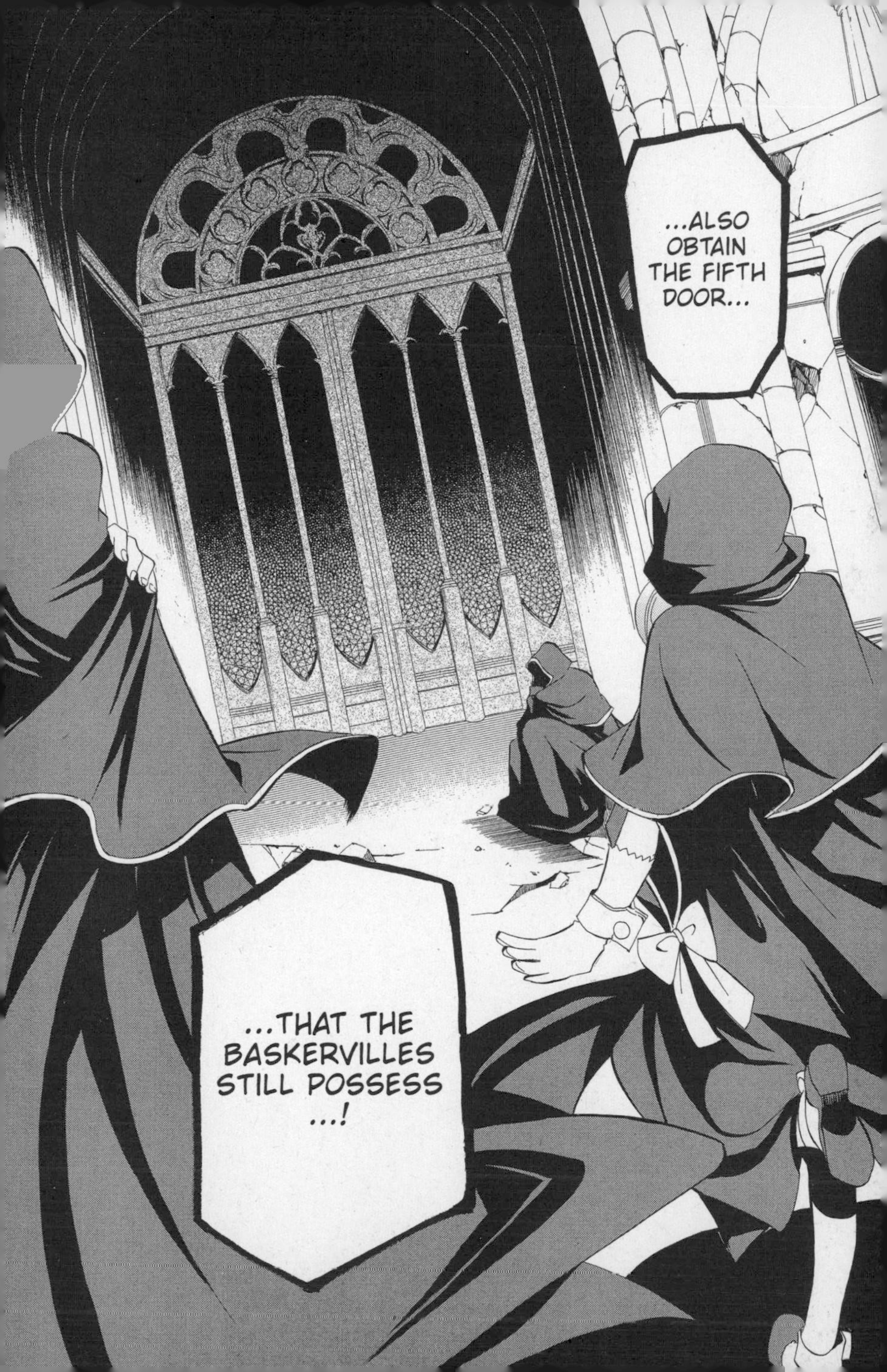
...ALSO OBTAIN THE FIFTH DOOR...
...THAT THE BASKERVILLES STILL POSSESS ...!

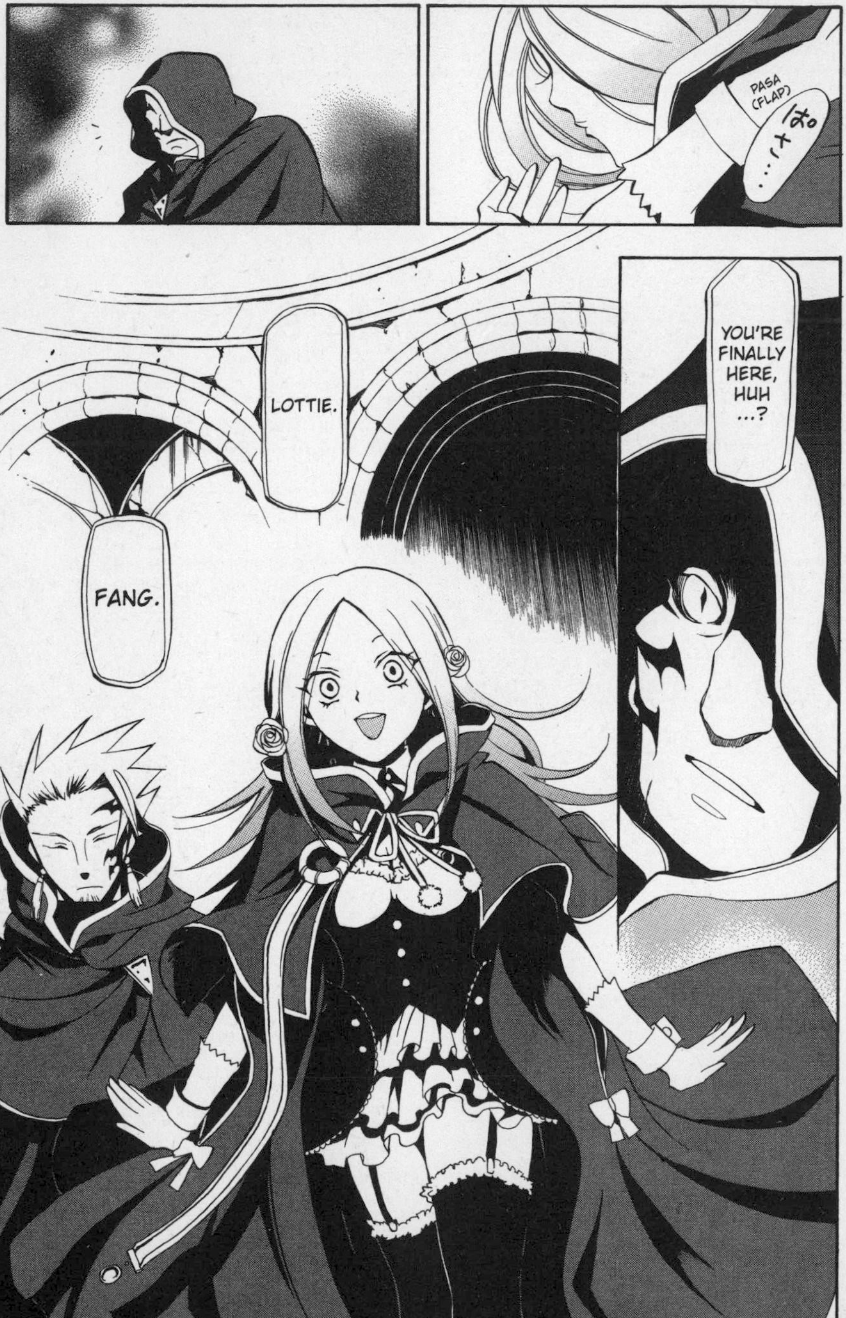
PASA (FLAP)
ぱさ…
YOU'RE FINALLY HERE, HUH ...?
LOTTIE.
FANG.

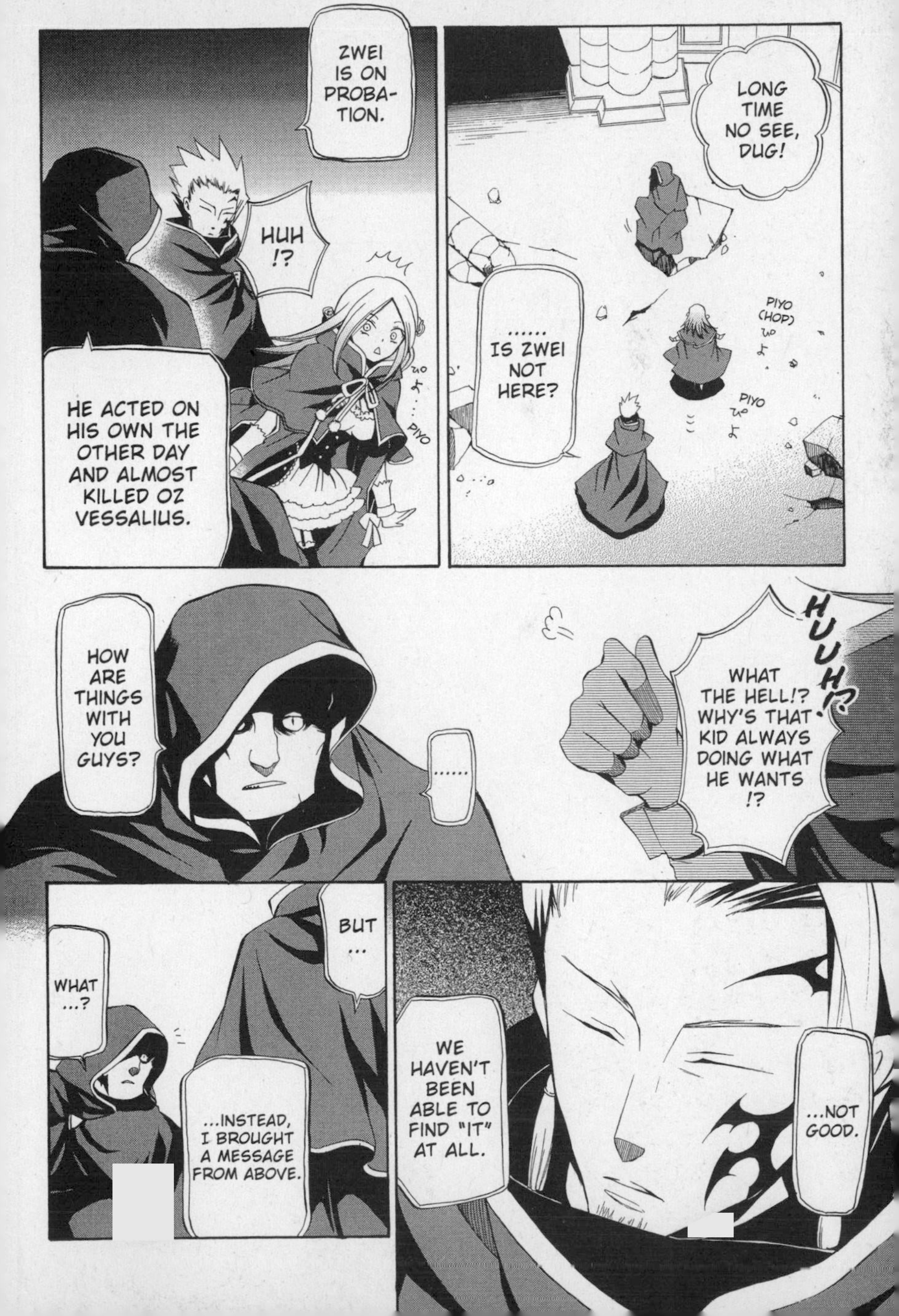
LONG TIME NO SEE, DUG!
...... IS ZWEI NOT HERE?
PIYO (HOP)
PIYO
ZWEI IS ON PROBA-TION.
HUH !?
HE ACTED ON HIS OWN THE OTHER DAY AND ALMOST KILLED OZ VESSALIUS.
PIYO
HUUH!?
WHAT THE HELL!? WHY'S THAT KID ALWAYS DOING WHAT HE WANTS !?
HOW ARE THINGS WITH YOU GUYS?
......
...NOT GOOD.
WE HAVEN'T BEEN ABLE TO FIND "IT" AT ALL.
BUT ...
...INSTEAD, I BROUGHT A MESSAGE FROM ABOVE.
WHAT ...?

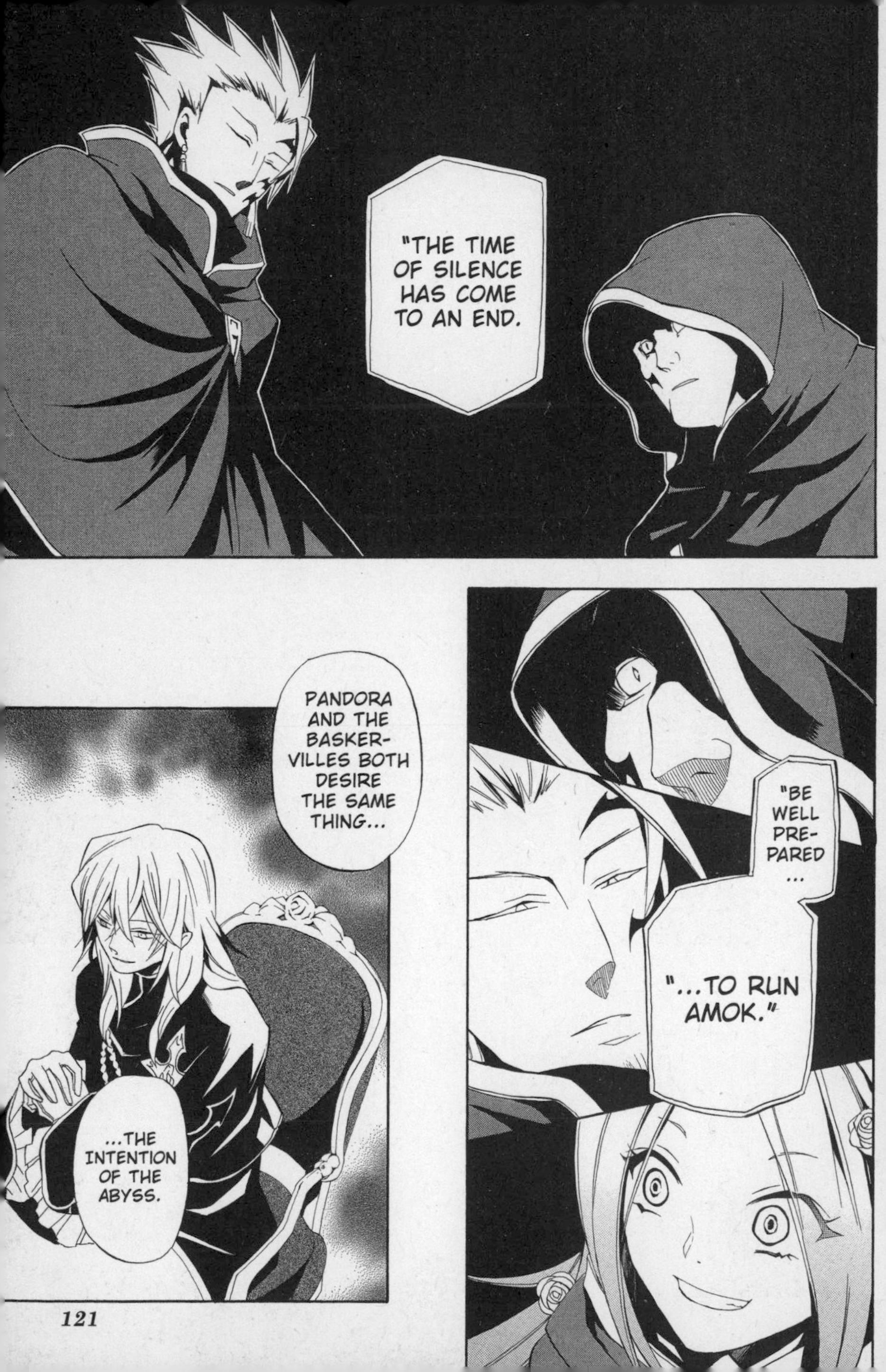
"THE TIME OF SILENCE HAS COME TO AN END.
"BE WELL PREPARED...
"...TO RUN AMOK."
PANDORA AND THE BASKERVILLES BOTH DESIRE THE SAME THING...
...THE INTENTION OF THE ABYSS.

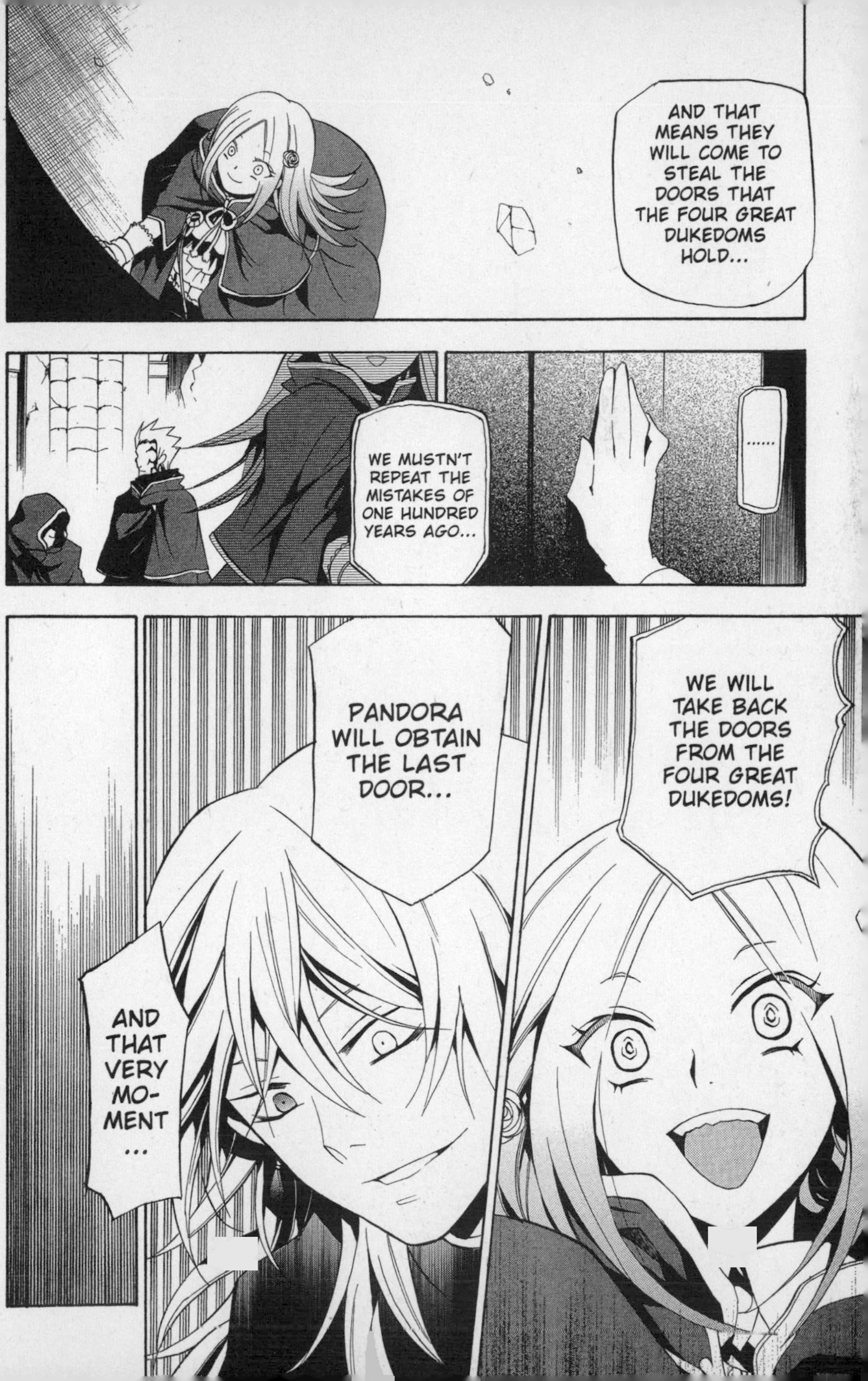
AND THAT MEANS THEY WILL COME TO STEAL THE DOORS THAT THE FOUR GREAT DUKEDOMS HOLD...
......
WE MUSTN'T REPEAT THE MISTAKES OF ONE HUNDRED YEARS AGO...
WE WILL TAKE BACK THE DOORS FROM THE FOUR GREAT DUKEDOMS!
PANDORA WILL OBTAIN THE LAST DOOR...
AND THAT VERY MO-MENT ...

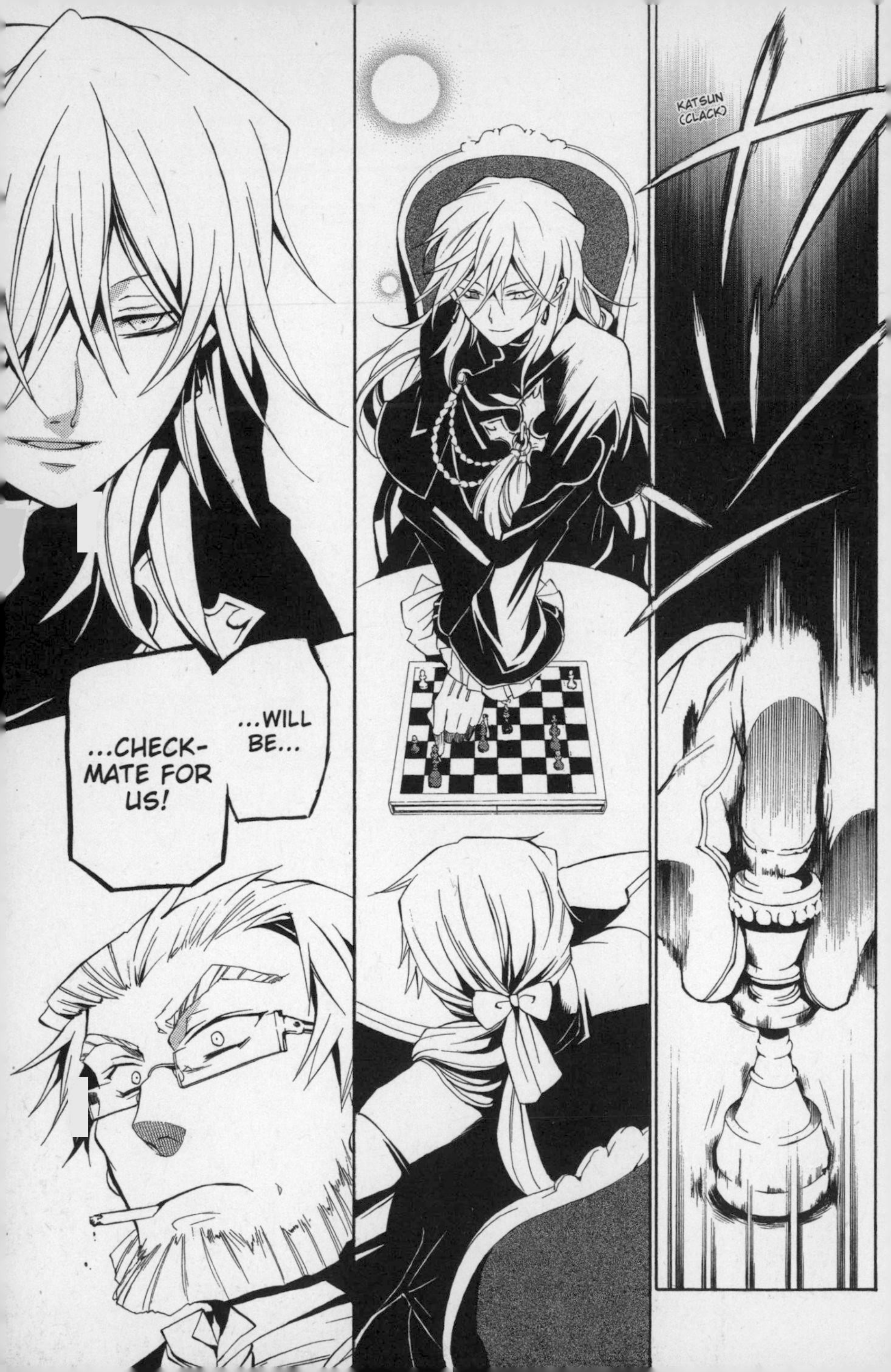
KATSUN (CLACK)
...WILL BE...
...CHECK-MATE FOR US!

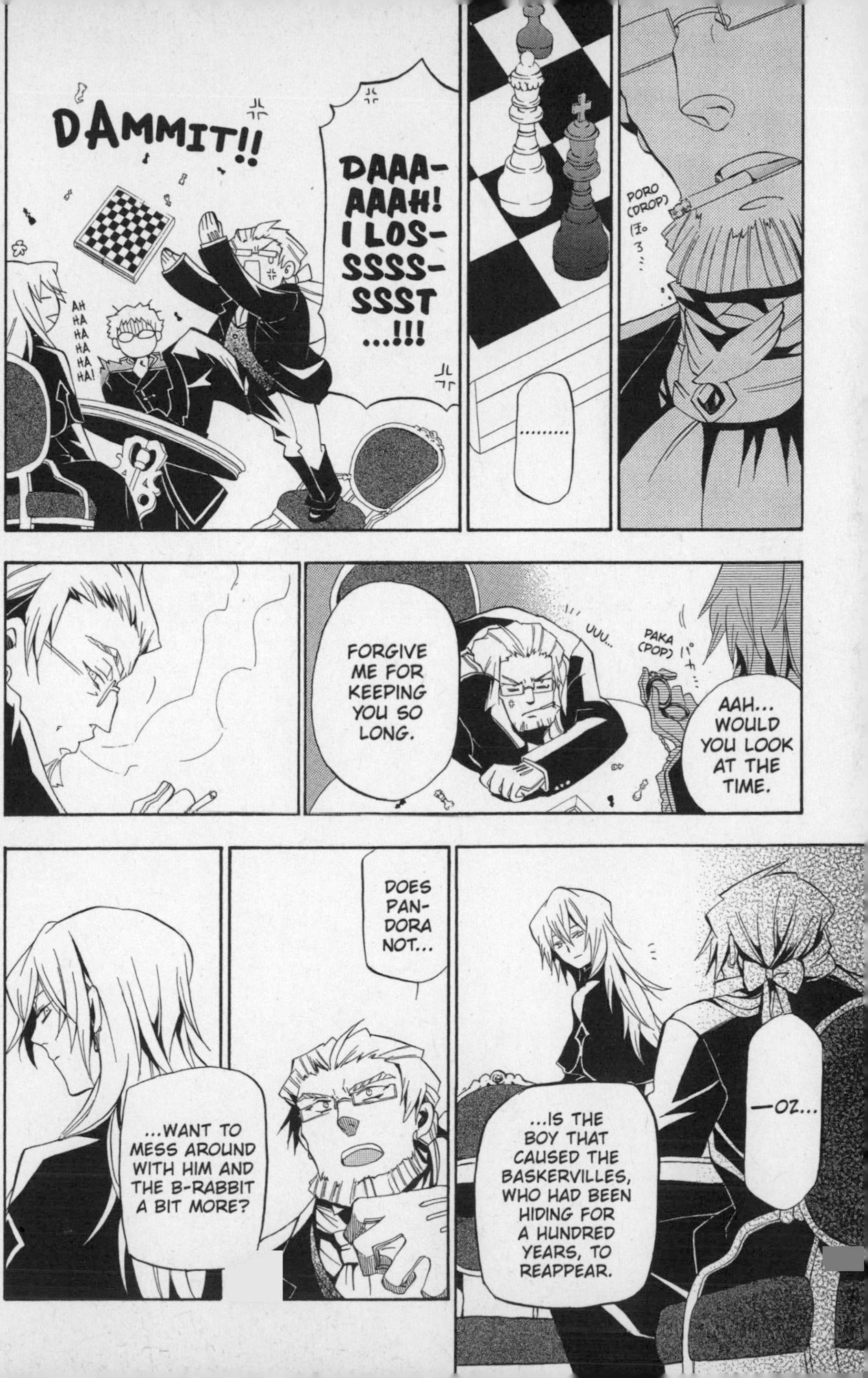
PORO (DROP)
ぽろ
....
DAAA-AAAH! I LOS-SSSS-SSST ...!!!
DAMMIT!!
AH HA HA HA HA HA!
PAKA (POP)
パカ
AAH... WOULD YOU LOOK AT THE TIME.
UUU...
FORGIVE ME FOR KEEPING YOU SO LONG.
—OZ...
...IS THE BOY THAT CAUSED THE BASKERVILLES, WHO HAD BEEN HIDING FOR A HUNDRED YEARS, TO REAPPEAR.
DOES PANDORA NOT...
...WANT TO MESS AROUND WITH HIM AND THE B-RABBIT A BIT MORE?

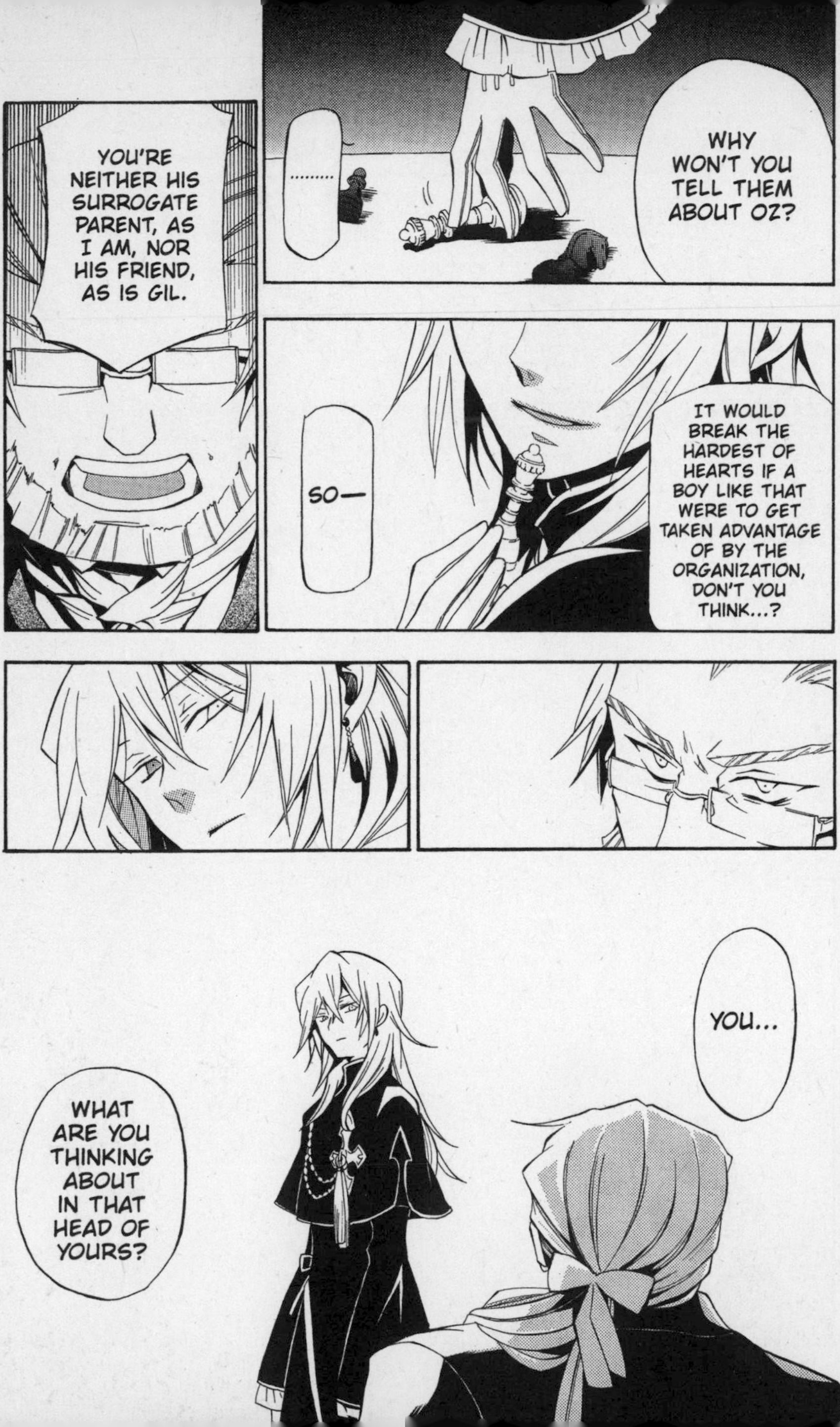
WHY WON'T YOU TELL THEM ABOUT OZ?
....
IT WOULD BREAK THE HARDEST OF HEARTS IF A BOY LIKE THAT WERE TO GET TAKEN ADVANTAGE OF BY THE ORGANIZATION, DON'T YOU THINK...?
SO—
YOU'RE NEITHER HIS SURROGATE PARENT, AS I AM, NOR HIS FRIEND, AS IS GIL.
YOU...
WHAT ARE YOU THINKING ABOUT IN THAT HEAD OF YOURS?

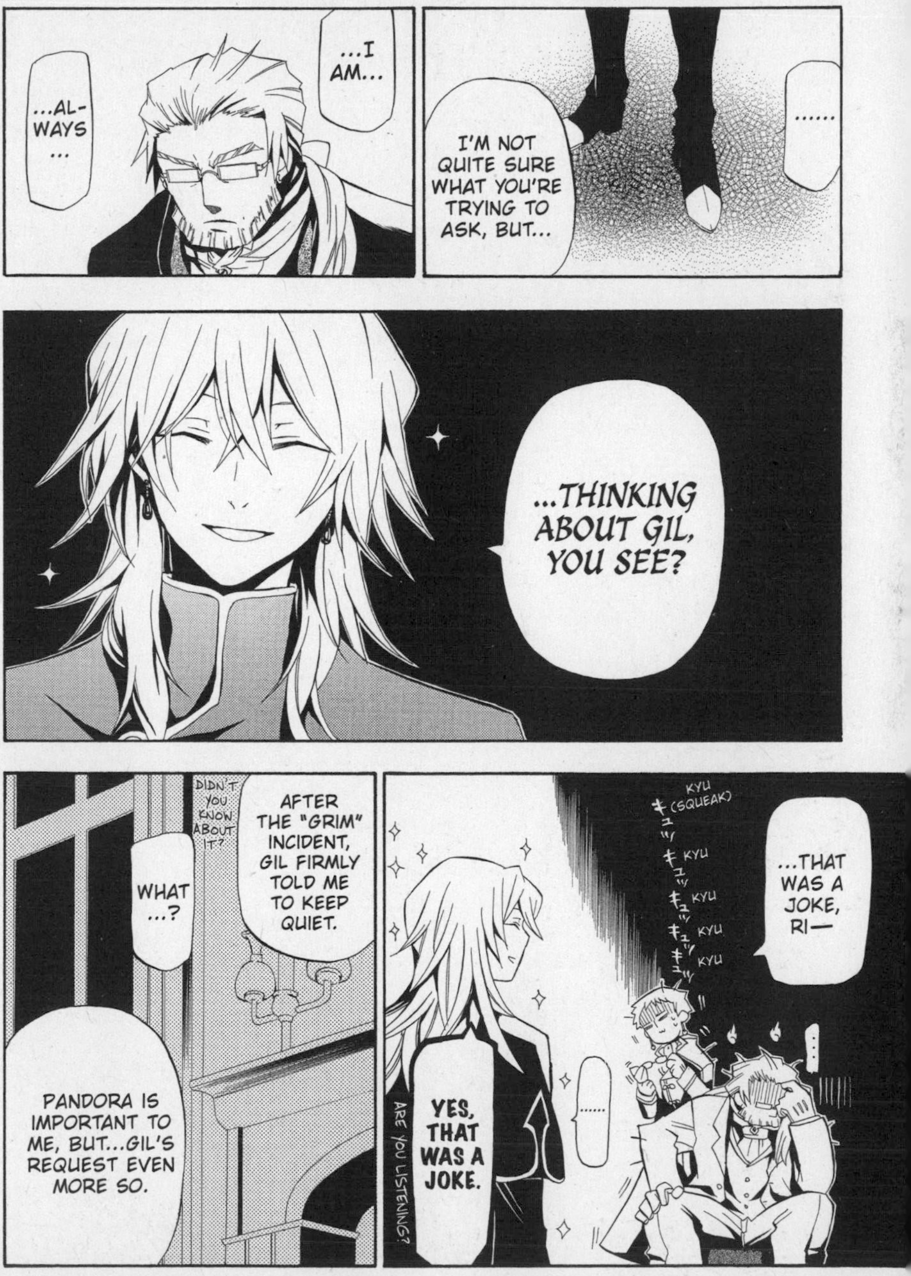
......
I'M NOT QUITE SURE WHAT YOU'RE TRYING TO ASK, BUT...
...I AM...
...AL-WAYS...
...THINKING ABOUT GIL, YOU SEE?
...THAT WAS A JOKE, RI—
KYU (SQUEAK)
KYU
KYU
KYU
KYU
!
......
YES, THAT WAS A JOKE.
ARE YOU LISTENING?
AFTER THE "GRIM" INCIDENT, GIL FIRMLY TOLD ME TO KEEP QUIET.
DIDN'T YOU KNOW ABOUT IT?
WHAT...?
PANDORA IS IMPORTANT TO ME, BUT...GIL'S REQUEST EVEN MORE SO.

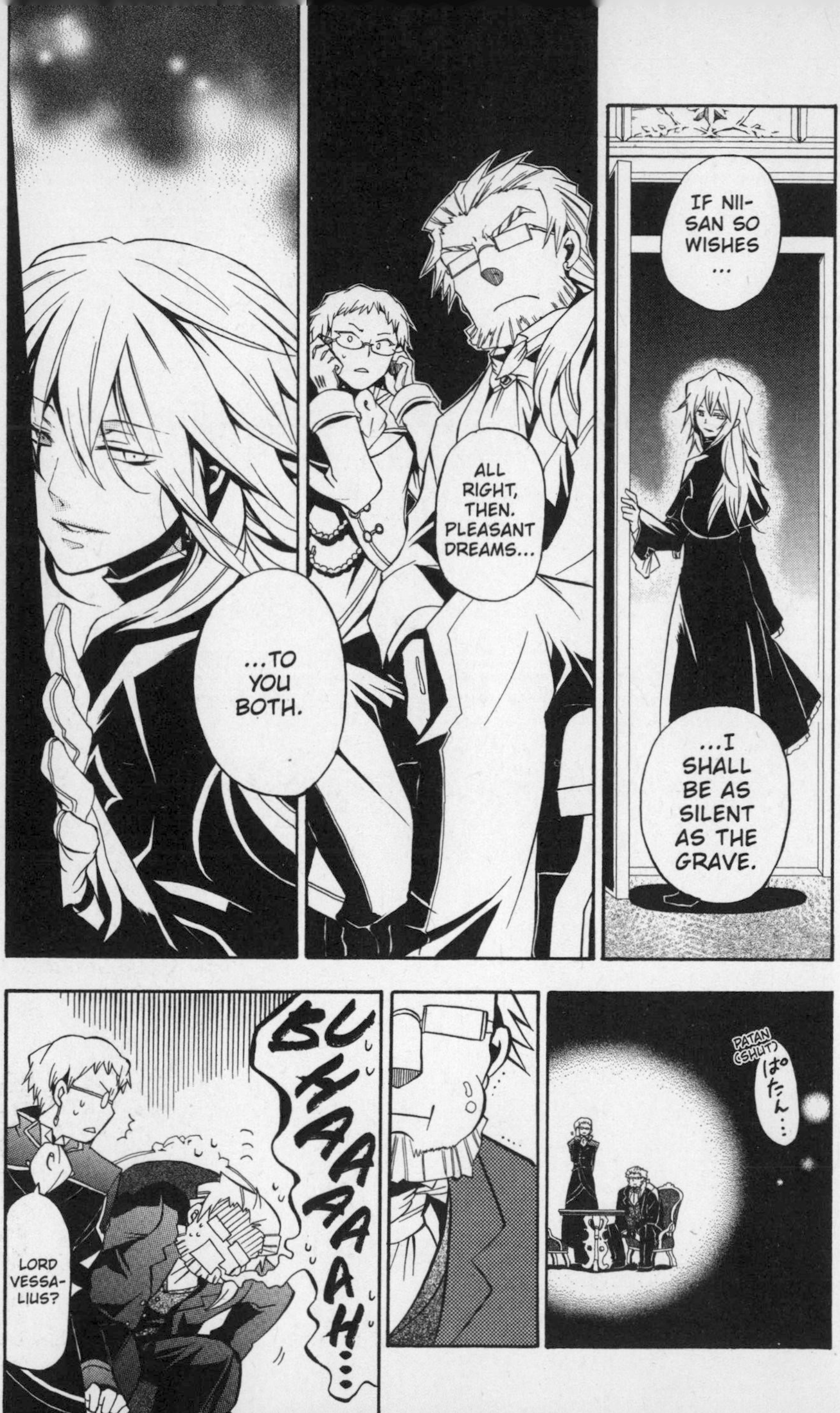
IF NII-SAN SO WISHES ...
...I SHALL BE AS SILENT AS THE GRAVE.
ALL RIGHT, THEN. PLEASANT DREAMS...
...TO YOU BOTH.
PATAN (SHUT)
ぱたん…
BUHAAAAAAAH...
LORD VESSALIUS?

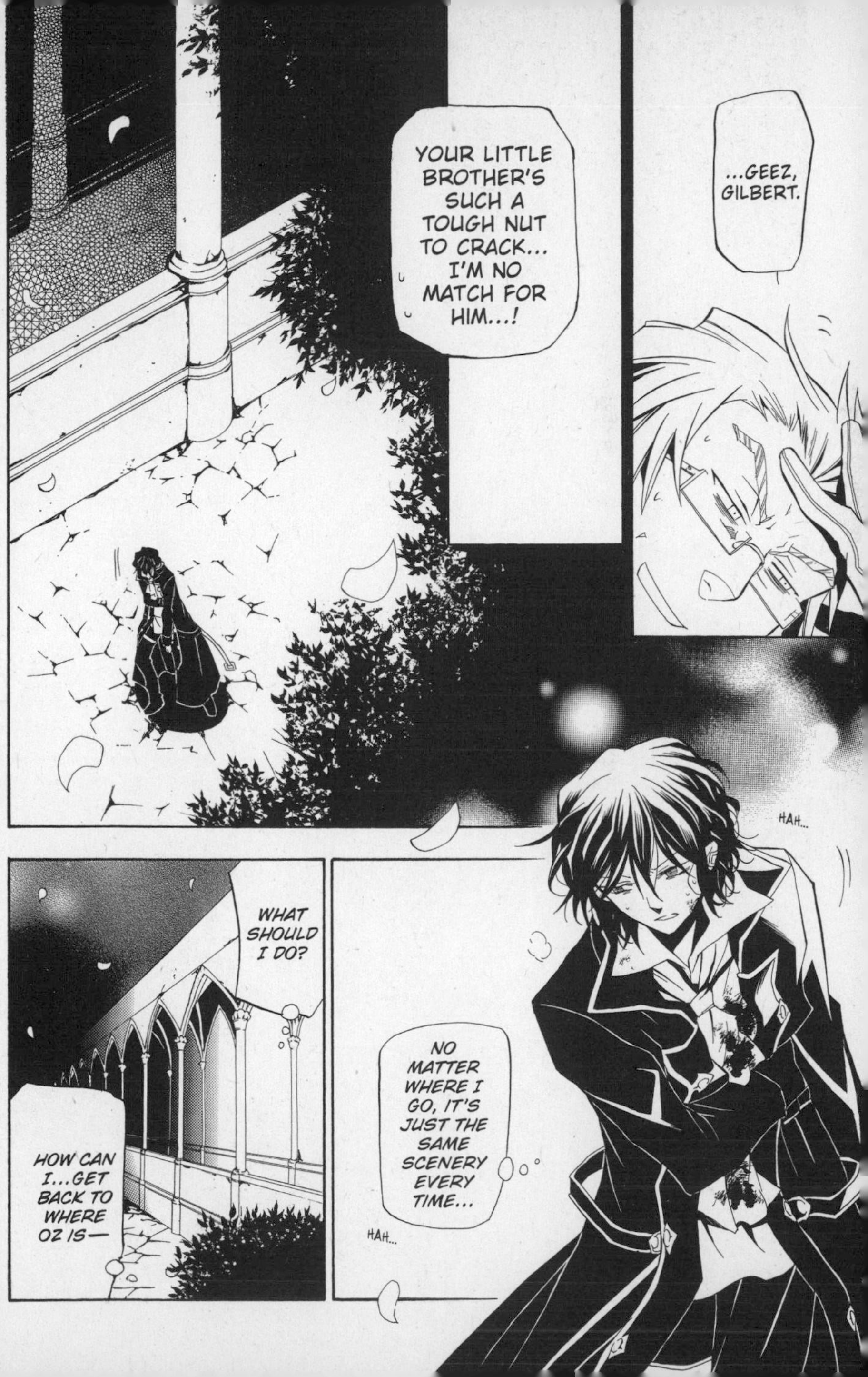
...GEEZ, GILBERT.
YOUR LITTLE BROTHER'S SUCH A TOUGH NUT TO CRACK... I'M NO MATCH FOR HIM...!
HAH...
NO MATTER WHERE I GO, IT'S JUST THE SAME SCENERY EVERY TIME...
HAH...
WHAT SHOULD I DO?
HOW CAN I...GET BACK TO WHERE OZ IS—

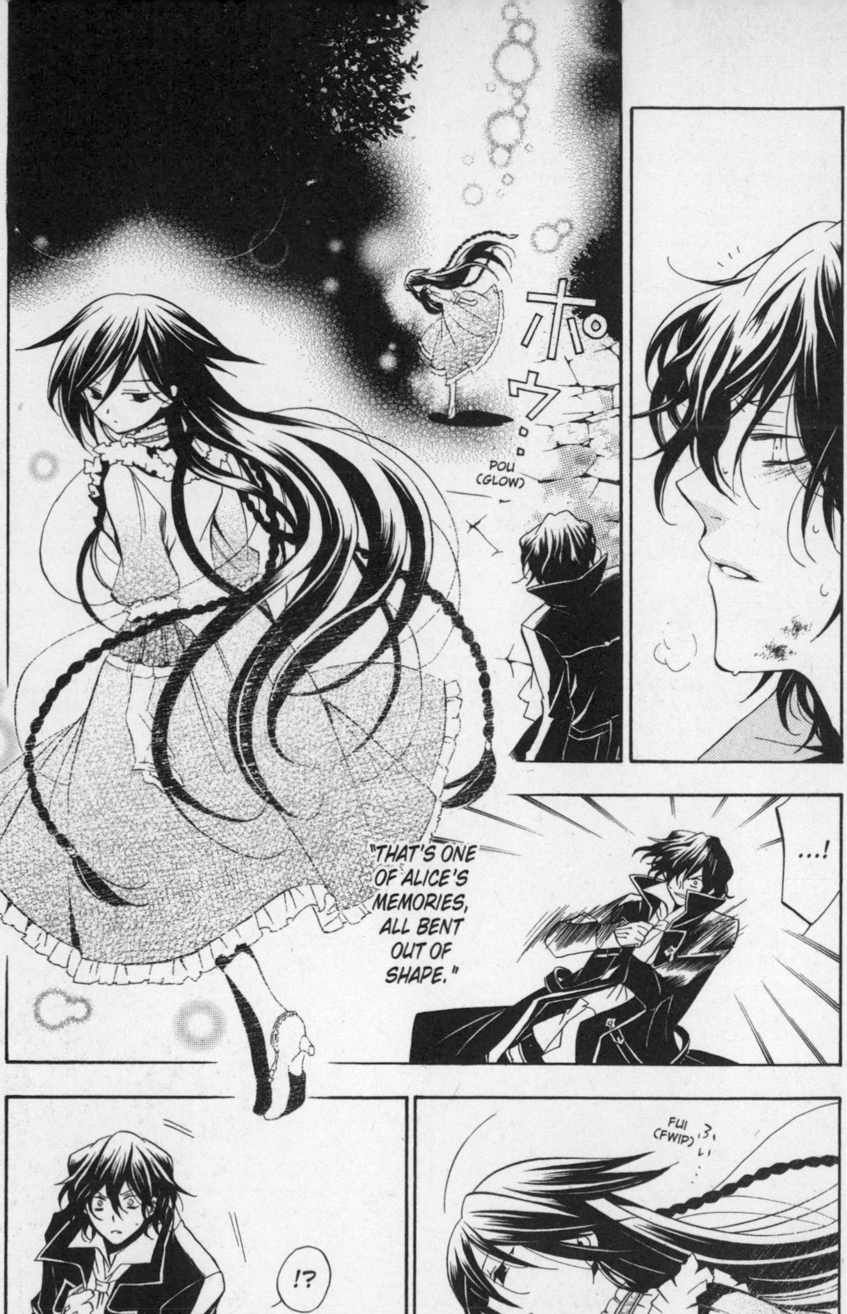
ポウ
POU (GLOW)
...!
"THAT'S ONE OF ALICE'S MEMORIES, ALL BENT OUT OF SHAPE."
FUI (FWIP)
!?

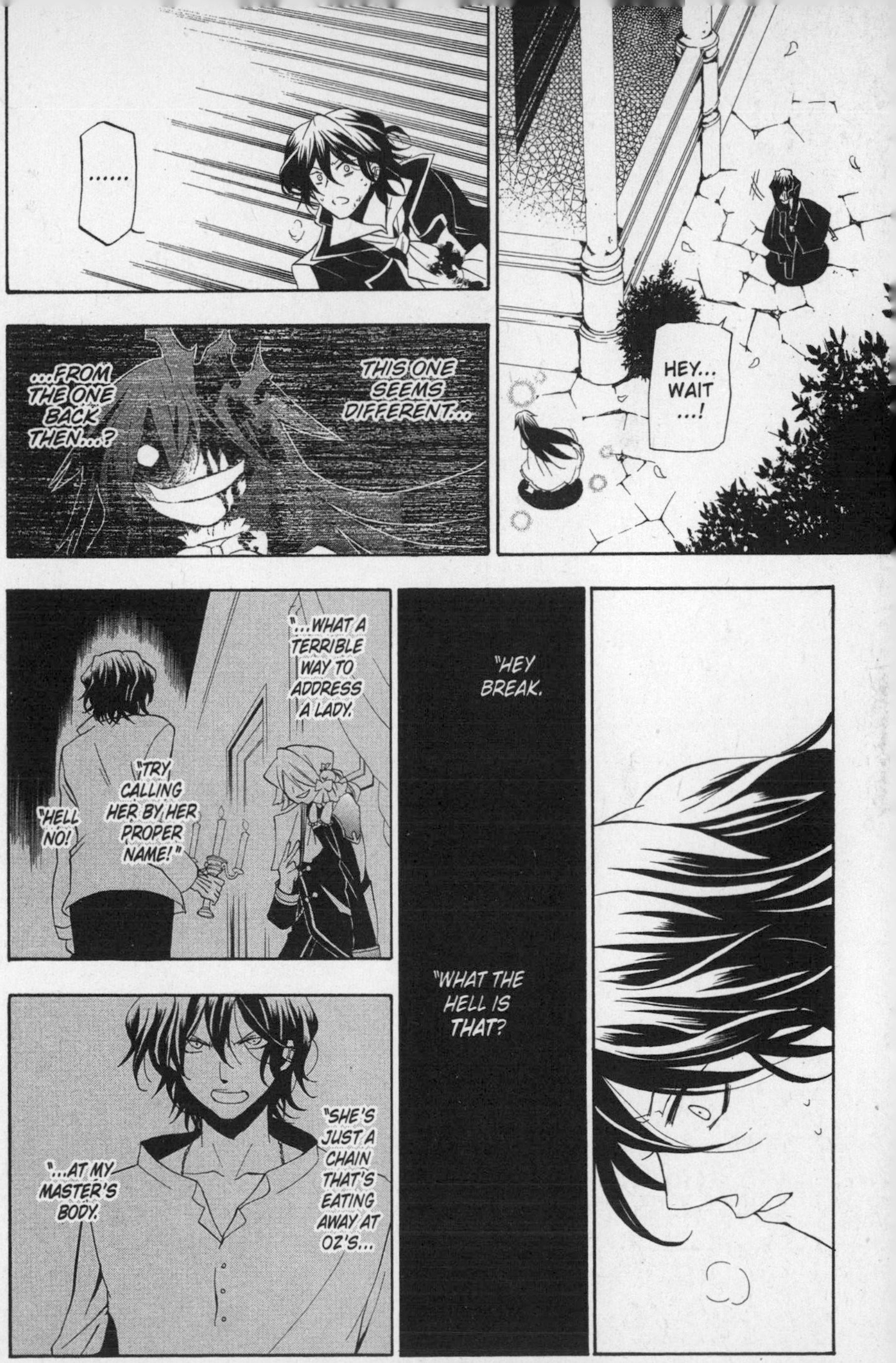
HEY... WAIT ...!
......
THIS ONE SEEMS DIFFERENT...
...FROM THE ONE BACK THEN...?
"HEY BREAK.
"WHAT THE HELL IS THAT?
"...WHAT A TERRIBLE WAY TO ADDRESS A LADY.
"TRY CALLING HER BY HER PROPER NAME!"
"HELL NO!
"SHE'S JUST A CHAIN THAT'S EATING AWAY AT OZ'S...
"...AT MY MASTER'S BODY.

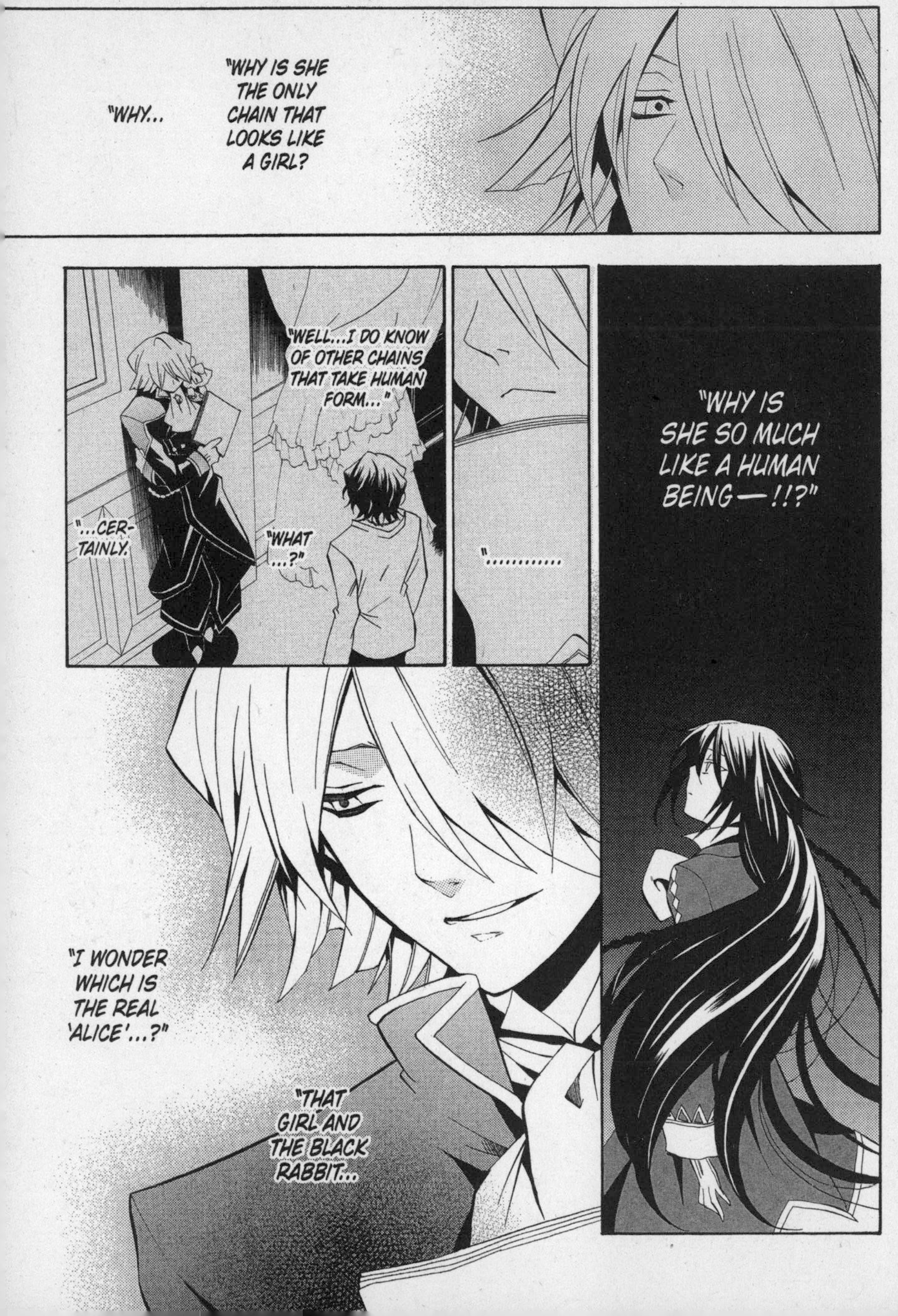
"WHY IS SHE THE ONLY CHAIN THAT LOOKS LIKE A GIRL?
"WHY...
"WHY IS SHE SO MUCH LIKE A HUMAN BEING—!!?"
"..........
"WELL...I DO KNOW OF OTHER CHAINS THAT TAKE HUMAN FORM..."
"WHAT ...?"
"...CER-TAINLY.
"I WONDER WHICH IS THE REAL 'ALICE'...?"
"THAT GIRL AND THE BLACK RABBIT...

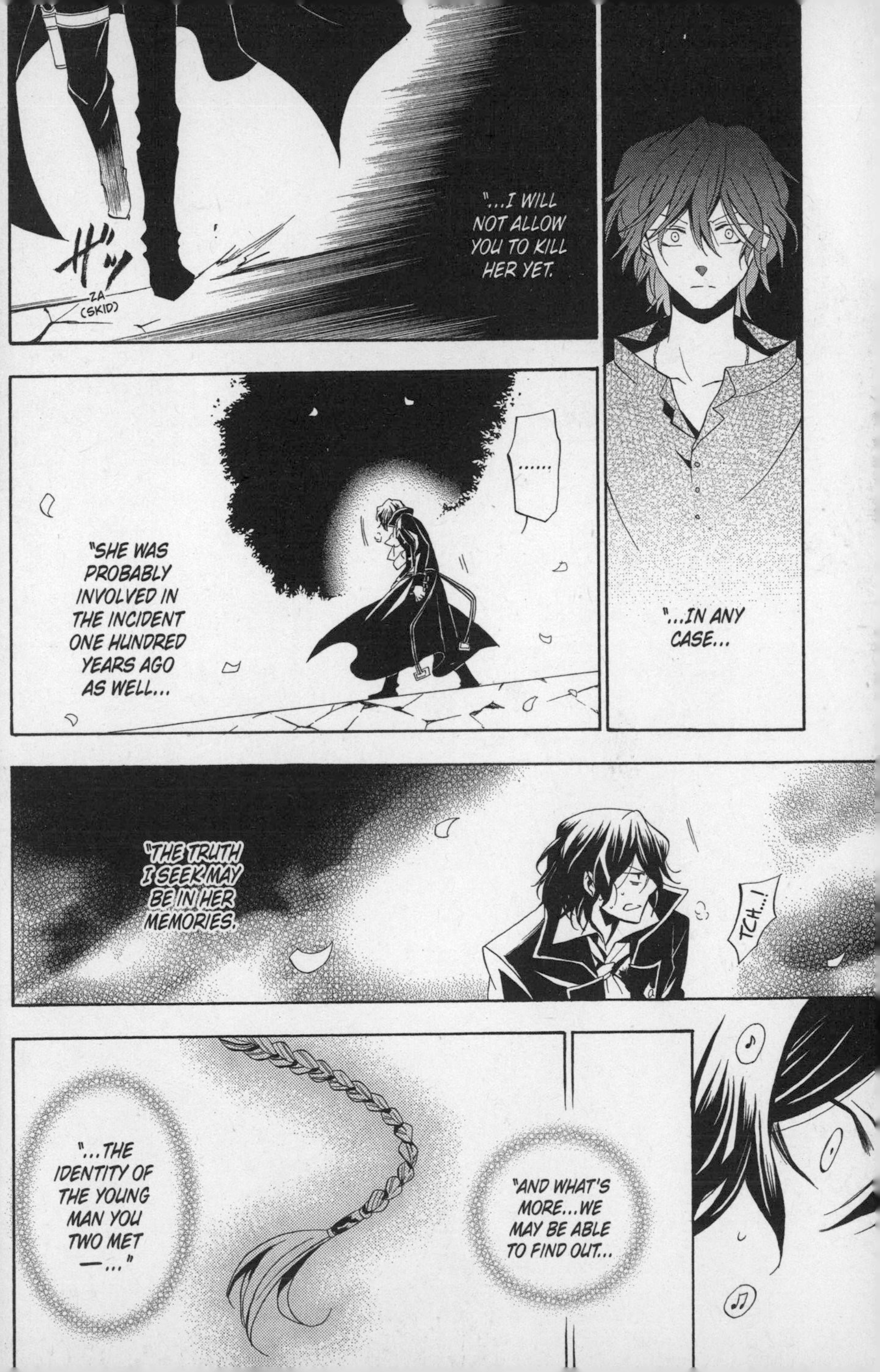
"...IN ANY CASE...
ザッ
ZA (SKID)
"...I WILL NOT ALLOW YOU TO KILL HER YET.
......
"SHE WAS PROBABLY INVOLVED IN THE INCIDENT ONE HUNDRED YEARS AGO AS WELL...
TCH...!
"THE TRUTH I SEEK MAY BE IN HER MEMORIES.
"AND WHAT'S MORE...WE MAY BE ABLE TO FIND OUT...
"...THE IDENTITY OF THE YOUNG MAN YOU TWO MET—..."

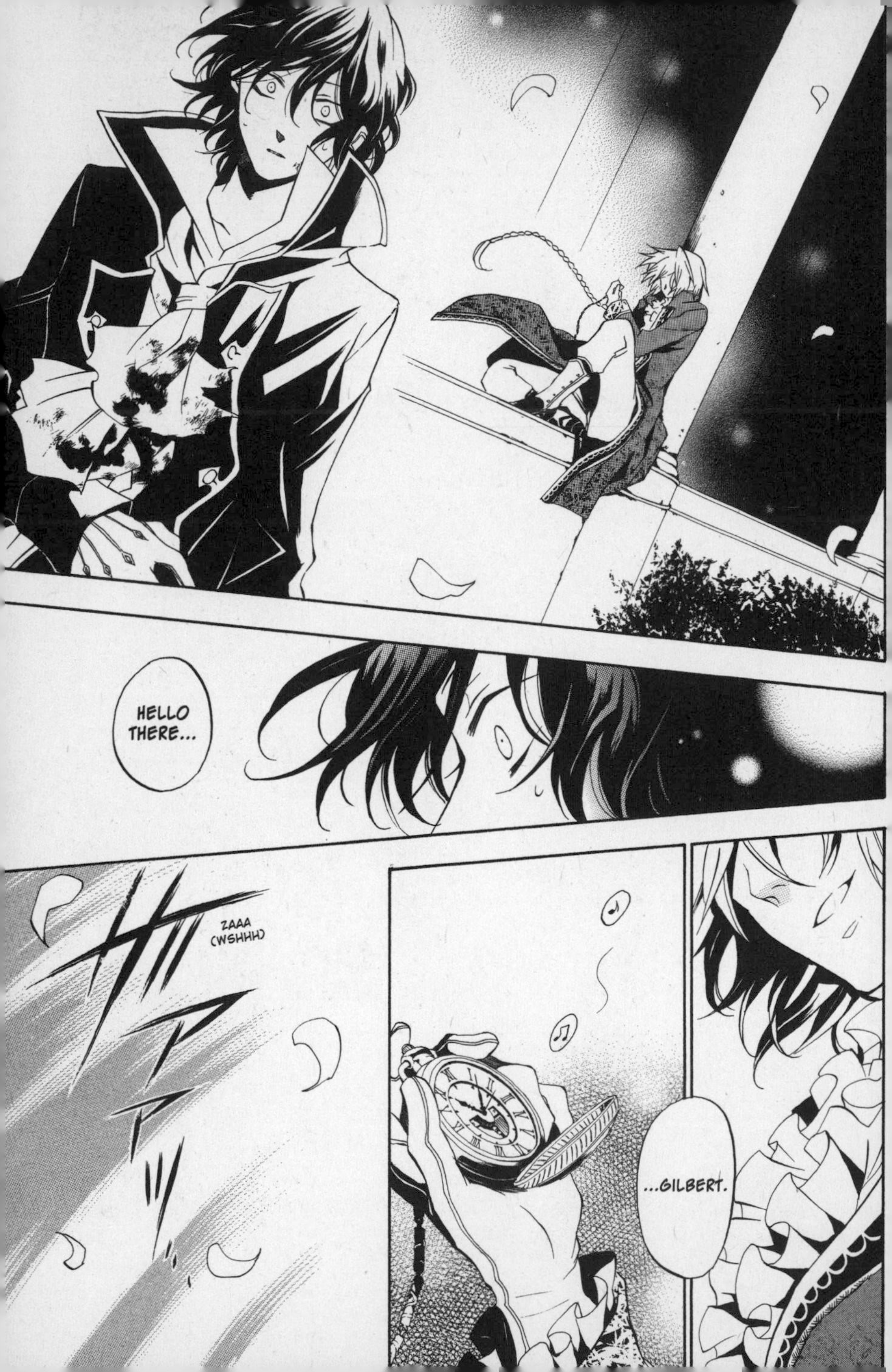
HELLO THERE...
...GILBERT.
ZAAA
(WSHHH)

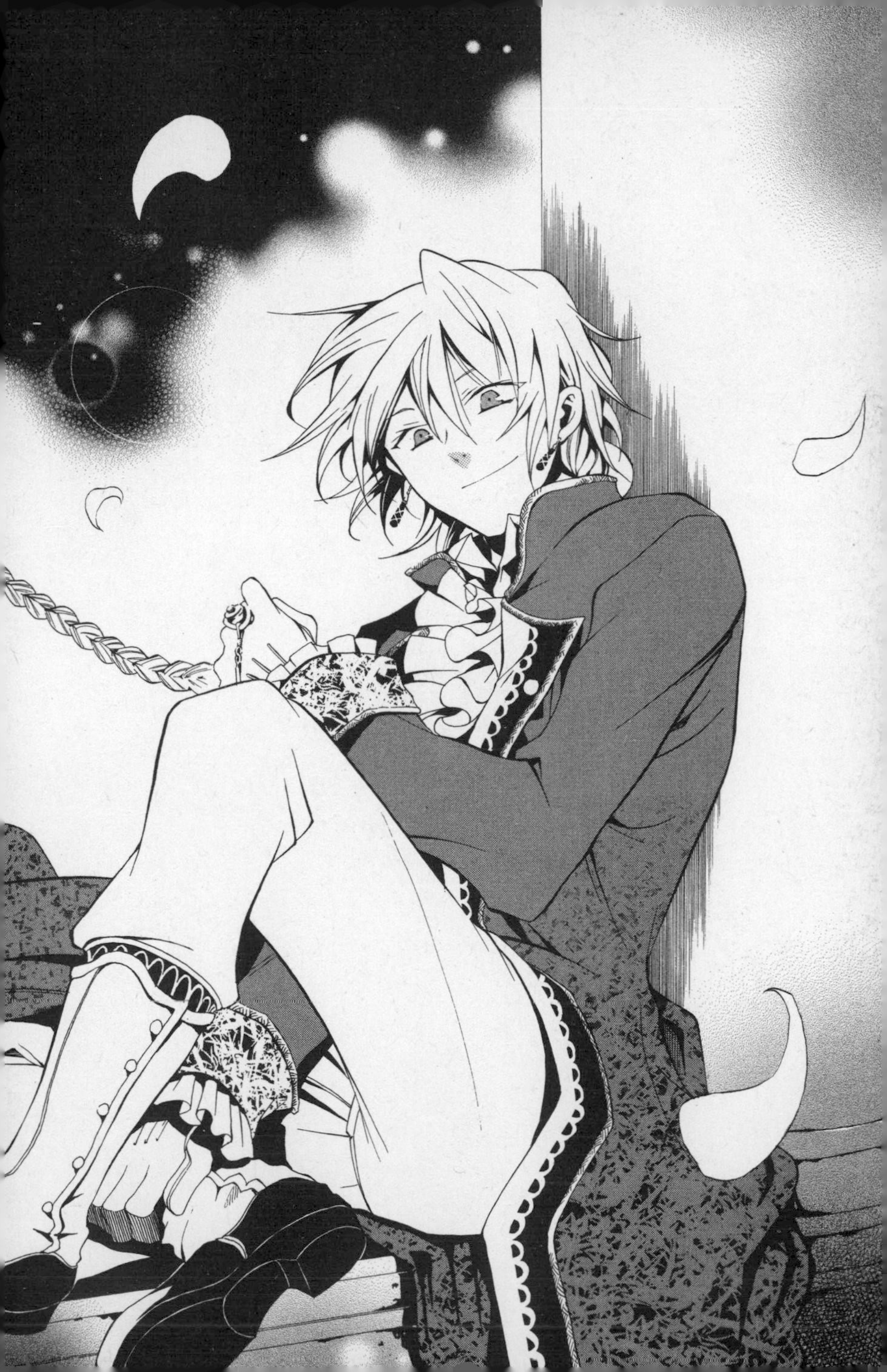

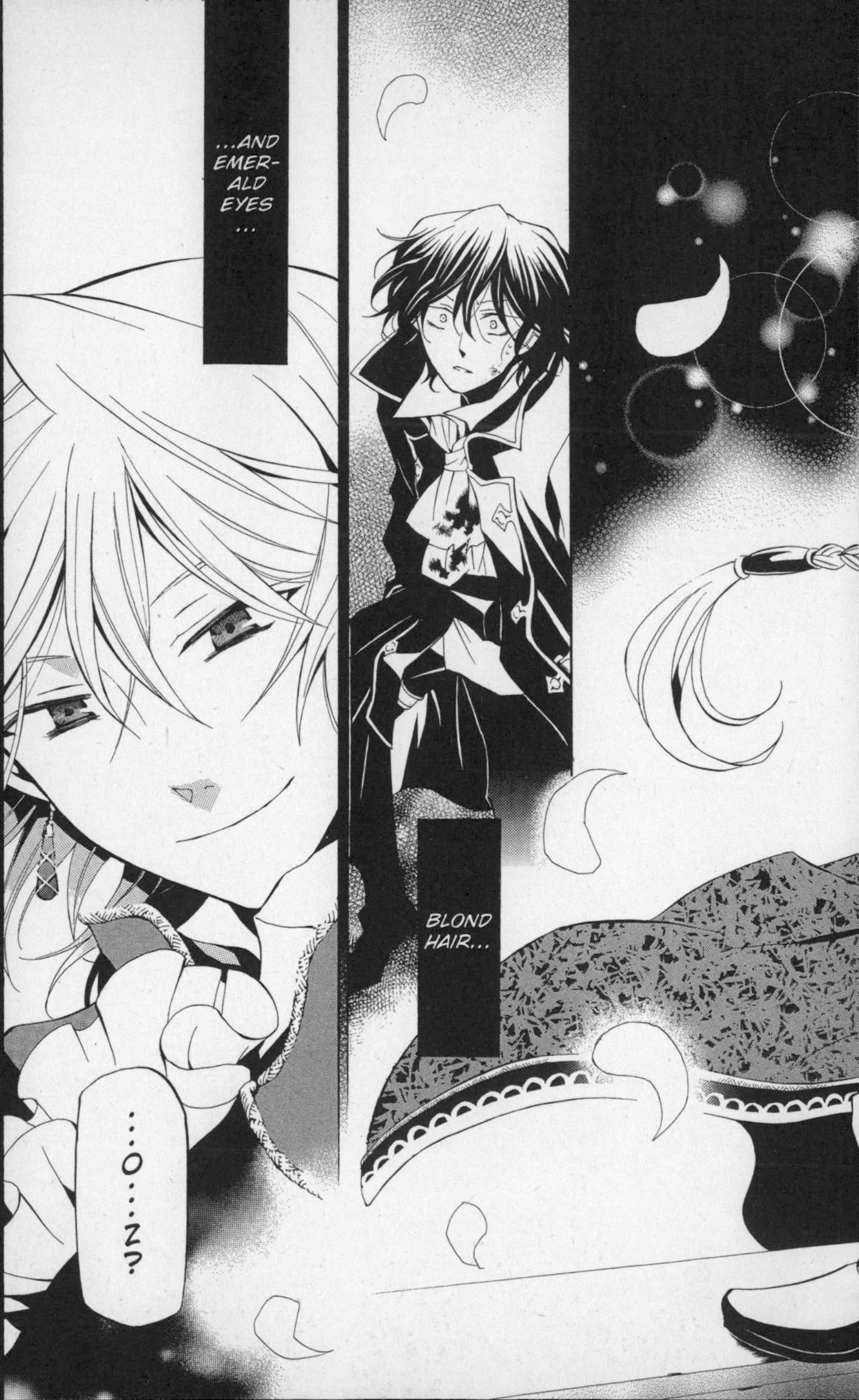
BLOND HAIR...
...AND EMER-ALD EYES ...
...O...Z?

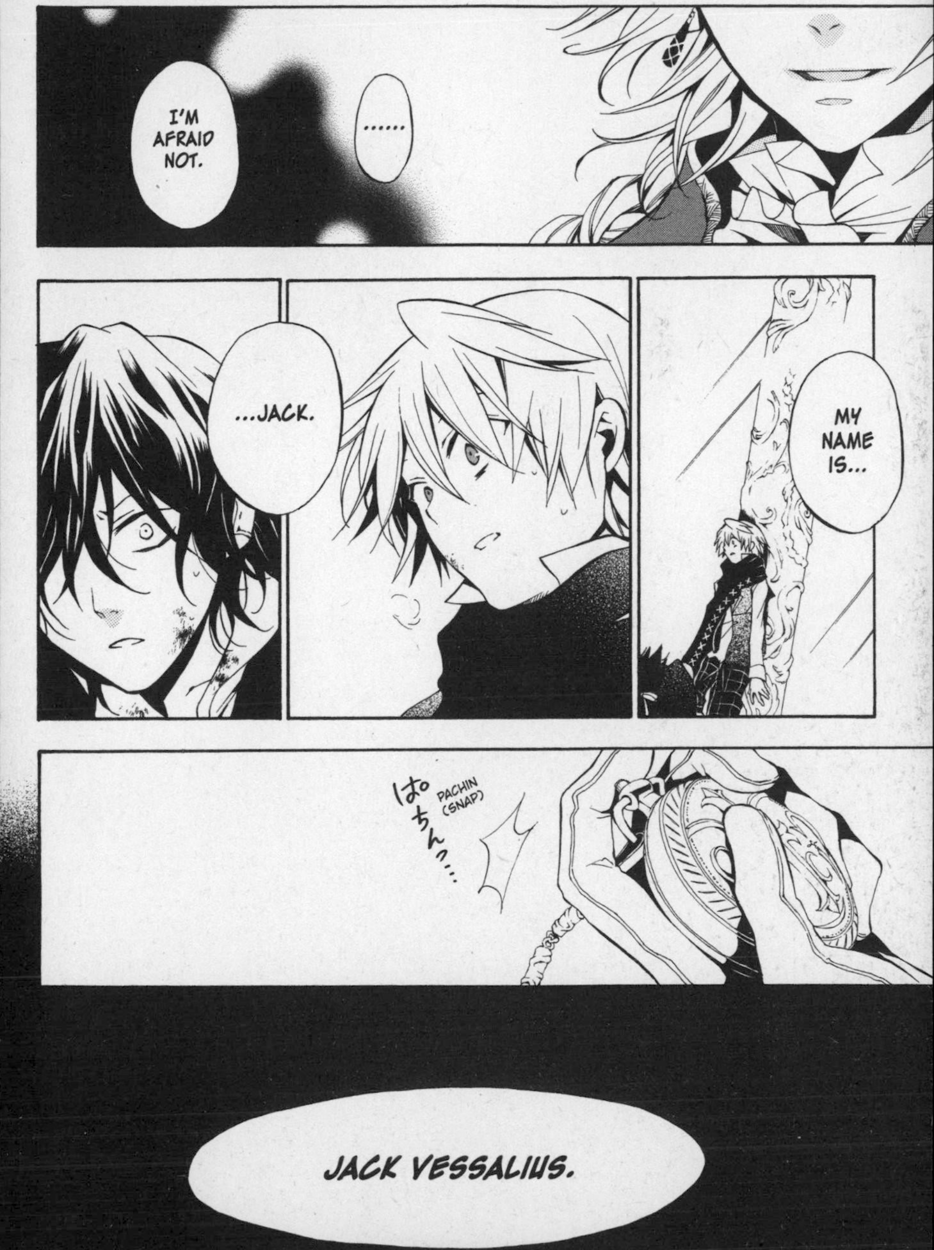

......
I'M AFRAID NOT.
MY NAME IS...
...JACK.
ぱちんっ...
PACHIN (SNAP)
JACK VESSALIUS.

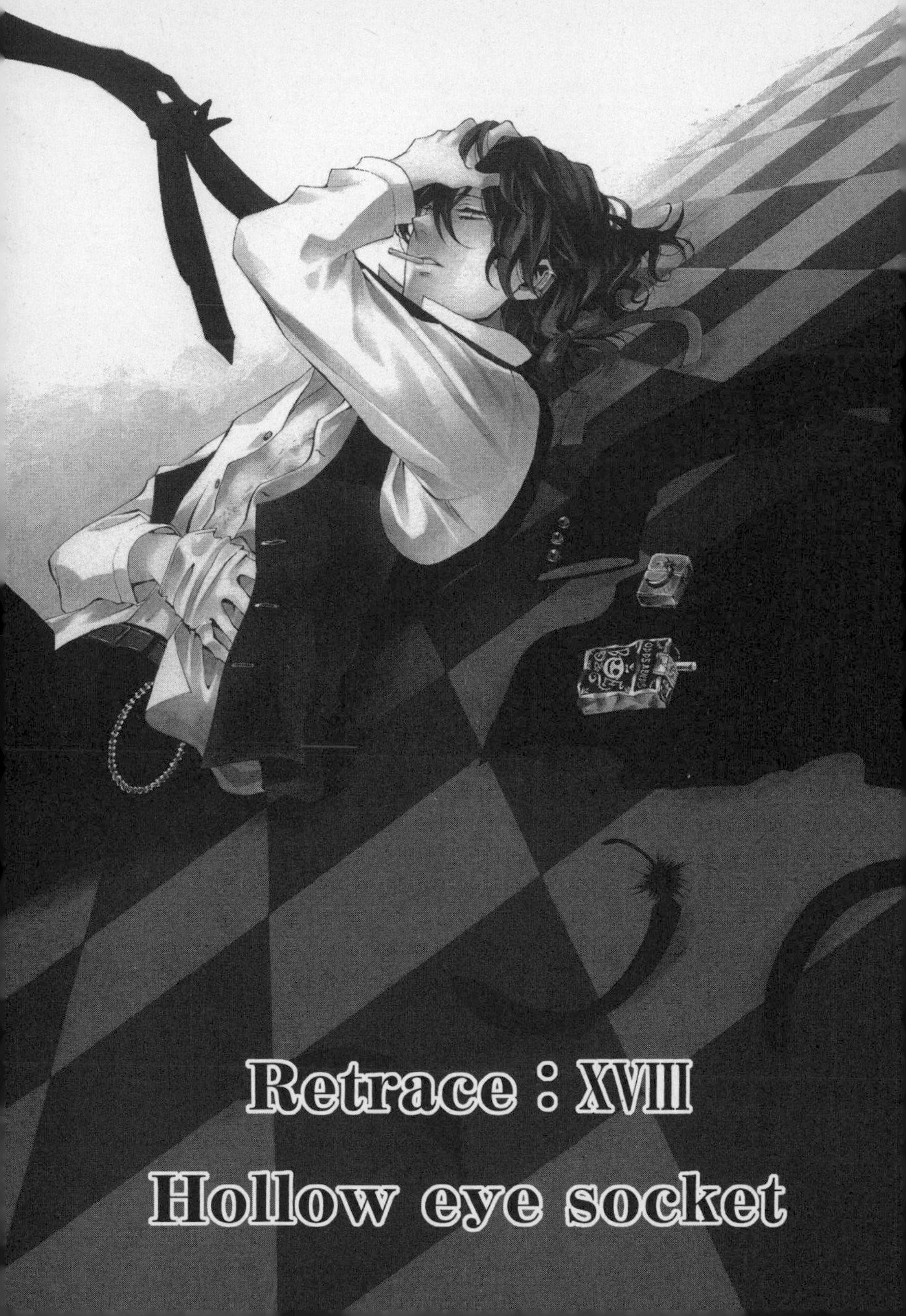

Retrace : XVIII
Hollow eye socket

BONUS: "LITTLE BROTHER...NII-CHAN'S DYING TO KNOW, SO THERE'S NO HELPING IT!"

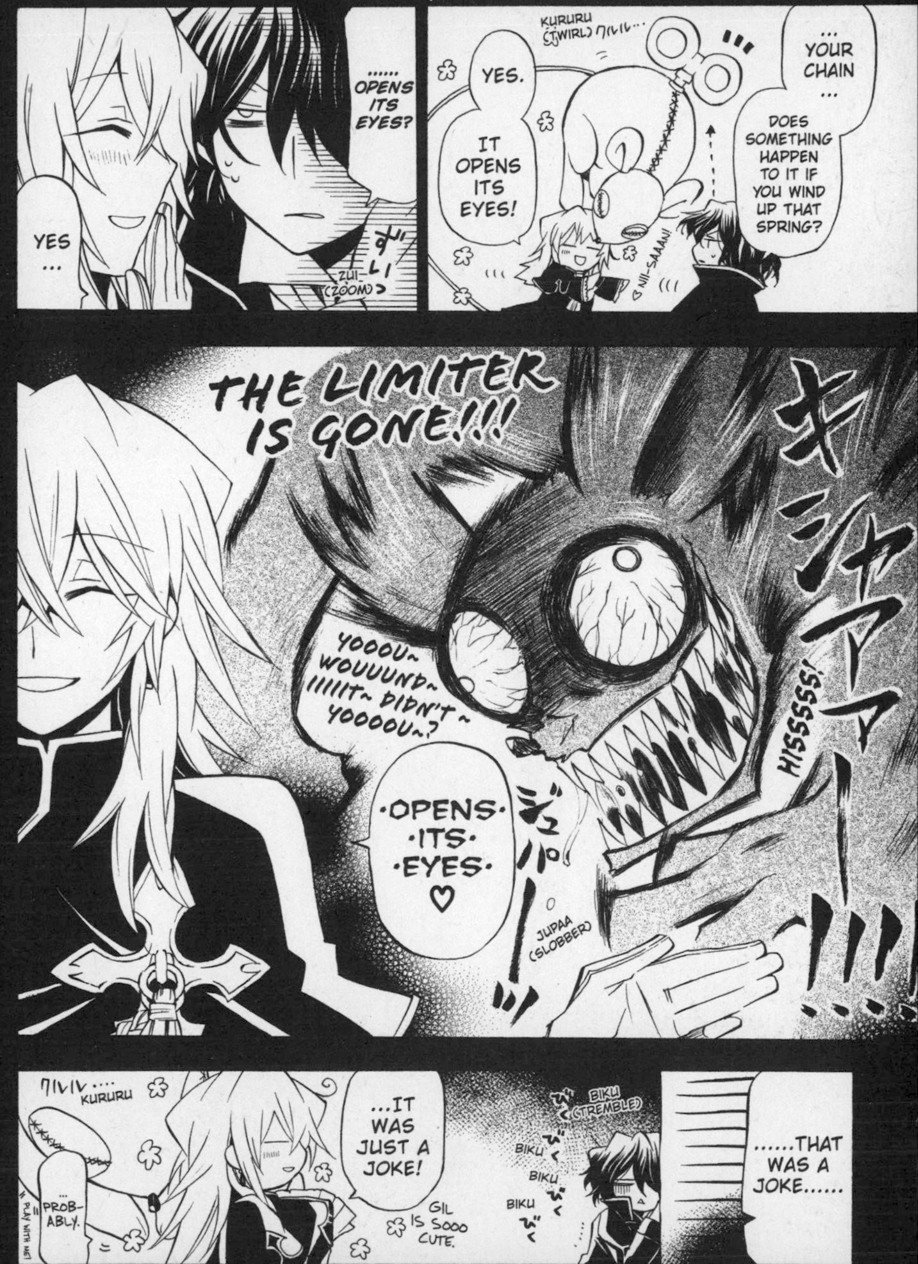

... YOUR CHAIN ... DOES SOMETHING HAPPEN TO IT IF YOU WIND UP THAT SPRING?
KURURU (TWIRL) クルル…
YES.
IT OPENS ITS EYES!
NII-SAAAN!
...... OPENS ITS EYES?
ZUI- (ZOOM)
YES ...
THE LIMITER IS GONE!!!
HISSSSS!
YOOOU~ WOUUUND~ IIIIIT~ DIDN'T~ YOOOOU~?
·OPENS· ·ITS· ·EYES· ♡
JUPAA (SLOBBER)
......THAT WAS A JOKE......
BIKU (TREMBLE)
BIKU
BIKU
BIKU
...IT WAS JUST A JOKE!
クルル.... KURURU
GIL IS SOOO CUTE.
... PROB-ABLY.
PLAY WITH ME!

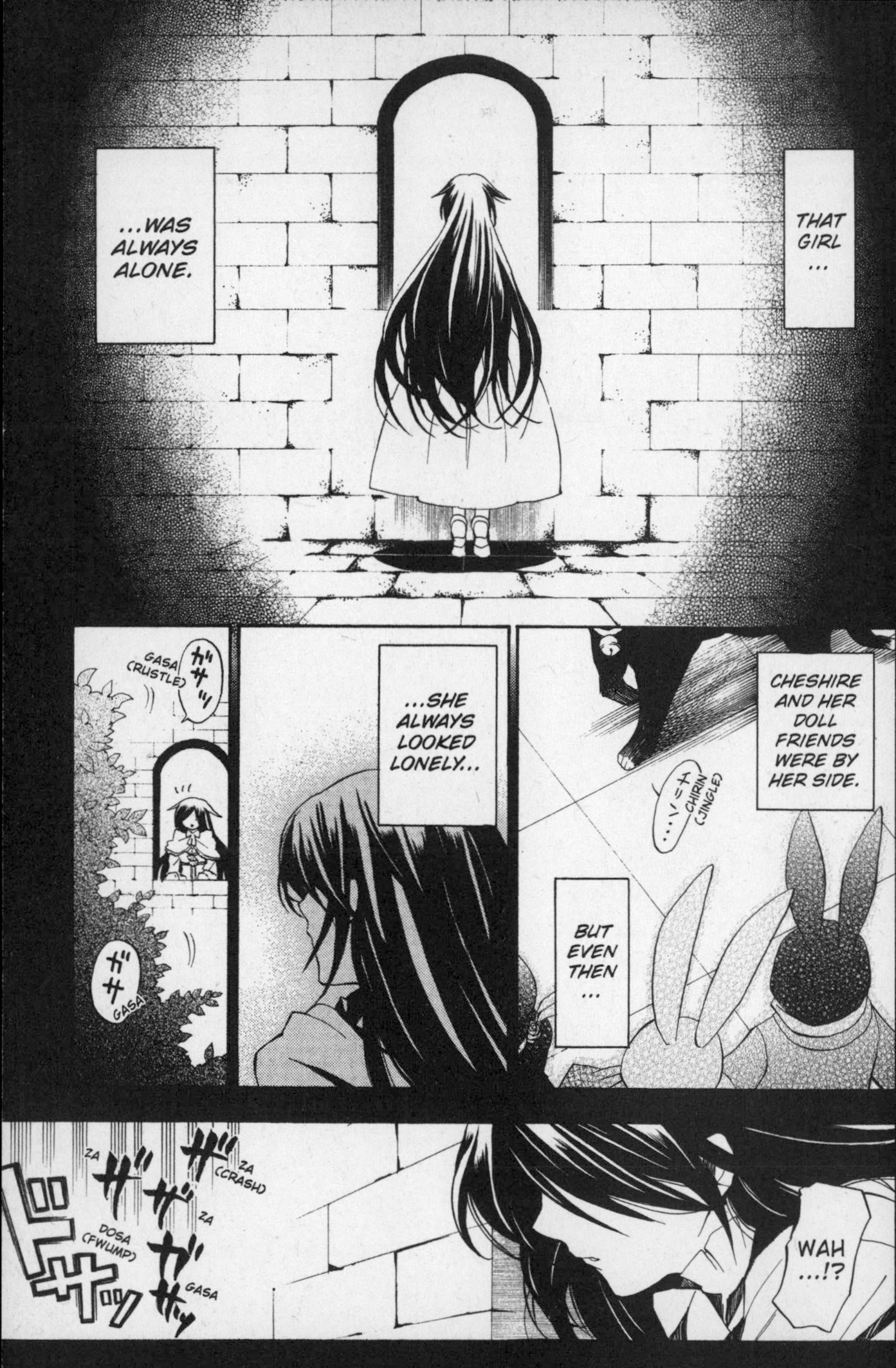

THAT GIRL ...
...WAS ALWAYS ALONE.
CHESHIRE AND HER DOLL FRIENDS WERE BY HER SIDE.
CHIRIN (JINGLE)
BUT EVEN THEN ...
...SHE ALWAYS LOOKED LONELY...
ガサッ
GASA (RUSTLE)
ガサ
GASA
WAH ...!?
ZA (CRASH)
ZA
ZA
GASA
DOSA (FWUMP)

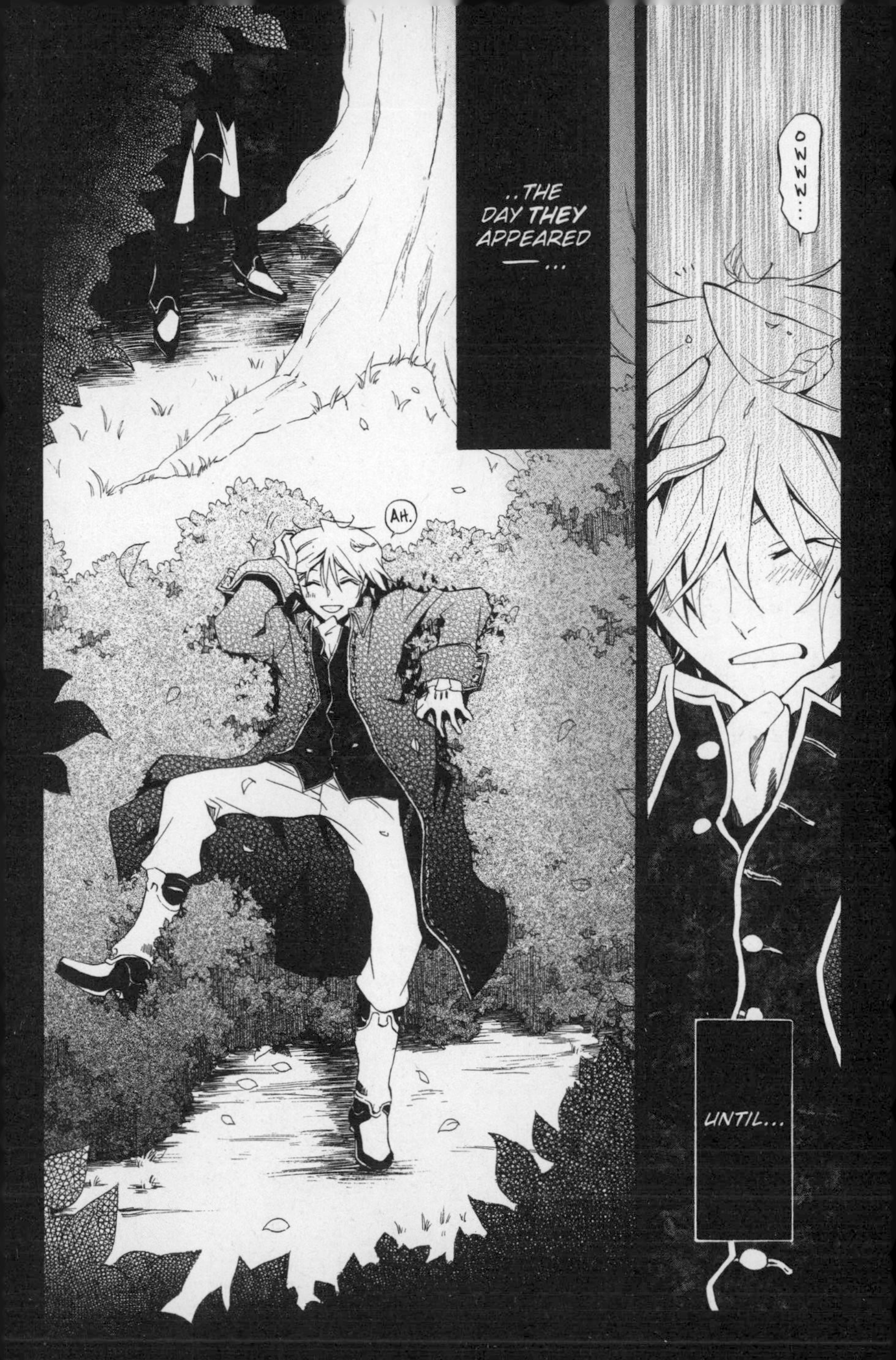
OWWW...
UNTIL...
..THE DAY THEY APPEARED —...
AH.

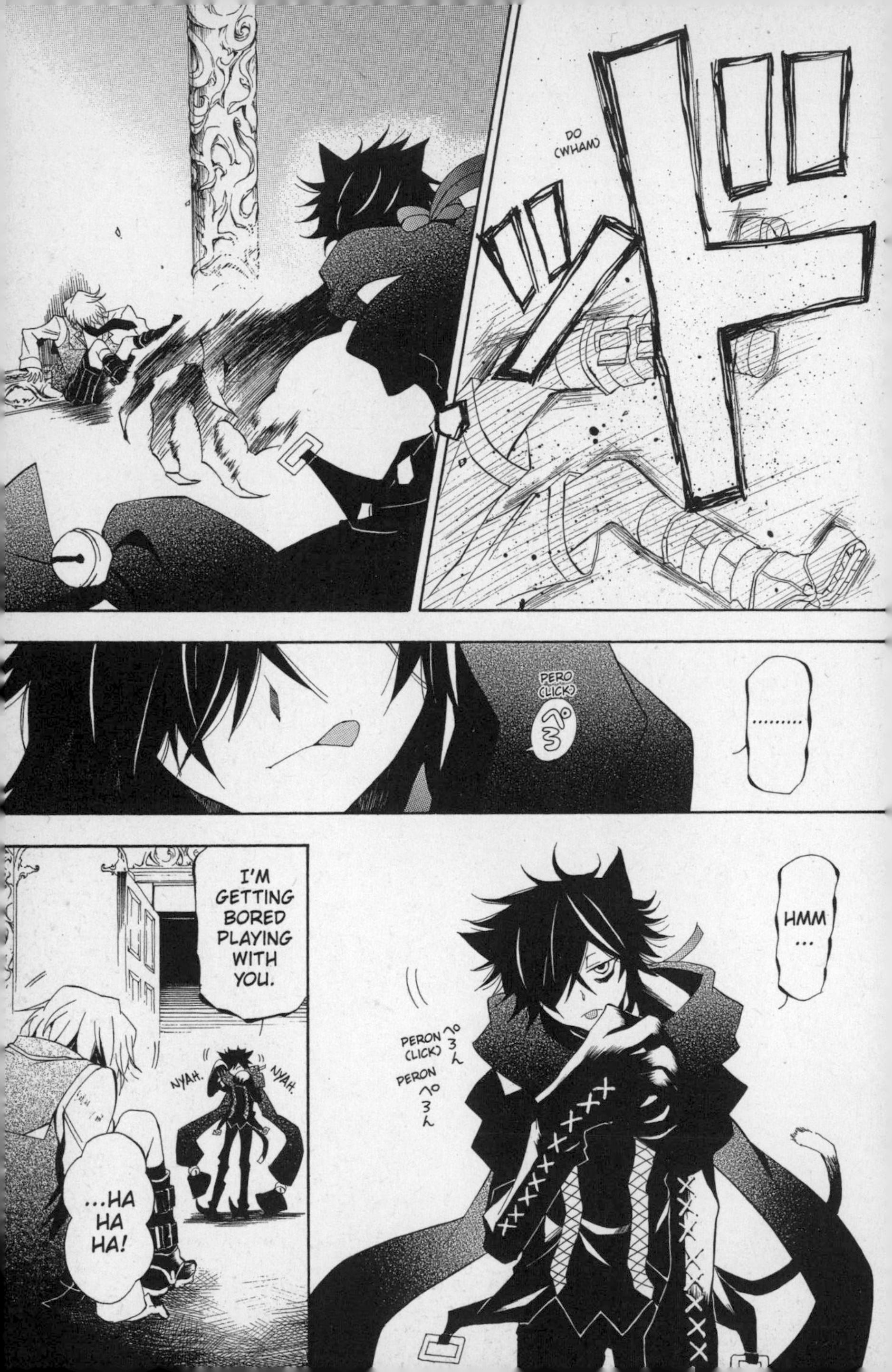
DO (WHAM)
....
PERO (LICK) ぺろ
HMM ...
PERON (LICK) ぺろん
PERON ぺろん
I'M GETTING BORED PLAYING WITH YOU.
NYAH.
NYAH.
...HA HA HA!

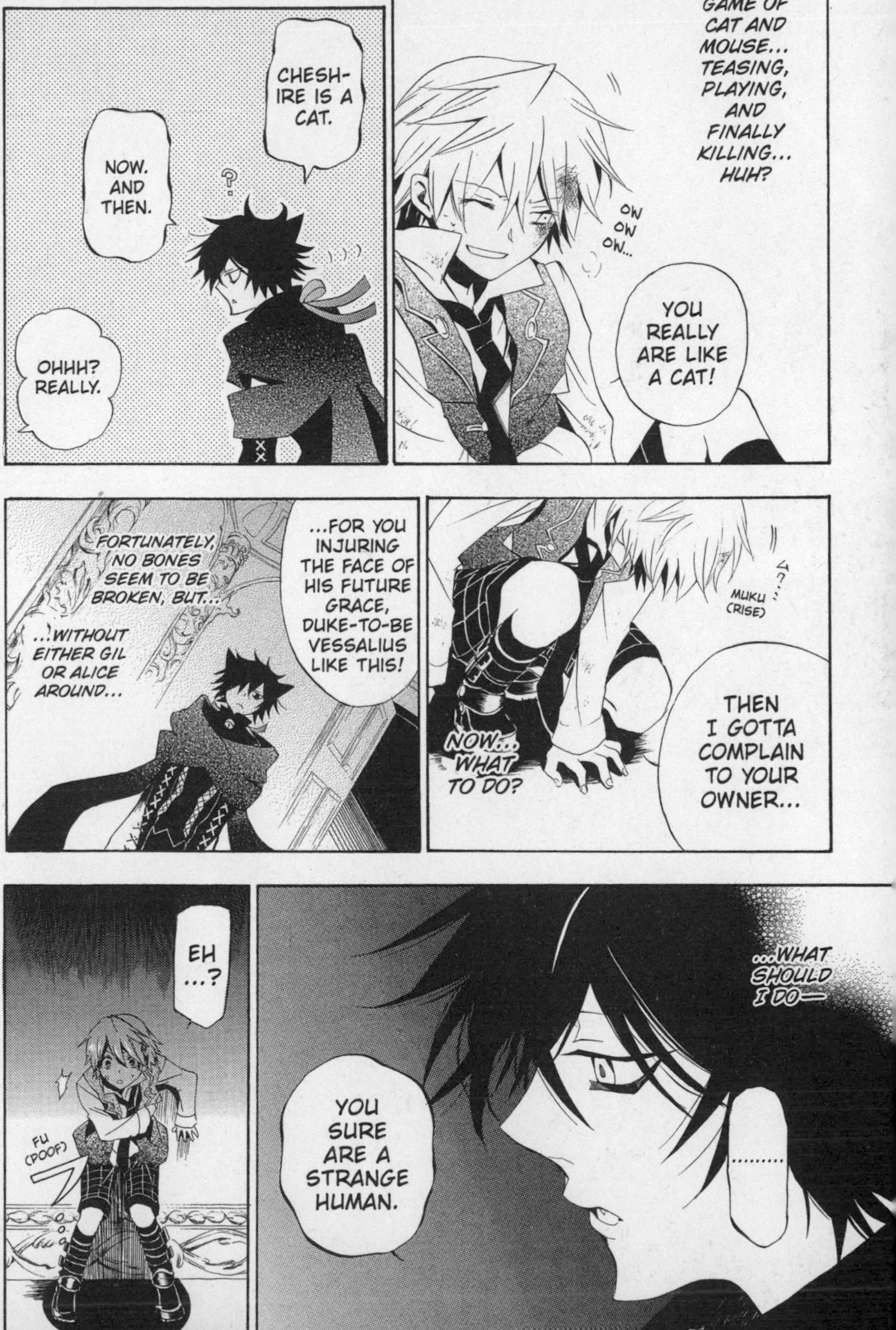
LIKE A GAME OF CAT AND MOUSE... TEASING, PLAYING, AND FINALLY KILLING... HUH?
OW OW OW...
YOU REALLY ARE LIKE A CAT!
CHESH-IRE IS A CAT.
NOW. AND THEN.
OHHH? REALLY.
MUKU (RISE)
THEN I GOTTA COMPLAIN TO YOUR OWNER...
NOW... WHAT TO DO?
...FOR YOU INJURING THE FACE OF HIS FUTURE GRACE, DUKE-TO-BE VESSALIUS LIKE THIS!
FORTUNATELY, NO BONES SEEM TO BE BROKEN, BUT...
...WITHOUT EITHER GIL OR ALICE AROUND...
...WHAT SHOULD I DO—
....
YOU SURE ARE A STRANGE HUMAN.
EH ...?
FU (POOF)

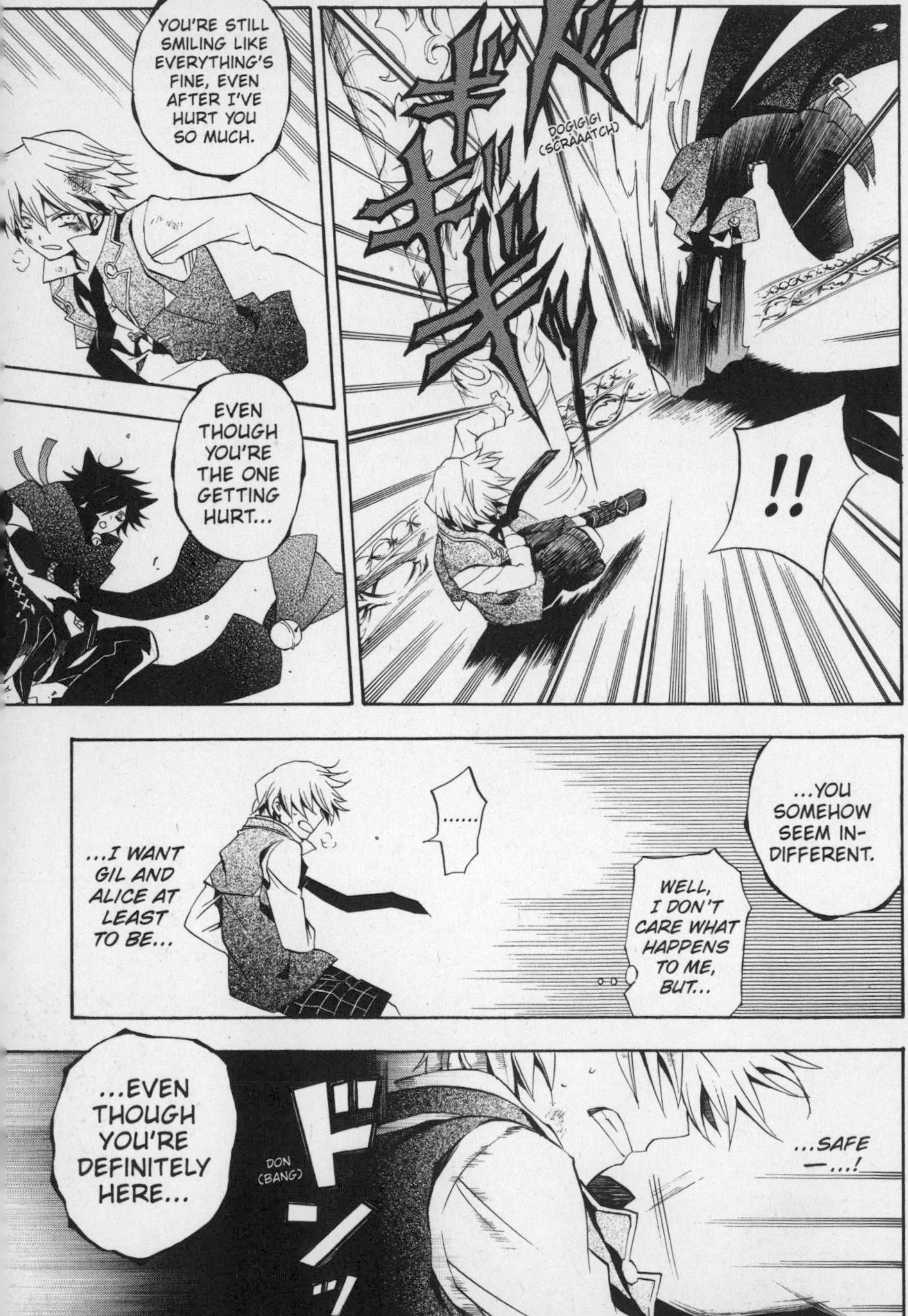
DOGIGIGI (SCRAAATCH)
!!
YOU'RE STILL SMILING LIKE EVERYTHING'S FINE, EVEN AFTER I'VE HURT YOU SO MUCH.
EVEN THOUGH YOU'RE THE ONE GETTING HURT...
...YOU SOMEHOW SEEM IN-DIFFERENT.
WELL, I DON'T CARE WHAT HAPPENS TO ME, BUT...
......
...I WANT GIL AND ALICE AT LEAST TO BE...
...SAFE—...!
DON (BANG)
...EVEN THOUGH YOU'RE DEFINITELY HERE...

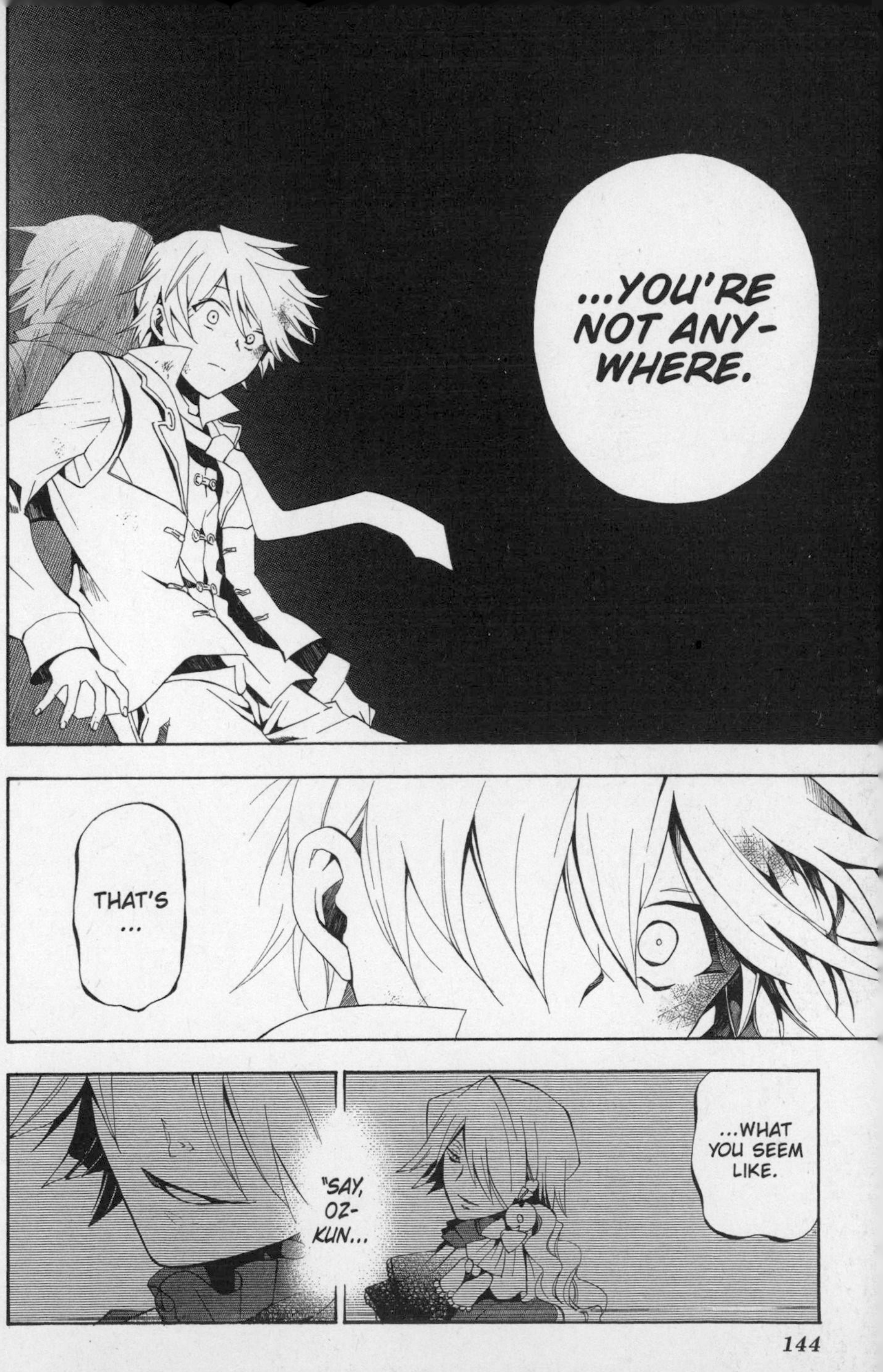
...YOU'RE NOT ANY-WHERE.
THAT'S ...
...WHAT YOU SEEM LIKE.
"SAY, OZ-KUN...

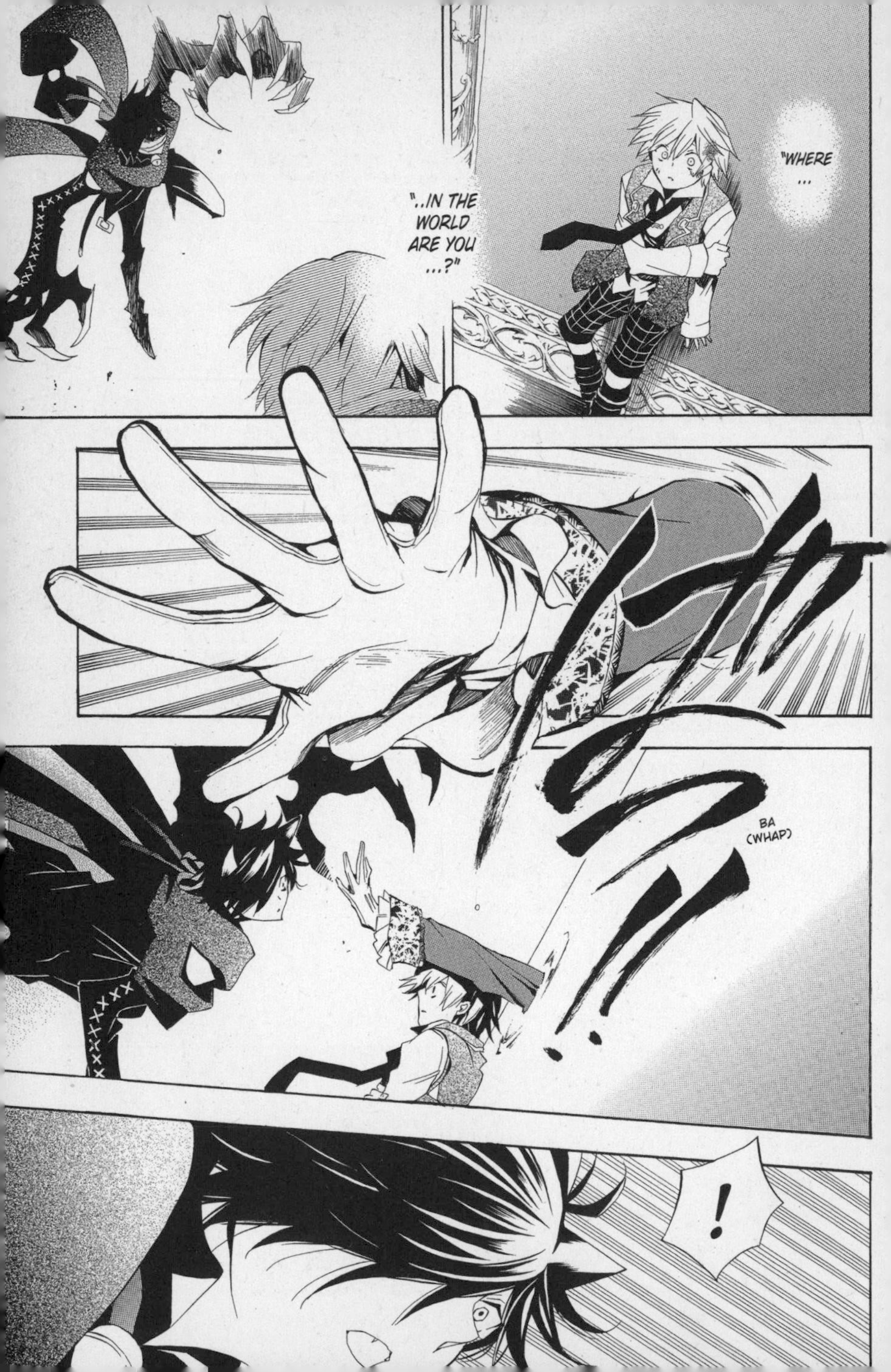
"WHERE ...
"..IN THE WORLD ARE YOU ...?"
BA (WHAP)
!

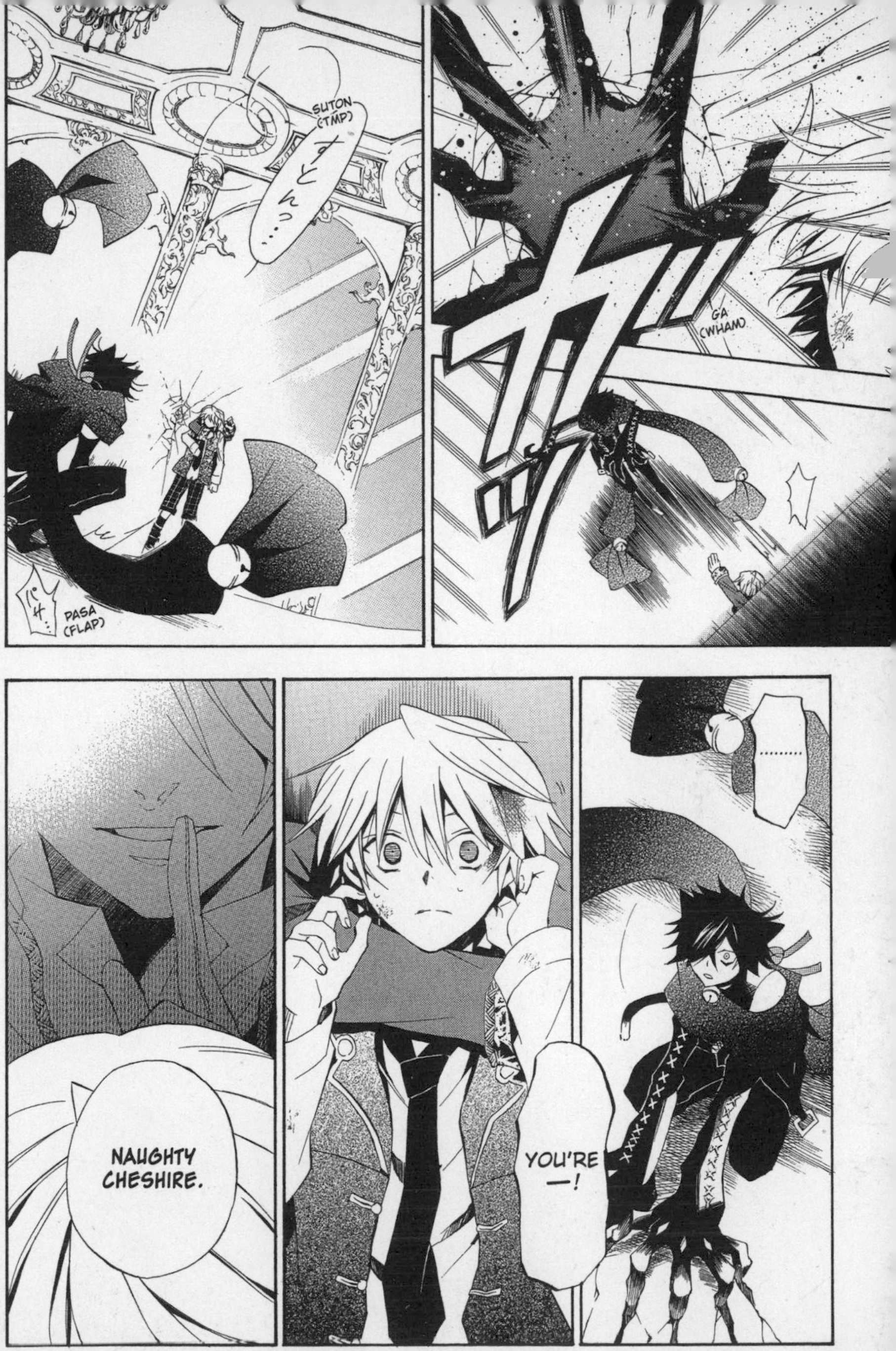
GA
(WHAM)
!
SUTON
(TMP)
すとんっ…
パサ…
PASA
(FLAP)
......
YOU'RE —!
NAUGHTY CHESHIRE.

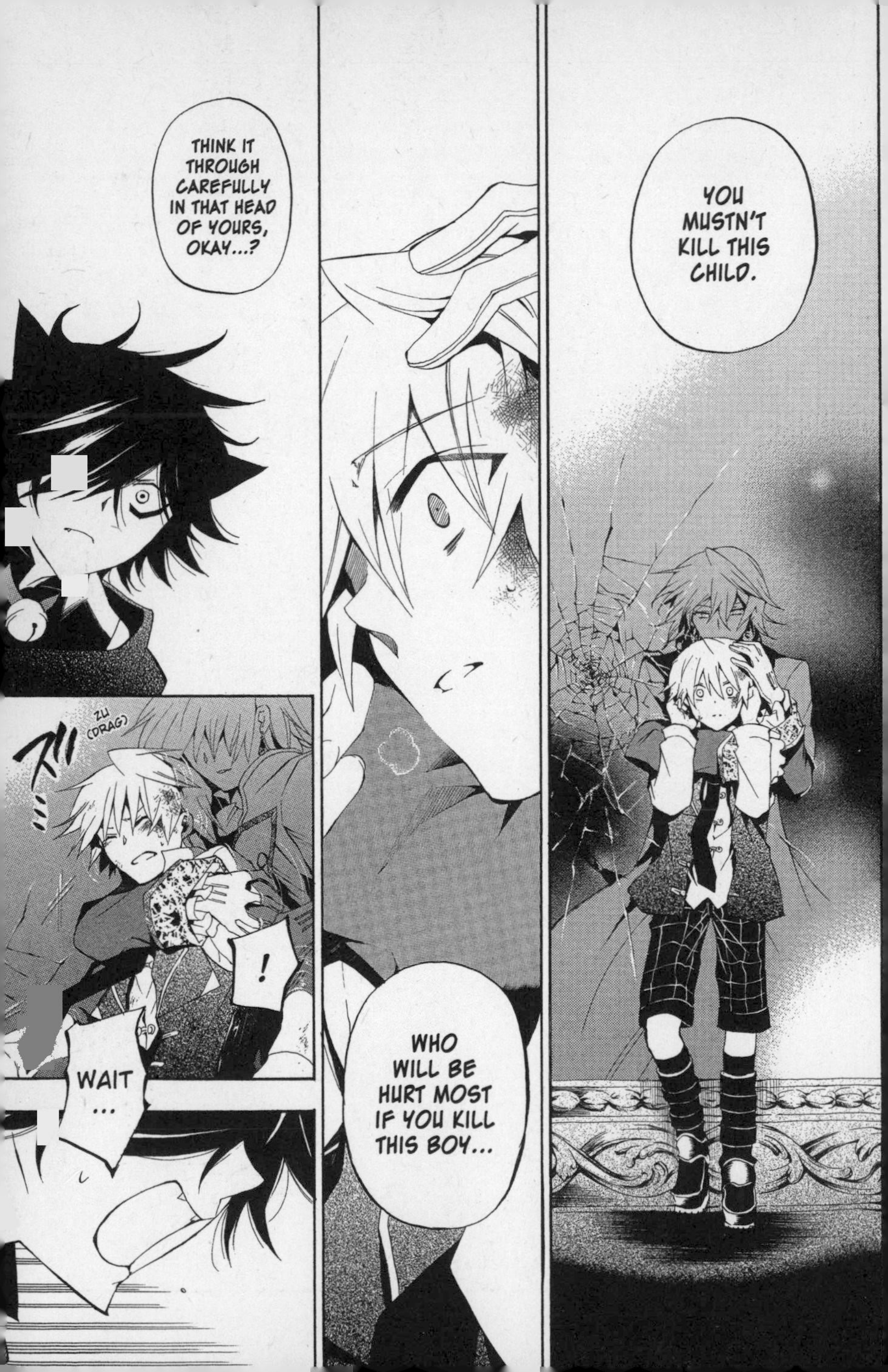
YOU MUSTN'T KILL THIS CHILD.
WHO WILL BE HURT MOST IF YOU KILL THIS BOY...
THINK IT THROUGH CAREFULLY IN THAT HEAD OF YOURS, OKAY...?
ZU (DRAG)
!
WAIT ...

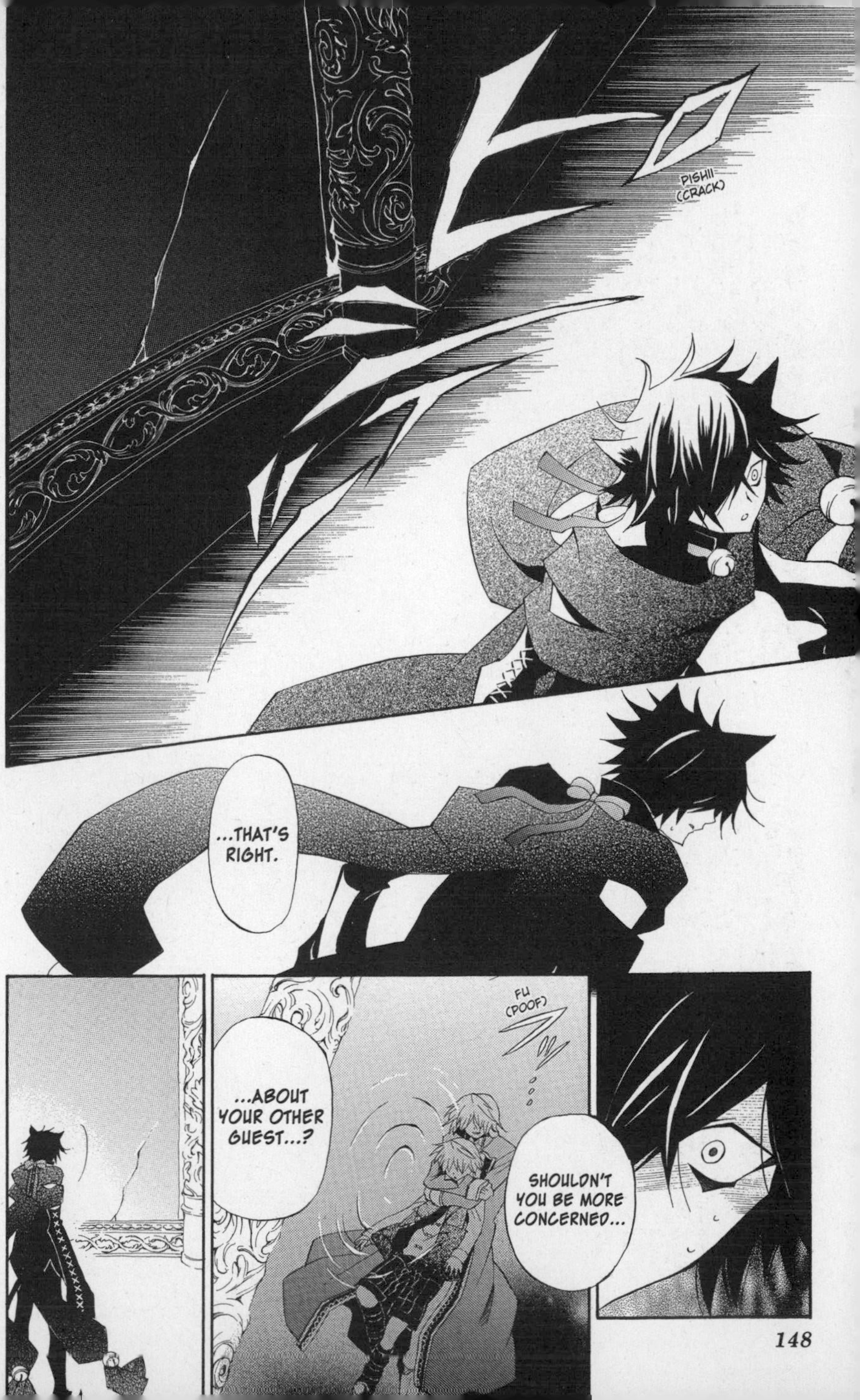
PISHII (CRACK)
...THAT'S RIGHT.
FU (POOF)
SHOULDN'T YOU BE MORE CONCERNED...
...ABOUT YOUR OTHER GUEST...?

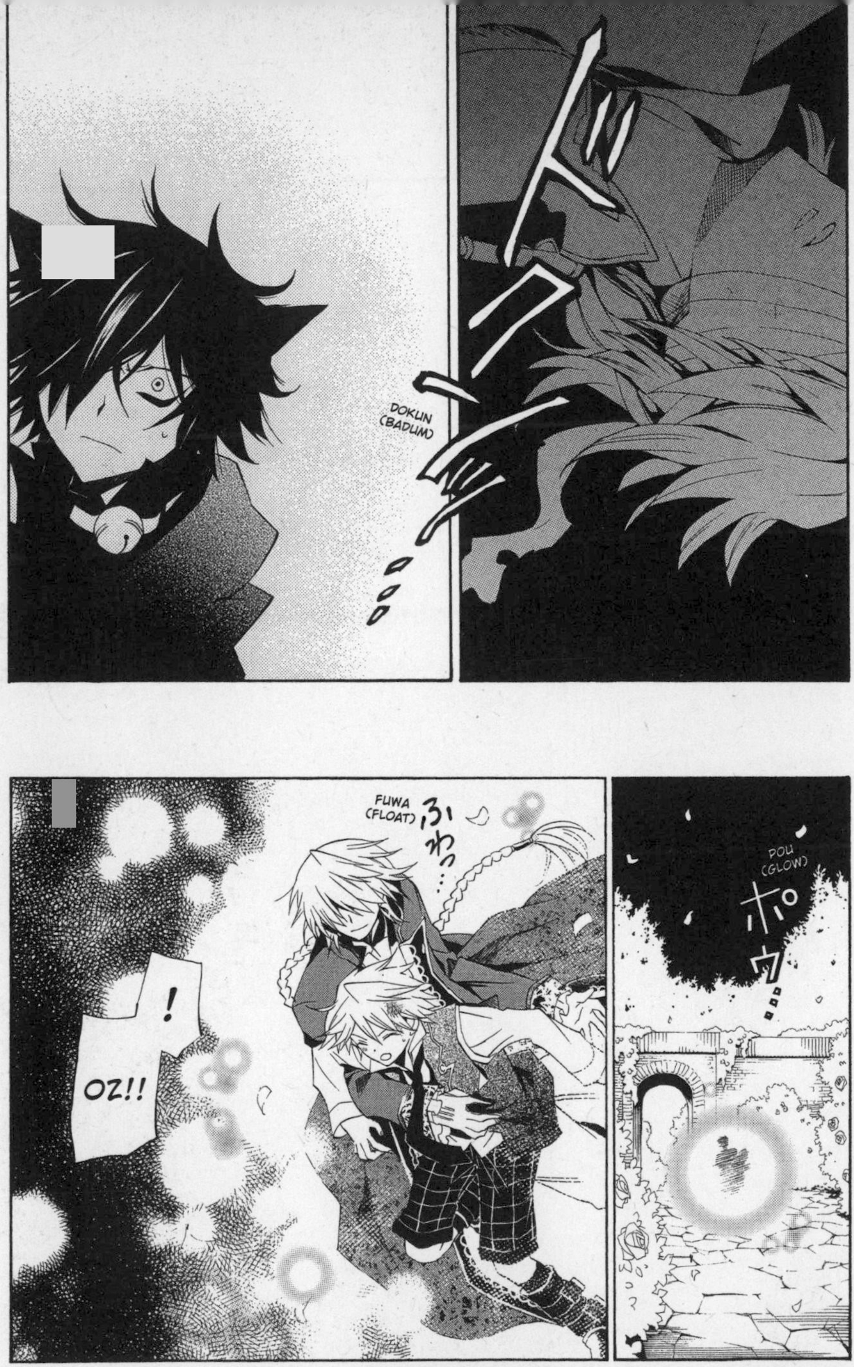
DOKUN (BADUM)
POU (GLOW)
ポゥ…
FUWA (FLOAT)
ふわっ…
!
OZ!!

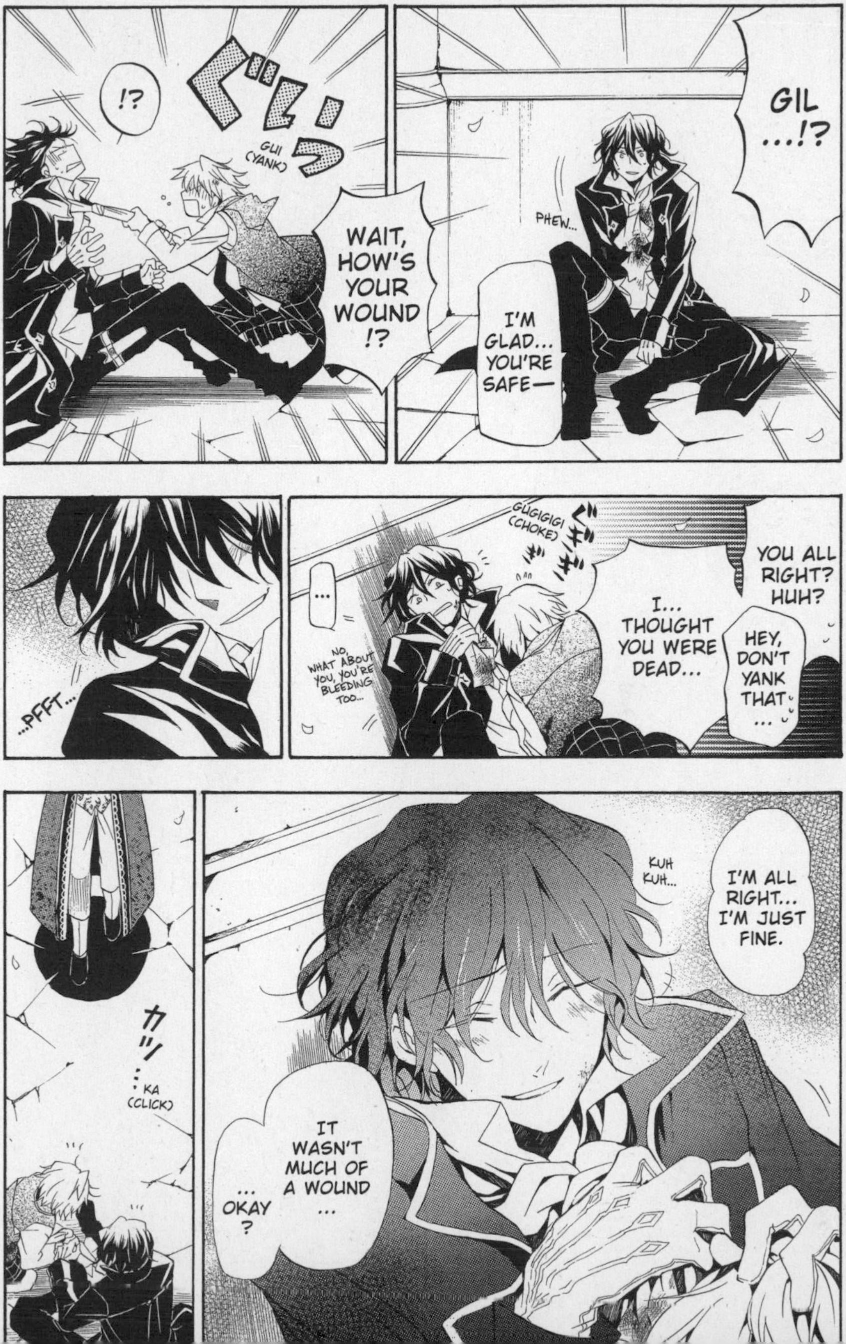
GIL ...!?
PHEW...
I'M GLAD... YOU'RE SAFE—
ぐいっ
GUI (YANK)
!?
WAIT, HOW'S YOUR WOUND !?
YOU ALL RIGHT? HUH?
HEY, DON'T YANK THAT ...
I... THOUGHT YOU WERE DEAD...
GUGIGIGI (CHOKE)
...
NO, WHAT ABOUT YOU, YOU'RE BLEEDING TOO...
...PFFT...
KUH KUH...
I'M ALL RIGHT... I'M JUST FINE.
IT WASN'T MUCH OF A WOUND ...
... OKAY ?
カッ
KA (CLICK)

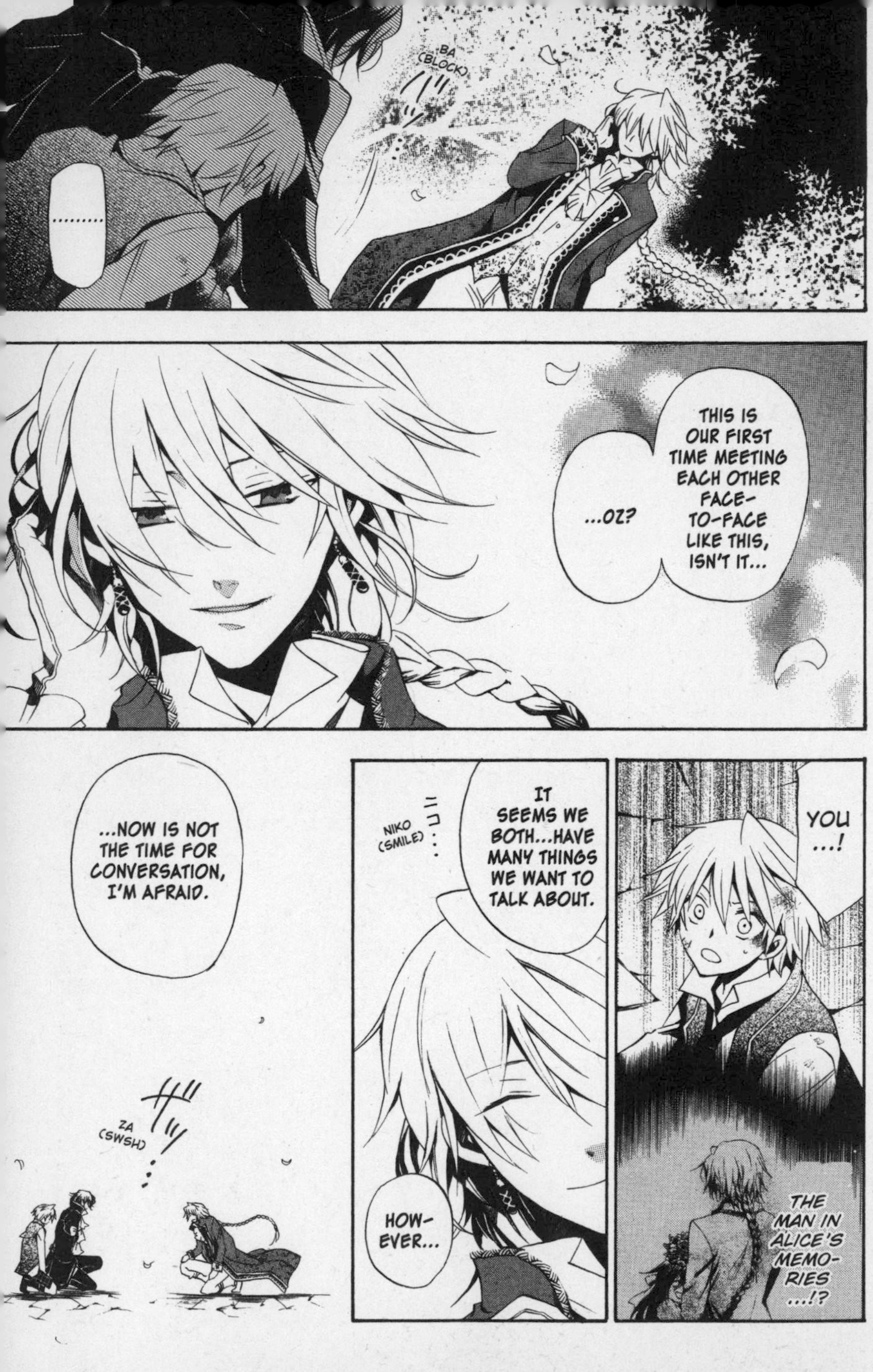
BA (BLOCK)
....
THIS IS OUR FIRST TIME MEETING EACH OTHER FACE-TO-FACE LIKE THIS, ISN'T IT...
...OZ?
YOU ...!
THE MAN IN ALICE'S MEMORIES ...!?
IT SEEMS WE BOTH...HAVE MANY THINGS WE WANT TO TALK ABOUT.
NIKO (SMILE)
HOW-EVER...
...NOW IS NOT THE TIME FOR CONVERSATION, I'M AFRAID.
ZA (SWSH)

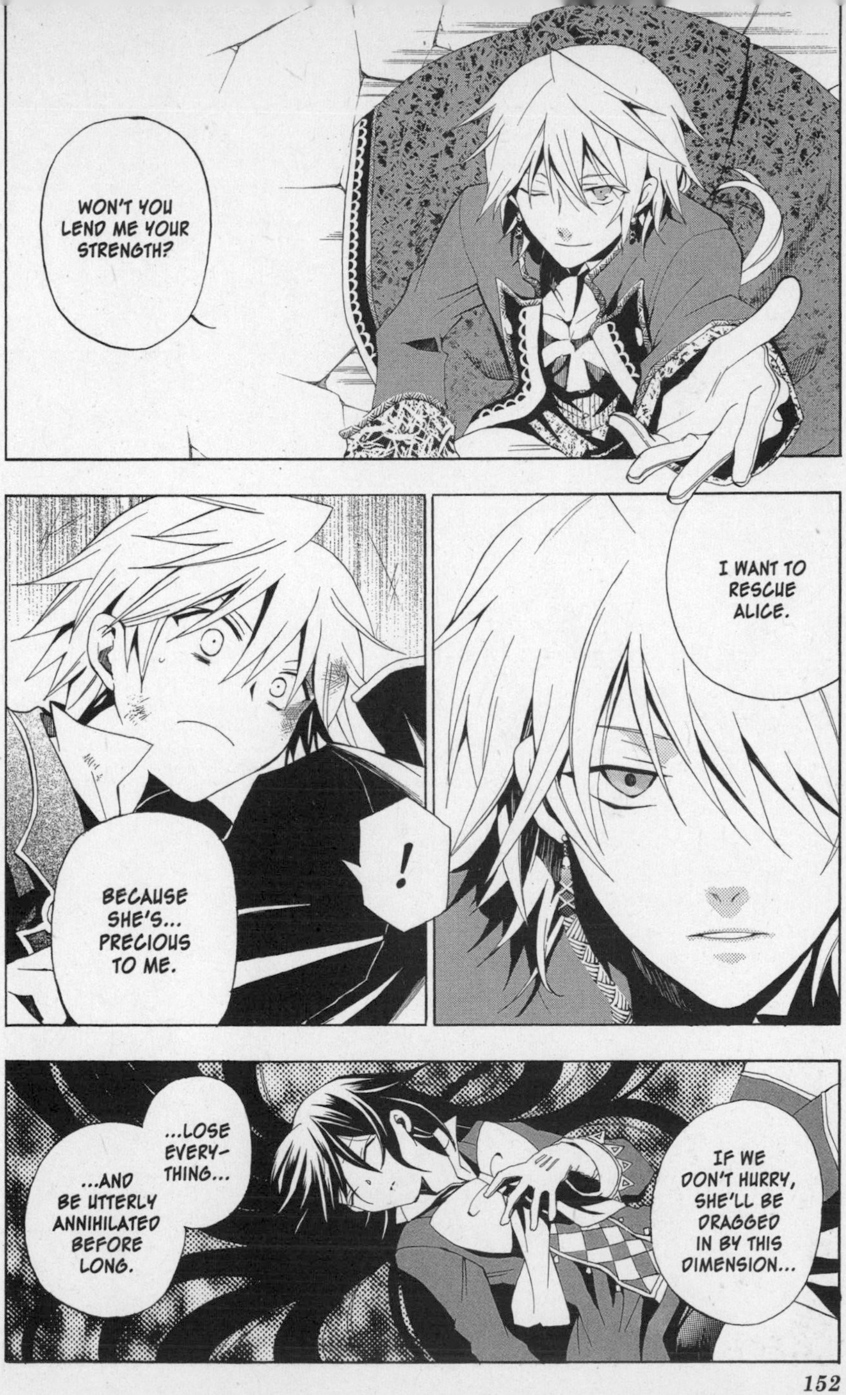
WON'T YOU LEND ME YOUR STRENGTH?
I WANT TO RESCUE ALICE.
!
BECAUSE SHE'S... PRECIOUS TO ME.
IF WE DON'T HURRY, SHE'LL BE DRAGGED IN BY THIS DIMENSION...
...LOSE EVERY-THING...
...AND BE UTTERLY ANNIHILATED BEFORE LONG.

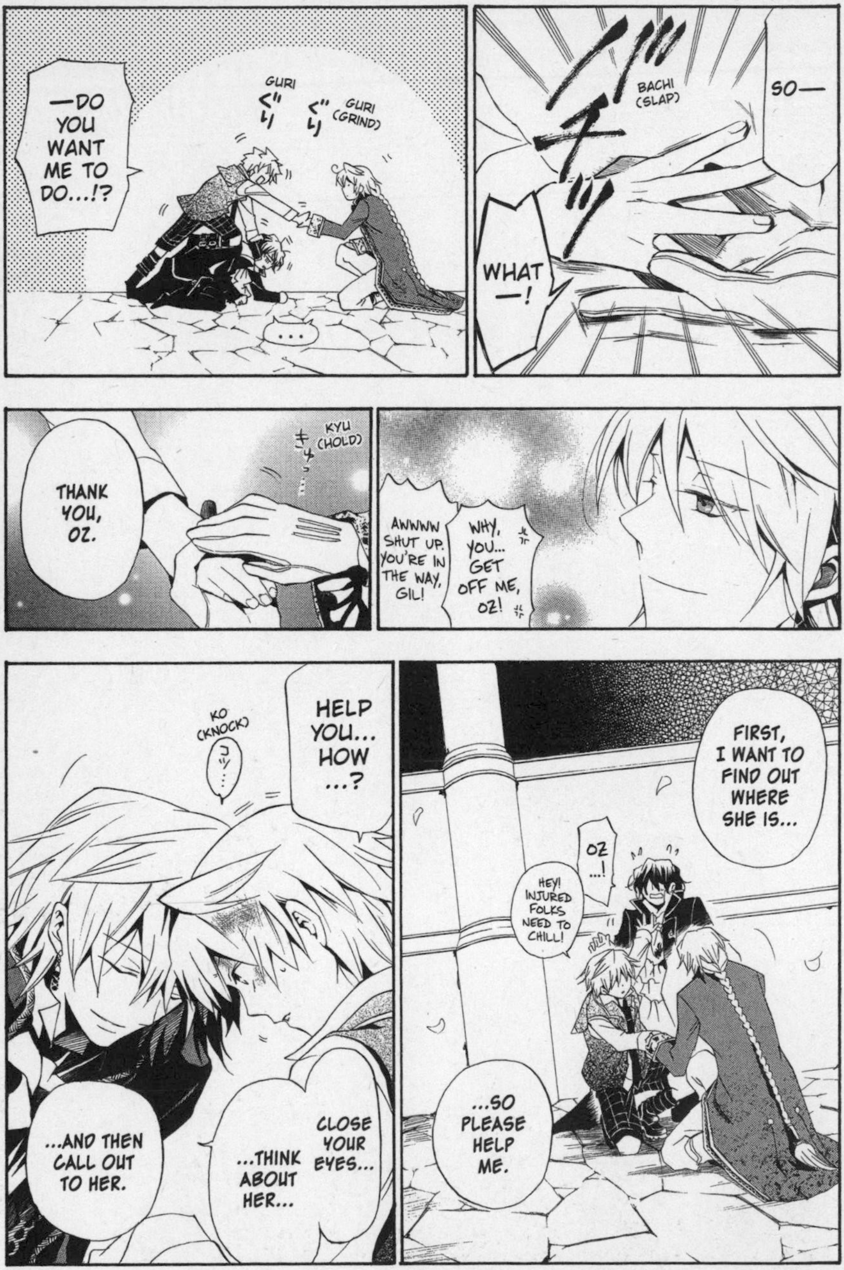
SO—
BACHI (SLAP)
WHAT—!
—DO YOU WANT ME TO DO...!?
GURI
GURI (GRIND)
...
WHY, YOU... GET OFF ME, OZ!
AWWWW SHUT UP. YOU'RE IN THE WAY, GIL!
KYU (HOLD)
THANK YOU, OZ.
FIRST, I WANT TO FIND OUT WHERE SHE IS...
OZ...!
HEY! INJURED FOLKS NEED TO CHILL!
...SO PLEASE HELP ME.
HELP YOU... HOW...?
KO (KNOCK)
CLOSE YOUR EYES...
...THINK ABOUT HER...
...AND THEN CALL OUT TO HER.

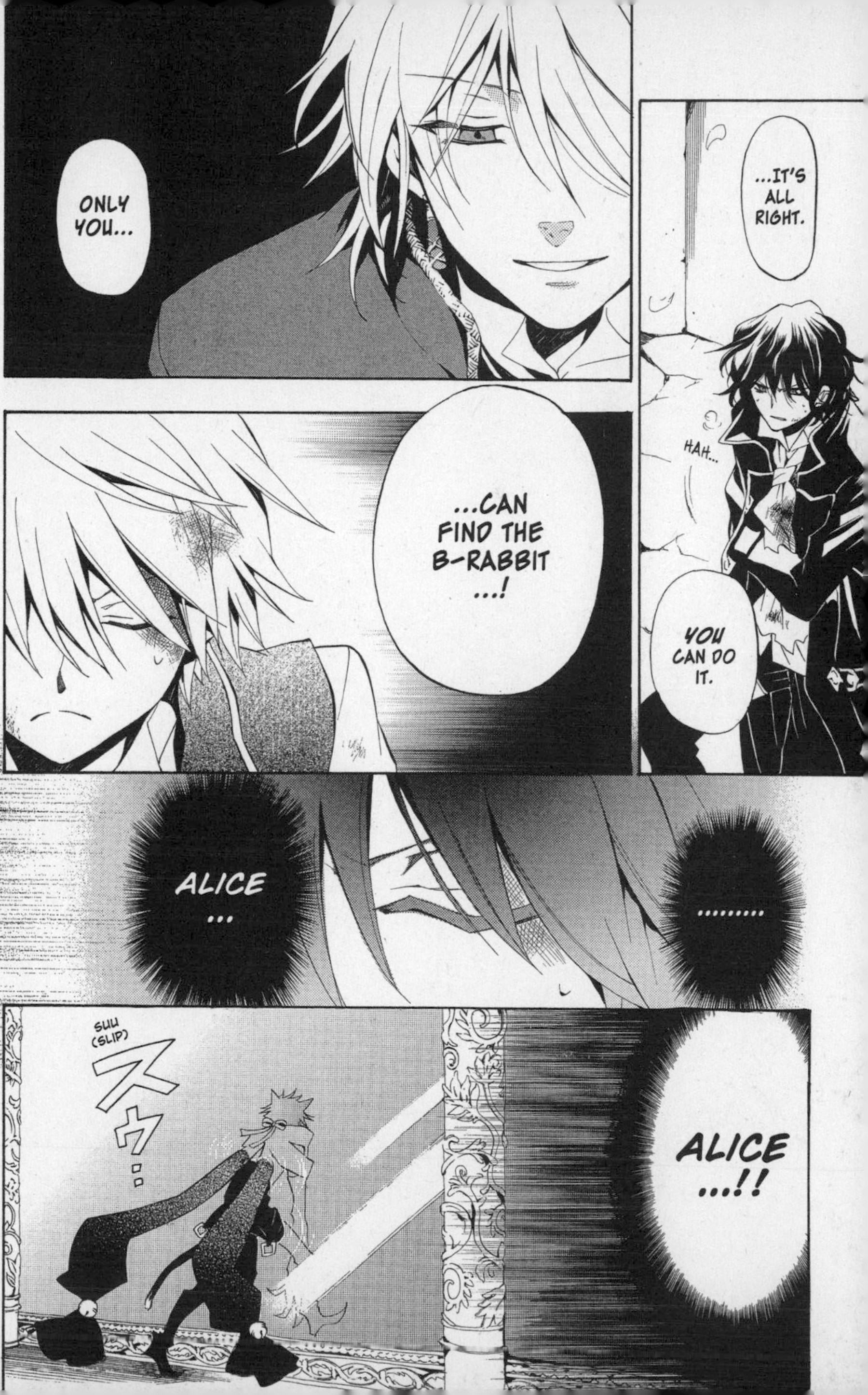
...IT'S ALL RIGHT.
HAH...
YOU CAN DO IT.
ONLY YOU...
...CAN FIND THE B-RABBIT ...!
....
ALICE ...
ALICE ...!!
SUU (SLIP)
スゥ..

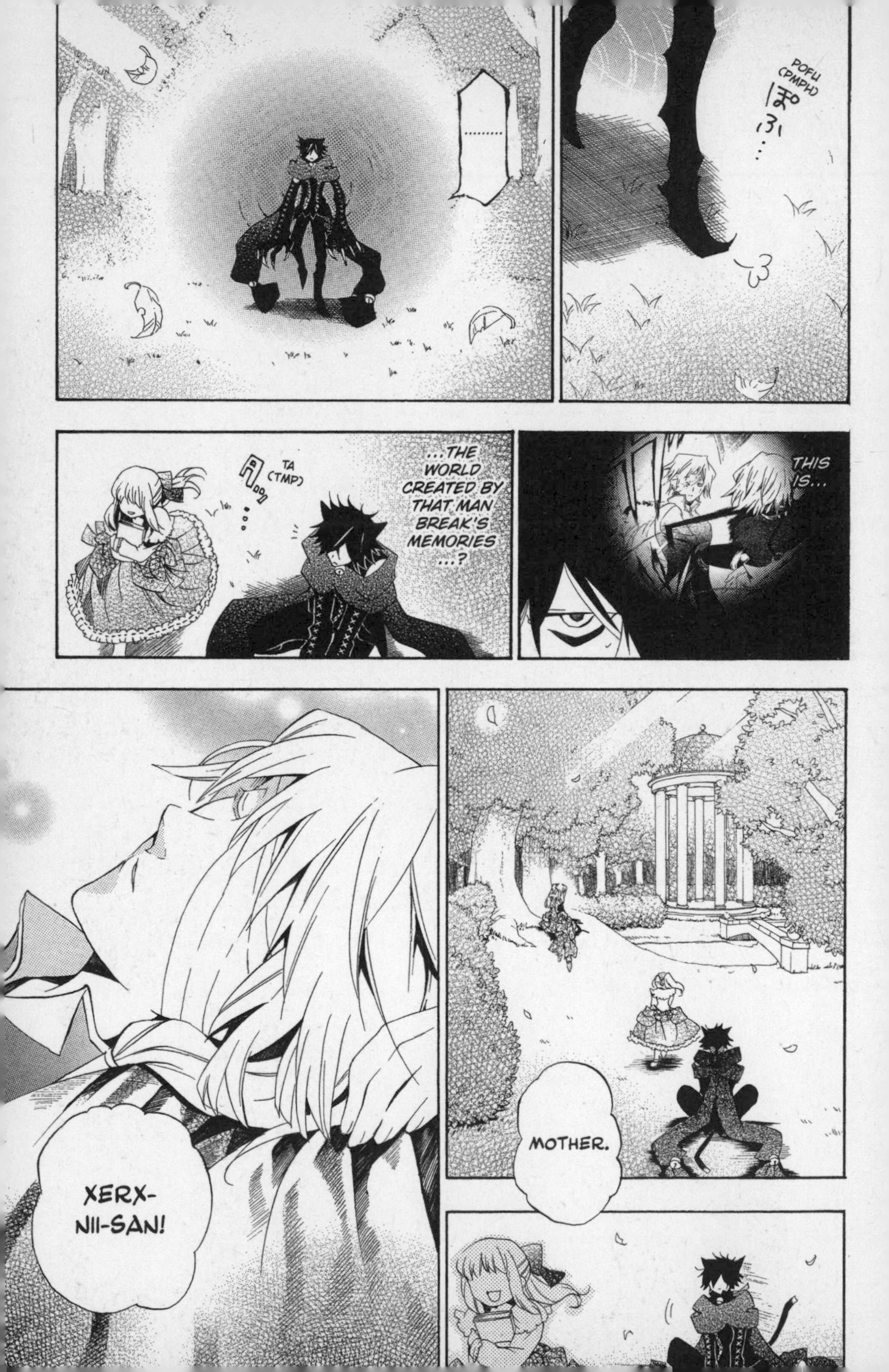
POFU (PMPH)
ぽふ…
……
THIS IS…
…THE WORLD CREATED BY THAT MAN BREAK'S MEMORIES …?
TA (TMP)
MOTHER.
XERX-NII-SAN!

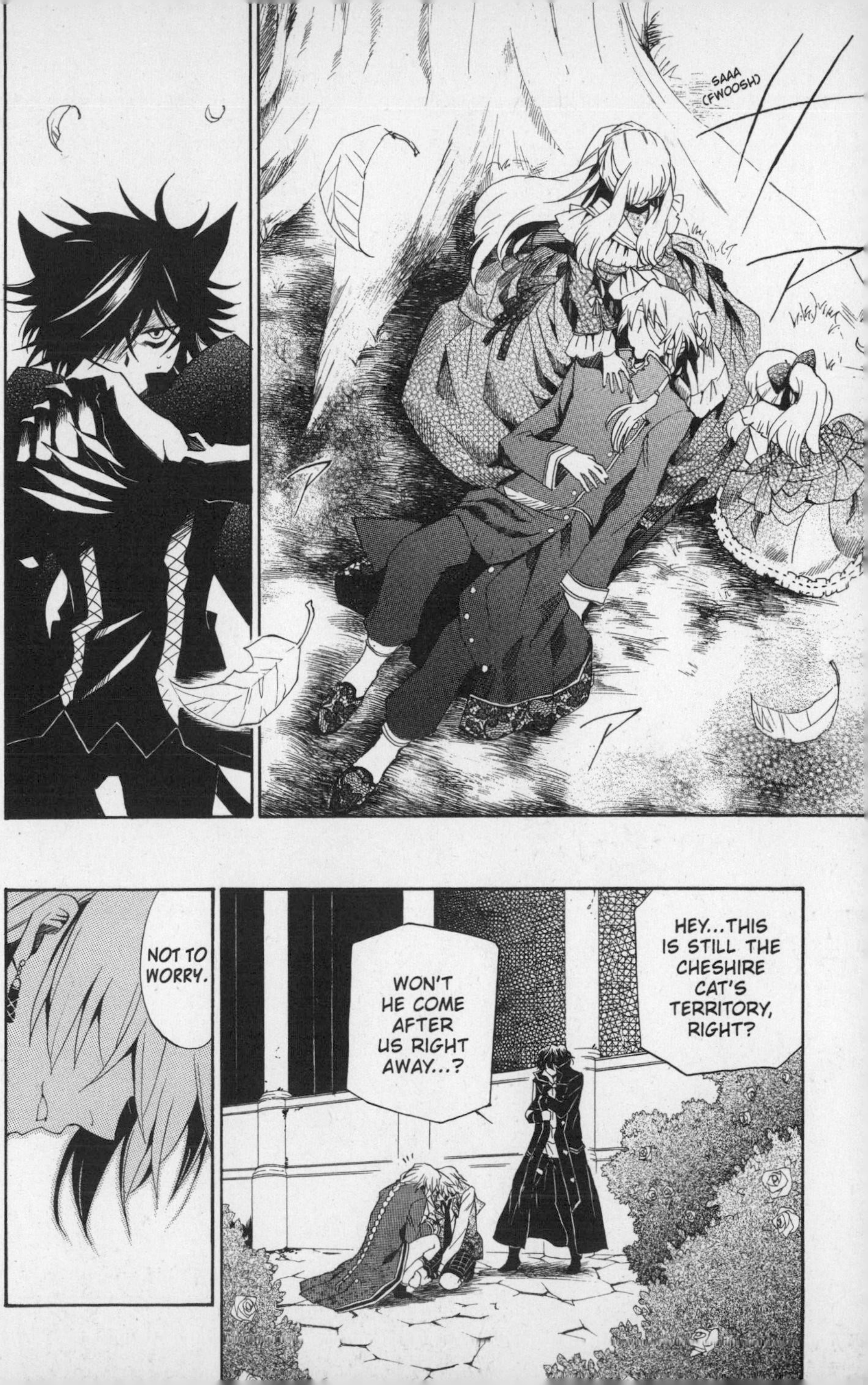
SAAA (FWOOSH)
HEY...THIS IS STILL THE CHESHIRE CAT'S TERRITORY, RIGHT?
WON'T HE COME AFTER US RIGHT AWAY...?
NOT TO WORRY.

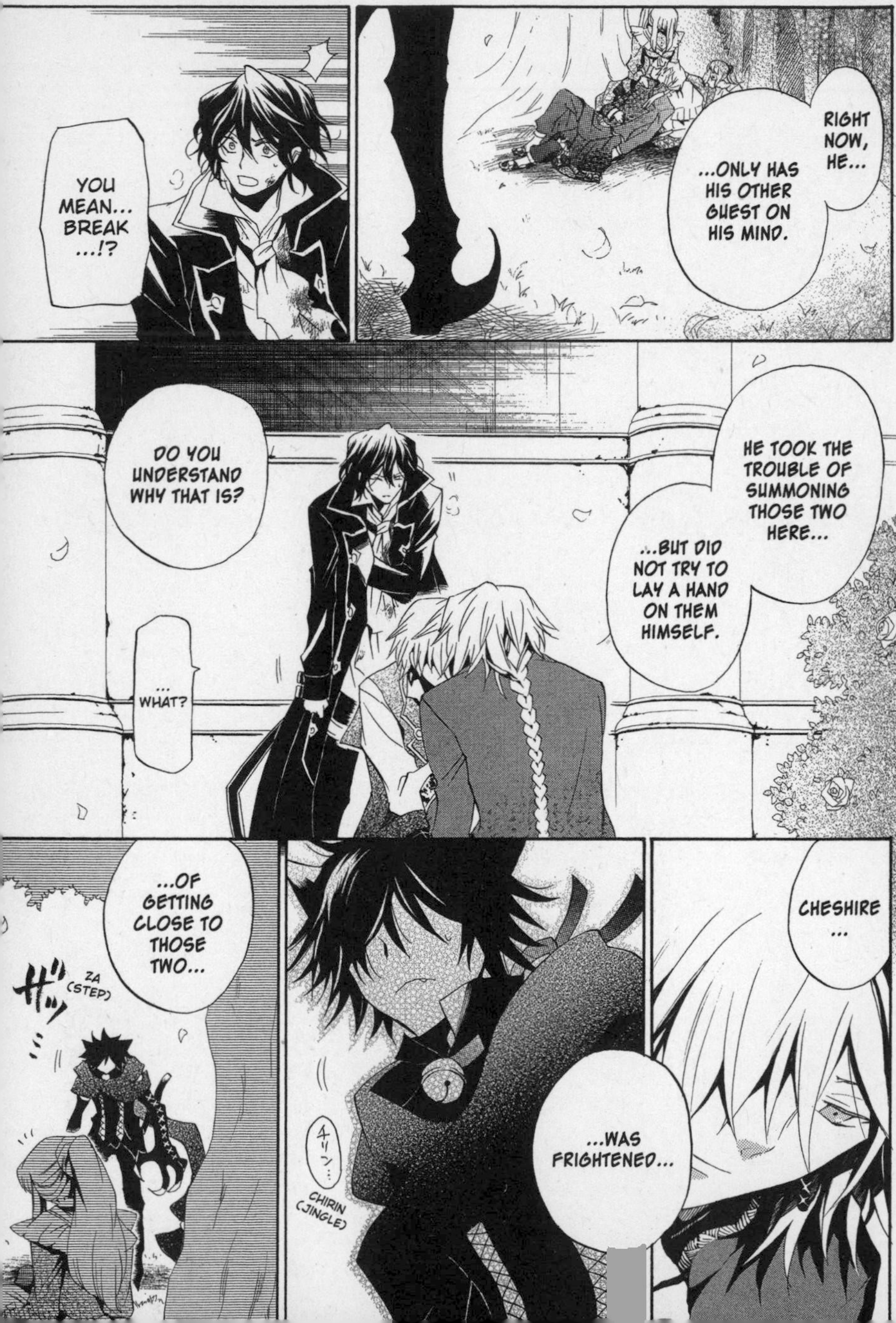
RIGHT NOW, HE...
...ONLY HAS HIS OTHER GUEST ON HIS MIND.
YOU MEAN... BREAK ...!?
HE TOOK THE TROUBLE OF SUMMONING THOSE TWO HERE...
...BUT DID NOT TRY TO LAY A HAND ON THEM HIMSELF.
DO YOU UNDERSTAND WHY THAT IS?
... WHAT?
CHESHIRE ...
...WAS FRIGHTENED...
チリン…
CHIRIN (JINGLE)
...OF GETTING CLOSE TO THOSE TWO...
ザッ
ZA (STEP)

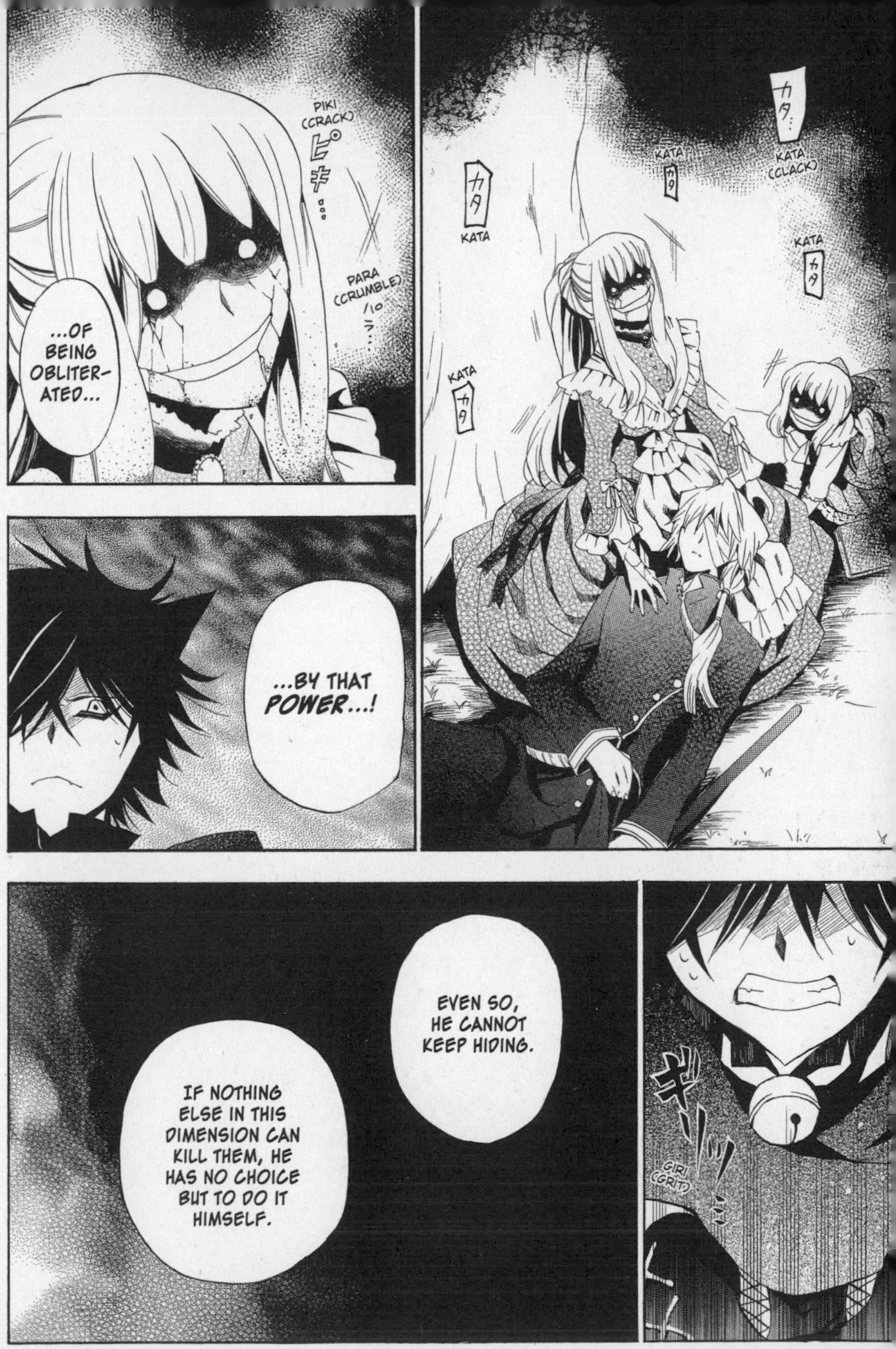
カタ…
KATA (CLACK)
KATA
カタ
カタ
KATA
KATA
カタ
KATA
カタ
PIKI (CRACK)
ピキ…
PARA (CRUMBLE)
パラ…
...OF BEING OBLITER-ATED...
...BY THAT POWER...!
ギリッ!!
GIRI (GRIT)
EVEN SO, HE CANNOT KEEP HIDING.
IF NOTHING ELSE IN THIS DIMENSION CAN KILL THEM, HE HAS NO CHOICE BUT TO DO IT HIMSELF.

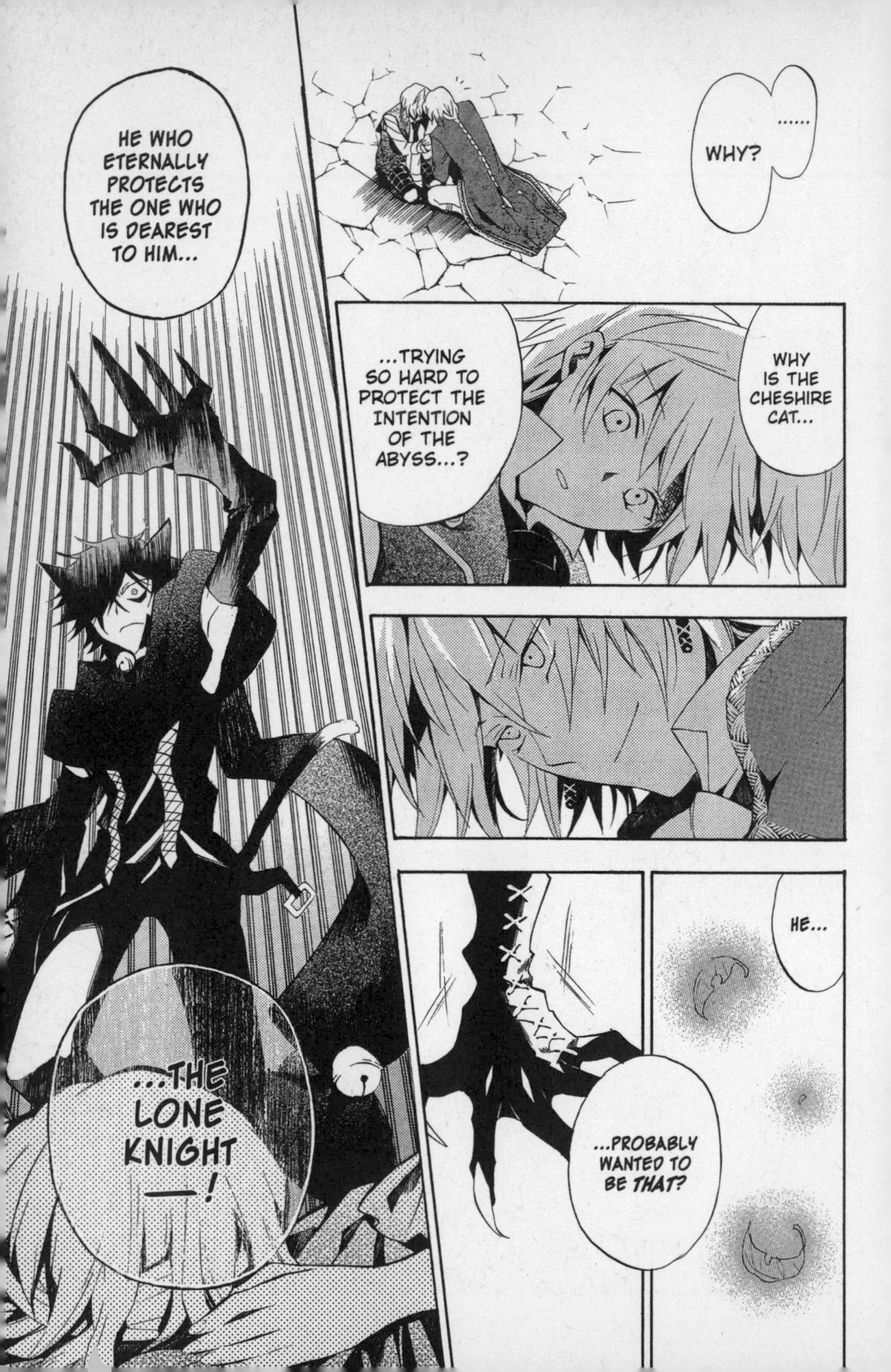

...... WHY?
WHY IS THE CHESHIRE CAT...
...TRYING SO HARD TO PROTECT THE INTENTION OF THE ABYSS...?
HE...
...PROBABLY WANTED TO BE *THAT*?
HE WHO ETERNALLY PROTECTS THE ONE WHO IS DEAREST TO HIM...
...THE LONE KNIGHT—!

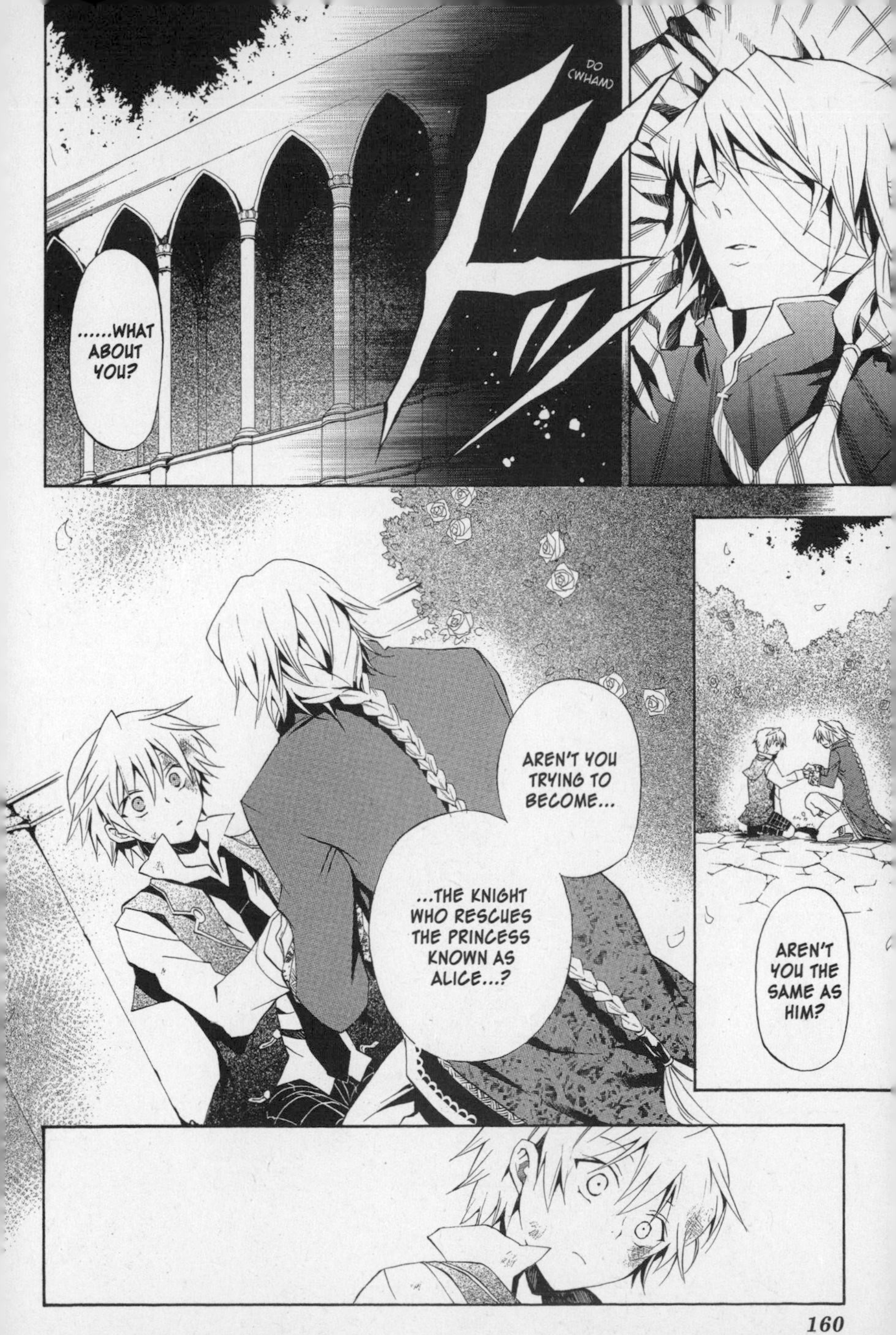
DO (WHAM)
......WHAT ABOUT YOU?
AREN'T YOU THE SAME AS HIM?
AREN'T YOU TRYING TO BECOME...
...THE KNIGHT WHO RESCUES THE PRINCESS KNOWN AS ALICE...?

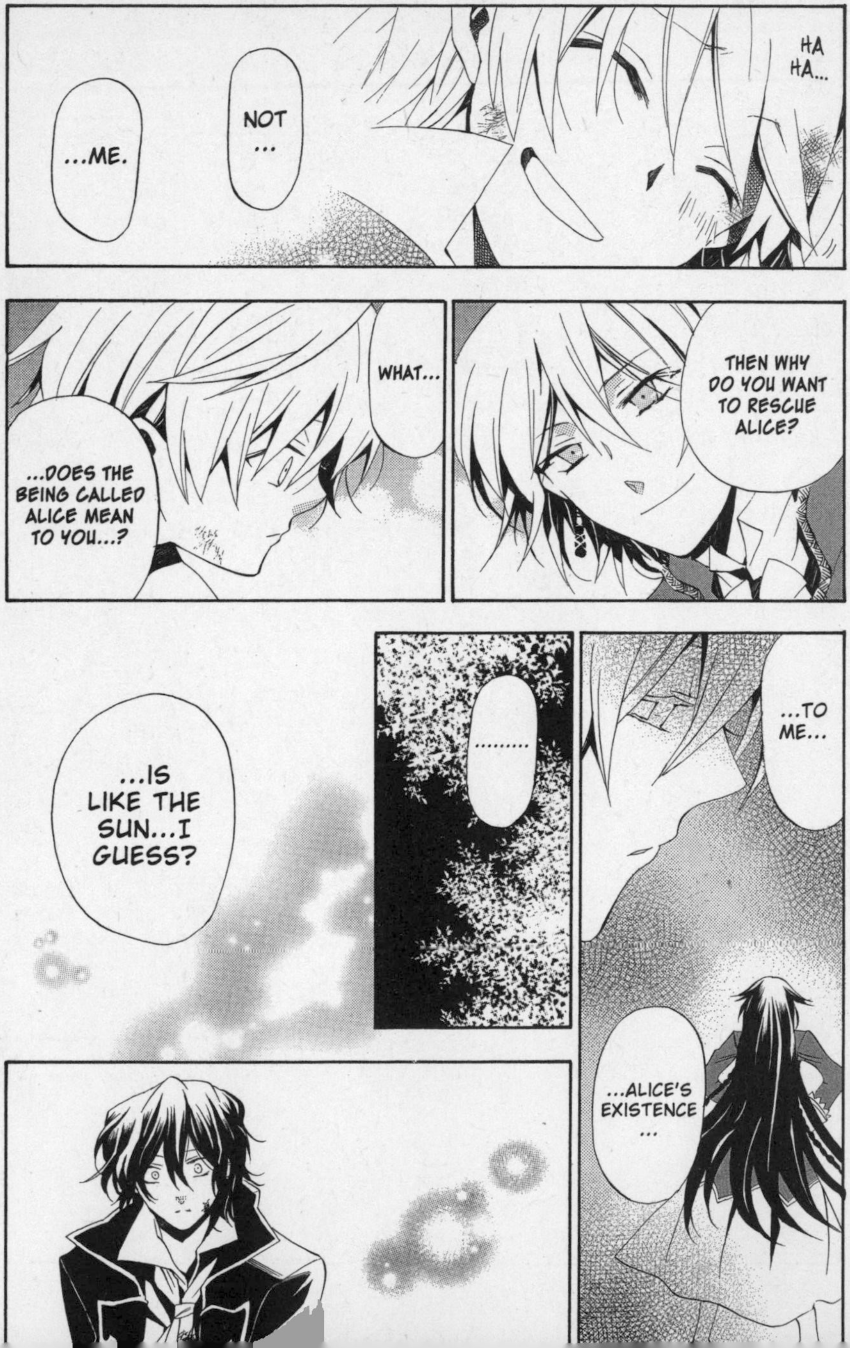
HA HA...
NOT ...
...ME.
THEN WHY DO YOU WANT TO RESCUE ALICE?
WHAT...
...DOES THE BEING CALLED ALICE MEAN TO YOU...?
...TO ME...
...ALICE'S EXISTENCE ...
....
...IS LIKE THE SUN...I GUESS?

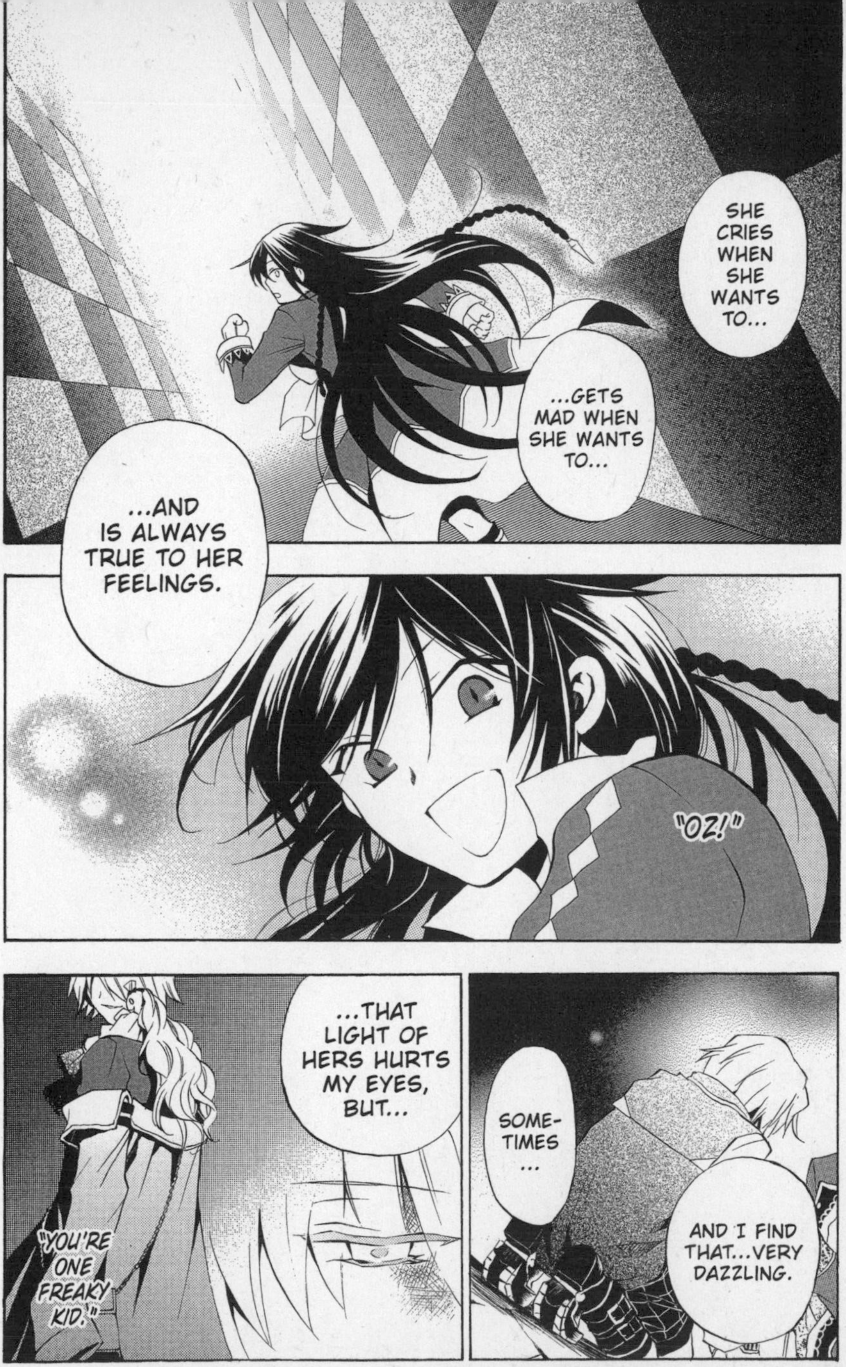

SHE CRIES WHEN SHE WANTS TO...
...GETS MAD WHEN SHE WANTS TO...
...AND IS ALWAYS TRUE TO HER FEELINGS.
"OZ!"
SOME-TIMES...
...THAT LIGHT OF HERS HURTS MY EYES, BUT...
AND I FIND THAT...VERY DAZZLING.
"YOU'RE ONE FREAKY KID."

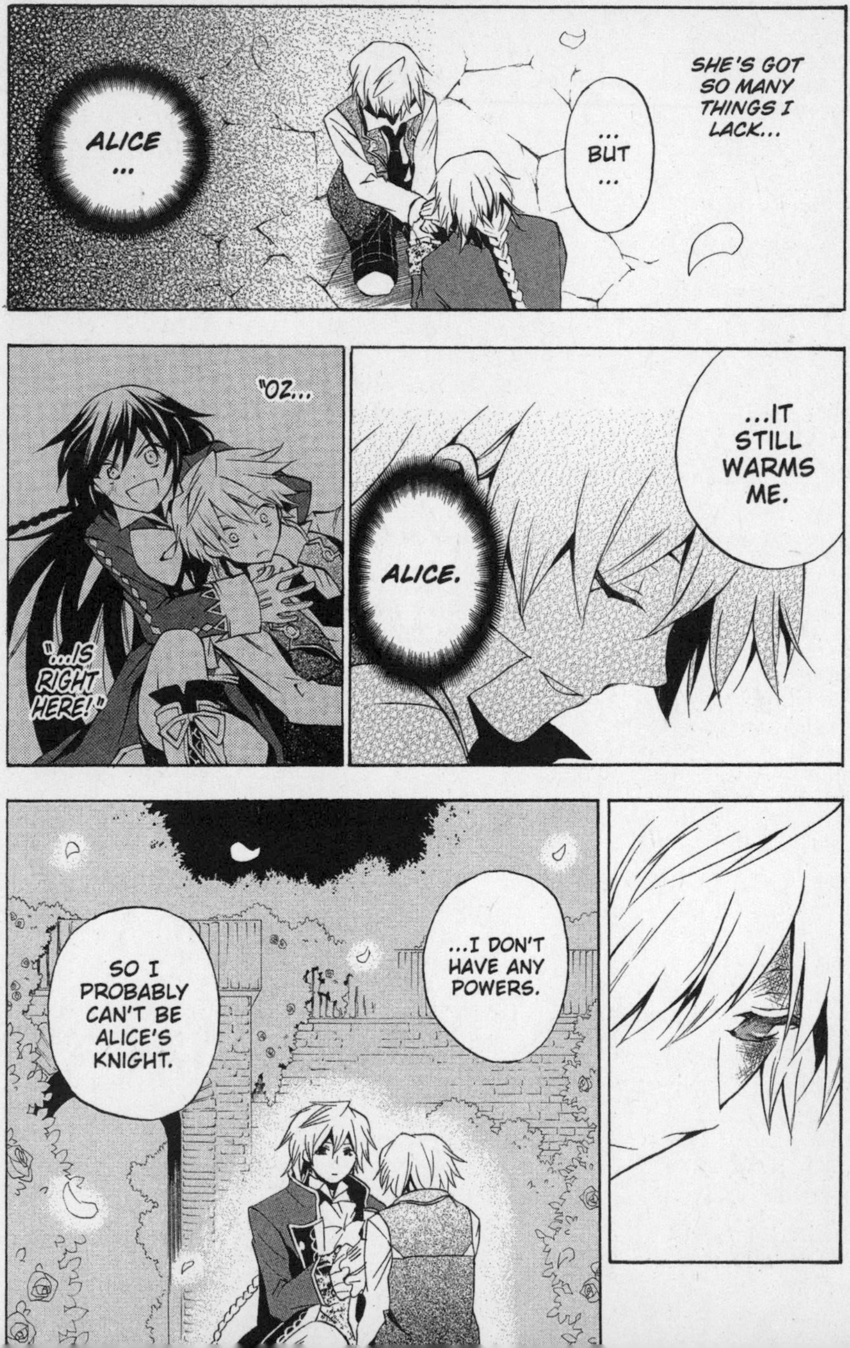
SHE'S GOT SO MANY THINGS I LACK...
...BUT...
ALICE...
...IT STILL WARMS ME.
ALICE.
"OZ...
"...IS RIGHT HERE!"
...I DON'T HAVE ANY POWERS.
SO I PROBABLY CAN'T BE ALICE'S KNIGHT.

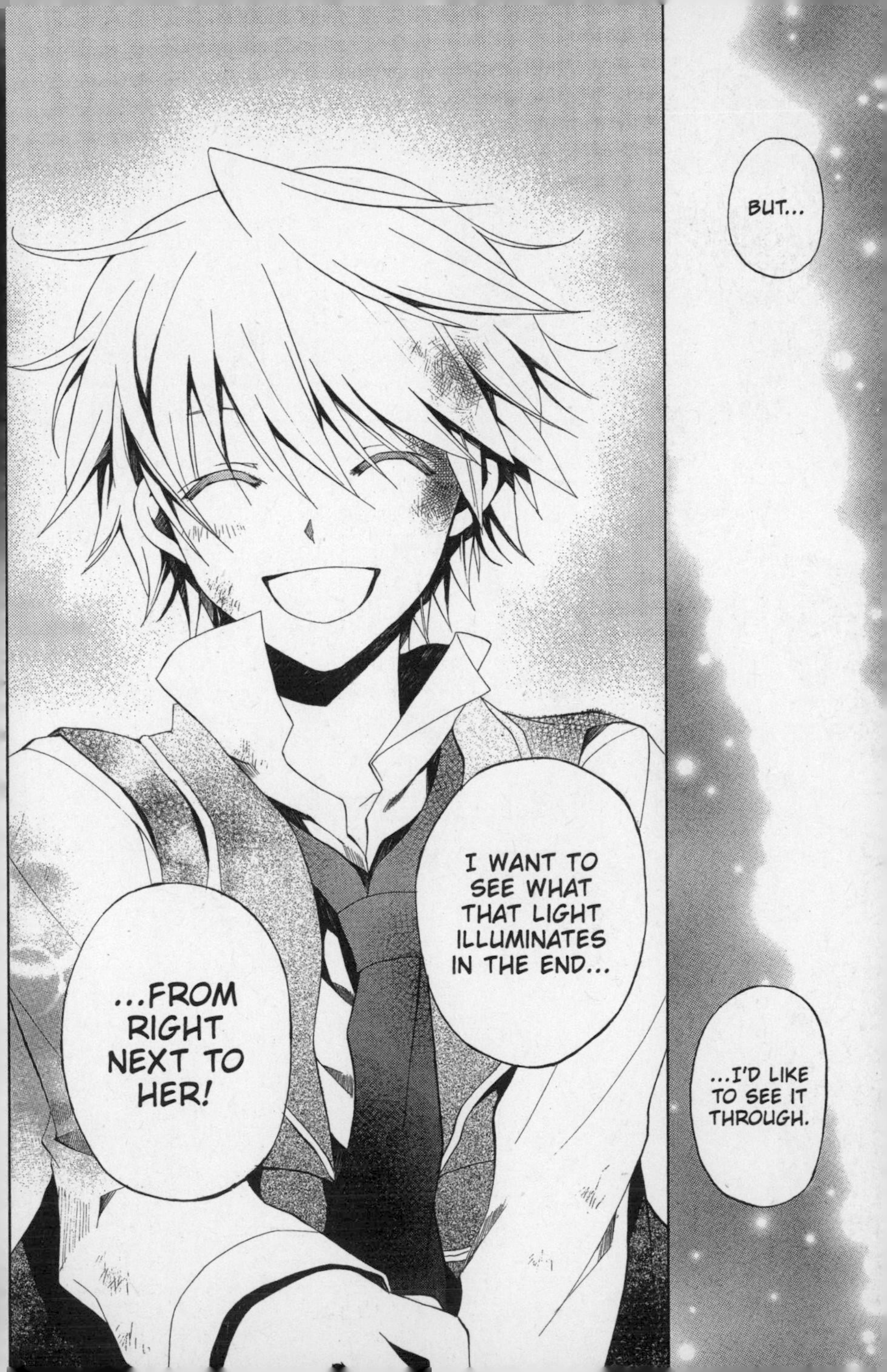
BUT...
...I'D LIKE TO SEE IT THROUGH.
I WANT TO SEE WHAT THAT LIGHT ILLUMINATES IN THE END...
...FROM RIGHT NEXT TO HER!

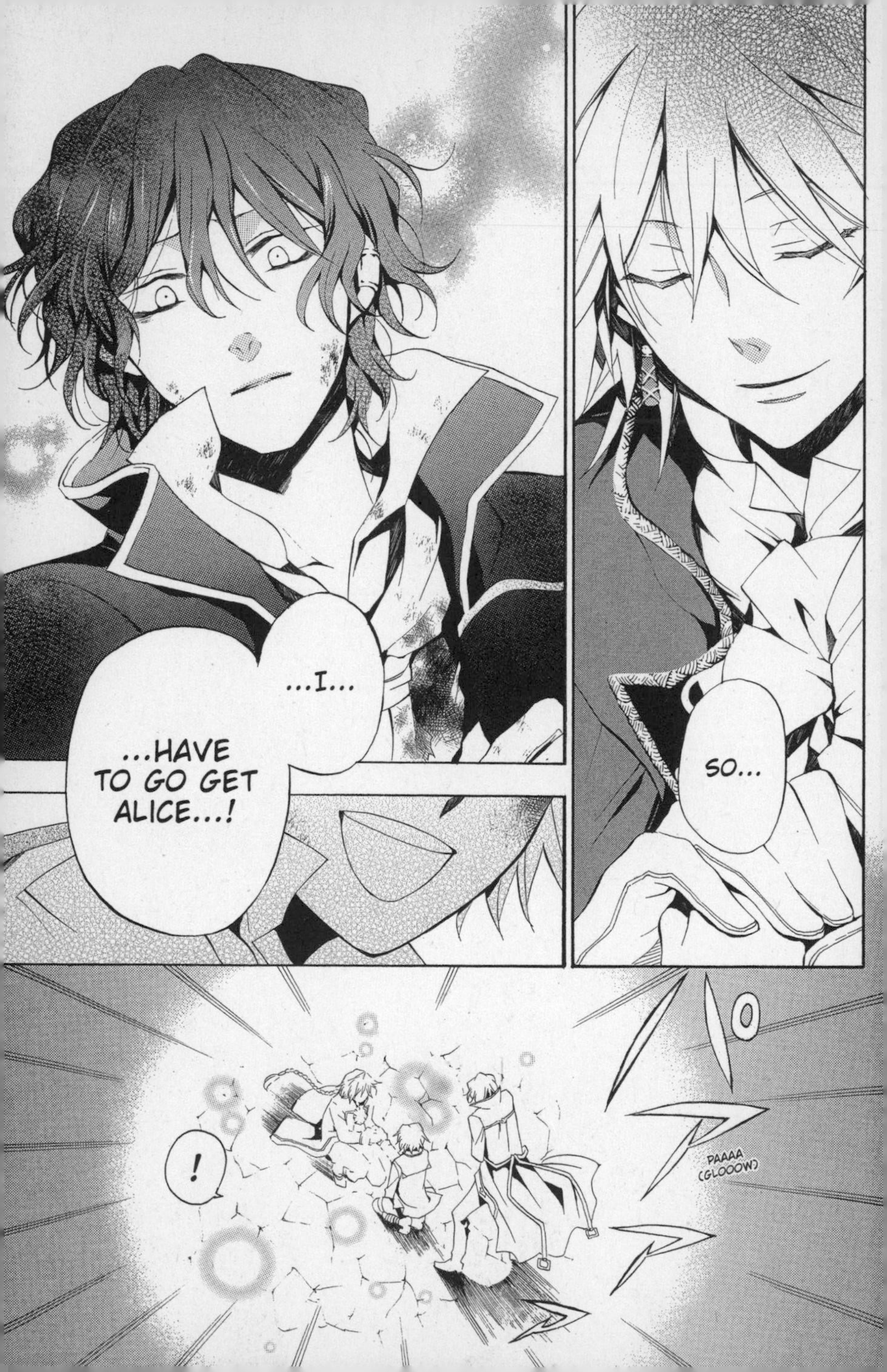
SO...
...I...
...HAVE TO GO GET ALICE...!
PAAAA (GLOOOW)
!

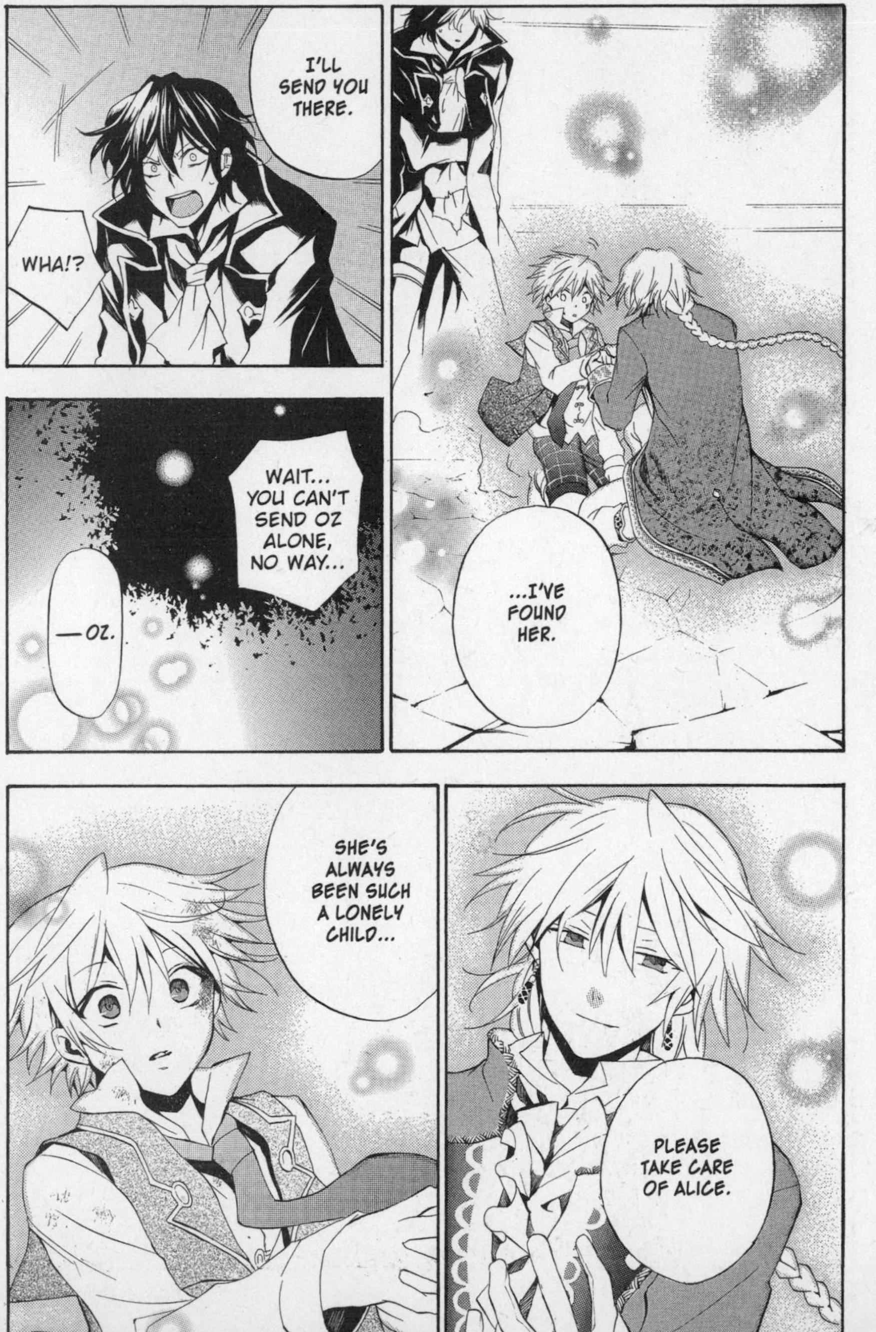
...I'VE FOUND HER.
I'LL SEND YOU THERE.
WHA!?
WAIT... YOU CAN'T SEND OZ ALONE, NO WAY...
—OZ.
PLEASE TAKE CARE OF ALICE.
SHE'S ALWAYS BEEN SUCH A LONELY CHILD...

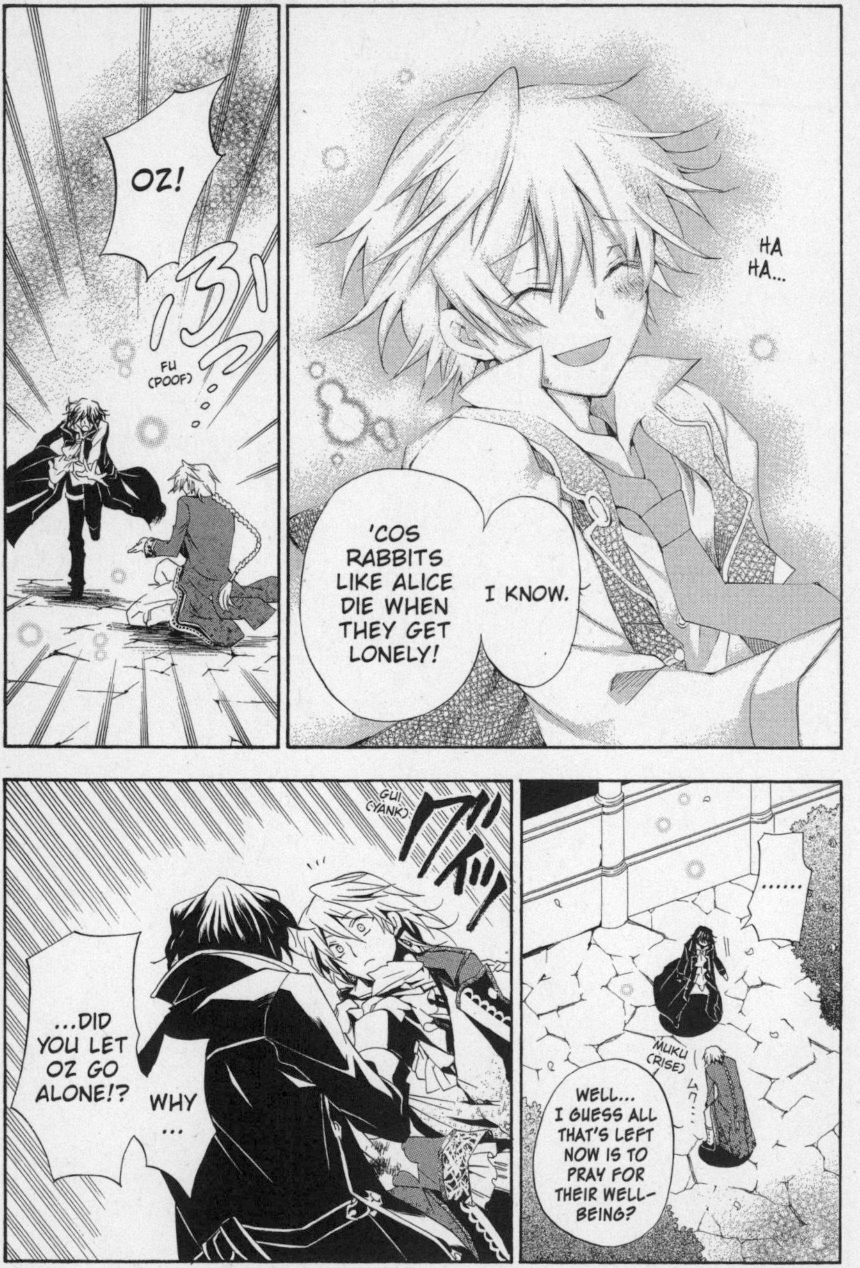
HA HA...
I KNOW.
'COS RABBITS LIKE ALICE DIE WHEN THEY GET LONELY!
OZ!
FU (POOF)
......
MUKU (RISE)
WELL... I GUESS ALL THAT'S LEFT NOW IS TO PRAY FOR THEIR WELL-BEING?
GUI (YANK)
WHY ...
...DID YOU LET OZ GO ALONE!?

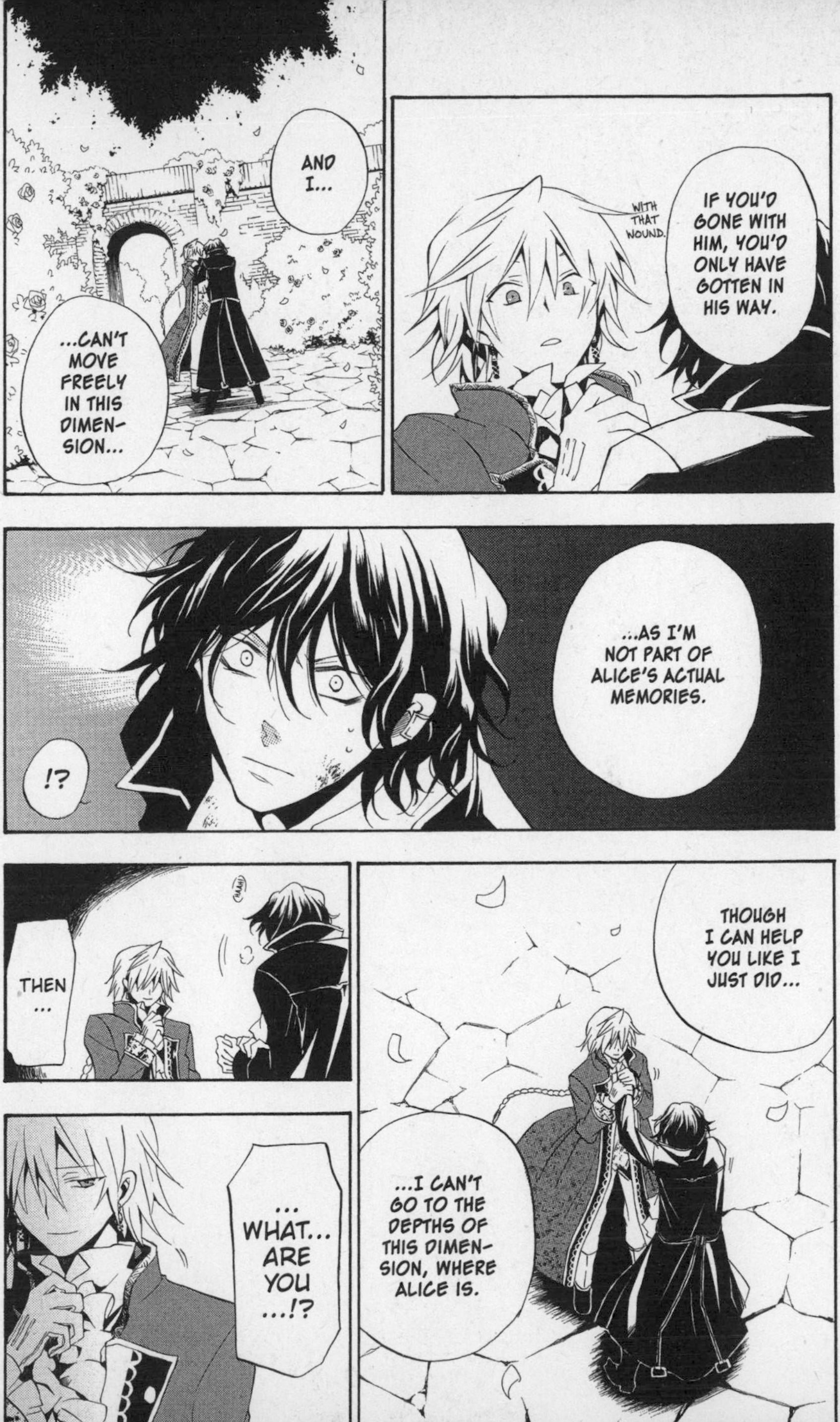
IF YOU'D GONE WITH HIM, YOU'D ONLY HAVE GOTTEN IN HIS WAY.
WITH THAT WOUND.
AND I...
...CAN'T MOVE FREELY IN THIS DIMENSION...
...AS I'M NOT PART OF ALICE'S ACTUAL MEMORIES.
!?
THOUGH I CAN HELP YOU LIKE I JUST DID...
...I CAN'T GO TO THE DEPTHS OF THIS DIMENSION, WHERE ALICE IS.
HAAH
THEN...
... WHAT... ARE YOU ...!?

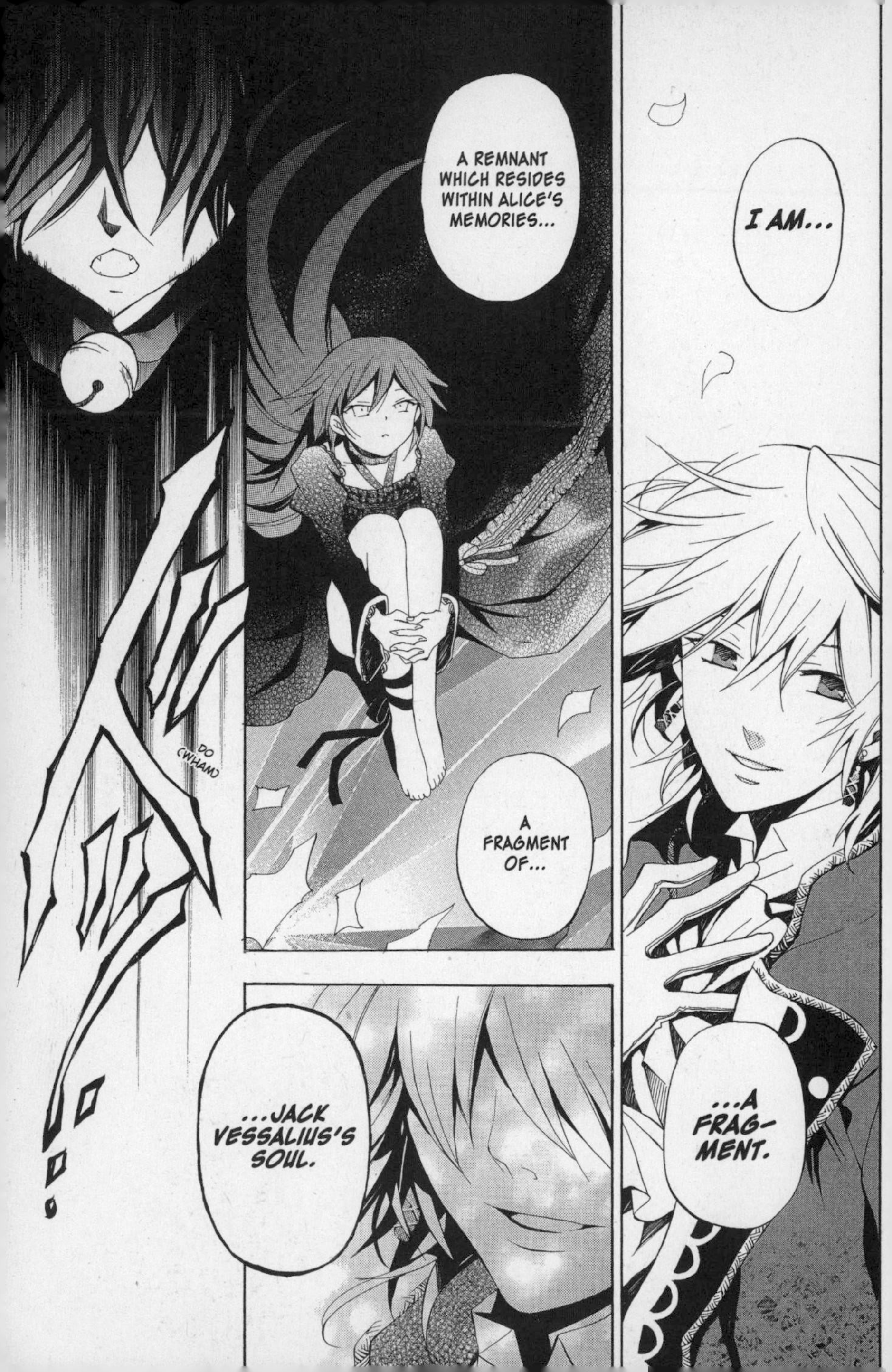
I AM...
...A FRAGMENT.
A REMNANT WHICH RESIDES WITHIN ALICE'S MEMORIES...
A FRAGMENT OF...
...JACK VESSALIUS'S SOUL.
DO (WHAM)

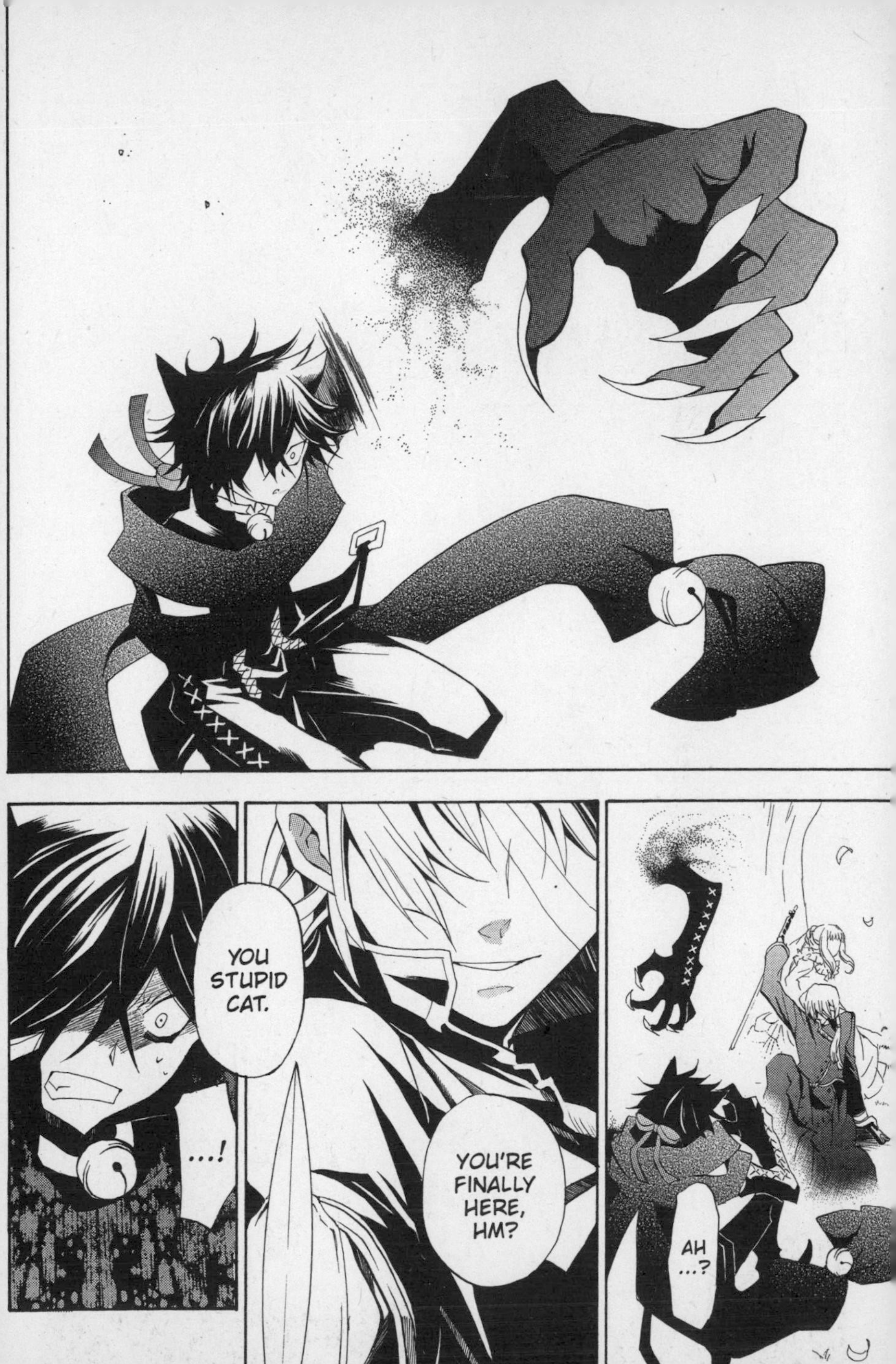
AH ...?
YOU STUPID CAT.
YOU'RE FINALLY HERE, HM?
...!

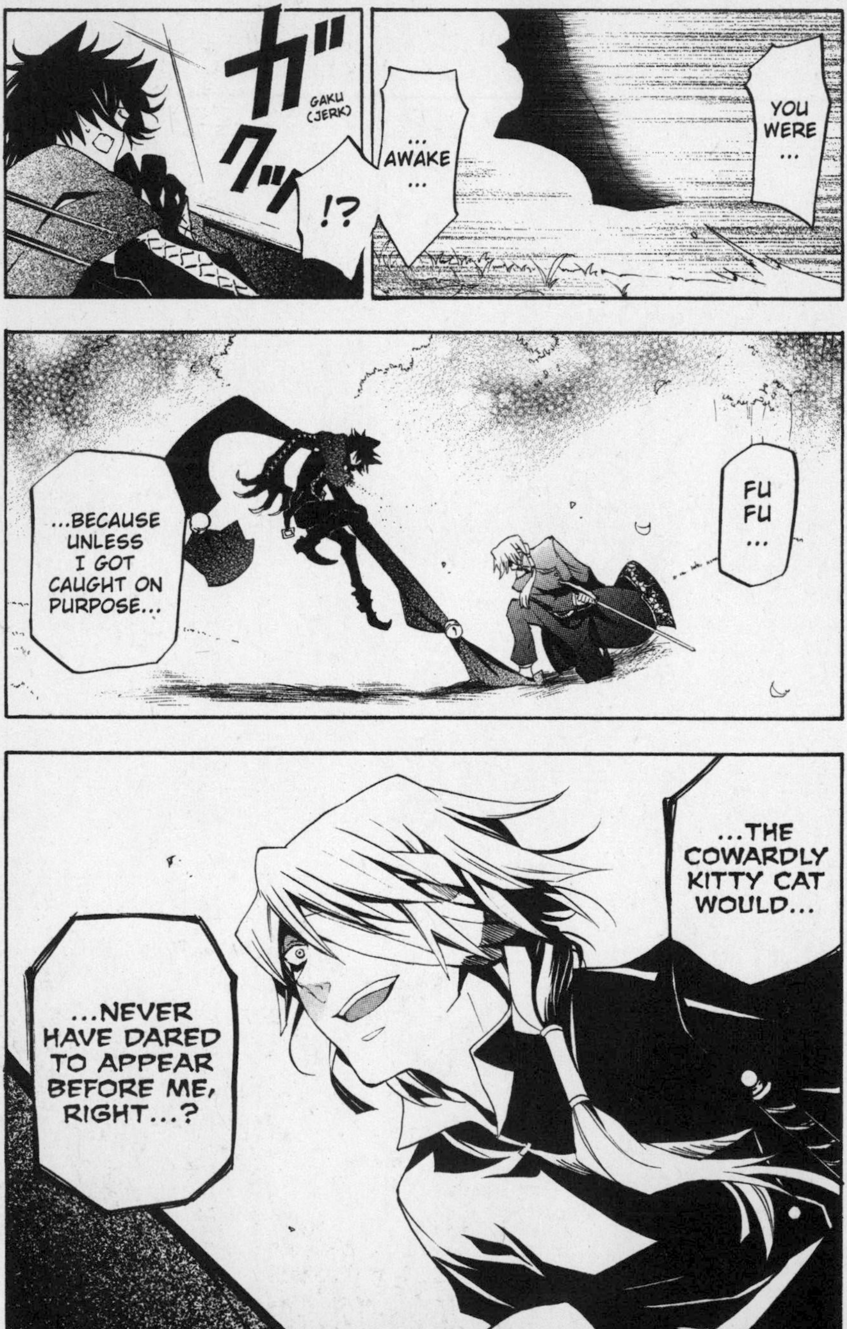
YOU WERE...
...AWAKE...
ガクッ
GAKU (JERK)
!?
FU FU...
...BECAUSE UNLESS I GOT CAUGHT ON PURPOSE...
...THE COWARDLY KITTY CAT WOULD...
...NEVER HAVE DARED TO APPEAR BEFORE ME, RIGHT...?

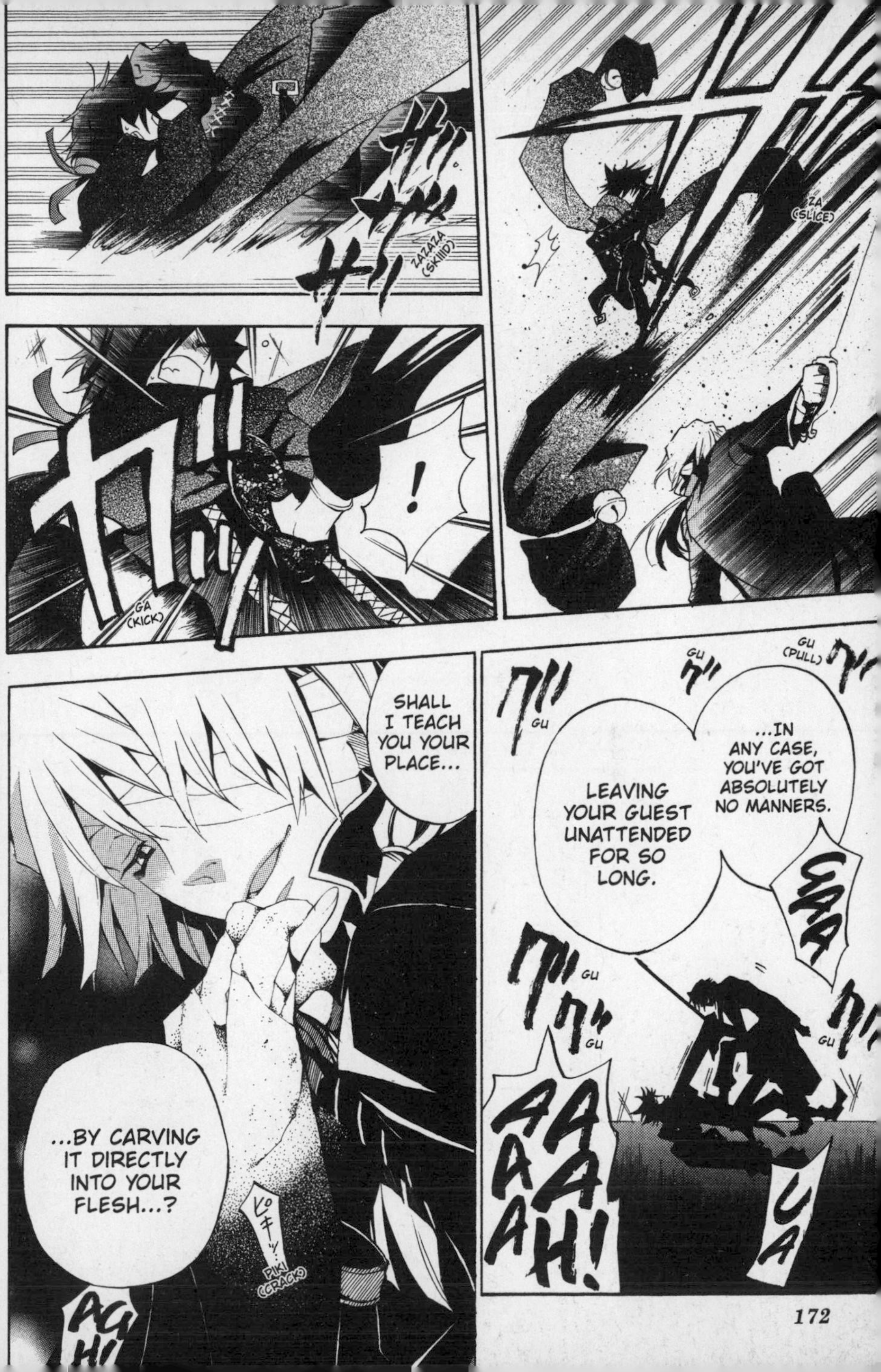
ZA (SLICE)
ZAZAZA (SKIIID)
GA (KICK)
!
GU (PULL)
GU
GU
...IN ANY CASE, YOU'VE GOT ABSOLUTELY NO MANNERS.
LEAVING YOUR GUEST UNATTENDED FOR SO LONG.
GAA
GU
GU
GU
AAAAAAH!
UA
SHALL I TEACH YOU YOUR PLACE...
...BY CARVING IT DIRECTLY INTO YOUR FLESH...?
PIKI (CRACK)
AGH

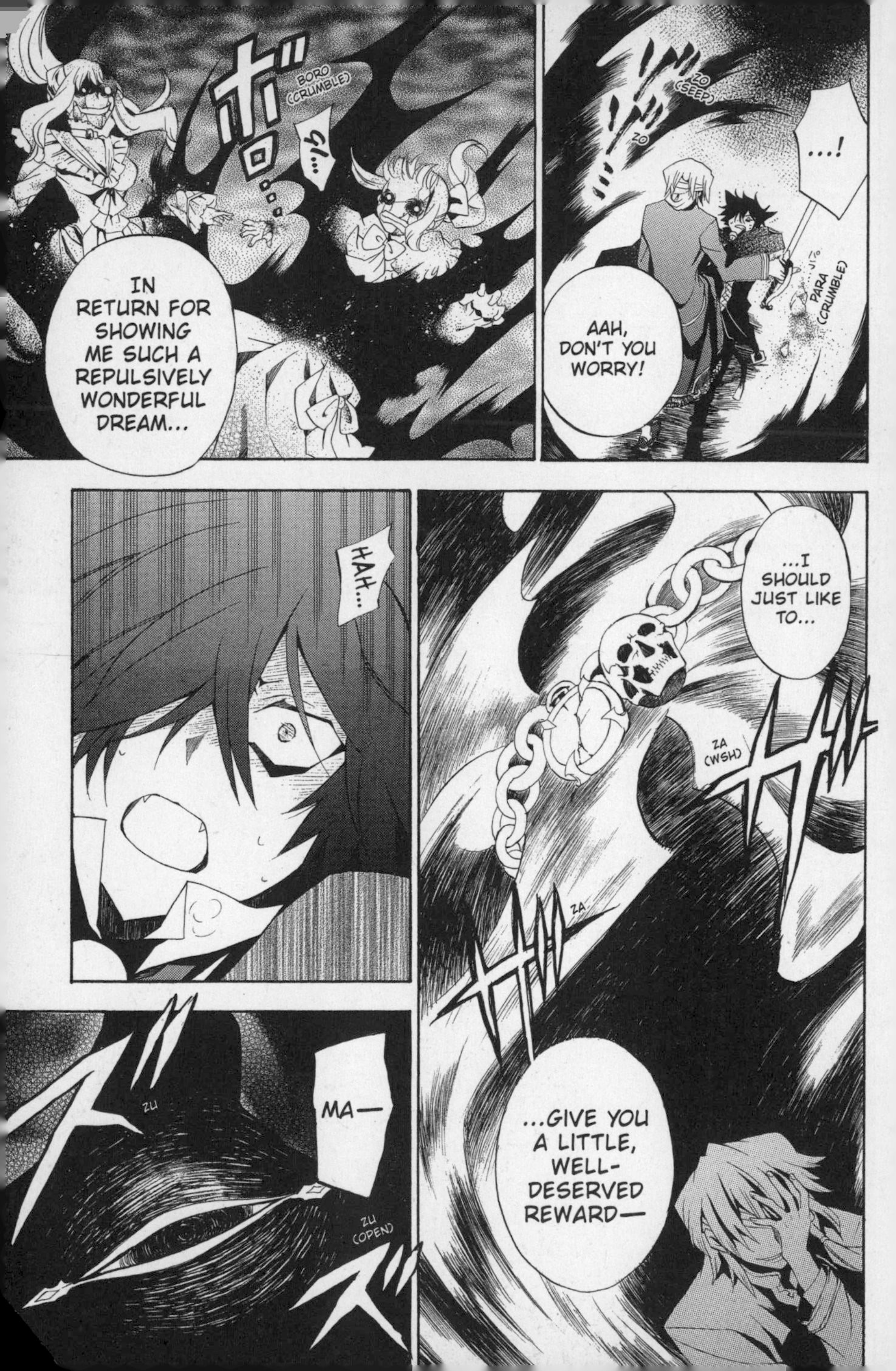

ZO (SEEP)
ZO
...!
AAH, DON'T YOU WORRY!
PARA (CRUMBLE)
BORO (CRUMBLE)
G!...
IN RETURN FOR SHOWING ME SUCH A REPULSIVELY WONDERFUL DREAM...
...I SHOULD JUST LIKE TO...
ZA (WSH)
ZA
...GIVE YOU A LITTLE, WELL-DESERVED REWARD—
HAH...
MA—
ZU
ZU (OPEN)

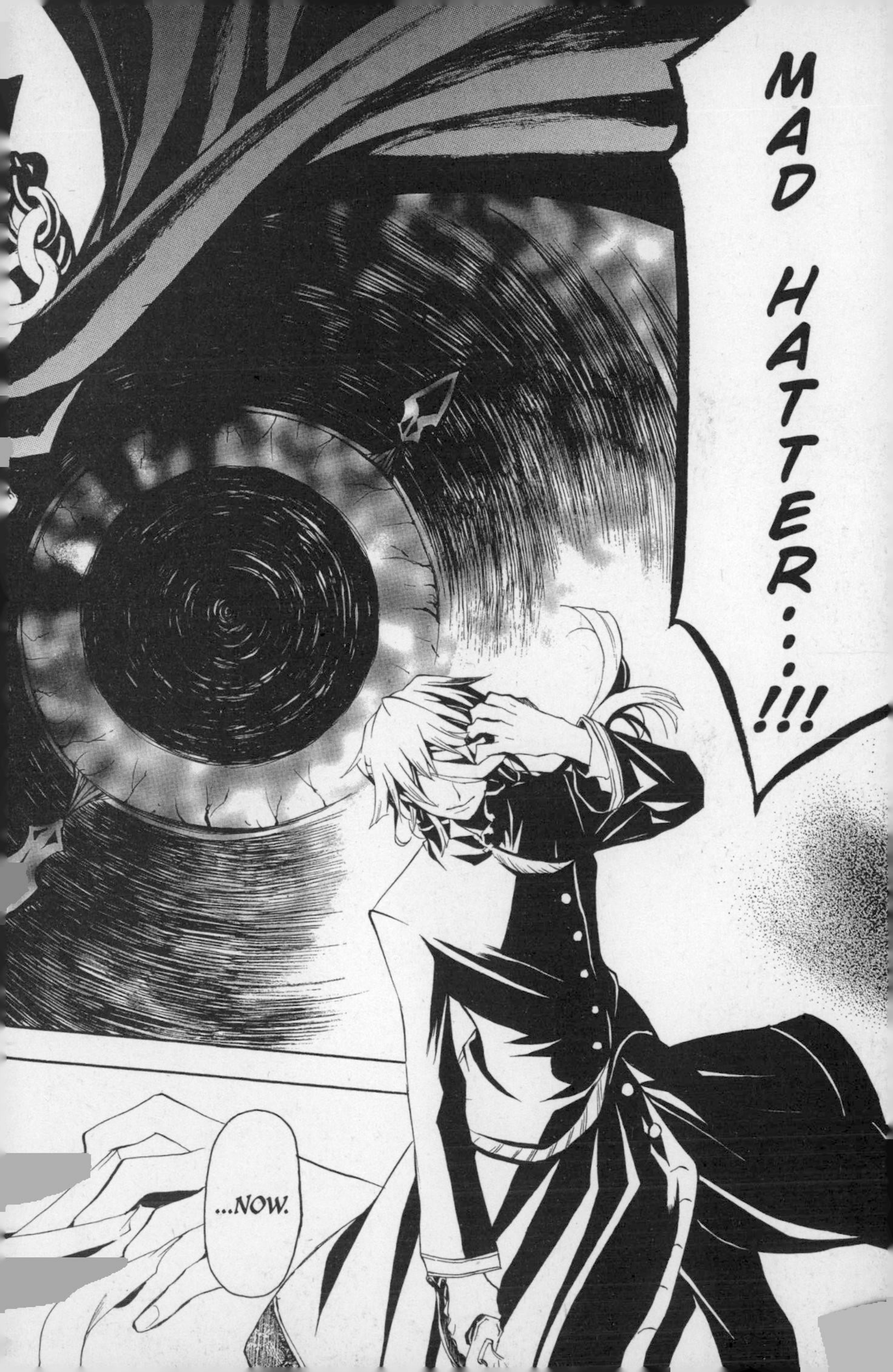
MAD HATTER...!!!
...NOW.

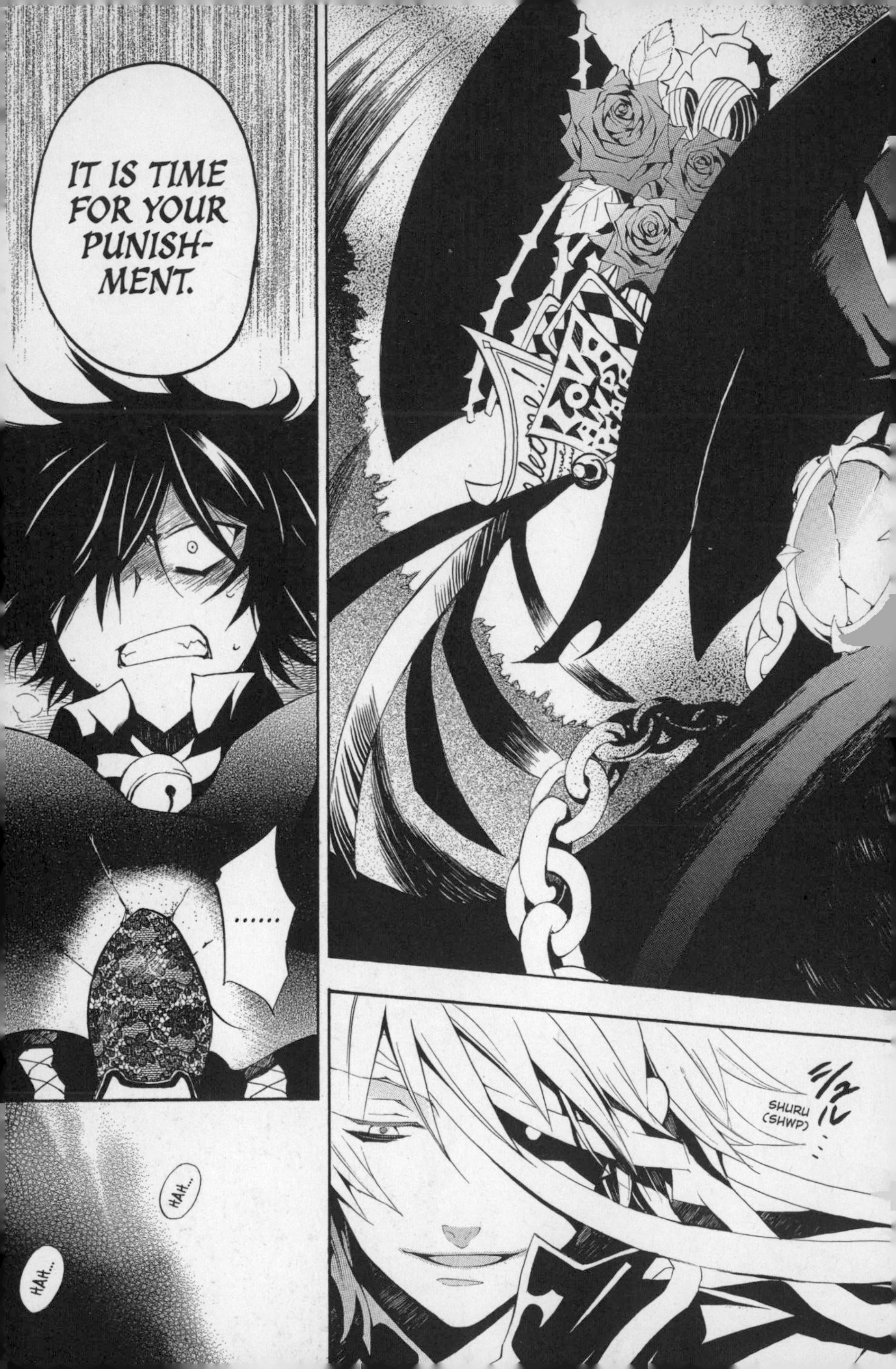
IT IS TIME FOR YOUR PUNISH-MENT.
......
シュル
SHURU (SHWP)
HAH...
HAH...

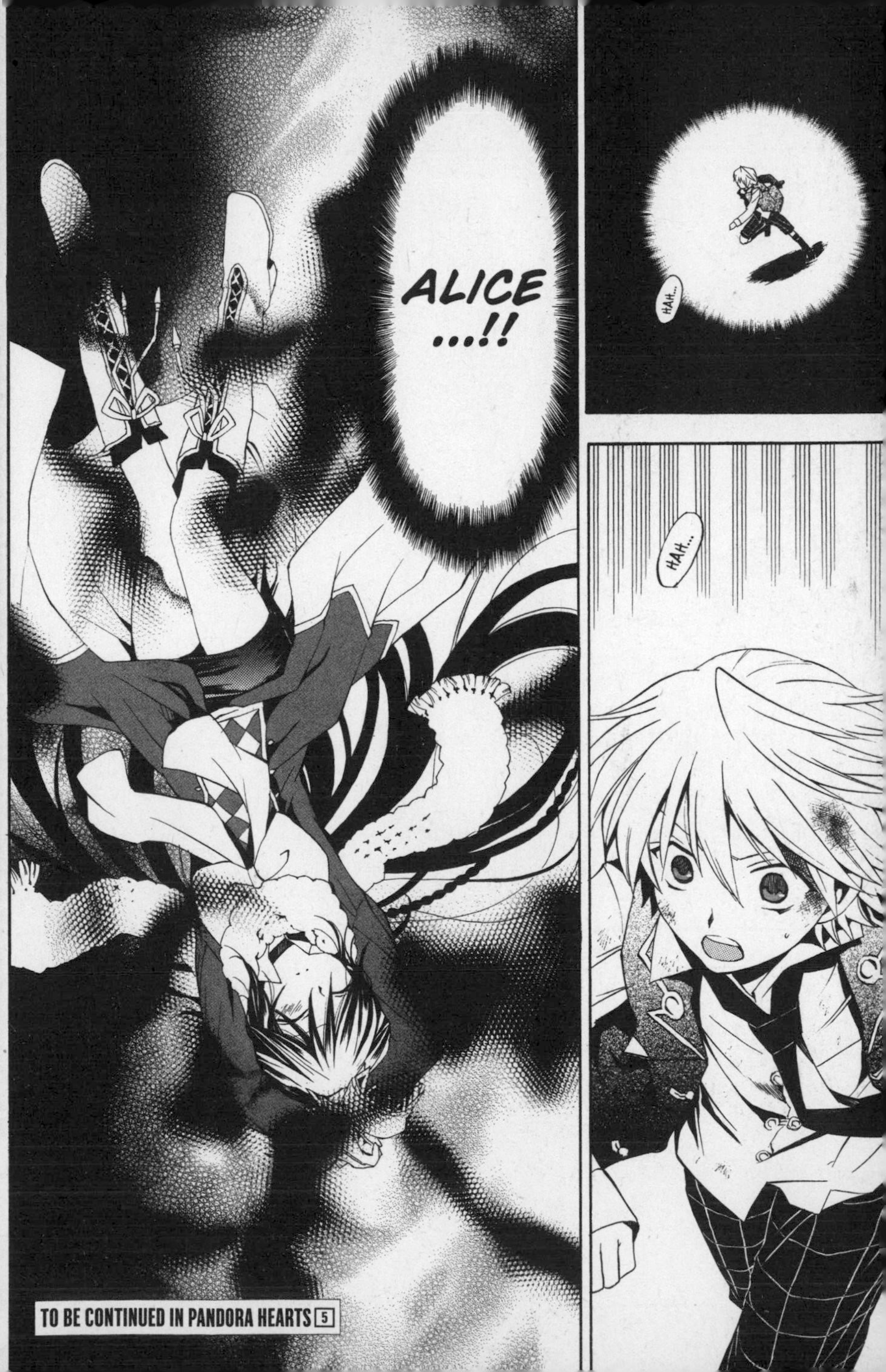
HAH...
HAH...
ALICE ...!!
TO BE CONTINUED IN PANDORA HEARTS 5

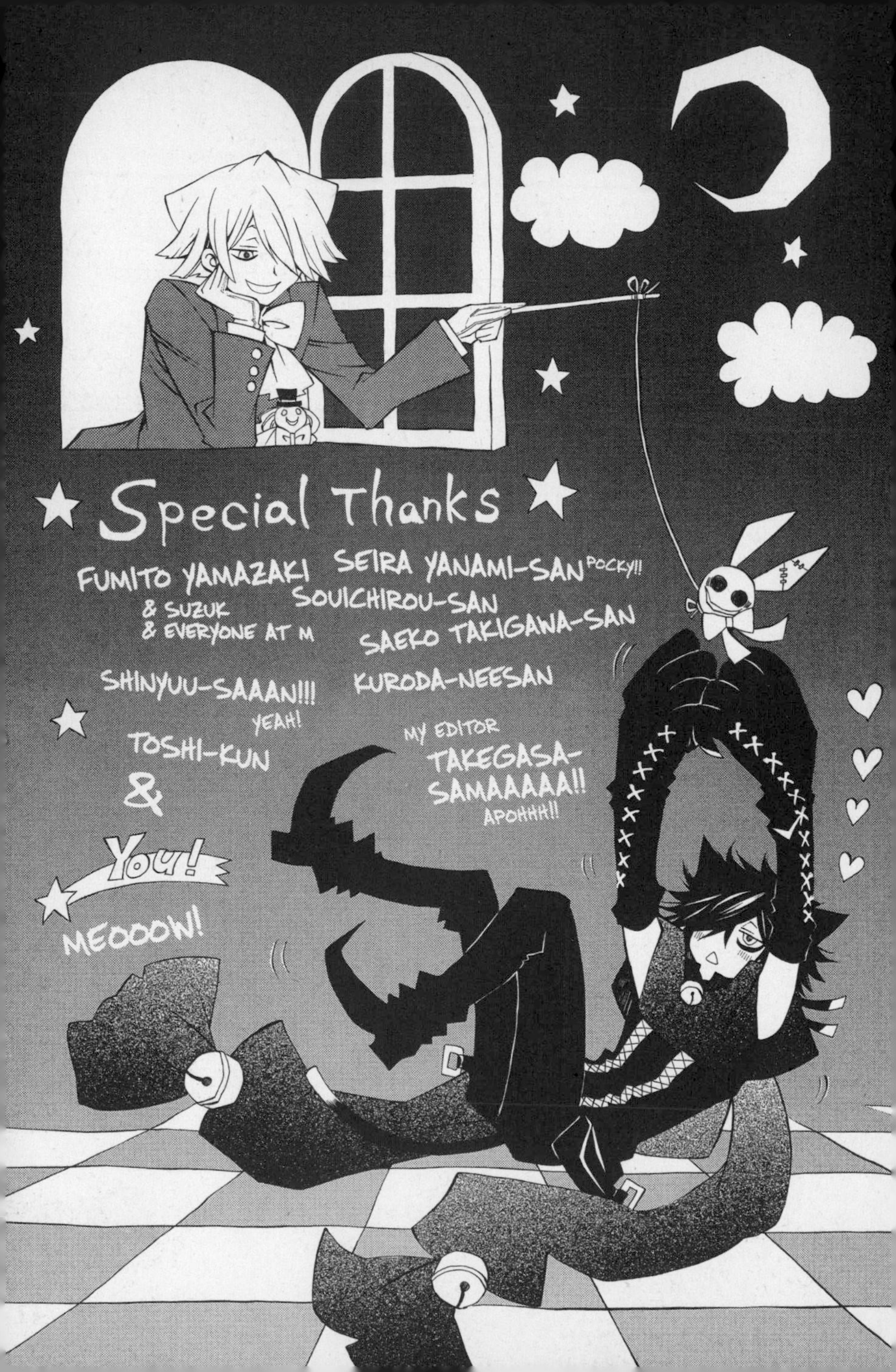
Special Thanks
FUMITO YAMAZAKI
& SUZUK
& EVERYONE AT M
SEIRA YANAMI-SAN POCKY!!
SOUICHIROU-SAN
SAEKO TAKIGAWA-SAN
SHINYUU-SAAAN!!!
KURODA-NEESAN
YEAH!
TOSHI-KUN
MY EDITOR
TAKEGASA-SAMAAAAA!!
APOHHH!!
&
You!
MEOOOW!

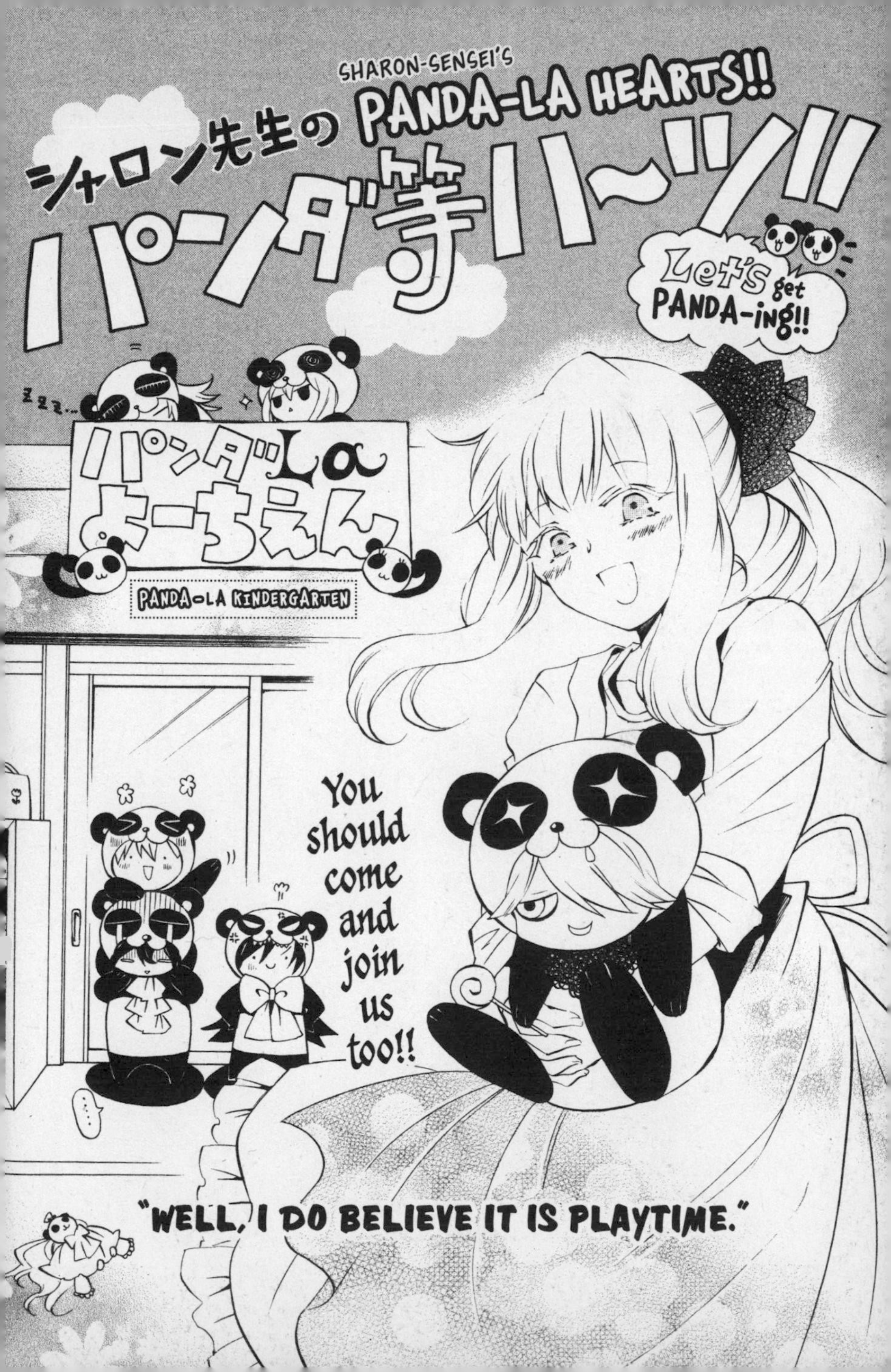
シャロン先生の
SHARON-SENSEI'S PANDA-LA HEARTS!!
Let's get PANDA-ing!!
ZZZ...
パンダLa よーちえん
PANDA-LA KINDERGARTEN
You should come and join us too!!
"WELL, I DO BELIEVE IT IS PLAYTIME."

SHARON-SENSEI SAYS LET'S MEET YOUR NEW FRIENDS!♡

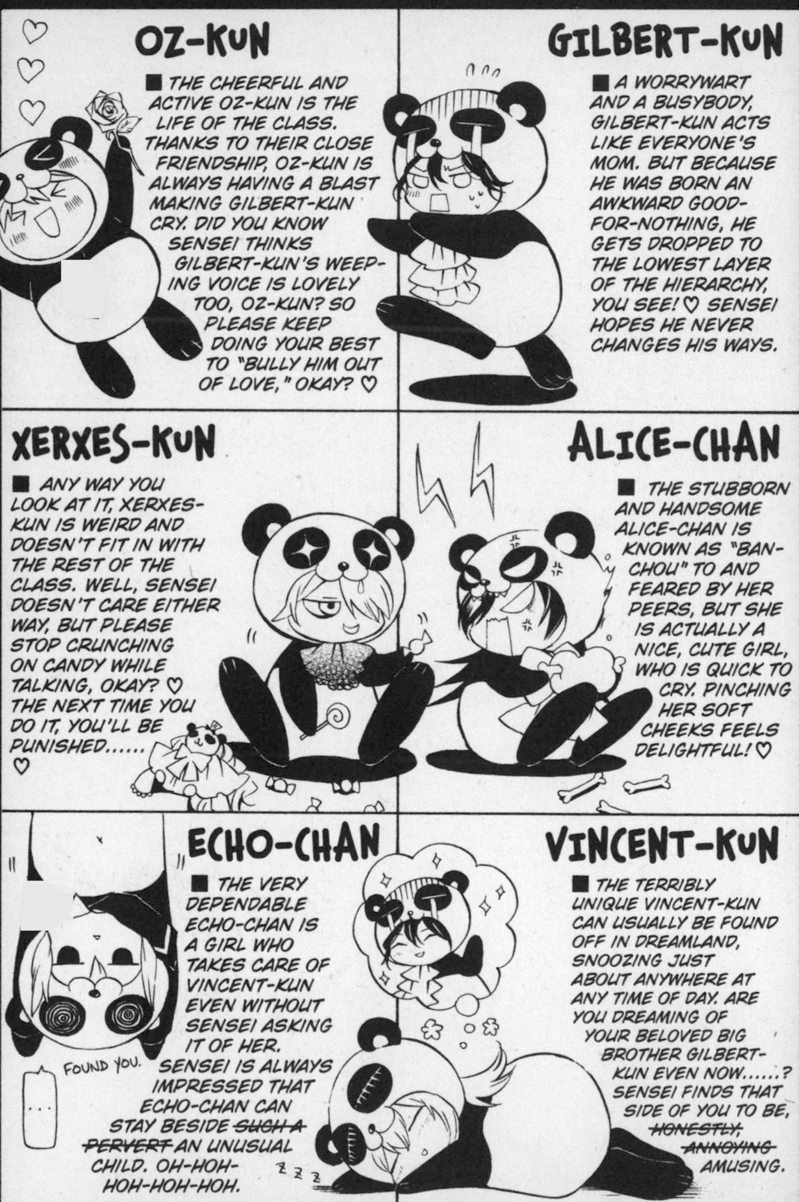
GILBERT-KUN
■ A WORRYWART AND A BUSYBODY, GILBERT-KUN ACTS LIKE EVERYONE'S MOM. BUT BECAUSE HE WAS BORN AN AWKWARD GOOD-FOR-NOTHING, HE GETS DROPPED TO THE LOWEST LAYER OF THE HIERARCHY, YOU SEE! ♡ SENSEI HOPES HE NEVER CHANGES HIS WAYS.
OZ-KUN
■ THE CHEERFUL AND ACTIVE OZ-KUN IS THE LIFE OF THE CLASS. THANKS TO THEIR CLOSE FRIENDSHIP, OZ-KUN IS ALWAYS HAVING A BLAST MAKING GILBERT-KUN CRY. DID YOU KNOW SENSEI THINKS GILBERT-KUN'S WEEPING VOICE IS LOVELY TOO, OZ-KUN? SO PLEASE KEEP DOING YOUR BEST TO "BULLY HIM OUT OF LOVE," OKAY? ♡
ALICE-CHAN
■ THE STUBBORN AND HANDSOME ALICE-CHAN IS KNOWN AS "BANCHOU" TO AND FEARED BY HER PEERS, BUT SHE IS ACTUALLY A NICE, CUTE GIRL, WHO IS QUICK TO CRY. PINCHING HER SOFT CHEEKS FEELS DELIGHTFUL! ♡
XERXES-KUN
■ ANY WAY YOU LOOK AT IT, XERXES-KUN IS WEIRD AND DOESN'T FIT IN WITH THE REST OF THE CLASS. WELL, SENSEI DOESN'T CARE EITHER WAY, BUT PLEASE STOP CRUNCHING ON CANDY WHILE TALKING, OKAY? ♡ THE NEXT TIME YOU DO IT, YOU'LL BE PUNISHED...... ♡
VINCENT-KUN
■ THE TERRIBLY UNIQUE VINCENT-KUN CAN USUALLY BE FOUND OFF IN DREAMLAND, SNOOZING JUST ABOUT ANYWHERE AT ANY TIME OF DAY. ARE YOU DREAMING OF YOUR BELOVED BIG BROTHER GILBERT-KUN EVEN NOW......? SENSEI FINDS THAT SIDE OF YOU TO BE, ~~HONESTLY, ANNOYING~~ AMUSING.
ZZZ
ECHO-CHAN
■ THE VERY DEPENDABLE ECHO-CHAN IS A GIRL WHO TAKES CARE OF VINCENT-KUN EVEN WITHOUT SENSEI ASKING IT OF HER. SENSEI IS ALWAYS IMPRESSED THAT ECHO-CHAN CAN STAY BESIDE ~~SUCH A PERVERT~~ AN UNUSUAL CHILD. OH-HOH-HOH-HOH-HOH.
FOUND YOU.
...

COMMON HONORIFICS

no honorific: Indicates familiarity or closeness; if used without permission or reason, addressing someone in this manner would constitute an insult.

-san: The Japanese equivalent of Mr./Mrs./Miss. If a situation calls for politeness, this is the fail-safe honorific.

-sama: Conveys great respect; may also indicate that the social status of the speaker is lower than that of the addressee.

-kun: Used most often when referring to boys (though it can be applied to girls as well), this indicates affection or familiarity. Occasionally used by older men among their peers, but it may also be used by anyone referring to a person of lower standing.

-chan: An affectionate honorific indicating familiarity used mostly in reference to girls; also used in reference to cute persons or animals of either gender.

ninjutsu — page 31

The skills, tactics, and strategy employed by trained ninja.

Pocky — page 177

A Japanese cookie snack shaped like a long, thin stick usually covered in some variety of chocolate.

neesan — page 177

Though this usually means "sister," here it's used as a term of respect in a gang or yakuza sense to address a female higher-up in the organization ranks.

Apohhh!! — page 177

This could refer to several things. Apple (the fruit or the brand) is written this way in Japanese characters if written as it would be pronounced by a native speaker. It could also refer to Appo, the clone commander in *Star Wars*.

banchou — page 179

The leader of a juvenile gang, alternately feared and respected.

PandoraHearts

I'm not comfortable using a computer, but I finally bought something online. It's easy... too easy...! And I can get crazy amounts of books easily too. And so, my room is about to be taken over by reference texts I bought when I got carried away. Well, next I guess I need to buy a bookshelf online...

MOCHIZUKI'S MUSINGS

VOLUME 4

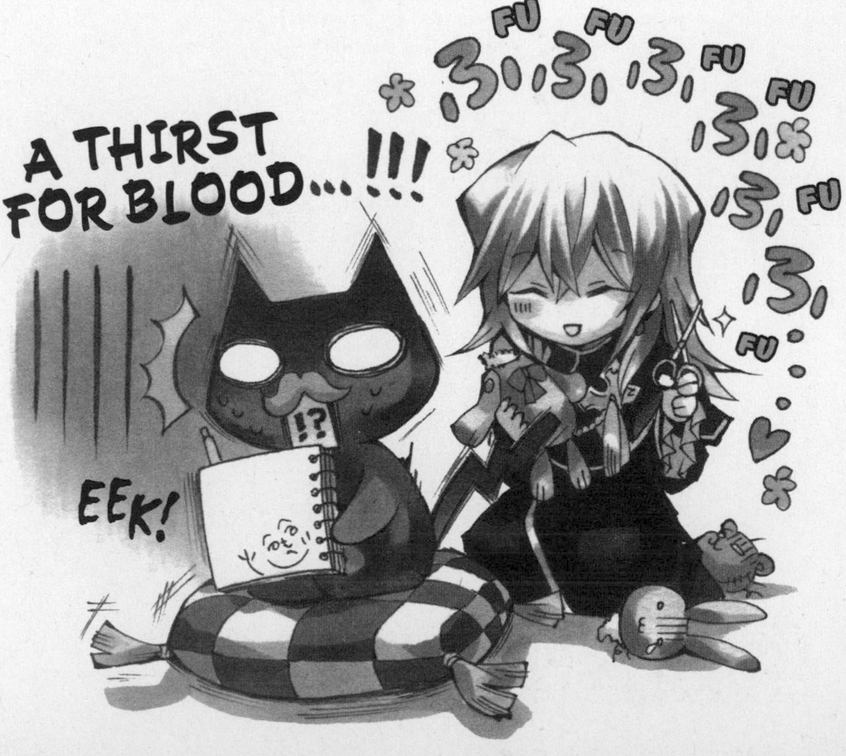
FU FU FU FU FU FU
A THIRST FOR BLOOD...!!!
!?
EEK!

PandoraHearts

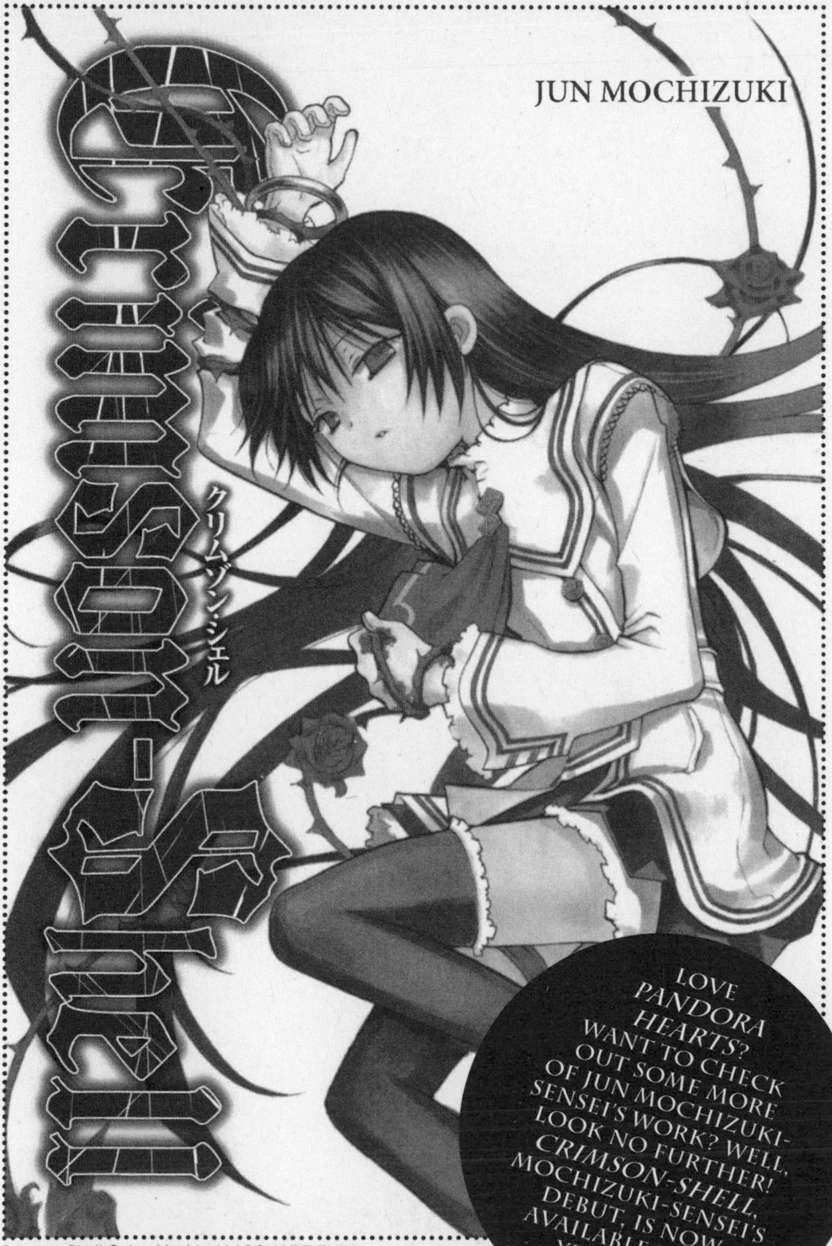
JUN MOCHIZUKI
Crimson-Shell
クリムゾン・シェル
LOVE *PANDORA HEARTS*? WANT TO CHECK OUT SOME MORE OF JUN MOCHIZUKI-SENSEI'S WORK? WELL, LOOK NO FURTHER! *CRIMSON-SHELL*, MOCHIZUKI-SENSEI'S DEBUT, IS NOW AVAILABLE FROM YEN PRESS!